Orwell in *Tribune*

Orwell in *Tribune*

'As I Please' and other writings 1943–7

compiled and edited by Paul Anderson

POLITICO'S

First published in Great Britain 2006 by
Politico's Publishing Ltd, an imprint of
Methuen Publishing Ltd
11–12 Buckingham Gate
London
SW1E 6LB

10 9 8 7 6 5 4 3 2

A CIP catalogue record for this book is available from the British Library.

ISBN-10: 1-84275-155-7
ISBN-13: 978-1-84275-155-8

Typeset by SX Composing DTP, Rayleigh, Essex
Printed and bound in Great Britain by St Edmundsbury Press, Bury St Edmunds, Suffolk

Contents

Foreword by Michael Foot

A famous photograph of George Orwell – as famous as any ever taken of him – bore the heading 'National Union of Journalists' and asserted: 'This is to certify that Mr George Orwell of *The Tribune* is a member of the National Union of Journalists.' The card was dated 29 December 1943.

Tribune gave Orwell political shelter at a most important moment in his career; each bestowed favours on the other, the full significance of which, however, could only be appreciated years later. Orwell had already developed his own brand of writing and his own brand of socialism. But his association with *Tribune* happened at an especially crucial time for both. He joined when *Tribune* was suddenly securing a quite unexpected fame – or notoriety – under the direction of Aneurin Bevan. And it was in Orwell's years on the staff of *Tribune* between 1943 and 1945, when no other paper in the land for which he was prepared to write would have printed what he wanted, that he also wrote *Animal Farm* and struggled painfully and at first vainly to find a publisher. *Tribune* sustained his pride when all establishment doors, right, left and especially centre, were slammed in his face.

It might be thought that that association between Orwell and Bevan, so fortunate for them both, derived from some natural affinity and outlook or way of living in wartime London, but it was not so. Bevan took his politics extremely seriously, especially at that period in the war when he and *Tribune* carried aloft the banner of democratic socialism with few allies in high places. But he was always ready to relax and enjoy himself in the company of kindred spirits, the more so indeed if they knew too how to escape the suffocations of parliamentary politics. Yet somehow no magical sympathy in the relationship between him and Orwell was discovered, there or thereafter. All the more remarkable was the political trust and understanding which they did establish there and then, and which survived all the political buffetings of the next few years. The insight and the steadfastness with which Bevan judged Orwell were something rare indeed.

The group of friends Orwell gathered around himself before and during the war fortified his spirit just when he most needed it: Tosco Fyvel, George Woodcock, Paul Potts, Jack Common, Julian Symons, Arthur Koestler. I would gladly lend my own name to this list of honour, if I could, but it would be shamefully misleading. Aneurin Bevan was my mentor and when I argued with him about Orwell, I was more than probably joining with other *Tribune* readers protesting about Orwell's increasingly bitter attacks on the Soviet Union. But in the end I was convinced by Orwell's case, less by Orwell himself than by Arthur Koestler, who was more and more becoming a second mentor, sweeping aside all opposition with his unmatched polemical power.

In 1958, on *Tribune*'s twenty-first anniversary, I wrote of Orwell that he was

> the sharpest thorn in the side of editorial complacency, the greatest of modern iconoclasts, a new and much more humane Swift with a deadly lash for all hypocrisies, including socialist hypocrisies. How many readers he offended no one can calculate (the circulation manager made her rough-and-ready weekly estimate), but certainly nothing comparable with his column has been seen in recent journalistic history.

Nearly fifty years on, I see no reason to change that opinion.

Abbreviations in notes

References to work by Orwell not reproduced in this collection are to the relevant volumes of Peter Davison (ed), *The Complete Works of George Orwell* (London: Secker and Warburg, 2001):

CWGO X	*Volume X: A Kind of Compulsion (1903–36)*
CWGO XI	*Volume XI: Facing Unpleasant Facts (1937–39)*
CWGO XII	*Volume XII: A Patriot after All (1940–41)*
CWGO XIII	*Volume XIII: All Propaganda Is Lies (1941–42)*
CWGO XIV	*Volume XIV: Keeping Our Little Corner Clean (1942–43)*
CWGO XV	*Volume XV: Two Wasted Years (1943)*
CWGO XVI	*Volume XVI: I Have Tried to Tell the Truth (1943–44)*
CWGO XVII	*Volume XVII: I Belong to the Left (1945)*
CWGO XVIII	*Volume XVIII: Smothered under Journalism (1946)*
CWGO XIX	*Volume XIX: It Is What I Think (1947–48)*
CWGO XX	*Volume XX: Our Job Is to Make Life Worth Living (1949–50)*

Introduction

When George Orwell joined the staff of *Tribune* at the end of November 1943 it was with a sense of liberation. He had spent the previous two years working as a talks producer in the Indian Section of the BBC's Eastern Service, and he'd had enough of it. He was a competent and innovative radio broadcaster, and the money was good, £720 a year when he left, three times the pay of the average manual worker. He was also rather proud of what he had achieved, and for the rest of his life he defended the BBC against what he saw as ill-informed criticism.[1]

But he hated the BBC's niggling bureaucracy and was tired of being a propagandist, not least because of the increasingly intrusive censorship imposed by the wartime Ministry of Information on what went out to India. He was forty, his health was poor and he desperately wanted time to do his own work. As he put it in a letter to Philip Rahv, editor of the American magazine *Partisan Review*, shortly after taking on the *Tribune* job at an annual salary of £500:

> I have left the BBC after two wasted years in it and have become literary editor of the *Tribune*, a leftwing weekly which you may have seen. It leaves me a little spare time, which the BBC didn't, so I have got another book under weigh which I hope to finish in a few months if nothing intervenes.[2]

The book was *Animal Farm*, which he finished in March 1944 and which established Orwell's global reputation, although it did not come out for another sixteen months: a succession of publishers rejected it, most of them because its anti-Stalinist political message was inconvenient at a time when the Soviet Union was Britain's ally, and it was then delayed by paper shortages. It was not only the spare time to write the book, however, that attracted Orwell to *Tribune*. He was broadly in sympathy with its politics - he was already a reader and a more-than-occasional contributor - and the job was in itself an opportunity to express himself as a writer and as an editor. Both Aneurin Bevan, the left-wing Labour MP who was the weekly's political director and nominal editor, and Jon Kimche, who actually edited it, were prepared to give him a degree of editorial freedom he had never had before. Over the next thirteen months as literary editor, and over the next three-and-a-half years as columnist, feature writer and reviewer, he did precisely what he wanted.

As often happens in journalism, Orwell got the job at least partly because of his connections. He knew Kimche from years before, when Orwell was still Eric Blair to everyone he came across. They had worked together in a Hampstead bookshop in the early 1930s, had met again in Spain during the civil war and had renewed the acquaintance in 1942, when Kimche became *Tribune*'s assistant editor. Orwell was also a close friend of one of Kimche's best friends, Tosco Fyvel.[3] Orwell, Fyvel and the publisher Fredric Warburg had collaborated in 1940–1 on a series of books making the case for a socialist transformation of Britain as the goal of the war. When John Atkins, the *Tribune* literary editor, resigned to join Mass Observation, the organisation that pioneered the monitoring of public opinion in Britain, Fyvel lobbied Kimche to take on Orwell in his place. Kimche and Bevan agreed; Orwell was hired.

The overwhelming majority of Orwell's contributions to *Tribune* in 1943–7 were instalments of his aptly named column 'As I Please', the first of which appeared on 3 December 1943 and the last, the eightieth, on 4 April 1947. There was a break in the continuity of the column after 16 February 1945 – the next Orwell 'As I Please' did not appear for twenty-one months – because Orwell left the *Tribune* staff to become a war correspondent for the *Observer* and in his absence 'As I Please' was taken over by Jennie Lee, Bevan's wife and political co-conspirator, who became a Labour MP in the July 1945 general election. But Orwell was back as a *Tribune* contributor writing more or less weekly in autumn 1945, and most of the features he wrote between then and the next spring were 'As I Please' columns under other names. He eventually reclaimed the title of the column from Lee in November 1946, after another six-month break from writing for *Tribune* in summer 1946.

Orwell's columns for *Tribune* are justly feted. The range of subjects he covered is extraordinary: it is difficult to think of anyone before or since who could write about so many different things. As his friend Julian Symons wrote: 'He discussed a hundred subjects, ranging from the comparative amounts he spent on books and cigarettes or lamenting the decline of the English murder from the days of Crippen to a casual wartime killing to the spawning of toads in spring.'[4]

But it isn't just Orwell's versatility that stands out. The columns are also remarkably original and written in a taut, demotic journalistic style. As another friend, George Woodcock, put it: 'He could always find a subject on which there was something fresh to say in a prose that, for all its ease and apparent casualness, was penetrating and direct.'[5] Moreover, despite the diversity of subject matter, they form a single coherent body of work. In the words of the literary critic D. J. Taylor in his recent Orwell biography: 'One of the most engaging features of the column, read sequentially, is the sense of dialogue, points taken up, conceded or refuted, continuity rather than a trail of pronouncements which the reader could take or leave as he or she chose.'[6]

Tribune was, as it remains, a political paper, but Orwell rarely dealt directly in his columns with the subject matter of most political journalists: elections, debates in parliament, legislation, policy pronouncements, ministerial appointments and so on. Nor, for the most part, did he use his *Tribune* column to examine in detail the latest developments in world affairs.

It would be wrong, however, to suggest that his columns were not political. They were intensely so – even, paradoxically, when they appeared to have nothing to do with politics. Orwell was writing as a democratic socialist for democratic socialist readers, and his role as he saw it was to provoke them, to get them to think about what politics is and what it can and cannot achieve.[7] If there is a single theme that runs all the way through Orwell's *Tribune* columns from 1943 to 1947, it is that the left needs a more nuanced conception of politics. Democratic socialism is not *just* a matter of the Labour Party adopting the right manifesto, winning a general election, nationalising the means of production and creating a comprehensive welfare state (although it is all these). It also involves telling inconvenient truths – about the nature of Soviet communism, about the economic consequences of decolonisation, about the extent of popular anti-Americanism in Britain. It means, among other things, reforming the press, defending the right of anarchists to sell seditious literature and countering racial prejudice. Moreover, a lot that is important in life cannot be reduced to politics. Great writers can be very right wing; people will never tire of celebrating Christmas by eating and drinking too much; and the arrival of spring will always be a source of wonder.

Sixty-odd years on, Orwell's emphases on the lacunae of left politics and principles, rather than the programmatic core of 1940s democratic socialism or the week-by-week flow of events, make his *Tribune* columns more accessible than anything written by his contemporaries. Not everything he discussed is still current. The Soviet Union and British empire are long over, the Cold War has been and gone, and the best writers in Britain have not been right wing for some time. But totalitarianism and imperialism are still very much live issues, and Orwell's commitment to telling inconvenient truths, his warnings about the slipperiness of political language and the sensationalism of the popular press, his concerns with racism and religious intolerance and his conviction that there is more to life than politics are as relevant today as they were in the 1940s.

* * *

Orwell did more as a *Tribune* staffer than write columns. Apart from 'As I Please' and his run of weekly pieces in 1945–6, he also contributed occasional reviews and longer essays on literary themes, mostly critical accounts of writers he liked – Tobias Smollett, Oliver Goldsmith, William Makepeace Thackeray, Winwood Reade, Henry Miller.[8] And from December 1943 to February 1945 he commissioned and edited the contributions to *Tribune*'s literary pages – the book reviews, literary essays and short stories that made up, in journalists' jargon, the 'back of the book'.

Looking back in the piece he wrote for *Tribune*'s tenth anniversary issue, Orwell was self-deprecating about his ability as a literary editor:

> It was interesting, but it is not a period that I look back on with pride. The fact is that I am no good at editing. I hate planning ahead, and I have a psychical or even physical inability to answer letters. My most essential memory of that time is of pulling out a drawer here and a drawer there, finding it in each case to be stuffed with letters and manuscripts which ought to have been dealt with weeks earlier, and hurriedly shutting it up again. Also, I have a fatal tendency to accept manuscripts which I know very well are too bad to be printed. It is questionable whether anyone who has had long experience as a freelance journalist ought to become an editor. It is too like taking a convict out of his cell and making him governor of the prison.[9]

Tosco Fyvel concurred in a memoir published in 1982:

> When I went with Orwell to his little office at *Tribune* to take over, I found to my surprise that the drawers of his desk were stuffed with unpublished manuscripts of reviews, literary articles and poems.
>
> 'What on earth are all these?' I asked.
>
> He sighed. 'Most of them are unspeakably bad,' he said, 'but I could not bring myself to send them back.'
>
> I could see his dilemma, hovering between the high standards he set for his own writing and his desire not to hurt a struggling fellow-writer to whom a small *Tribune* fee might mean the difference between eating and not eating – or so he explained to me with what I thought considerable exaggeration. Torn between his high standards and generosity he let his famous honesty desert him. He had not answered some letters and in others had written that he had not yet got round to deciding about the particular piece but would do so presently.[10]

Most commentators and critics have taken Orwell at his word on his failings as a literary editor, but he was not the naïf he made himself out to be. It's true that the short stories he published most weeks in 1944 were, with a few exceptions, at best competent and at worst embarrassing. But publishing them was a worthy attempt to reverse the decline of the short story in Britain and to encourage new writers. Orwell felt that British writing was in a dire state. 'This place is a literary desert at present,' he wrote to Philip Rahv just before joining *Tribune*. 'No new people who are worth much seem to be coming along, and nearly everyone is either in the forces or being drained dry by writing muck for one of the ministries.'[11] And the short story was a form that was on its uppers. 'Few people would claim that the short story has been a successful art form in England during the past twenty years,' Orwell told the readers of *Tribune* in January 1944, announcing a competition that he hoped would help the 'rehabilitation of the short story in this country'.[12]

The experiment did not work. He reported disappointedly in a piece in May 1944 on the entries to the competition: 'Of the five or six hundred stories that were sent in, the great majority were, in my judgment, very bad.'[13] By the beginning of 1945, he had admitted defeat. 'Regular readers of *Tribune* will have noted that during recent months we have printed short stories only intermittently,' he wrote. 'In future we shall probably abandon short stories almost completely . . . It was only unwillingly that we decided on the dropping of short stories, but the quality of the stories sent in to me makes them, in much more than nine cases out of ten, simply not worth ink and paper.'[14]

But if the short stories Orwell published were uninspiring, the book reviews on his literary pages were erudite, stylish and snappy. He wrote reviews only rarely for *Tribune*, but he recruited what he rightly described as 'a first-rate team of reviewers',[15] most of them either friends or contacts he had made while at the BBC. The best known today are probably the novelists Mulk Raj Anand, Arthur Koestler and Julian Symons, the literary critics and poets Herbert Read, Stephen Spender and Alex Comfort, the poet Stevie Smith and the art critic David Sylvester.[16] Others less familiar now but prominent in the 1940s or soon after include the critics R. C. Churchill and Michael Roberts, the poet Paul Potts, the historian and polemicist Franz Borkenau, the translator Elisaveta Fen, the novelist Rayner Heppenstall, the wit Hugh Kingsmill, the communist novelist, translator and pamphleteer Jack Lindsay and the broadcaster Antony Brown.[17] Orwell also commissioned occasional longer articles on literary and cultural themes, among them pieces by the critic William Empson and the novelist Anthony Powell.[18] Orwell failed to persuade T. S. Eliot to contribute - but he got E. M. Forster to write the lead review for his autumn books special in September 1944.[19] Even if his reviewers for the most part did not do their best work for him, Orwell brought an élan to the *Tribune* books pages that they had never had before and retained long after he left.

While he was literary editor, Orwell worked three days a week for *Tribune*. The offices were on the third floor of an imposing late-Victorian building, largely occupied by lawyers, at 222 Strand, opposite the Royal Courts of Justice and a few yards west of Temple Bar and the beginning of Fleet Street. To reach them from the street involved climbing eight flights of stairs or risking a journey in an ancient hydraulic lift that had to be stopped and started manually.[20] The editorial staff - which consisted only of Jon Kimche, Orwell and Evelyn Anderson, the assistant editor - occupied three rooms arranged in a row, with Orwell in the middle one, a 'cramped little office looking out on a backyard' as he described it.[21] Orwell generally wrote his column at home and went into the paper's offices every Wednesday to see off his pages and do the routine work of contacting publishers and sending out review copies.[22] He was also a regular at the paper's weekly editorial meetings, which were attended by Aneurin Bevan and George Strauss, a rich Labour MP who provided much of *Tribune*'s funding, as well as the editorial staff. More than thirty years later, Kimche described the meetings as rather like a stage play by Harold Pinter, with Bevan and Orwell speaking in monologues about what each would be writing for the next issue.[23]

It is difficult to avoid the conclusion that Kimche never really liked Orwell. 'He wasn't a phony but he was affected,' he recalled.[24] One reason for the coolness might have been that he thought Orwell anti-Semitic. Kimche was Jewish and a keen Zionist, Orwell an opponent of Zionism who (by one secondhand account) thought the Zionists were 'Wardour Street Jews who have a controlling influence over the British press'.[25] But Anderson - who was also Jewish - became Orwell's close personal friend, as did Sally McEwen, his editorial secretary, with whom he appears to have had an affair.[26] Bevan liked Orwell a lot, and the feeling was reciprocated, though they never became close. In October 1945, Orwell wrote a profile of Bevan anonymously for the *Observer*:

> Bevan thinks and feels as a working man. He knows how the scales are weighted against anyone with less than £5 a week . . . But he is remarkably free - some of his adversaries would say dangerously free - from any feeling of personal grievance against society. He shows no sign of ordinary class consciousness. He seems equally at home in all kinds of company. It is difficult to imagine anyone less impressed by social status or less inclined to put on airs with subordinates . . . He does not have the suspicion of 'cleverness' and anaesthesia to the arts which are generally regarded as the mark of a practical man. Those who have worked with him in a journalistic capacity have remarked with pleasure and astonishment that here at last is a politician who knows that literature exists and will even hold up work for five minutes to discuss a point of style.[27]

Strauss, another Jew, also remembered Orwell warmly: 'I found him very pleasant . . . He never imposed himself on you. He talked very easily, fluently, on a variety of matters and was a most agreeable person to get on with.'[28]

When he was not doing *Tribune* work in 1943–5, Orwell wrote at home, completing *Animal Farm* and half a dozen substantial essays, including four instalments of his 'London Letter' to *Partisan Review*, as well as doing jobbing freelance work - dozens of reviews for the *Observer* and the *Manchester Evening News* and an essay for a Collins illustrated book series, *The English People*, which he described as 'a piece of propaganda for the British Council'. (It was not published until 1947.)

His productivity is all the more remarkable given his personal and domestic circumstances. He was in poor health - the tuberculosis that eventually killed him made him short of breath at the best of times - and the business of finding a publisher for *Animal Farm* was extremely time-consuming: it was only in late summer 1944 that Fredric Warburg agreed to take the book.

As if that were not enough, in early summer Orwell and his wife Eileen (who was also ill) adopted a newborn baby boy who had been found for them by Eileen's brother's widow Gwen, a doctor, in Newcastle upon Tyne. No sooner had the Blairs completed the paperwork, naming the baby Richard Horatio Blair, than their flat in Kilburn – a 53 bus-ride away from *Tribune* – was hit by a German flying bomb. For the next three months they borrowed the flat of their friend Inez Holden in Marylebone, just north of Marble Arch, travelling regularly to the north-east to visit Richard, who stayed with Gwen.

It was another three months before Orwell found the family somewhere more-or-less permanent to live, a flat at 27b Canonbury Square, near Highbury and Islington station, with a choice of four buses and two trams to Aldwych and *Tribune*. Through all this Orwell also kept up a hectic social life, regularly lunching and drinking with friends and contacts – mainly in the pubs and restaurants around Fleet Street and in Soho.

* * *

Tribune was not yet seven years old when Orwell joined it – but it already had a complex and colourful history. It was by late 1943 on its fourth editor and had gone through two radical changes in editorial direction and at least three life-threatening financial crises.

The Tribune – the definite article was dropped from the masthead in late 1938, returned in summer 1940 and was abandoned for good in early 1942 – was launched in January 1937 to support the Unity Campaign, an attempt by the left-wing Labour MP Sir Stafford Cripps and the Labour-affiliated ginger group he bankrolled and chaired, the Socialist League, to secure a 'United Front' between Labour and the small parties to its left, the Communist Party of Great Britain (CPGB) and the Independent Labour Party (ILP), 'against fascism, reaction and war and against the National government', as the campaign's manifesto put it.

Cripps, the 'Red Squire', MP for Bristol East since 1931 and Solicitor General in the dying days of the 1929–31 Labour government, was chairman of the new weekly's editorial board. An impetuous Christian socialist, then in his late forties, he had become fabulously wealthy as a barrister specialising in patent law and, together with George Strauss, was the paper's main source of money.[29] Cripps was notably ascetic in his personal life, a teetotaller who ate little and whose only self-indulgences were tobacco and luxurious holidays.

The paper's editor was William Mellor, a little older than Cripps and with a history of twenty-five years' activity on the radical left. He had been a founder member of the CPGB as a young man and editor of the *Daily Herald* in the late 1920s. Mellor was Cripps's de facto deputy in the Socialist League, an accomplished speaker who had a volcanic temper and was an unrepentant hedonist. The other board members were Strauss, MP for North Lambeth and a prominent left-wing councillor on the London County Council, whose fortune derived from his family's metal merchant business;

Bevan, MP for Ebbw Vale; Ellen Wilkinson, MP for Jarrow; the veteran journalist H. N. Brailsford; the political scientist Harold Laski (who was also a leading light in the publisher Victor Gollancz's Left Book Club, of which more anon); and Ben Greene, a campaigner for constituency parties' rights in the Labour Party.[30] The journalists included two keen Oxford graduates in their twenties, Michael Foot and Barbara Betts. Foot had been a student at Oxford with Cripps's son John and had worked as researcher on Cripps's 1936 book *The Struggle for Peace*; Betts, the future Barbara Castle, was Mellor's lover (no matter that he was married with two children).

Seventy years on, the Unity Campaign appears a quixotic venture. The Labour leadership - which in 1936–7 meant not only the leader of the Parliamentary Labour Party, the unassuming Clement Attlee, but also his most senior colleagues in Parliament (notably Hugh Dalton, the party chairman and foreign affairs spokesman, and Herbert Morrison, leader of London County Council), as well as the two main trade union power brokers, Ernest Bevin, general secretary of the Transport and General Workers' Union, and Walter Citrine, general secretary of the TUC - had little or no enthusiasm for the CPGB and the ILP joining its broad church.[31]

In early 1937, Labour had more than 400,000 individual members and 158 MPs. The CPGB had just 10,000 members (though it was growing fast) and a single MP, Willie Gallagher in West Fife.[32] It was considered by Labour's big guns as an unreliable nuisance, a cuckoo in the nest that took its orders from Moscow. They remembered only too well that the CPGB in the 1920s had a policy of infiltrating the Labour Party and that between 1928 and 1932, on the instructions of the Communist International, it had denounced Labour as 'social fascists'. Labour's conference had ruled that members should refuse joint work with the CPGB and had repeatedly rejected its applications for affiliation, most recently in 1936.

The ILP for its part was little more than a fractious irrelevance for the Labour leadership: it had been in catastrophic decline since its decision to disaffiliate from Labour after the debacle of 1931, when Ramsay MacDonald had created a national government with the Tories and Labour had slumped to an ignominious defeat in the subsequent general election. In 1937 the ILP had four MPs, all in Scotland, and perhaps 3,500 members, down from nearly 17,000 in 1932.[33]

Nor did the Labour leadership have much time for Cripps and the Socialist League. The league, which had its origins in the minority of the ILP that had rejected disaffiliation, had no more than 3,000 members and, after a brief period in 1932–3 when Labour, stunned by MacDonald's apostasy, swung sharply to the left, had been opposed to the whole thrust of Labour policy.[34] Cripps had been a big fish in the small pool of the Parliamentary Labour Party after 1931, as one of only three former ministers from the 1929–31 Labour government to be returned as Labour MPs. (The others, in a PLP reduced to forty-seven MPs at its lowest point, were George Lansbury, who became Labour leader in 1932, and Attlee.) But he had earned the enmity of the Labour right with his incendiary rhetoric for an all-or-nothing socialist programme, to be imposed by a Labour government that assumed dictatorial powers. Cripps had flounced out of the Labour National Executive Committee (NEC) as long ago as autumn 1935 and had been marginalised by the return to Parliament of several of the Labour right's major players, including Dalton and Morrison, in the November 1935 general election.

Cripps and his allies were particularly at odds with Bevin, Dalton and Citrine, the Labour leaders with greatest influence on foreign policy, on two crucial and related questions: how to deal with the growing threat to peace posed by militarist Japan, fascist Italy and, particularly, Nazi Germany; and what to do about the civil war in Spain. On the first of these, to simplify somewhat, in the course of 1935 and 1936 Bevin, Dalton and Citrine had been convinced by events – the Japanese invasion of Manchuria in 1931, Hitler's withdrawal from the League of Nations and his initiation of a massive rearmament programme in 1934, Mussolini's invasion of Abyssinia in 1935–6, Hitler's reoccupation of the Rhineland in March 1936 – that Labour should abandon its long-standing emphasis on negotiating disarmament agreements and should disavow pacifism. Instead, while supporting 'collective security' through the League of Nations to face down aggression, it should back British rearmament. Cripps and the Socialist League, by contrast, saw the League of Nations as a tool of imperialism and vehemently opposed both collective security and British rearmament, unless it were done by a 'workers' government'. The Labour conference, overwhelmingly dominated by trade union block votes, had emphatically backed collective security in 1935, prompting the resignation of the pacifist Lansbury as parliamentary leader, and (rather more ambiguously) had endorsed rearmament in 1936: on all this, Cripps and the Socialist League were fighting a losing battle.

On Spain, however, the momentum was with them and the CPGB. The civil war had begun in July 1936 with an attempted right-wing coup against the centre-left Popular Front government, a coalition of reformist socialists and anti-clerical radicals, elected earlier in the year. The coup had limited success except in Spanish Morocco, but from there General Francisco Franco and the colonial army, airlifted and then supplied by Mussolini and Hitler, invaded mainland Spain. The British government declared a policy of non-intervention, supported by the newly elected Popular Front government in France, and organised an international non-intervention pact, to which France, Italy, Germany, Portugal, the Soviet Union and the United States signed up alongside Britain. On the insistence of Bevin and Dalton, the Labour leadership initially backed non-intervention (on the grounds that it would prevent the war spreading to the whole of Europe) even though Italy and Germany blatantly contravened the pact from the start, continuing to supply Franco's Nationalist rebels. Cripps and the Socialist League, by contrast, immediately saw through the sham and demanded an end to the de facto one-sided arms embargo on the Republican side to allow the elected government to defend itself against the Nationalist insurgency – exactly the same position as that of the CPGB, whose sponsor, the Soviet Union, announced it would adhere to the non-intervention pact only as much as others and began to supply the Republicans. The October 1936 Labour conference in Edinburgh voted for non-intervention but then heard an impassioned speech against it by a Spanish visitor, Isabel de Palencia, which delegates greeted with wild enthusiasm. The left demanded that the vote be retaken: the leadership refused.

Even though Labour was in opposition and in no position to change government policy on Spain, disgust at the leadership's stance swept the left – fuelled by official Labour's failure, as the left saw it, to take on domestic fascism in the shape of Sir Oswald Mosley and the British Union of Fascists (BUF).[35] Mosley and the BUF were at this point running a vicious anti-Semitic campaign in the East End of London. On the eve of the Labour conference, it was the ILP and the CPGB that took to the streets to stop Mosley marching through the East End in what became known as the battle of Cable Street – and for their efforts they were immediately disowned by Morrison.

More than 2,000 young Britons, among them Orwell, volunteered to fight for the Spanish Republic – most of them (unlike Orwell) recruited by the Communist Party for the International Brigades. (Orwell travelled independently to Spain carrying letters of recommendation from H. N. Brailsford and Fenner Brockway, general secretary of the ILP, and joined the militia of the ILP's sister party in Spain, the POUM, the Partido Obrero de Unificación Marxista.)[36] Rather less heroically, Cripps and his allies resolved to seize the opportunity to press ahead with a simultaneous launch of a new weekly paper, a project with which Cripps had been toying for some months, and a vigorous campaign for a United Front.

Driven by Cripps's enthusiasm, negotiations with the CPGB and the ILP secured agreement to create a campaign on the basis of a programme of arms for Spain, anti-fascism, alliance with the Soviet Union and opposition to rearmament and war. The first issue of *The Tribune* duly appeared on Friday 1 January 1937. Cripps presented a Socialist League conference that weekend with a unity deal it could either accept or reject; and the conference backed it. The Unity Campaign was formally launched a fortnight later at a packed-out rally at Manchester's Free Trade Hall, addressed by Cripps, the CPGB's general secretary, Harry Pollitt, and the ILP's chairman, James Maxton, which was followed by enthusiastic meetings up and down the country.[37]

The problem was that the constituent parts of the Unity Campaign had incompatible expectations – so that when the Labour leadership decided to crush it, the campaign was helpless to resist. Cripps and most of the Socialist League saw the campaign as a means of shifting the balance of power in the Labour Party to the left. Pollitt and the CPGB saw it as a stepping stone on the way to affiliation with Labour (so were desperate for the campaign not to upset the Labour leadership) and to the creation of a 'Popular Front' against the National Government involving Liberals and perhaps even anti-appeasement Tories. By contrast, the ILP and several prominent members of the Socialist League, among them Aneurin Bevan and William Mellor, thought the campaign should be the prelude to the creation of a new socialist party to Labour's left and were eager to push confrontation with the Labour leadership to the point of schism. Neither the ILP nor much of the Socialist League would sanction a Popular Front with 'bourgeois' parties under any circumstances because it would be an alliance to sustain capitalism; and a significant minority of ILPers and Socialist Leaguers, most notably Brailsford and Brockway, were appalled by the CPGB's subservience to Moscow and had already questioned the validity of the first of the Soviet show trials, that of Zinoviev, Kamenev and other old Bolsheviks in August 1936.[38] The CPGB for its part detested the ILP – Pollitt thought Brockway was an MI5 spy – and wanted no part in the creation of a new left-wing workers' party. Pollitt suspected that the Socialist League was keen on the Unity Campaign solely to get a mass readership for *The Tribune*, and despised the paper's editorial board: Cripps, he declared, was 'the only clean man in the whole of that bunch'.[39]

Shunned by the Labour leadership and internally divided, the Unity Campaign proved a short-running farce. Labour's NEC responded to its launch by disaffiliating the Socialist League and then a few weeks later – after Cripps made an idiotic speech from a Unity Campaign platform calling for workers to refuse to work on the rearmament programme – declared membership of the league to be incompatible with Labour Party membership. Cripps, under Pollitt's influence, decided it was time to wind up the league – to the dismay of Mellor, Strauss and the ILP – and at an emotional conference in April 1937, the league voted to dissolve itself. A hastily constructed National Unity Campaign Committee to continue agitation for the United Front collapsed in less than three weeks after the NEC ruled that any Labour member appearing on a joint platform with a member of the CPGB or the ILP would be expelled. By the end of June relations between the ILP and the CPGB had all but collapsed after the Stalinist suppression of the ILP's sister party in Spain, the POUM. The Labour conference in October 1937 rejected even the proposal to keep open the option of a United Front, though it did vote Cripps back on to the Labour NEC. As Brockway put it: 'Thus ended ingloriously the Unity Campaign. Its result was the destruction of the Socialist League, the loss of influence of Cripps, Bevan, Strauss and other "lefts", the strengthening of the reactionary leaders and the disillusionment of the rank and file.'[40]

* * *

All that survived from the wreckage was *The Tribune*. In its first nine months, it had been of variable quality. Much of its writing was jargon ridden and formulaic, and - even allowing for the left's mood of the time - it was obsessive and at best short sighted in its enthusiasm for the Soviet Union, in its often hysterical warnings of the dangers of British fascism and, above all, in its overarching opposition to British rearmament. But it had its good points too. It was lively and irreverent and featured big names from the left firmament: as well as Cripps, Bevan, Strauss and Laski, it carried G. D. H. Cole, George Lansbury, Pollitt and Brockway, alongside a smattering of left-leaning journalists from the liberal press, among them John Langdon-Davies, the *News Chronicle*'s main man in Spain, and an impressive range of foreign socialist leaders - largely thanks to Julius Braunthal, an Austrian socialist exile.[41] It had a letters page that allowed the expression of opinion that deviated from its line, and several of its regular contributors - notably Bevan, who revealed considerable talent as a parliamentary columnist - wrote directly and entertainingly.

It was, however, incontrovertibly a commercial disaster. Cripps, Strauss and Mellor had expected the paper to hit a break-even circulation of 50,000 in a matter of weeks. But it had reached barely half that before exhausting the £18,000 launch capital - the equivalent of more than £800,000 today - and it was still losing money. Cripps and Strauss were forced to dig deep again to keep it alive. Politically, too, *The Tribune* was in a hole. With the acrimonious collapse of the Unity Campaign, Brailsford, the ILP and many of the big Labour Party names drifted away and political differences erupted between Cripps and Mellor, who were already at odds over what Cripps saw as Mellor's cavalier enthusiasm for spending his money. Cripps, under the influence of Pollitt, became increasingly open to the idea of a Popular Front, particularly after the German annexation of Austria in March 1938. Mellor remained vehemently opposed to any alliance with non-socialist parties.

The Mellor–Cripps dispute came to a head in summer 1938. With losses continuing to mount, the paper launched a desperate appeal to its supporters to recruit new readers. 'We must double our existing circulation within the next 12 weeks,' exclaimed a statement from the editorial board, adding disingenuously that '*The Tribune* has behind it no millionaire'.[42] The appeal failed miserably and Cripps decided that the only hope was to turn to the publisher Victor Gollancz and the Left Book Club (LBC).[43]

Gollancz had made a fortune publishing popular fiction, but from the early 1930s had expanded into political publishing, driven by a sense of desperation at the growing international crisis. A strong advocate of the Popular Front and, like Cripps, very much under the influence of Pollitt and the CPGB, he had set up the LBC in May 1936: the idea had come to him over lunch with Cripps and the Marxist intellectual John Strachey, then the CPGB's most loyal fellow-traveller, to discuss Cripps's idea for a new left weekly.[44] Within a year the club had 45,000 members, each receiving at least one book a month. By spring 1938 membership was 58,000 and there were more than 700 local discussion groups holding fortnightly meetings spread around the country. A panel comprising Gollancz, Laski and Strachey selected the books. Most were by communist authors; the others included books by Cripps and by Orwell, whose *The Road to Wigan Pier* was a massive success for the club in May 1937. Gollancz was intolerant of criticism of the Communist Party in British politics - he added an introduction to *The Road to Wigan Pier* attacking Orwell's mildly critical remarks on the party in the second part of the book - and on the Soviet Union would publish only encomiums to the wonders of socialist construction.[45] On Spain, he would countenance only books that stuck to the communist line: he turned down Orwell's *Homage to Catalonia* unseen. Partly because he distrusted the ILP on Russia and Spain, partly because he was desperate to keep in with the Labour leadership (he even published Clement Attlee's achingly dull *The Labour Party in Perspective*), Gollancz kept a respectable distance from the Unity Campaign and *The Tribune* at their launch. But by summer 1938, with Cripps coming round to the idea of a Popular Front, the ILP off the scene and the LBC in need of a membership-boosting initiative - growth had slowed and it was still losing money - Gollancz was open to a deal. Cripps agreed that, in return for two pages of what would now be called advertorial in *The Tribune* for the LBC, he would fire Mellor, replace him with a more amenable editor and give Gollancz a seat on the board.

Cripps's first choice as new editor was the young Michael Foot - but Foot would have none of it, and resigned in solidarity with Mellor, despite Brailsford's pleading with him to stay and fight.[46] Cripps brushed aside Foot's protests at the way Mellor had been treated as 'one of those unavoidable happenings that do occur in life and for which no one can be blamed!' and told him: 'I think you may give me credit for the fact that I don't propose to pay many thousands a year to run a paper which is not in harmony - broadly - with my views.' Cripps and Gollancz duly appointed as editor H. J. Hartshorn, a secret member of the CPGB who had been working on the *Sunday Pictorial*, the *Daily Mirror*'s sister paper. Brailsford wrote sadly to Foot: 'The socialist left is allowing itself to be driven from all its strategical positions by the Communist Party. With great subtlety it drove the Socialist League to suicide and now it is capturing *The Tribune*.'[47]

Foot's break with the paper was only temporary, and his resignation did his career no harm. On the recommendation of Bevan, Lord Beaverbrook invited him over to his country house, Cherkley Court, for the weekend and immediately hired him to write for the *Evening Standard*. Foot was soon the *Standard*'s star writer, becoming its editor in 1942 at the age of twenty-nine.

* * *

Under Hartshorn, *Tribune* really did become 'Cripps' Chronicle', as it had been nicknamed at its launch. Hartshorn tried to ape the populist style of his erstwhile boss Hugh Cudlipp on the *Sunday Pictorial* – but he had none of Cudlipp's flair and the result was a badly designed mess. The Hartshorn *Tribune* followed loyally in the footsteps of Cripps as his calls for a Popular Front grew louder in the wake of the Munich crisis, supporting independent candidates in the Oxford and Bridgwater by-elections in October and November 1938. It stuck with him in January 1939 when, after failing to get the Labour NEC to accept a memorandum backing the Popular Front, he distributed the document throughout the party – an act that led to his expulsion. (Cripps also declared that Labour had no hope of winning the next election, expected later in the year.) *Tribune* then became the organ of Cripps's 'Petition Campaign' for the Popular Front in February–May 1939 – a poorly organised national speaking tour, supported by Bevan and Strauss (who were also expelled), that was disbanded after the May 1939 Labour conference voted in favour of the expulsions. Bevan and Strauss were soon back; Cripps remained outside the Labour Party until 1945.

Through all this, *Tribune* took an unquestioningly pro-Soviet line. Under Mellor, the paper had been an enthusiastic Soviet fellow-traveller. At the height of Stalin's purges, it sent the young Barbara Betts out to Russia to find out about women in the Soviet Union, and when she returned she was given a page a week for seven weeks to regale readers with the joys of sexual equality and state nurseries.[48] It even allowed the Communist Party ideologue Pat Sloan a whole page to denigrate as Trotskyist some very mild criticism of the Soviet Union by Norman Thomas, the American Socialist Party leader. 'For over 30 years,' declared Sloan, 'Trotsky has been one of the most vitriolic of all the enemies of Bolshevism.'[49] But at least under Mellor the paper ignored the show trials and purges rather than endorsed them. As Foot put it:

> We said nothing or next to nothing on the subject, refusing to join the communist claque which hailed these infamies as triumphs of popular justice but lamentably failing to assist H. N. Brailsford in *Reynolds News* as he stripped aside the curtain of lies and saved the honour of socialist journalism in face of the inconvenient horror.[50]

Under Hartshorn, *Tribune* – he dropped the *The* a couple of months after becoming editor – pretty much joined the communist claque. Through late 1938 and 1939, it published nothing even remotely critical of the Soviet Union. It faithfully praised every Soviet diplomatic initiative, not even expressing doubt over the Molotov–Ribbentrop pact of August 1939, which it described as 'a great reinforcement for peace in Eastern Europe'.[51] In Foot's words: 'J. R. Campbell's apologia for the Moscow trials, *Soviet Policy and its Critics*, was favourably reviewed, Trotsky was incessantly denounced, and Stalin's unscrupulous redrafting of recent history, *The History of the CPSU* (1939), was praised in lavish terms.'[52]

When war finally came with the Nazi invasion of Poland on 1 September, the paper at first, like the CPGB, proclaimed its support for victory against Nazism but then - after the CPGB abruptly changed tack on Moscow's instructions at the end of the month - denounced the war as imperialist. The CPGB went through agonies over its change of line: Harry Pollitt, who had produced a pamphlet setting out the case for rallying to the war effort, was deposed as general secretary in favour of the ultra-Stalinist Rajani Palme Dutt.[53] Cripps appears to have been oblivious, enthusiastically taking up the new line and affecting ignorance as to why Pollitt had fallen out with his party. He defended the Soviet occupation of eastern Poland in a piece entitled 'Why Blame Russia?'[54] and spent the next two months agitating for a negotiated peace with 'the German people' - though he never identified how this could happen. Then he went off on a semi-official visit to India, Burma and China (the Foreign Office appears to have believed he might persuade Indian nationalists to hold off their campaign for independence for the duration of the war) that ended up lasting five months and to which he added an unofficial trip to Moscow. His parting shot was a leader with a headline that said it all: 'Put yourselves in Russia's place'.

To be fair to Cripps, this was the period of the 'phoney war', when neither Britain and France nor Germany seemed altogether committed to fighting and plenty of people expected the war to end soon with some sort of deal among the great powers. But just as he left Britain, Russia attacked Finland - and *Tribune* was thrown into crisis. If Cripps had remained blindly pro-Soviet, the other members of the *Tribune* board, Bevan, Strauss and Gollancz, along with Konni Zilliacus, a former League of Nations official who had become the Hartshorn *Tribune*'s main foreign affairs commentator, already had their doubts about Soviet policy.[55] Bevan in particular had from the start of the war been convinced that there was no alternative to fighting Hitler with or without Stalin, though he thought the Soviet Union would eventually be drawn in against the Nazis, and he had felt nothing but contempt for the British Communist Party's volte-face. Now, with Cripps away, the *Tribune* board made a break with the CPGB, denouncing the Soviet invasion of Finland. 'We deplore her for her aggression, but we support her for her socialism,' they wrote in the issue of 8 December, going on to make it clear that they were against Britain assisting the Finns militarily. Hartshorn commissioned Dutt to write an article for the same issue of the paper calling on *Tribune* readers to disown the *Tribune* board - as Strauss put it, effectively advising them 'to stop buying the paper. Surely an editorial request unique in the history of journalism.'[56]

For a couple of months, Hartshorn and his staff continued to press the CPGB line in *Tribune*'s pages, maintaining, as Strauss put it, 'a communist tone in every issue' and attempting to turn the paper into 'an organ of the Nazi-Soviet pact'. They advocated a policy of 'revolutionary defeatism', arguing that the war was an imperialist war in which the enemy of the working class was the ruling class at home, and commissioned letters from CPers and fellow-travellers attacking the board for daring to criticise the Soviet Union. But in February 1940, with circulation in free fall, Strauss pulled the plug after Hartshorn wrote a piece for the paper explicitly making the case for a negotiated settlement with Hitler.[57] He fired Hartshorn and asked the journalist Raymond Postgate to take over. Postgate, like Mellor a member of the CPGB in its infancy who had worked on the *Daily Herald*, accepted on condition that he would not only change the paper's policy to back the war but also take it upmarket to compete with the *New Statesman*. The CPGB's *Daily Worker* was apoplectic about the appointment, denouncing Postgate as 'an anti-Soviet journalist' and mourning the end of an era in which *Tribune* had been 'following a vigorous socialist policy and brilliantly edited' and 'had achieved a deserved reputation as a genuinely progressive organ'.[58]

For a few issues, the paper continued to give space to supporters of the CPGB line. But by the time the 'phoney war' was brought abruptly to an end by the momentous events of April to May 1940 – Hitler's invasion of Denmark and Norway, the replacement of Neville Chamberlain with Winston Churchill as British Prime Minister and Labour's entry into the wartime coalition government, the rapid German advances through Holland, Belgium and then France, the evacuation of the British Expeditionary Force from Dunkirk – *Tribune* had definitively abandoned the fellow-travelling camp. So too had Gollancz and John Strachey. Straight after the fall of Chamberlain, Gollancz commissioned Foot, Frank Owen (Foot's editor at the *Standard*) and Peter Howard (a journalist on the *Daily Express*) to write an instant polemical book attacking the appeasers of the 1930s and by implication the defeatists of 1939–40. The result, *Guilty Men*, published under the pseudonym of 'Cato' because the authors wanted to conceal their identities from Lord Beaverbrook, their employer, was a runaway bestseller. Gollancz himself wrote and published a pamphlet, *Where Are You Going?*, an excoriating assault on the communists, who only a year before had been his closest political allies.

* * *

Orwell had nothing to do with *Tribune* at its launch or for the first three years of its life. By his own account, in a piece for the tenth anniversary issue of the paper, he 'did not learn of the existence of *Tribune* till some time in 1939': 'It had started early in 1937, but of the thirty months that intervened before the outbreak of war I spent five in hospital and thirteen abroad. What first drew my attention to it, I believe, was a none-too-friendly review of a novel of mine.'[59]

And indeed he did spend the first half of 1937 fighting for the POUM in Spain, was hospitalised with a tuberculosis lesion in a Kent sanatorium between March and September 1938 and then spent six months in Morocco resting and writing *Coming Up for Air*. It is quite possible that these long periods out of circulation - along with the fact that he spent most of the nine months between returning from Spain and being hospitalised secluded in his cottage in Wallington, Hertfordshire, writing *Homage to Catalonia* - meant that Orwell remained completely oblivious to *Tribune* until Winifred Horrabin's review of *Coming Up for Air* appeared in July 1939.[60] There is certainly no evidence to the contrary.

But it is difficult to avoid the suspicion that Orwell was diplomatically drawing a veil over *Tribune*'s first few years so as not to spoil the birthday party. It would be odd if Orwell really did first hear of the paper three months after returning from Morocco, even if he didn't read it. He knew several people associated with *Tribune* - notably Gollancz, his publisher, and Fenner Brockway - and belonged to the left-wing milieu in which the paper circulated, although he was very much a dissident member. (He spoke at an ILP summer school in August 1937 when the Unity Campaign was still nominally alive, later went to LBC meetings while researching for *Coming Up for Air* and joined the ILP in summer 1938.) After his experience in Spain, moreover, he had become an obsessive reader of the left press - not least because he felt a burning urge to counter the lies that had been spread about his comrades in arms.

In May 1937, on leave in Barcelona from the front, he had taken to the barricades to defend the POUM and the anarchists against what they saw (rightly, though Orwell demurred) as a Soviet-inspired attempt by the local Stalinists to crush them. For this resistance the POUM had been denounced by the Stalinists as 'Trotskyist-fascist' fifth columnists and then, some weeks later, ruthlessly hunted down by the secret police, under the direction of the Soviet NKVD, and arrested or shot. Orwell and his wife Eileen were lucky to escape: unknown to them, they were on a wanted list as '*trotzquistas pronunciados*' (confirmed Trotskyists).[61] On his return from Spain, Orwell was outraged to find that most of the left was not interested in the story of the POUM and was repeating Stalinist propaganda against it. Kingsley Martin, the editor of the *New Statesman*, spiked the account of the May events in Barcelona he had commissioned because it contravened the paper's editorial policy and then refused to run Orwell's review of Franz Borkenau's *The Spanish Cockpit*.[62] Gollancz turned down *Homage to Catalonia* before Orwell had started writing it because he wouldn't publish anything 'which could harm the fight against fascism'. The same attitude, Orwell discovered, was prevalent everywhere on the British left except in the ILP and among the anarchists. While writing *Homage to Catalonia* in late 1937 he actively searched out examples of Stalinist propaganda masquerading as the truth about the POUM in the left and liberal press - and it would be surprising if he didn't come across *Tribune* then or in the course of 1938.

If he did, it is unlikely he thought much of it. He shared *Tribune*'s rejection of British rearmament, its opposition to war and its gloomy prognosis that the National Government in Britain would probably turn fascist. He was as excoriating as any *Tribune* writer about the Labour leadership's faith in collective security and its support for rearmament, as dismissive as Stafford Cripps of Labour's prospects in the election that should have happened in 1939 or 1940. But, unlike *Tribune* right up to the end of 1939, after his experience in Spain he saw the Communist Party as part of the problem rather than as part of the solution. As he wrote immediately after returning from Spain:

> It is unfortunate that so few people in England have yet caught up with the fact that communism is now a counter-revolutionary force; that communists everywhere are in alliance with bourgeois reformism and using the whole of their powerful machinery to crush or discredit any party that shows signs of revolutionary tendencies.[63]

He was convinced that the only way fascism could be defeated was through socialist revolution. As he wrote to a friend in September 1937: 'After what I have seen in Spain I have come to the conclusion that it is futile to be "anti-fascist" while attempting to preserve capitalism.'[64] As for the Popular Front - which *Tribune* advocated from 1938 - it was, he declared in February 1938, nothing more than a euphemism for class collaboration, 'an unholy alliance between the robbers and the robbed' to trick the working class into supporting an imperialist war. He ridiculed 'the nauseous spectacle of bishops, communists, cocoa-magnates, publishers, duchesses and Labour MPs marching arm in arm to the tune of "Rule Britannia" and all tensing their muscles for a rush to the bomb-proof shelter when and if their policy begins to take effect'.[65] He was still on the same track in June 1939, attacking the 'monstrous harlequinade' of 'Quakers shouting for a bigger army, communists wearing union jacks, Winston Churchill posing as a democrat'. 'Nothing is likely to save us,' he declared, 'except the emergence within the next two years of a real mass party whose first pledges are to refuse war and to right imperial injustice.'[66]

Precisely when Orwell changed his mind on the need to 'refuse war' is unclear - but change it he did. By his own account, he had a dream one night in August 1939 that war had started, which made him realise that the onset of war would come as a relief and that he would support it as a patriot. The next morning, he claimed, he 'came downstairs to find the newspaper announcing Ribbentrop's flight to Moscow'.[67] As John Newsinger remarks in *Orwell's Politics*, this has the air of an apocryphal story, but there can be no doubt that Orwell's conversion to pro-war patriotism was sudden and visceral.[68] As Orwell put it himself:

> If I had to defend my reasons for supporting the war, I believe I could do so. There is no real alternative between resisting Hitler and surrendering to him, and from a

> socialist point of view I should say that it is better to resist; in any case I can see no argument for surrender that does not make nonsense of the Republican resistance in Spain, the Chinese resistance to Japan, etc, etc. But I don't pretend that that is the emotional basis of my actions. What I knew in my dream that night was that the long drilling in patriotism which the middle classes go through had done its work, and that once England was in a serious jam it would be impossible for me to sabotage. But let no one mistake the meaning of this. Patriotism has nothing to do with conservatism. It is devotion to something that is changing but is felt to be mystically the same, like the devotion of the ex-White Bolshevik to Russia. To be loyal both to Chamberlain's England and to the England of tomorrow might seem an impossibility, if one did not know it to be an everyday phenomenon.[69]

Orwell's volte-face put him even more at odds with *Tribune* in the first months of the war as Cripps pleaded for understanding for Russia and H. J. Hartshorn spread defeatism. But after Raymond Postgate took Hartshorn's place Orwell suddenly found himself more or less in sympathy with *Tribune* for the first time.

When he became *Tribune* editor, Postgate was forty-three, with a long history of involvement in left-wing politics. Educated at public school and Oxford, he had been a conscientious objector in the First World War and had started in journalism on the *Daily Herald* after marrying Daisy Lansbury, whose father George was its editor. Postgate had joined the CPGB when it was launched in 1920 and briefly edited its weekly paper, the *Communist*, but resigned from the party in 1922 when Moscow insisted that the CPGB adopt a 'democratic centralist' structure and become a truly Bolshevik party - and his apostasy had earned him the undying enmity of the CPGB. During the 1930s he had established a reputation as a biographer and popular historian, and from 1937 to 1939 had edited *Fact*, an independent left-wing monthly in the form of a small book, usually containing one major article on a key issue of the day alongside reviews and shorter pieces. *Fact* had been notably free of the kowtowing to the Communist Party that was such a feature of the late-1930s left: Postgate responded sympathetically to a suggestion from Orwell (whom he had met at a party at Fredric Warburg's) for an article about the POUM, although it was never published, and like Orwell he had a run-in with Victor Gollancz, who refused to publicise *Fact* to LBC members because Postgate had promised to run an '"objective examination" of the Trotsky–Stalin controversy'.[70]

Orwell, whose book of literary essays, *Inside the Whale and Other Essays*, was published on 11 March 1940, was one of the first writers Postgate recruited for his relaunch of *Tribune*, along with John Lehman, the editor of *New Writing*.[71] Orwell's first contribution to the paper, a review of a soldier's eyewitness account of Napoleon's disastrous Russian campaign in 1812–13, appeared in Postgate's second issue on 29 March.[72] For the next six months, initially from Wallington and then from a dingy flat in Marylebone where he and Eileen moved in mid-May, Orwell produced a book review for *Tribune* on average every three weeks, occasionally visiting the paper's offices in Chiswell Street, near Moorgate. Most of the reviews were round-ups of fiction, either new or reprinted, some of them of wholly unrelated books. Although competently written - and generally given a cover line by *Tribune* - they are unremarkable except for odd glimpses of humour and occasional toying with themes developed by Orwell at greater length and in greater depth elsewhere. In a piece published on 12 July on new editions of dystopian novels, he noted of Aldous Huxley's *Brave New World* that although it 'was a brilliant caricature of the present (the present of 1930), it probably casts no light on the future': 'No society of that kind would last more than a couple of generations, because a ruling class that thought principally in terms of a "good time" would soon lose its vitality.'[73] Four weeks later he teased *Tribune* readers in a round-up that included his friend Ethel Mannin's novel *Rolling in the Dew*, 'a high-spirited satire on the teetotal, vegetarian fringe of "enlightened" society':

> There is a charming picture of a colony of nudists, higher thinkers and theosophists having the time of their lives on goat's milk and bran in a chateau in the Swiss mountains. To satirise these people may seem a little like shooting a sitting rabbit, but the fact that they are so numerous - or rather, by their untiring missionary efforts they make themselves seem so numerous - that an occasional counter-attack is justified. They have done the socialist movement appreciable harm by spreading the notion that a socialist is a person who either lives on nuts, wears sandals or abjures alcohol.[74]

On 23 August, in a discussion of Mark Benney's 'underclass' novel, *The Lights Go Down*, Orwell declared: 'Burglars, as is well known, usually vote Conservative.'[75]

Tribune was not a priority for Orwell in 1940. 'I was not paid,' he recalled in 1947, 'and I only saw the paper on the somewhat rare occasions when I went up to London and visited Postgate in a bare and dusty office near London Wall.' Far more important to him - because they did pay - were two other weeklies for which he reviewed regularly, *New Statesman* and *Time and Tide*. He was more in sympathy politically with *Tribune*: he had not forgiven Kingsley Martin, whom he hated with a vengeance, for refusing to carry his articles on Spain (although he had made his peace with the *Statesman*'s literary editor, Raymond Mortimer), and *Time and Tide* was liberal rather than socialist in its politics.

But Orwell was at the extreme left-wing edge of *Tribune*'s political circle and - along with Gollancz and John Strachey, strangely enough - one of its most trenchant critics of the Communist Party and the Soviet Union.[76] At least at the start of Postgate's editorship he felt that it still carried far too much Popular Front baggage. As he put it in 1947: 'The futile controversy between "supporters" and "opposers" of the war continued to rumble in its columns while the German armies gathered for the spring offensives.'[77] Although there is nothing in his *Tribune* reviews that shows it, during the course of 1940

Orwell became convinced that Britain was growing ripe for a socialist revolution and that the Home Guard, which he joined in June, could play the role of a workers' militia in that revolution. *Tribune*, although very much in favour of the Home Guard's 'citizen soldiers', saw them playing a rather more limited role.

Orwell's first expressed this 'revolutionary patriotism' well away from *Tribune*, in an essay published in *Folios of New Writing* in autumn 1940, 'My Country Right or Left':

> Only revolution can save England, that has been obvious for years, but now the revolution has started, and it may proceed quickly if only we can keep Hitler out . . . I dare say the London gutters will run with blood. All right, let them, if it is necessary. But when the red militias are billeted in the Ritz I shall still feel that the England I was taught to love so long ago and for such different reasons is somehow persisting.[78]

He developed the theme at length in the essay *The Lion and the Unicorn*, written between August and October 1940 and published by Warburg in early 1941 as the first in a series of Searchlight Books that were commissioned and edited by Orwell and the young left-wing author Tosco Fyvel to make the case for radical socialist war aims.[79] 'England is a family with the wrong members in control,' wrote Orwell. 'It is only by revolution that the native genius of the English people can be set free.' Possibly the most forceful of Orwell's revolutionary patriotic polemics was 'Our Opportunity', first published in early 1941 in *Left News*, the LBC's magazine, and then republished as 'Patriots and Revolutionaries' in *The Betrayal of the Left*, Gollancz's collection of writings against the People's Convention of January 1941, a London conference organised by the CPGB that was the nearest it came to organising a defeatist movement during the period of the Nazi-Soviet pact.[80] 'Either we turn this war into a revolutionary war,' Orwell declared, 'or we lose it.'

There is only one piece he wrote for *Tribune* that expresses these sentiments, 'The Home Guard and You', published on 20 December 1940: 'We are in a strange period of history in which a revolutionary has to be a patriot and a patriot has to be a revolutionary. We know, even if the Blimps don't, that without a radical change in our social system the war cannot be won.'[81]

* * *

'The Home Guard and You' was the last piece Orwell wrote for *Tribune* for twenty-one months, and it was not until spring 1943 that he again became a regular in the paper. It is possible that he was piqued by Postgate's review of *The Betrayal of the Left*, which appeared on 14 March 1941 under the headline 'A book to make you sick': Postgate dismissed one of Orwell's essays in the book, 'Freedom and Democracy' as 'probably the worst thing he ever wrote', although he also said that 'Patriots and Revolutionaries' was 'perhaps the best thing he ever wrote and should be read and re-read'.[82] Certainly, Orwell was less worried than Aneurin Bevan and Postgate about the government's response to the People's Convention, the banning of the Communist Party's *Daily Worker* and the *Week*, Claud Cockburn's Stalinist gossip sheet. *Tribune* had been vigorous in its denunciations of the People's Convention, and Bevan had described the *Worker* as 'now among the ranks of those helping Hitler to win' – 'It is doing it as openly and deliberately as it dares.'[83] But after Herbert Morrison, the Home Secretary, closed down the *Worker*, both Bevan and *Tribune* attacked him, with Postgate declaring that 'the Cabinet has made the worst mistake of the war' and that 'the suppression of the *Daily Worker* is the suppression of *opinion*, nothing more'.[84] Orwell, by contrast, noted in his diary that he was 'only very doubtfully pleased' about the ban.

But the main reason for Orwell's absence from *Tribune* in 1941–2 was simply that he had too much else on. He spent the first eight months of 1941 earning a living as a jobbing freelance – mainly churning out reviews, but also writing several substantial essays, including his first three 'London Letters' to the American magazine *Partisan Review*. Then from August he worked full time at the BBC, with a contract stipulating that he could not 'undertake work for any other person or firm whatsoever . . . without the previous written consent of the Corporation'. All his free time, he wrote later, was taken up with the Home Guard.

In the meantime, *Tribune* went on without him. Either Postgate was not very confident when it came to magazine design or wartime conditions rendered aesthetic considerations secondary, but the look of *Tribune* changed with disturbing frequency and seldom for the better. Nevertheless, he consolidated the paper's position as an upmarket rival to the *New Statesman* – he never went back to tabloid populism – and circulation recovered. Stafford Cripps had dropped out altogether from *Tribune* on being appointed ambassador to Moscow by Winston Churchill in May 1940, leaving Bevan as the senior politician associated with it. During late 1940 and the early months of 1941, with Labour's leaders in Churchill's government and bound by collective responsibility, he found a role for himself in Parliament as the government's most outspoken and persistent left-wing critic, and he increasingly harnessed *Tribune* to his campaigns.

From the failure of the attempt of the British and Free French to capture the Vichy stronghold of Dakar in French West Africa in September 1940, Bevan and *Tribune* relentlessly criticised the inadequacies of the British war effort. In June 1941, when Hitler attacked the Soviet Union, Bevan used the pages of *Tribune* to demand immediate action by Britain against Germany to take the heat off the Russians. On the home front, *Tribune* demanded that the 'men of Munich' be dumped from the government and accused Churchill of amassing himself unaccountable powers.

It was not all plain sailing. One night at the end of December 1940, a German bomb destroyed the *Tribune* offices in Chiswell Street. No one was hurt, but *Tribune* found itself homeless. It survived thanks to luck in finding new premises within a week at 222 Strand, an emergency appeal to readers and an influx of cash from Strauss. Despite rising circulation, *Tribune* continued to lose money, and some time in summer 1941 the board warned Postgate that it might have to do without him. He stayed, but only until the end of the year. Bevan and he fell out - Postgate later said that 'there were two explosions and one unjustified accusation' - and Strauss, apparently reluctantly, gave Postgate his notice. Gollancz was also sympathetic with Postgate and soon afterwards resigned from the board.[85]

Bevan initially took over as editor himself. 'I shall edit the paper myself without salary,' he wrote to Jennie Lee, then on a speaking tour in the US, 'and I shall scour Fleet Street giving journalists with good information and bad consciences the privilege of burning candles for their souls on the same financial terms as myself.'[86] But it soon became apparent that he had neither the time nor the technical expertise to do it properly, and on the advice of Michael Foot hired Jon Kimche as assistant editor. Kimche, whom Foot had met when Kimche was running the ILP bookshop, had been writing articles on military strategy for the *Evening Standard*. Soon after, Strauss resigned from the *Tribune* board to become parliamentary private secretary to Cripps, who returned from Moscow in the middle of January 1942 to an extraordinary welcome from the press and within a month - amid speculation that he would set himself up as leader of the opposition or even somehow mount a challenge for the premiership - was brought into the war Cabinet by Churchill. Strauss's place on the board was taken by his wife Patricia.

Japan entered the war in December 1941, bringing the United States in on the Allied side with its attack on Pearl Harbor, and for the next six months defeat followed defeat for the Allies everywhere but Russia, where the Red Army held and then began to reverse the German advance. The Germans won victory after victory in north Africa, threatening British-held Egypt, and Japan swept through south-east Asia and the Pacific. Bevan sharpened his criticisms of British military policy, from early 1942 playing a leading role in the campaign for a west European 'second front' to relieve the pressure on the Soviet Union. And *Tribune*, redesigned elegantly under the new Bevan-Kimche regime, at last found real success despite a doubling of price to sixpence. The paper created a sensation in May 1942 by publishing three articles by Thomas Rainsboro' (a pseudonym for Frank Owen) laying into Churchill's record of military blunders and demanding a change of strategy. Bevan led the subsequent charge against Churchill in the Commons with what his biographer John Campbell describes as 'his greatest speech of the war': 'First, the main strategy of the war has been wrong; second, the wrong weapons have been produced; and third, those weapons are being managed by men who are not trained in the use of them and who have not studied the use of modern weapons.'[87] He and *Tribune* kept up the pressure in print and in Parliament over the ensuing two years, calling again and again for the US and Britain to open a second front and then castigating them for adopting a 'Mediterranean strategy' of attacking Axis Europe through Italy.

As the war went on, Bevan and *Tribune* also argued ever more resolutely for Labour to come out on the attack on the need to create a comprehensive welfare state and extend public ownership after the war. They defended unofficial strikers, lampooned the Tories and demanded that Labour abandon the agreement not to put up candidates in seats previously held by Tories in by-elections.

Orwell returned to *Tribune*'s pages with a review essay on Thomas Hardy's poetic drama *The Dynasts*, published on 16 September 1942,[88] and contributed a background piece on French Morocco – in the news because of the Allied landings in north Africa – two months later,[89] but it was not until the next year that he started doing regular pieces. Between March and November 1943, when he took up the post of literary editor, he wrote something every month or so, including four pieces that were much more substantial than the routine reviews he had turned out in 1940: essays on George Gissing, Thomas Mann and Mark Twain;[90] and 'Literature and the Left', a trenchant assault on the leftist habit of judging literary work by the politics of its author that is almost a manifesto for the approach taken by Orwell as *Tribune*'s literary editor:

> If you consult any sporting manual or yearbook you will find many pages devoted to the hunting of the fox and the hare, but not a word about the hunting of the highbrow. Yet this, more than any other, is the characteristic British sport, in season all the year round and enjoyed by rich and poor alike, with no complications from either class-feeling or political alignment.
>
> For it should be noted that in its attitude towards 'highbrows' – that is, towards any writer or artist who makes experiments in technique – the left is no friendlier than the right. Not only is 'highbrow' almost as much a word of abuse in the *Daily Worker* as in *Punch*, but it is exactly those writers whose work shows both originality and the power to endure that Marxist doctrinaires single out for attack. I could name a long list of examples, but I am thinking especially of Joyce, Yeats, Lawrence and Eliot. Eliot, in particular, is damned in the left-wing press almost as automatically and perfunctorily as Kipling – and that by critics who only a few years back were going into raptures over the already forgotten masterpieces of the Left Book Club . . .
>
> Left-wing literary criticism has not been wrong in insisting on the importance of subject matter . . . Where it has been wrong is in making what are ostensibly literary judgements for political ends. To take a crude example, what communist would dare to admit in public that Trotsky is a better writer than Stalin – as he is, of course? To say 'X is a gifted writer, but he is a political enemy and I shall do my best to silence him' is harmless enough. Even if you end by silencing him with a tommy-gun you are not really sinning against the intellect. The deadly sin is to say 'X is a political enemy:

> therefore he is a bad writer.' And if anyone says that his kind of thing doesn't happen, I answer merely: look up the literary pages of the left-wing press, from the *News Chronicle* to the *Labour Monthly*, and see what you find.[91]

* * *

By the time Orwell joined the *Tribune* staff and started writing his 'As I Please' column, the war in Europe was reaching the beginning of the end. On the eastern front, the Soviet advance that had begun in early 1943 with the destruction of the German armies besieging Stalingrad and the expulsion of the Germans from the Caucasus continued relentlessly, with extraordinary loss of life, through 1943 and 1944. After inflicting a crushing defeat on the Germans in the battle of Kursk in summer 1943, the Soviet juggernaut rolled west. By the end of 1943, most of the Ukraine was in Soviet hands. In January 1944 the siege of Leningrad was lifted and the Red Army reached the 1939 Polish border. During spring and summer 1944, a massive offensive smashed the German Army Group Central and brought the Russians to the gates of Warsaw. There they paused - allowing the German SS to crush the uprising of the Polish home army in Warsaw - but by the beginning of 1945, having cleared the Germans from the Baltic states and most of the Balkans, the Russians were advancing on Germany itself.

Meanwhile, in the west, the Allied advance through Italy, begun with the invasion of Sicily from north Africa in July 1943, moved painfully slowly towards Rome (liberated in June 1944) and then north, reaching a line north of Florence by the end of 1944. The long-awaited Allied liberation of north-western Europe began with the Normandy landings of June 1944. Paris was taken within three months, and by the middle of September the Germans had been driven from nearly all of France, Belgium and Luxembourg. The Allied advance was then slowed by the failure of the British airborne assault on Arnhem and briefly reversed by the German Ardennes offensive of December 1944, but by January 1945 the western Allies were, like the Russians, beginning their invasion of Germany.

As victory came within sight, the Allies attempted to reach agreement on the shape of the post-war settlement in Europe. The deals struck between the western powers and Stalin in 1943–5 remain controversial today: whether through pusillanimity or a grudging acceptance of facts on the ground, at Tehran and Yalta Roosevelt and Churchill acquiesced in the establishment of Soviet hegemony in east-central Europe and Soviet annexation of substantial areas of pre-1939 Poland and East Prussia (with Poland taking the rest of East Prussia, Pomerania and Silesia from Germany) and agreed to the division of Germany and Austria into four occupation zones.

On the home front, with the Blitz a distant memory - though from June 1944 the Germans found a new means of terrorising the population of London, the V-1 flying bomb, and then added the V-2 rocket at the end of the year – politics was dominated by arguments about what should happen after the war.

Bevan and *Tribune* again played a noisy oppositional role. They relentlessly pressed the case for Labour to leave the coalition government and adopt a bold socialist programme in preparation for the general election due as soon as the war was won, denouncing the coalition's post-war reconstruction planning – including the 1944 White Paper laying down the central objective of full employment – as a means of merely preserving capitalism. They were equally vigorous in their condemnation of the consensus among the Labour leadership, Churchill, the Communist Party and Stalin that Germany should be dismembered and punished and that east-central Europe should be left to Soviet domination. Throughout 1943–5, Bevan and *Tribune* consistently attacked the Allied policy of accepting only unconditional surrender from Germany, disavowed dismemberment of Germany and opposed punishment of the German people as a whole. Bevan, who in 1941–2 had been one of the most forceful proponents of immediately opening a second front, became increasingly critical of the Soviet Union's behaviour as just another cynical great power, intent, like Britain and the United States, on carving out the maximum sphere of influence with scant regard for the wishes of its subject peoples.

Orwell's 'As I Please' column was conceived as a means of providing relief from the diet of political polemic and policy analysis that dominated the pages of *Tribune*, and only one of the columns written while he was literary editor deals directly and at length with events on the battlefields of Europe – an excoriating polemic published at the beginning of September 1944 against unthinking leftist acceptance of Soviet propaganda about the Warsaw uprising. It includes this memorable warning (almost certainly directed at Kingsley Martin of the *New Statesman*, who telephoned *Tribune* threatening libel action):

> First of all, a message to English left-wing journalists and intellectuals generally: 'Do remember that dishonesty and cowardice always have to be paid for. Don't imagine that for years on end you can make yourself the boot-licking propagandist of the Soviet régime, or any other régime, and then suddenly return to mental decency. Once a whore, always a whore.'[92]

But the columns are littered with asides that make clear his broad agreement with the paper's opposition to the punitive Allied policy towards Germany and to Soviet designs on eastern Europe. In December 1943, he ridiculed the notion of imposing a humiliating 'Carthaginian peace' on Germany;[93] a couple of months later he insisted that 'what is important is that "revenge" and "punishment" should have no part in our policy or even in our day-dreams' and denounced 'the left associating itself with schemes to partition

Germany, enrol millions of Germans in forced-labour gangs and impose repatriations which will make the Versailles reparations look like a bus fare'.[94] Early in 1945 he despaired of the double standards that led the pro-Soviet left-wing press to ignore the depredations of Stalin and the anti-Soviet right-wing press to ignore those of Churchill:

> When it comes to such issues as Poland, the Baltic countries, Yugoslavia or Greece, what difference is there between the Russophile press and the extreme Tory press? The one is simply the other standing on its head. The *News Chronicle* gives the big headlines to the fighting in Greece but tucks away the news that 'force has had to be used' against the Polish Home Army in small print at the bottom of a column. The *Daily Worker* disapproves of dictatorship in Athens, the *Catholic Herald* disapproves of dictatorship in Belgrade. There is no one who is able to say – at least, no one who has the chance to say in a newspaper of big circulation – that this whole dirty game of spheres of influence, quislings, purges, deportation, one-party elections and hundred per cent plebiscites is morally the same whether it is done by ourselves, the Russians or the Nazis.[95]

On the eve of the Yalta conference, Orwell laid into 'the scheme to remove all Poles from the areas to be taken over by the USSR, and, in compensation, all Germans from the portions of Germany to be taken over by Poland' as an 'enormous crime' and warned:

> With the acquiescence of all of us, the world is splitting up into the two or three huge super-states . . . One cannot draw their exact boundaries as yet, but one can see more or less what areas they will comprise. And if the world does settle down into this pattern, it is likely that these vast states will be permanently at war with one another, though it will not necessarily be a very intensive or bloody kind of war . . . If these two or three super-states do establish themselves, not only will each of them be too big to be conquered, but they will be under no necessity to trade with one another, and in a position to prevent all contact between their nationals. Already, for a dozen years or so, large areas of the earth have been cut off from one another, although technically at peace.[96]

The first run of 'As I Please' is intensely political in other ways too. The columns reverberate with reflections on the relationship between politics and literature and with observations of public opinion and political culture – the unreported rise of popular anti-Americanism, the impact of official pro-Russian propaganda, the effects of rationing and shortages, the influence of the flying bombs on morale, attitudes to the treatment of war criminals. There are barbs directed at Orwell's bugbears: reactionary Catholics, pro-Hitler pacifists, lying communists and apologists for Stalinism.

What Orwell never addressed even in asides in *Tribune* in 1943–5 was the political situation in Britain. It is clear from his writing elsewhere, notably his 'London Letters' to *Partisan Review* and the short book *The English People*, that he had long since given up his high hopes of 1940–1 that Britain was on the verge of a socialist revolution. As he put it to *Partisan Review* in October 1944, looking back on his previous contributions to the magazine:

> I fell into the trap of assuming that 'the war and the revolution are inseparable'. There were excuses for this belief, but still it was a very great error . . . I over-emphasised the anti-fascist character of the war; exaggerated the social changes that were actually occurring; and underestimated the enormous strength of the forces of reaction.[97]

As John Newsinger argues in his *Orwell's Politics*, it is nevertheless questionable how far Orwell embraced left Labour reformism in this period.[98] Orwell's political thinking was rooted in a very different left tradition to that of Bevan and most of the Labour left. Orwell came from and was still engaged with the dissident anti-Stalinist revolutionary socialist left that was obsessed with the degeneration of the Bolshevik revolution, the influence of which is apparent not only in his journalism but also in his last two novels, *Animal Farm* and *Nineteen Eighty-Four*. He was not fundamentally a parliamentary socialist: in his spring 1944 'London Letter' to *Partisan Review* he declared: 'As a legislative body parliament has become relatively unimportant, and it has even less control over the executive than over the government. But it still functions as a kind of uncensored supplement to the radio – which, after all, is something worth preserving.'[99]

Nor was he optimistic about Labour's electoral prospects. Unlike Bevan, who in 1944–5 was insistent that the tide of public opinion was running to the left and that Labour would win a famous general election victory if only it broke with the coalition, Orwell took the view that because of the 'weakness of the Labour leaders' the party probably wouldn't break with the coalition and, even if it did, it would not make a 'serious effort to win' the general election.[100] 'I have predicted all along that the Conservatives will win with a small majority,' declared Orwell just before Labour won a massive landslide in July 1945.[101]

But it would be wrong to draw from any of this that Bernard Crick's description of Orwell's 1940s political stance as '*Tribune* socialism' is too wide of the mark even during Orwell's time on the paper's staff, when he was much more sceptical about Labour than he became after the party won in 1945.[102] Socialism might not be 'what Labour governments do', in Herbert Morrison's immortal phrase, but '*Tribune* socialism' has never been more or less than what the paper has done. Orwell, as literary editor for fifteen months, during which time he controlled a third of *Tribune*'s pages and occupied its most prominent bylined space, defined *Tribune* socialism almost as much as Bevan. The wartime *Tribune* was a far more eclectic and open paper than it had been in its first three years and far less attached to left Labour parliamentary socialism than it became after 1945 (and particularly after 1951, when it became to a large extent the organ of the

Bevanite fraction of the Parliamentary Labour Party). As George Woodcock put it, '*Tribune* gave space, particularly in its literary pages, to many writers far closer in their views to the independent attitudes of the anarchists, Trotskyists and Independent Labour Party than they were to the policy of the official Labour Party.'[103] Orwell was by no means the only revolutionary or former revolutionary far-leftist who found a berth there. Others included the editor who first commissioned Orwell to write for the paper, Raymond Postgate; Orwell's contemporaries on the journalistic staff when he was literary editor, Jon Kimche and Evelyn Anderson; his successor as literary editor, Tosco Fyvel; and, among contributors, Arthur Koestler, Tom Wintringham, Hugh Slater, Franz Borkenau, Reg Reynolds, Alex Comfort and Herbert Read.[104]

* * *

Orwell left the literary editorship of *Tribune* on 15 February 1945 to become a war correspondent for the *Observer*. He had written for the *Observer* since 1942, when he first made friends with David Astor (its proprietor's son and its de facto controller, who later became its editor and owner) and since leaving the BBC had contributed fortnightly reviews and occasional features.[105] Astor had asked him to cover the Allied landings in Italy in late 1943 and Orwell had agreed enthusiastically; but he had been turned down by the authorities because of his poor health. Now he leapt at a second chance to get into the thick of the action – in the expectation, according to Astor, that he would be able to 'pick up the atmosphere of a dictatorship'. Instead he found just devastation.

He travelled first to Paris, staying at the Hotel Scribe in the ninth *arrondissement*, where he met Malcolm Muggeridge, A. J. Ayer and Ernest Hemingway, and then on to the ruins of Cologne, where he was so ill he was briefly hospitalised.[106] Returning to Paris, he received the shattering news that his wife Eileen had died during what both he and she thought – or perhaps just hoped – would be a routine hysterectomy operation. He rushed back to England for the funeral, made arrangements for the care of Richard, then spent a few days in London before setting off again for Germany via Paris, telling friends that he needed to keep busy. He eventually returned to London at the end of May after a brief visit to occupied Austria.

On Eileen's advice, Orwell had decided not to return to his job at *Tribune*, and he wrote nothing for it over the summer of 1945 apart from a couple of letters for publication – one of them (not published) taking issue with an article on Poland and one responding to a piece repeating the old canard that he had said in *The Road to Wigan Pier* that the working class stank.[107] Orwell claimed that the reason he stopped writing for the paper was that 'Bevan was terrified there might be a row over *Animal Farm* which might have been embarrassing if the book had come out before the election, as it was first intended to'.[108] But there is no supporting evidence for this. Two much more plausible explanations for Orwell's absence from *Tribune* in summer 1945 are that *Tribune* was in a state of chaos during the run-up to and immediate aftermath of Labour's 1945 general election victory – Kimche had left the editor's chair to join Reuters as a foreign correspondent at about the time Orwell went to France, and Bevan, out on the stump during the campaign, was given a Cabinet post as Minister of Health[109] – and that Orwell yet again simply had too much else on his plate. Devastated by Eileen's death, he spent the summer of 1945 in frantic activity, churning out journalism for money (both reviews and longer pieces, including two 'London Letters' for *Partisan Review*), immersing himself in canvassing for Labour during the election, setting up a civil libertarian campaign with his anarchist friends, searching for a live-in nanny to look after Richard and starting the novel that would become *Nineteen Eighty-Four*. *Animal Farm* was published on 17 August, two days after the war ended with Japan's surrender. He then went up to the Scottish island of Jura for a holiday and to check up on progress on the renovation of an isolated and abandoned farmhouse he had discovered on a trip the previous year, to which he was planning to move. While he was away *Tribune* published Fyvel's asinine review of *Animal Farm*, which described it as 'one of the best and most simply written books for the child of today'. It was, wrote Fyvel, 'a gentle satire on a certain state'. He failed even to mention that it was all about the Soviet Union, as Julian Symons pointed out angrily on the letters page.[110]

Orwell returned to *Tribune* with a review published on 7 September, resuming his column on 19 October, though it wasn't published as 'As I Please' because Jennie Lee had appropriated the title. There had been other big changes on the paper in his absence. Only Anderson of the old editorial team was still in place. The young Frederic Mullally had replaced Kimche, Fyvel was in Orwell's old job and Bevan's role as political director had been taken over by Michael Foot. The general political line remained the same, however – with the obvious difference that Labour was now in power – as did most of the contributors, particularly on the books pages. For the next six months, Orwell wrote nearly every week for the paper, usually taking a single theme for each article rather than choosing multiple topics as he had before. He remained as extraordinarily prolific as ever. As well as writing his *Tribune* pieces, he had resumed regular book reviewing, weekly for the *Manchester Evening News* and fortnightly for the *Observer*, and he continued to accept commissions for longer essays (among them 'The Prevention of Literature', published in Humphrey Slater's magazine *Polemic* in January 1946, and 'Politics and the English Language', published by Cyril Connolly's magazine *Horizon* in April 1946) as well as one-off journalistic articles.[111]

Orwell was a deeply unhappy man in the winter of 1945–6. He had several brief affairs, one of them with Sonia Brownell, the editorial secretary on *Horizon*, and made several unsuccessful passes at women. He was repeatedly ill. But there is little sign of his unhappiness in his columns for *Tribune*. They include a dozen or more pieces that are among his most incisive and memorable journalistic writing, and although many are deadly serious, many have a remarkable lightness of tone. In 'You and the Atom Bomb', Orwell raises the possibility that the bomb will 'put an end to large-scale wars at the cost of prolonging indefinitely a "peace that is no peace"' – a 'cold war' as he puts it (possibly coining the phrase).[112] 'Revenge is Sour', 'Through a Glass, Rosily' and 'The Politics of Starvation' all deal with aspects of the desperate situation in Europe.[113] In 'Freedom of the Park', Orwell comes to the defence of anarchists arrested for selling newspapers in Hyde Park; 'The Sporting Spirit' dissects the ill will surrounding the visit to Britain of the Moscow Dynamo football team; and 'Pleasure Spots' explores the grim prospect of mass leisure resorts.[114] 'Books v Cigarettes' is a bizarrely compelling comparison of Orwell's expenditure on books and tobacco, 'Confessions of a Book Reviewer' a hilarious account of the futility of hack reviewing.[115] Best of all are 'Decline of the English Murder', a masterpiece of dark nostalgia for the good old days of middle-class poisoners brought on by the publication of an account of a particularly sordid recent murder, and 'Some Thoughts on the Common Toad', a rumination on the delights of spring.[116]

Politically, Orwell was as in agreement with *Tribune* in 1945–6 as he ever was. The Labour government elected in July 1945 was still enjoying its honeymoon with the voters, and both *Tribune* and Orwell were close to its thinking on most aspects of domestic and foreign affairs. At home, the paper gave wholehearted backing to the government's programme of nationalisations, beginning with the Bank of England and the coal industry, and the legislation to create the National Health Service and a 'cradle to grave' welfare state. Although he didn't say as much in his *Tribune* pieces – the only articles dealing with domestic high politics were 'Freedom of the Park' and 'On Housing'[117] – Orwell was also fully supportive. In an essay in *Commentary* in late 1945 he declared that 'the Labour government has at least five years in hand, and the men at the top of it, as a body, are at least as able and determined as any government we have had for decades past. It is too early to cheer, but a hopeful attitude is justified.' His main worries in this period were that the government was insufficiently committed to maintaining civil liberties and was not moving quickly enough to introduce socialism. 'Even allowing for the fact that everything takes time,' he wrote in *Partisan Review* in 1946, 'it is astonishing how little change seems to have happened in the structure of society. In a purely economic sense, I suppose, the drift is towards socialism, or at least state ownership . . . But in the social set-up there is no symptom by which one could infer that we are not living under a Conservative government.'[118]

The only major issue on which *Tribune* disagreed with the government was on the terms of the loan negotiated with the US in autumn 1945 to keep the war-crippled British economy afloat, which Bevan opposed in Cabinet and which prompted a flurry of anti-American polemic in *Tribune*. Orwell's views, if any, on the loan are unrecorded. On foreign policy more generally the paper stuck close to Ernest Bevin, now Foreign Secretary, as summer 1945's grand hopes of international co-operation gave way to the first signs of the division of Europe into two hostile blocs and the beginning of the Cold War. Although Bevan had declared just before joining the government that 'friendship with the Soviet Union is the key to world peace',[119] *Tribune* was above all committed to democracy. Unlike much of the Labour left, which saw the Soviet Union simply as a benign force in world politics, it remained sceptical about Stalin's intentions in eastern Europe and the Middle East, and its scepticism was reinforced by Soviet military intervention in Iran and, particularly, by the growing evidence that the Soviet occupiers of eastern Europe had scant regard for democracy.[120] Foot repeatedly made it clear he saw Soviet actions as the main reason east-west tensions were increasing. In early March 1946, for example, he declared:

> The agreement on the reconstitution of the Bulgarian government was never put into force . . . In Poland the communists have successfully blackmailed the socialists into agreeing to joint electoral lists . . . In Yugoslavia men like Subasic, who promoted the idea of cooperation with Britain as well as with the Soviet Union, have been dropped . . . In East Germany . . . by a mixture of intimidation, terror, censored propaganda and despicable tricks the communists have achieved control of all life in the Russian zone.[121]

This was precisely in line with Orwell's reading of the situation. Like Foot, he wanted democratic socialism to prevail throughout Europe and warned consistently that the main threat to it came from Stalin carving out a sphere of influence. His anti-Stalinism echoes through his writing in this period, both in *Tribune* – in 'Through a Glass, Rosily' and 'The Politics of Starvation'[122] – and elsewhere.[123] His other great political concern in foreign policy, decolonisation, in particular independence for India, was also shared by *Tribune*.

* * *

In May 1946, with Barnhill, the house on Jura he had agreed to rent, ready to move into, Orwell decided to give up all his journalistic commitments and head off there to get stuck into his next novel, which he had started the previous year. But there was so much else to do – work on the house and garden, shooting rabbits, fishing, entertaining visitors from London and helping his crofter neighbours with the harvest – that he managed to do virtually nothing before he returned to London in the autumn.

Once again he resumed writing weekly for *Tribune*, to which Jon Kimche had come back as managing editor. This time, he wrote under the title 'As I Please' again, the first one of the new series appearing on 8 November 1946.

The final run of Orwell's *Tribune* columns is as varied as before in its subject matter and as stylish. His topics include women's magazines, immigration, the method used to hang war criminals, the state of the press, laundries, how you cannot prove the earth is a globe, starvation in Germany, famous writers' handwriting and the birth-rate.

Politically, however, Orwell again began to find bones to pick with *Tribune*. By late 1946, *Tribune* was starting to have doubts about Bevin's conduct of foreign policy, in particular over his consistent pro-Americanism and his opposition to creation of a Jewish state in Palestine. Orwell disagreed on both, and he continued to disagree for some time after he wrote his last piece for the paper in spring 1947.

A key role in all this was played by someone who had nothing formally to do with *Tribune*: Richard Crossman, newly elected MP for Coventry East and *New Statesman* journalist.[124] A brilliant but devious intellectual, Crossman had worked as a government propagandist during the war. (One of his colleagues was Tosco Fyvel.) In 1946–7 he found himself leading the Labour left in a revolt against Bevin, demanding the adoption of a distinctively democratic socialist foreign policy rather than alliance with American capitalism.

The rebellion came about because most of the Labour left thought that Labour foreign policy should be different from what went before whereas Bevin appeared simply to be continuing the policy inherited from the wartime coalition. It began in November 1946, when Crossman led fifty-seven backbench MPs in tabling an amendment to the King's Speech proposing 'a democratic and constructive socialist alternative to an otherwise inevitable conflict between American capitalism and Soviet communism in which all hope of world government would be destroyed'. It continued in April 1947 when seventy-two Labour MPs – not including Crossman – voted against peacetime conscription and he used it to persuade the government to reduce the term of national service from eighteen to twelve months. It reached its climax the next month when the *New Statesman* published *Keep Left*, a pamphlet making the case for a 'third force' foreign policy, written by Crossman, Foot and Ian Mikardo over Easter weekend 1947 and signed by twelve other MPs.[125]

Tribune's role in the revolt was ambiguous. Foot was one of the King's Speech rebels and a co-author of *Keep Left*, but the paper was ill at ease lining up with some of the conscription rebels, whom it saw as 'near communists'.[126] Orwell, however, felt that *Tribune*'s involvement with Crossman's initiatives gave succour to the fellow-travelling left and caught a whiff of a nascent Popular Front with the CPGB. There were perhaps twenty Labour MPs in the 1945 parliament – out of more than 400 – who were reliably pro-Soviet, half of whom straightforwardly followed the Communist Party line, and they all enthusiastically joined in the King's Speech and conscription rebellions (though they did not sign *Keep Left*). From late 1946, *Tribune* started to run contributions from them

- including, in late January 1947, a letter from Konni Zilliacus, now MP for Gateshead, who had reverted to the fervent Russophilia he displayed before the war. In it, he attacked Orwell for an article in *Partisan Review* six months before in which Orwell had named Zilliacus as one of Labour's '"underground" Communist MPs - that is, MPs elected as Labour men, but secretly members of the CP or reliably sympathetic to it'.

It is unusual for any newspaper to publish correspondence on a contributor's writing in another publication - but *Tribune* went to town, filling its letters pages for four weeks with acrimonious diatribes on the subject, three from Zilliacus, two from Orwell and a handful from other readers, running to a total of 4,500 words.[127]

Zilliacus charged:

> I am not a member of the CP, never have been a member of the CP, and would consider it a disgraceful thing to do, to be secretly a member of any party or organisation, membership of which was not compatible with membership of the Labour Party . . . Can Mr Orwell suggest any explanation not wholly discreditable to himself, for having uttered the silly and offensive falsehood in an American publication that Labour MPs who feel it their duty to oppose the Bevin-Churchill under-the-counter coalition in foreign policy, are 'secretly members of the CP'?[128]

Orwell replied:

> If you strip Mr Zilliacus's letter of its abusive words . . . the substance of it boils down to this: that he says he is not a 'crypto-communist'. But of course he does! What else could he say? A pickpocket does not go to the races wearing a label 'pickpocket' on his coat-lapel, and a propagandist does not describe himself as a propagandist . . . I do not think Mr Zilliacus's past record is evidence . . . Nor do I care whether he has a Communist Party ticket or any direct connection with the CP. What I believe, and will go on believing until I see evidence to the contrary, is that he and others like him are pursuing a policy barely distinguishable from that of the CP, that they are in effect the publicity agents of the USSR in this country, and that when Soviet and British interests appear to them to clash, they will support the Soviet interest.[129]

And so it went on, the only notable subsequent development coming with Zilliacus shooting himself in the foot with his final riposte to a critic (not Orwell):

> What I actually said in both the Soviet zone of Germany and Poland was that what I had seen was not parliamentary democracy as we knew it in the west, which was the most mature and highly developed form of democracy, but revolutionary democracy, democracy in the primitive and original sense of Abraham Lincoln's great definition of 'government of the people, by the people, for the people'.[130]

Tribune was not really toying with a Popular Front. *Keep Left*, published just as Orwell gave up his column and went off to Jura again, was in no way sympathetic to the Soviet

Union or the Communist Party – and the fellow-travellers did not sign it. It was a manifesto for a democratic socialist Europe, neither capitalist nor communist, with its own independent foreign policy. The problem was that its time had gone two months before. In March 1947, after the British government made it plain that it could no longer sustain its intervention against the communist insurgency in Greece, US President Harry Truman had announced that America would take over the British role in the Mediterranean – the declaration of the 'Truman doctrine' of containment of communism. The 'third force' was, by the time its most coherent defence appeared, wishful thinking.

At the Labour conference in May 1947, Bevin arraigned his critics in the most brutal speech he had made since his assault on George Lansbury in 1935, claiming to have been 'stabbed in the back' by the King's Speech rebels. Crossman and the left had nothing to offer against him but complaints that a pamphlet demolishing their argument, Denis Healey's *Cards on the Table*, had been published by Labour headquarters without proper approval of the party's NEC.[131] Meekly, they accepted defeat. Then, in early June, the US Secretary of State, George Marshall, announced a plan to revive the war-devastated European economy with American money. That put an end to the argument. *Tribune* rallied to Bevin. 'If the Russians . . . contract out, then they alone will be the architects of a divided Europe,' wrote Foot on 13 June.[132] The next week he was even more enthusiastic:

> Then, into the midst of this world of darkened hopes, tedious wranglings and cut-throat competing strategies, came a new offer: the offer of a fresh start: one which presented the chance to Britain, France, the Soviet Union and the United States of honourable association in the work of bringing sustenance to the hunger-stricken peoples of this tragic postwar epoch. This and nothing less is the meaning of the Marshall Plan.[133]

Orwell, up in Jura, was still grumbling about the failure of *Tribune* to embrace reality earlier in the year. He wrote an open letter to the paper, 'In Defence of Comrade Zilliacus', that was blistering about the impossibility of the 'third force' in the real world:

> Surely, if one is going to write about foreign policy at all, there is one question that should be answered plainly. It is: 'If you *had* to choose between Russia and America, which would you choose?' It will not do to give the usual quibbling answer, 'I refuse to choose.' In the end the choice may be forced upon us. We are no longer strong enough to stand alone, and if we fail to bring a western European union into being, we shall be obliged, in the long run, to subordinate our policy to that of one great power or the other. And in spite of all the fashionable chatter of the moment, everyone knows in his heart that we should choose America. The great mass of people in this country would, I believe, make this choice almost instinctively. Certainly there is a small minority that would choose the other way. Mr Zilliacus, for instance, is one of

> them. I think he is wrong, but at least he makes his position clear. I also know perfectly well what *Tribune's* position is. But has *Tribune* ever made it clear?[134]

The open letter was never sent: Orwell fell ill while writing it and by the time it was finished it was redundant. *Tribune* had by summer 1947 made its choice very clear, and it was, like Orwell's, for America. It stuck to it for the next four years, backing the creation of NATO and denouncing the Berlin blockade, only rethinking its Cold War anti-communism during the Korean War. Orwell accepted that its attitude to the Soviet Union was fundamentally sound. As he put it in an article for a small American journal a year after he wrote his final piece for *Tribune*:

> Unavoidably, *Tribune* has lost some of its vigour since Labour took office. It suffers from the embarrassment that always besets rebels when their own side has won, and in addition, its attacks on Ernest Bevin's foreign policy have been somewhat unreal, since on the all-important issue of standing up to Russia it is not genuinely in opposition. A few communists and fellow-travellers occasionally write for *Tribune*, but all of those who have anything to do with determining its policy are extremely anti-communist. In spite of surface appearances, it is much the most reliable supporter that the present government has among weekly papers.[135]

Orwell continued to complain that *Tribune* was sometimes stupidly anti-American until the beginning of 1948, but his big differences with the paper were on Palestine. *Tribune* had from the beginning backed a Jewish homeland of some description in Palestine, but in the mid-1940s it became a militant advocate of Zionism in opposition to Bevin's desperate attempts to keep a lid on Jewish emigration from Europe to Palestine and to prevent partition of Palestine on ethnic lines. Both Jon Kimche and Tosco Fyvel were ardent left-wing Zionists, and Aneurin Bevan and Michael Foot were sympathetic. So, importantly, was Crossman, who had worked with Fyvel as a British government propagandist during the war. Crossman had been converted to the Zionist case while serving on the 1945–6 Anglo-American Commission of Inquiry on Palestine, which opened the gates for mass Jewish migration to Palestine with its recommendation – against Bevin's policy at the time – that 100,000 Jewish refugees from Europe be allowed into Palestine at once. Crossman and Foot, with the unacknowledged help of Arthur Koestler, co-authored a pamphlet demanding a change in British policy in late 1946, *A Palestine Munich?*, and in 1946–8, *Tribune* campaigned enthusiastically for Britain to allow mass Jewish emigration from Europe to Palestine and for the creation of a Jewish state.[136]

Orwell had little sympathy with the Zionist position. In 1945, he had written that 'few English people realise that the Palestine issue is partly a colour issue and that an Indian nationalist, for example, would probably side with the Arabs'.[137] He and Fyvel argued repeatedly on the issue, and he complained to other friends repeatedly about

Tribune's line. He told Julian Symons - wrongly - that Fyvel rather than Kimche was responsible for *Tribune*'s 'over-emphasis on Zionism', complaining that Crossman had been 'the evil genius of the paper', influencing it through Foot and Fyvel.[138]

It would be a mistake, however, to give the impression that Orwell's disagreements with *Tribune* were the reason he wrote nothing for it between his last 'As I Please' in May 1947 and his death in January 1950. Indeed, he had planned to return to its pages but was simply too busy with *Nineteen Eighty-Four* and too ill with tuberculosis to do so. He spent December 1947 to July 1948 hospitalised near Glasgow, returned to Jura to finish the book and fell ill again, completing the typescript in bed. He handed it over in December 1948 and was almost immediately hospitalised again, this time in Gloucestershire. He was transferred to University College Hospital in London in September 1949 and never left.

During this period he remained a regular reader of the paper, referred favourably to it in print on a couple of occasions[139] and stayed on good personal terms with his *Tribune* friends Evelyn Anderson and Fyvel, with whom he kept up a frequent correspondence. He asked Fyvel to remember him to 'everyone at the office' in December 1948, and when, on the publication of *Nineteen Eighty-Four* in June 1949, the paper ran a short item wishing him a speedy recovery asked Fyvel to 'thank the others at *Tribune* for putting in such a kind par'.

Bruce Bain's review of *Nineteen Eighty-Four* in *Tribune* had reservations about its virtues as a novel. Orwell was 'not in full command of his material, and the importance of what he has to say splits the novel at the seams'. But it was in no doubt about the urgency of the book's satire: 'George Orwell is a prophet of the larger pessimism, one of the most perceptive moralists of our time, and his brilliant tract should provoke us all to take our heads out of the sand and look into his crystal ball.'[140]

Orwell died at the age of forty-six on 21 January 1950, exactly fifteen weeks after marrying Sonia Brownell in hospital. Symons wrote his obituary for *Tribune*:

> The particular time of his death was, one feels, especially tragic; he was at last to leave hospital and go with his wife to Switzerland. When I saw him on the Thursday before he died he was worrying, with fine Johnsonian insularity, about the problem of tea. 'I don't know if I shall get proper tea in Switzerland,' he said. 'They have that filthy China stuff, you know. I like Ceylon tea, very strong.' He was pleased because for some time he had not been allowed to write, and he thought that in Switzerland this ban might be raised. He spoke of a short novel that was in his mind, and a study of Joseph Conrad's political books, *The Secret Agent* and *Under Western Eyes*. He also elaborated a thesis that the Communist Party's object in putting up a hundred election candidates was to help defeat the Labour Party. 'I shall go to Switzerland next Wednesday,' he said, and laughed, 'if I don't catch cold.'
>
> Thirty-six hours later he was dead.[141]

* * *

All the articles in this collection appear - of course - in Peter Davison's magisterial twenty-volume *The Complete Works of George Orwell*, without which the production of this book would have been much more difficult. Many also appear in the third and fourth volumes of *The Collected Essays, Journalism and Letters of George Orwell* edited by Ian Angus and Sonia Orwell and published in 1968.

So why reproduce them here? The most important reason is that collecting Orwell's *Tribune* columns in one volume presents him, as never before, as one of the greatest practitioners in the English language of the craft of turning out 800–2,000 words a week - more usually 1,200–1,400 - week in, week out. Orwell's *Tribune* columns are by no means his only journalism: he wrote hundreds of reviews, scores of essays on literary, cultural and political themes, three great books of reportage and even a clutch of news reports, most of them for the *Observer*. But, along with the essays and the books, the *Tribune* columns are his best journalism, and they have never appeared before in a single volume. They are spread across six volumes of Davison's *Complete Works*, in which they are presented amid a mass of letters, notes and pieces for other publications. And the Angus/Orwell *Collected Essays, Journalism and Letters* volumes miss out far too much.

It is also *Tribune*'s seventieth anniversary, and there can be no better way of celebrating it than republishing its greatest contribution to the world of letters. *Tribune* has been extraordinarily generous with permissions to reprint Orwell - it has said yes to every request for reproduction of anything in its copyright and has never to my knowledge demanded a fee from anyone. But until the advent of optical character recognition software it was beyond the resources of the paper to do what Douglas Hill, Bernard Crick and many others urged and put Orwell's 'As I Please' and other columns out as a book. This volume owes a lot to Abby FineReader. Needless to say, it has also required serious attention to detail in copy editing, for which Jonathan Wadman deserves the highest praise. Many thanks to all those friends who read through earlier drafts of this introduction and pointed out where they made no sense, in particular Kevin Davey and Michelle Bhatia. And thanks too to the staff of *Tribune* for giving me a desk, tea and biscuits while I was doing the research. All proceeds from this book will go to *Tribune*. I hope it not only survives but thrives for another seventy years.

Finally, a note on the texts. Everything is taken from the *Tribune* originals and has been checked meticulously against them. But unlike Davison, and against the enthusiasm of Crick for preserving 1940s habits of using initial capitals for Socialism, Anarchism, the Government and so forth - though I have reluctantly accepted Orwell's own strictures on initial caps for Negro - I have taken the liberty of rendering Orwell into 21st-century style, with lower case the norm. I make no apologies. This is an edition to be read above all, and there is nothing to be gained by sticking to what is now archaic usage. The notes here are all attempts to explain Orwell's references and the context of arguments rather than to provide biographical detail on Orwell or clarification of textual ambiguities. As such, they are different from but in no sense supplant Davison's.

June 2006

Notes

1. See, for example, pp. 86 & 289.
2. Letter to Philip Rahv, 9 December 1943, in *CWGO* XVI, p. 22. Rahv (1908–73) was an American literary critic and editor. Born into a Jewish family in the Ukraine, he arrived in the US via Palestine at the age of fourteen, joined the American Communist Party in 1932 and the next year, with William Phillips (1908–2002), co-founded the literary-political journal *Partisan Review*. Phillips and Rahv broke with the CP in 1937, adopting a broadly Trotskyist political position, then moved away from Trotskyism to support the American war effort from 1941. During the 1950s *PR* was one of the bastions of American Cold War liberalism. Orwell wrote fifteen 'London Letters' to *PR* between 1941 and 1946.
3. For details of Bevan, Kimche and Fyvel, see '*Tribune* biographies', pp. 389–98 of this volume.
4. Julian Symons, 'An Appreciation', in George Orwell, *Nineteen Eighty-Four* (London: Heron, 1970). Symons (1912–94) was a critic and novelist. He met Orwell in 1942 after Orwell attacked him for co-authoring a pacifist pamphlet that Orwell believed 'showed the overlap between fascism and pacifism'. Orwell apologised and they became close friends. Symons became a frequent *Tribune* contributor, reviewed *Nineteen Eighty-Four* in the *Times Literary Supplement* and wrote Orwell's obituary for *Tribune*.
5. George Woodcock, 'Recollections of George Orwell', *Northern Review*, August–September 1953, in Audrey Coppard and Bernard Crick (eds), *Orwell Remembered* (London: Ariel, 1984), p. 199. Woodcock (1912–95) was a Canadian poet, literary critic, biographer, historian and anarchist. He was editor of the journal *Now* in London in the late 1940s, to which Orwell contributed, and wrote a memoir of Orwell, *The Crystal Spirit: A Study of George Orwell* (London: Jonathan Cape, 1967).
6. D. J. Taylor, *Orwell: The Life* (London: Chatto and Windus, 2003), p. 327.
7. As Bernard Crick, author of the first comprehensive biography of Orwell, still in many respects the best, put it: 'He wrote for the faithful of the Labour movement, yet he refused to preach; rather he became adept at stinging them into thought, at being the Socratic gadfly to prevent "complacency and sloganising".' Bernard Crick, *George Orwell: A Life* (Harmondsworth: Penguin, 1982), p. 444.
8. These are not included in this volume, partly for reasons of space but mainly because they are not columns. They are of course published in *CWGO*.
9. 'As I Please', 31 January 1947, p. 358 of this volume.
10. T. R. Fyvel, *George Orwell: A Personal Memoir* (London: Hutchinson, 1982), pp. 139–40.
11. Letter to Philip Rahv, 14 October 1943, in *CWGO* XV, p. 273.
12. 'As I Please', 7 January 1944, p. 82 of this volume.
13. 'As I Please', 5 May 1944, p. 135 of this volume.
14. 'Books and the People: A New Year Message', 5 January 1945, p. 221 of this volume.
15. 'As I Please', 3 November 1944, p. 204 of this volume.

16. Mulk Raj Anand (1905–2004) was an Indian novelist and critic, best known for his novels dealing with themes of caste and class in India, among them *Untouchable* (London: Wishart, 1935), *Coolie* (London: Lawrence and Wishart, 1936) and *The Village* (London: Jonathan Cape, 1939). Like Orwell, he fought for the Republicans in the Spanish civil war, but they met when they were both working for the BBC. He contributed to the volume of broadcast talks to India edited by Orwell, *Talking to India* (London: George Allen and Unwin, 1943). Orwell had reviewed Anand's *The Sword and the Sickle* (London: Jonathan Cape, 1942) in *Horizon*.

Arthur Koestler (1905–83) was a Hungarian/British journalist and author, best known for his novel *Darkness at Noon* (London: Jonathan Cape, 1940), a fictional account of the destruction of the old Bolsheviks in Stalin's purges. A communist from 1931 to 1938, he was a war correspondent in Spain for the London *News Chronicle* and was imprisoned by the Nationalists, an experience related in his book *Spanish Testament* (London: Left Book Club, 1938), reviewed by Orwell in *Time and Tide* on 3 February 1938. He subsequently escaped from German-occupied France after being interned as an enemy alien, a story told in his *Scum of the Earth* (London: Victor Gollancz, 1941). Orwell gave favourable reviews to *Darkness at Noon* (*New Statesman and Nation*, 4 January 1941), *Arrival and Departure* (*Manchester Evening News*, 9 December 1943) and (briefly) *The Gladiators* (*Tribune*, 28 July 1944) and wrote a critique of Koestler which appeared in *Critical Essays* (London: Secker and Warburg, 1946). Koestler was a regular contributor to *Tribune* during the 1940s and a personal friend of Orwell. In the 1950s, he became a hardline Cold Warrior and then drifted away from politics to explore scientific and mystical themes. The best biography, much publicised because it revealed Koestler to have raped Jill Craigie, the wife of Michael Foot, is David Cesarani, *Arthur Koestler: The Homeless Mind* (London: Free Press, 1999).

Julian Symons (1912–94) was a novelist and critic, best known for his many crime novels. He met Orwell in 1942 after Orwell attacked him for co-authoring a pacifist pamphlet that Orwell believed 'showed the overlap between fascism and pacifism'. Orwell apologised and they became close friends. Symons became a frequent *Tribune* contributor, reviewed *Nineteen Eighty-Four* in the *Times Literary Supplement* and wrote Orwell's obituary for *Tribune*.

Herbert Read (1893–1968) was a poet and critic, the leading interpreter of modernist art in Britain from the 1930s and a prominent anarchist. He had corresponded with Orwell in the late 1930s and contributed to his BBC broadcasts.

Stephen Spender (1909–95) was a poet and critic, briefly a member of the Communist Party in the 1930s. Orwell had disparaged him at that time, infamously writing in 1937 to Nancy Cunard when asked for a contribution to her book *Authors Take Sides on the Spanish War* (London: Left Review): 'I am not one of your fashionable pansies like Auden and Spender, I was six months in Spain, most of the time fighting.' But Orwell met Spender through Cyril Connolly six months later, liked him and apologised. They became friends and Orwell got Spender to broadcast for the BBC. All the same, Orwell continued to consider Spender politically 'very unreliable', as his entry in Orwell's notebook on fellow travellers puts it.

Alex Comfort (1920–2000), a talented young pacifist novelist, poet and critic with whom Orwell had sparred in print since publishing an excoriating review of Comfort's novel *No Such Liberty* (London: Chapman and Hall, 1941) in the *Adelphi* in September 1941. They exchanged insults in verse (anonymously) in the pages of *Tribune* in June 1943 and kept up a friendly correspondence despite their differences. Comfort went on to write the anarchist classic *Authority and Delinquency in the Modern State* (London: Routledge, 1950), do serious work in gerontology and, most famously, write *The Joy of Sex: A Gourmet Guide to Lovemaking* (London: Mitchell Beazley, 1972).

Stevie Smith (1902–71) was a poet, novelist and friend of Orwell.

David Sylvester (1924–2001) went on to become one of Britain's most influential art critics during the 1950s and 1960s.

17. R. C. Churchill (1916–86) was a prominent literary critic during the 1950s and 1960s. He was recommended to Orwell by the Cambridge critic F. R. Leavis.

Michael Roberts (1902–48) was a poet, critic, editor and an anthologist of poetry, best known as editor of *The Faber Book of Modern Verse* (1936). His biography of T. E. Hulme (London: Faber, 1938) which is mentioned by Orwell in his 'As I Please' of 24 December 1943, p. 72 of this volume.

Paul Potts (1911–90) was a Canadian poet, author and bohemian. He became a close friend of Orwell, visiting him on Jura in summer 1946, and published a memoir of Orwell, 'Don Quixote on a Bicycle', in *Dante Called Me Beatrice* (London, Eyre and Spottiswoode, 1960).

Franz Borkenau (1900–57) was an Austrian socialist historian and polemicist. A member of the German Communist Party from 1921, he worked as a researcher for the Communist International in Berlin from 1924 to 1928, leaving the party over the Comintern's 'left turn', which saw communists attacking socialists as 'social fascists'. He joined the Institute for Social Research in Frankfurt and left Germany after the Nazi victory, briefly taking a teaching post in Panama before settling in England in 1936. He went to Spain in 1936 and again in 1937, on the second occasion criticising the actions of Soviet agents – for which he was denounced as a Trotskyist and arrested. His book on Spain, *The Spanish Cockpit* (London: Faber and Faber, 1937) was reviewed by Orwell for the *New Statesman* but his piece was rejected on political grounds by Kingsley Martin: the review appeared in *Time and Tide* instead. Orwell also reviewed Borkenau's *The Communist International* (London: Faber and Faber, 1938) in *New English Weekly*, and his *The Totalitarian Enemy* (London: Faber and Faber, 1940) in *Time and Tide*. Orwell's wife Eileen helped Borkenau edit his book *Socialism: National or International?* (London: Routledge, 1942).

Elisaveta Fen was the pen-name of Lydia Jackson (nee Jiburtovich, 1899–1983). Born and educated in Russia, she came to Britain in 1925 and became a close friend of Eileen O'Shaughnessy (who married Orwell in 1936). She broadcast for Orwell on the BBC and was a friend until his death, although she subsequently recalled his having made an unwelcome pass at her soon after he married Eileen. She translated Chekhov into English in the 1950s.

Rayner Heppenstall (1911–81) was a novelist and critic. He got to know Orwell while both were contributors to the *Adelphi* in the early 1930s and they shared a flat in 1935. Returning home drunk one night, he attacked Orwell, who responded by hitting him with a shooting stick. They nevertheless remained friends for the rest of Orwell's life. Heppenstall's memoir of Orwell appeared in *Four Absences* (London: Barrie and Rockcliff, 1960).

Hugh Kingsmill (1889–1949) was a critic, biographer and wit, a collaborator with

Malcolm Muggeridge in the 1930s. Orwell had reviewed his book of essays on the corrupting effects of power, *The Poisoned Crown* (London: Eyre and Spottiswoode, 1944) in the *Observer*.

Jack Lindsay (1900–90) was an extraordinarily prolific Australian Marxist classicist, novelist, critic and playwright, and was a member of the Communist Party of Great Britain from the late 1930s.

Antony Brown (1922–2001), a BBC scriptwriter in the 1940s, became a newscaster for ITN in the 1950s.

18. William Empson (1906–84) was a poet and critic. Educated at Winchester and Cambridge, he became a literary star in his twenties with the publication of *Seven Types of Ambiguity* (London: Chatto and Windus, 1930), his massively influential book on poetry criticism, and *Poems* (London: Chatto and Windus, 1935). During the 1930s he taught English literature at universities in Japan and China, and during the Second World War became the BBC's China editor, which is when he met Orwell. He went back to China in 1947, returning to become a professor at the University of Sheffield in 1953.

Anthony Powell (1905–2000) was a novelist and critic. Educated at Eton and Oxford, he worked in publishing in London during the 1920s and early 1930s, publishing his first novel in 1931. He met Orwell early in the Second World War and they became firm friends. He and Malcolm Muggeridge organised Orwell's funeral in 1950. Powell is best known today for his twelve-volume series of autobiographical novels, *A Dance to the Music of Time*, published from 1951 to 1975.

19. T. S. Eliot (1888–1965) was an Anglo-American poet and playwright who made London his home as a young man. Orwell was unsympathetic towards Eliot's reactionary politics and Anglo-Catholic religious beliefs, and he did not like Eliot's later work. But Eliot's early poetry, in particular 'The Love Song of J. Alfred Prufrock' (1917), 'The Waste Land' (1922) and 'Sweeney Agonistes' (1925), inspired Orwell, who consistently defended Eliot against left-wing critics who argued that Eliot's political views and anti-Semitism made him a bad writer. Orwell invited Eliot to contribute to *Tribune* when he became literary editor, but Eliot did not take up the offer. As editorial director of Faber and Faber, Eliot turned down both *Down and Out in Paris and London* and *Animal Farm*. Orwell made a point of taking him out to lunch in the 1940s.

E. M. Forster (1879–1970) was a novelist and critic. He is best known today for his novels *Howards End* (1910) and *A Passage to India* (1924). Orwell got him to broadcast while he was at the BBC.

20. Bob Edwards, *Goodbye Fleet Street* (London, Jonathan Cape, 1988).

21. *Tribune*, 31 January 1947, p. 359 of this volume.

22. Frederic Mullally, 'Fleet Street in the Forties', *British Journalism Review* (1999), vol. 10, no. 1, p. 49.

23. T. R. Fyvel, 'Orwell at *Tribune*', in Coppard and Crick (eds), *Orwell Remembered*, p. 214.

24. Stephen Wadhams, *Remembering Orwell* (Harmondsworth: Penguin, 1984), p. 140.

25. The account is Fyvel's report of what Kimche had told him (in *George Orwell: A Personal Memoir*, p. 140). This is one of several anecdotes that have been quoted to suggest that Orwell retained some of the anti-Semitism of his upbringing to his dying day – another *Tribune*-

related one is Frederic Mullally's story about Orwell making it clear in the pub that he was 'not at all comfortable with what he saw as the preponderant influence of émigré German Jews on the magazine's coverage of foreign affairs' (in Mullally, 'Fleet Street in the Forties'). There is certainly more than a trace of anti-Semitism in Orwell's description of 'a little Viennese Jew who had been enlisted in the branch of the American army which deals with the interrogation of prisoners' in 'Revenge is Sour' (*Tribune*, 9 November 1945, p. 256 of this volume) – a piece that Fyvel told Orwell trivialised the experience of the Jews under Nazism. But other evidence – not least his discussions of anti-Semitism in the pages of *Tribune* and his many Jewish friends – suggests at the very least that Orwell was trying to make amends for his previous prejudices. See 'Orwell and the Jews' in Taylor, *Orwell: The Life*, pp. 196–9.

26. Michael Shelden, *George Orwell: The Authorised Biography* (London: Heinemann, 1991), p. 419. McEwen (d. 1987) certainly visited Orwell on Jura in summer 1946.

27. *Observer*, 14 October 1945, in *CWGO* XVII, p. 310.

28. Wadhams, *Remembering Orwell*, p. 141.

29. According to Strauss in his unpublished autobiography, 'the paper had a nominal capital of £18,000, £12,000 of which was provided by Stafford and £6,000 by me'. George Strauss, unpublished autobiography, Churchill Archives Centre, Cambridge, p. 68. Cripps also subsidised *Tribune* at the rate of £5,000 a year. For a fascinating account of the role of moneyed men in inter-war left politics, see Kevin Morgan, *Bolshevism and the British Left, part 1: Labour Legends and Russian Gold* (London: Lawrence and Wishart, 2006).

30. For Cripps, Mellor, Bevan and Strauss, see *Tribune* biographies, pp. 389–98 of this volume.

Ellen Wilkinson (1891–1947) was Labour MP for Middlesbrough East (1924–31) and Jarrow (1935–47). She organised the 1936 Jarrow March to draw attention to the plight of the unemployed in depressed industrial areas of Britain. Born into a lower-middle-class Methodist family, 'Red Ellen' was educated at Manchester University, having already joined the Independent Labour Party at the age of sixteen. She was a founder member of the Communist Party in 1920 but left in 1924. She became a junior minister in the wartime coalition government in 1940, first as a pensions minister and later at the Home Office, and was made education secretary in the 1945 Labour government. She had a long affair with Herbert Morrison and died after taking an overdose of barbiturates. Her book on Jarrow, *The Town That Was Murdered* (1939), was a major success for the Left Book Club. Betty D. Vernon, *Ellen Wilkinson* (London: Croom Helm, 1982) is a thorough biography.

Harold Laski (1893–1950) was Professor of Politics at the London School of Economics 1926–50 and a member of the Labour Party's National Executive Committee from 1937 to 1949. Born into an affluent Jewish family in Manchester, he became involved in left-wing politics as a student at Oxford. His works include *Authority in the Modern State* (London: Oxford University Press, 1919), *A Grammar of Politics* (London: George Allen and Unwin, 1925), *Liberty in the Modern State* (London: Faber and Faber, 1930), *Reflections on the Revolution of Our Time* (London: George Allen and Unwin, 1943) and *The American Democracy: A Commentary and an Interpretation* (London: George Allen and Unwin, 1948). He was a contributor to *Tribune* up to his death but was more often to be found in the pages of the *New Statesman*. Kingsley

Martin, *Harold Laski* (London: Victor Gollancz, 1953) is hagiographic but still the best all-round biography.

Henry Noel Brailsford (1873–1958) was the most prominent British left-wing journalist of the first half of the twentieth century. The son of a Methodist preacher, he was born in Yorkshire and educated in Scotland. He rose to prominence as a foreign correspondent for the *Manchester Guardian*, the *Morning Leader* and then the *Daily News*. He joined the Independent Labour Party in 1907, was a prominent opponent of the First World War and stood unsuccessfully as a Labour candidate in the 1918 general election. He was editor of the ILP's newspaper, the *New Leader*, from 1922 to 1926, left the ILP in 1932 and during the 1930s and 1940s was a regular contributor to *Reynolds News* and the *New Statesman*. He was one of very few British left-wing writers in the late 1930s who was consistently critical of the Soviet show trials. His many books include *Shelley, Godwin and Their Circle* (London: Williams and Norgate, 1913), *The War of Steel and Gold: A Study of the Armed Peace* (London: G. Bell, 1914), *A League of Nations* (London: Headley Bros, 1917), *Across the Blockade: A Record of Travels in Enemy Europe* (London: George Allen and Unwin, 1919), *After the Peace* (London: Leonard Parsons, 1920), *The Russian Workers' Republic* (London: George Allen and Unwin, 1921), *Socialism for To-day* (London: ILP, 1925), *Rebel India* (London: Leonard Stein, 1931), *Property or Peace?* (London: Victor Gollancz, 1934), *Voltaire* (London: Thornton Butterworth, 1935), *Why Capitalism Means War* (London: Victor Gollancz, 1938), *America Our Ally* (London: Victor Gollancz, 1940), *Subject India* (London: Victor Gollancz, 1944) and *Our Settlement with Germany* (Harmondsworth: Penguin, 1944). F. M. Leventhal, *The Last Dissenter: H. N. Brailsford and His Times* (Oxford: Oxford University Press, 1985) is an excellent biography.

Ben Greene, the first cousin of the novelist Graham Greene, was an extrovert character who played a major part in the campaign to reform the Labour Party constitution to give constituency parties greater representation on the party's ruling National Executive Committee, which finally got its way in 1937. He did not last long on the *Tribune* board – he resigned in March 1937 – but the main reason he is not mentioned in most memoirs of the paper's early days is that he became a vociferous supporter of Hitler. In 1939, he became treasurer of the tiny anti-Semitic and pro-Nazi British People's Party; and he was interned during the Second World War. See Ben Pimlott, *Labour and the Left in the 1930s* (Cambridge: Cambridge University Press, 1977), pp. 116–40.

31. Clement Attlee (1883–1967) was Labour MP for Limehouse 1922–50 and for West Walthamstow 1950–5. He was a junior war minister in 1924, Chancellor of the Duchy of Lancaster 1929–31 and Postmaster General 1931, Labour deputy leader 1931–5 and Labour leader 1935–55. In the wartime coalition he served as Lord Privy Seal 1940–2, Secretary of State for the Dominions 1942–3 and deputy Prime Minister 1942–5. He was Prime Minister from 1945 to 1951. There are several good biographies, the best of which is still Kenneth Harris, *Attlee* (London: Weidenfeld and Nicolson, 1984).

Hugh Dalton (1887–1962) was Labour MP for Peckham 1924–9 and for Bishop Auckland 1929–31 and 1935–59. He was a Foreign Office minister in the 1929–31 Labour government, and in the wartime coalition government was minister of economic warfare 1940–42 and President of the Board of Trade 1942–5. In the 1945–51 Labour governments he was

Chancellor of the Exchequer 1945–7, Chancellor of the Duchy of Lancaster 1947–50 and Minister of Town and Country Planning 1950–1. See Ben Pimlott, *Hugh Dalton: A Life* (London: Jonathan Cape, 1985).

Herbert Morrison (1888–1965) was Labour MP for South Hackney 1923–4, 1929–31 and 1935–45, for East Lewisham 1945–50 and for South Lewisham 1950–9. He was also a member of London County Council 1922–45 and its leader 1934–40. He was Minister of Transport 1929–31, Minister of Supply 1940, Home Secretary 1940–5, Leader of the House of Commons 1945–51 and Foreign Secretary 1951. He was a member of the war Cabinet 1942–5 and deputy Prime Minister 1945–51. See Bernard Donoughue and George Jones, *Herbert Morrison: Portrait of a Politician* (London: Weidenfeld and Nicholson, 2001).

Ernest Bevin (1881–1951) was general secretary of the Transport and General Workers' Union 1921–40 and a member of the general council of the TUC 1925–40. He was Labour MP for Central Wandsworth 1940–50 and East Woolwich 1950–1. He was Minister of Labour 1940–5 and Foreign Secretary 1945–51. See Alan Bullock, *The Life and Times of Ernest Bevin* (three volumes) (London: Heinemann, 1960–83).

Walter Citrine (1887–1983) was general secretary of the TUC 1926–46 and president of the International Federation of Trade Unions 1928–45.

32. Willie Gallagher (1881–1965) was Communist MP for West Fife 1935–50. A militant shop steward on Clydeside during the First World War, he was a founder member of the CP in 1920 and one of its main leaders from then until his death. On the Communist Party in the 1930s and 1940s, see Kevin Morgan, *Harry Pollitt* (Manchester: Manchester University Press, 1994) and *Against Fascism and War: Ruptures and Continuities in British Communist Politics 1935-41* (Manchester: Manchester University Press, 1989); John Callaghan, *Rajani Palme Dutt: A Study in British Stalinism* (London: Lawrence and Wishart, 1997); Henry Pelling, *The British Communist Party: A Historical Profile* (London: A. and C. Black, 1958); Noreen Branson, *History of the Communist Party of Great Britain 1927–41* (London: Lawrence and Wishart, 1985); James Enden and David Renton, *The Communist Party of Great Britain since 1920* (Basingstoke: Palgrave Macmillan, 2002).

33. On the ILP, see Fenner Brockway, *Inside the Left* (London: George Allen and Unwin, 1942); R. E. Dowse, *Left in the Centre: The Independent Labour Party 1893–1940* (London: Longman, 1966).

34. On the Socialist League and the Labour left, see Ben Pimlott, *Labour and the Left in the 1930s* (Cambridge: Cambridge University Press, 1977); Kevin Morgan, *Bolshevism and the British Left, Part One: Labour Legends and Russian Gold* and *Part Two: The Webbs and Soviet Communism* (both (London: Lawrence and Wishart, 2006); Simon Burgess, *Stafford Cripps: A Political Life* (London, Victor Gollancz, 1999), chapters 7 and 8; John Campbell, *Nye Bevan and the Mirage of British Socialism* (London: Weidenfeld and Nicolson, 1987), chapter 6; Michael Foot, *Aneurin Bevan 1897–1945* (London: MacGibbon and Kee, 1962), chapters 5–8; Michael Bor, *The Socialist League in the 1930s* (London: Athena Press, 2005).

35. Sir Oswald Mosley (1896–1980) was leader of the BUF from 1932 to 1940, when he was interned. He was released from prison in November 1943 by Herbert Morrison. Mosley's political journey through the 1920s and 1930s was remarkable. Elected as Conservative MP

for Harrow in 1918, he left the Tories in 1920 and won election as an independent in 1922 before joining the Labour Party, in which, after a short hiatus caused by his failure to win a seat in the 1924 general election, he became the most outspoken leader of the left in the late 1920s as MP for Smethwick (1926–31). After failing to persuade the 1930 Labour conference to adopt a job creation programme based on the ideas of John Maynard Keynes (1883–1946), the 'Mosley manifesto', he set up the New Party, which failed miserably in the 1931 general election. Following a trip to Italy, Mosley dissolved it and set up the BUF. Robert Skidelsky, *Oswald Mosley* (London: Macmillan, 1975) is over-sympathetic but easy to follow; Stephen Dorril, *Blackshirt: Sir Oswald Mosley and British Fascism* (London: Penguin, 2006) is brilliantly researched and damning but rather dense.

36. Fenner Brockway (1888–1988) was a left-wing journalist and politician. He joined the ILP as a young man and was editor of its weekly, the *Labour Leader*, from 1912 to 1917. He was gaoled as a conscientious objector for most of the period 1916–19. He was a key figure in the inter-war ILP, serving as organising secretary (1922), general secretary (1928 and 1933–9) and chairman (1931–3) and again editing its weekly, renamed the *New Leader*, 1926–9 and 1931–46. He was Labour MP for East Leyton 1929–31, left the Labour Party when the ILP disaffiliated in 1932, rejoined Labour in 1946 and became Labour MP for Eton and Slough in 1950, serving until 1964, when he was made a life peer.

37. Harry Pollitt (1890–1960) was general secretary of the CPGB 1929–39 and 1941–56. Born near Manchester and a boiler maker by trade, he became a prominent member of the shop stewards' movement during the First World War and was national organiser of the Hands Off Russia campaign in 1920. Kevin Morgan, *Harry Pollitt* (Manchester: Manchester University Press, 1993) is an excellent biography.

James Maxton (1885–1946) was ILP MP for Bridgeton 1922–46, chairman of the party 1926–29 and, after it disaffiliated from the Labour Party, its parliamentary leader 1932–46.

38. There were three Moscow show trials in 1936–8. The first, held in August 1936, was of the two long-standing Bolshevik leaders with whom Stalin had created a triumvirate after the death of Lenin, Lev Kamenev (1883–1936) and Grigori Zinoviev (1883–1936), and fourteen others who were alleged to have created a 'Troskyite-Zinovievite terrorist centre' with the intention of killing Stalin and other Soviet leaders: all were shot. The second trial, of seventeen members of a supposed 'anti-Soviet Trotskyist centre', took place in January 1937: all but four were sentenced to death for plotting with the Germans to overthrow the Soviet government. Finally, in March 1938, came the trail of twenty-one supposed members of an 'anti-Soviet bloc of rights and Trotskyites', among them the two main leaders of the Communist Party 'right' in the late 1920s, Nikolai Bukharin (1888–1938) and Aleksei Rykov (1881–1938), and the secret police chief who had overseen the interrogations for the first trial, Genrikh Yagoda (1891–1938). All but three were shot.

The trials were bizarre spectacles in which the defendants, who had all previously occupied senior positions in the Communist Party and in the Soviet government, confessed to the most outlandish conspiracies. Very few on the left in Britain saw through the first two – even Brailsford and Brockway at first merely raised questions – and not even the small band of British Trotskyists realised that they were just the public face of (and excuse for) a massive wave of arrests, executions and deportations that swept the whole of Soviet society. (See Martin Upham's thesis *The History of British Trotskyism to 1949* at www.revolutionary-history.co.uk.) The sheer scale of the Great Terror slowly became apparent in the 1940s, but it was only in the 1960s that it became possible to make an educated guess at the number of its victims, and even now there are no precise figures. In the first account based on access to official archives, the historian Dmitri Volkogonov estimated that in 1937–8, 'between 4.5 million and 5.5 million people were arrested, of whom 800,000–900,000 were sentenced to death. Countless more died in concentration camps.' The effect of the purge on the Communist Party was immense: 'Of 139 members and candidate members of the central committee elected at the seventeenth congress [in 1934], 98, i.e. 70 per cent, were arrested and executed in 1937–38.' The armed forces also suffered almost incredible losses. See *Stalin: Triumph and Tragedy* (London: Weidenfeld and Nicolson, 1991).

39. Quoted in Morgan, *Harry Pollitt*, p. 92.

40. Brockway, *Inside the Left*, p. 269.

41. G. D. H. Cole (1889–1959) was a prolific socialist historian and publicist. Educated at St Paul's School and Oxford, where he became a lecturer, he was a conscientious objector during the First World War. An advocate of a decentralised self-managed guild socialism in the 1910s and 1920s, he had by the late 1930s returned to a rather orthodox Fabian gradualism, writing regularly for the *New Statesman*. His wife was Raymond Postgate's sister Margaret (1893–1980), herself a formidable socialist historian.

For John Langdon-Davies, see p. 231 and note 166 in the main text.

Julius Braunthal (1891–1972) joined the Austrian Social Democratic Party before the First World War, in which he fought in an artillery regiment. He became one of the most prominent socialist journalists in Austria in the 1920s and early 1930s. Imprisoned after the failure of the Vienna uprising against the authoritarian Dollfuss regime in 1934, he was expelled from the country in 1935 and lived briefly in Belgium before making his way to Britain. He became secretary of the Socialist International after the Second World War and wrote the monumental *History of the International* (London: Nelson, 1966 and 1967 and Victor Gollancz, 1980).

42. *Tribune*, 8 July 1938.

43. For Gollancz, see *Tribune* biographies, pp. 393–4 of this volume.

44. John Strachey (1901–63), son of the editor of the *Spectator*, St Loe Strachey, was educated at Eton and Oxford. A Tory at university, he was converted to socialism in his early twenties and became a prominent ILP publicist, working closely with Sir Oswald Mosley on proposals for combating unemployment. He was Labour MP for Birmingham Aston 1929–31, and followed Mosley into the New Party but swiftly resigned and gravitated towards the CPGB. During the 1930s, he was a tireless propagandist for an apocalyptic Marxism as understood by the CPGB: he wrote countless articles and several books, among them *The Coming Struggle for Power* (London: Victor Gollancz, 1932), *The Theory and Practice of Socialism* (London: Victor Gollancz, 1936) and the bestselling *Why You Should Be a Socialist* (London: Victor Gollancz, 1938). Strachey broke with the CPGB over its defeatism in 1940, drifted away from Marxism, rejoined the Labour Party and was elected MP for Dundee (1945–50) and then Dundee West

(1950–63), serving as air minister, food minister and war secretary in the 1945–51 Labour governments. His *Contemporary Capitalism* (London: Victor Gollancz, 1956) was a sophisticated rebuttal of the Marxism he had embraced in the 1930s. Hugh Thomas, *John Strachey* (London: Methuen, 1973) is good on his life; Noel Thompson, *John Strachey: An Intellectual Biography* (Basingstoke: Macmillan, 1993) is excellent on his thinking.

45. Among the LBC's titles on the Soviet Union were Dudley Collard's defence of the Moscow show trials, *Soviet Justice and the Trial of Radek and Others* (1937), Pat Sloan's fulsome account of the 1936 Soviet constitution, *Soviet Democracy* (1937), and the first cheap edition of Sidney and Beatrice Webb's *Soviet Communism: A New Civilisation* (1938).

46. Brailsford wrote to Foot: 'As to Mellor, I should agree that if you and he had been standing together against the proprietors on a matter of policy or principle, you would in honour have to go with him. But that I gather wasn't the fact . . . Why capitulate in advance? I assume that you would enjoy full editorial discretion . . . One may be too subjective – that's in the Liberal-Nonconformist tradition – and forget that to run a good paper matters more than to perform prodigies of conscience.' Quoted in Mervyn Jones, *Michael Foot* (London: Victor Gollancz, 1994), p. 62.

47. Quoted in Jones, *Michael Foot*, p. 63.

48. The pieces were published every week from 15 October to 26 November 1937.

49. *Tribune*, 11 June 1937.

50. Michael Foot, 'The Road to Ruin', in Elizabeth Thomas (ed.), *Tribune 21* (London: MacGibbon and Kee, 1958), p. 7. Foot went on: 'Our excuse was that we, along with the Independent Labour Party, were engaged in a unity campaign with the Communists on the supreme issue of Spain and the international crisis . . . Of course, the excuse was a bad one.'

51. *Tribune*, 25 August 1939.

52. Interview quoted in Mark Jenkins, *Bevanism: Labour's High Tide* (Nottingham: Spokesman, 1979), p. 36. J. R. Campbell (1894–1969) was a founder member of the CPGB in 1920 and a member of its central committee from 1923 to 1965. He was foreign editor of the *Daily Worker* 1932–4, its assistant editor 1937–9 and 1942–9 and its editor briefly in 1939 and again 1949–59.

53. Rajani Palme Dutt (1896–1974) was the CPGB's leading ideologue from the 1920s until the 1950s. Oxford educated, he was a founder member of the party and started *Labour Monthly* in 1921, editing it until his death. He was editor of the *Daily Worker* 1936–8.

54. *Tribune*, 22 September 1939.

55. Konni Zilliacus (1894–1967) was a Labour politician, MP for Gateshead 1945–50 and Manchester Gorton 1955–67. Born in Japan to a Finnish father and an American mother, he went to school in England and then to Yale University, ending the First World War as a cipher officer with the British forces intervening against the Bolsheviks in Siberia. He worked for the League of Nations in the 1920s and 1930s, all the while contributing anonymously to the left and liberal press. He started writing for *Tribune* in 1938 and was soon a regular in its pages. Zilliacus was generally pro-Soviet until the Molotov–Ribbentrop pact but then became a critic – a position that was reinforced by the Soviet attack on Finland in 1939. From 1941, however, he became once again militantly pro-Soviet, and from 1945 he was a vocal backbench critic of

Ernest Bevin's foreign policy, consistently taking the Moscow line. He was expelled from the Labour Party in 1948 for being so pro-Soviet - but then won the enmity of the Soviet Union and the CPGB by taking the side of Tito in the Soviet–Yugoslav split. He was readmitted to Labour in 1952. Archie Potts, *Zilliacus: A Life for Peace and Socialism* (London: Merlin, 2002) is an over-sympathetic biography. For Orwell's view of him in the 1940s, see p. 34.

56. Strauss, unpublished autobiography, p. 68. See also interview with Strauss in Bill Jones, *The Russia Complex: The British Labour Party and the Soviet Union* (Manchester: Manchester University Press, 1977), p. 48.

57. How low *Tribune*'s sales fell at this point is unclear. The paper claimed a 'certificated sale' of 30,000 in summer 1939. Orwell wrote in 1948 that circulation fell to 2,000 (see 'Britain's Left-wing Press', in *CWGO* XIX, pp. 294–8) but Strauss said the low point was 9,000. See Jones, *Russia Complex*, p. 48.

58. Quoted in John and Mary Postgate, *A Stomach for Dissent: The Life of Raymond Postgate* (Keele: Keele University Press, 1994), p. 209.

59. *Tribune*, 31 January 1947, pp. 356–7 of this volume.

60. *Tribune*, 21 July 1939. Why Orwell thought the review 'none-too-friendly' is a mystery. It described the novel as Orwell's 'in many ways best work'.

61. On the Blairs' experience in Spain, see Gordon Bowker, *George Orwell* (London: Little, Brown, 2003), chapter 11. The denunciation of the Blairs as Trotskyists is in *CWGO* XI, p. 30.

62. The article on the May events, 'Spilling the Spanish Beans', was published by *New English Weekly* in two parts on 29 July and 2 September 1937 (in *CWGO* XI, pp. 41–6). Kingsley Martin (1897–1969) was editor of the *New Statesman* from 1930 to 1960. A conscientious objector during the First World War, he was educated at Cambridge University and worked briefly as an academic before becoming a leader writer on the *Manchester Guardian*. Orwell detested him. C. H. Rolph, *Kingsley: The Life, Letters and Diaries of Kingsley Martin* (London: Victor Gollancz, 1973) is an over-sympathetic biography.

63. 'Spilling the Spanish Beans' part 1, *New English Weekly*, 29 July 1937, in *CWGO* XI, p. 42.

64. Letter to Geoffrey Gorer, 15 September 1937, in *CWGO* XI, pp. 80–1.

65. Review of *Workers' Front* by Fenner Brockway, *New English Weekly*, 17 February 1938, in *CWGO* XI, pp. 123–4.

66. 'Not Counting Niggers', *Adelphi*, July 1939, in *CWGO* XI, pp. 358–61.

67. 'My Country Right or Left', *Folios of New Writing*, autumn 1940, in *CWGO* XII, pp. 269–72.

68. John Newsinger, *Orwell's Politics* (Basingstoke: Macmillan, 1999), p. 62.

69. 'My Country Right or Left'.

70. For Postgate's response to Orwell, see *CWGO* XI, pp. 223–4. On Gollancz and *Fact*, see Ruth Dudley Edwards, *Victor Gollancz: A Biography* (London: Victor Gollancz, 1987), pp. 266–7. The piece on the 'Trotsky–Stalin controversy' appeared in *Fact* 10, January 1938, in which the main article was Evelyn Lend's 'The Underground Struggle in Germany'. Lend married a BBC journalist, Paul Anderson (no relation), and as Evelyn Anderson worked as assistant editor and then editor on *Tribune* in the 1940s.

71. John Lehman (1907–87) was a poet, critic and editor. He was the founder and editor of the magazines *New Writing* (1936–46) and *Penguin New Writing* (1940–50).

72. *CWGO* XII, pp. 119–20.
73. *Tribune*, 12 July 1940, in *CWGO* XII, pp. 210–13.
74. *Tribune*, 9 August 1940, in *CWGO* XII, pp. 227–9.
75. *Tribune*, 23 August 1940, in *CWGO* XII, pp. 238–40.
76. The best discussion of Orwell's political position in the early 1940s is Newsinger, *Orwell's Politics*, chapter 4.
77. *Tribune*, 31 January 1947, p. 357 in this volume.
78. 'My Country Right or Left'.
79. On Orwell's 'revolutionary patriotism', see Newsinger, *Orwell's Politics*, chapter 4.
80. The People's Convention was a front organisation for the Communist Party of Great Britain built around a conference held in London on 12 January 1941 to call for 'a People's Peace' and 'friendship with the Soviet Union' – which was then effectively allied with Nazi Germany under the terms of the 1939 Molotov–Ribbentrop pact. Attended by 2,000 delegates, the conference was the highest-profile event organised by the CPGB during the period of the pact, when it took an implicitly defeatist line on the war. Victor Gollancz (1893–1967), one of the most prominent fellow travellers of the Soviet Union pre-war, famously responded to the convention by putting together the book *Betrayal of the Left* (London: Victor Gollancz, 1941), an excoriating attack on the CPGB to which Orwell contributed two chapters.

The convention's chairman, the Hammersmith MP D. N. Pritt (1887–1972), had been a prominent defender of the legitimacy of the Moscow trials in the late 1930s and was expelled from the Labour Party in 1940 for supporting the Soviet invasion of Finland. He replied to this 'As I Please' with an ingenuous letter to *Tribune* protesting that the convention 'never ran a "stop the war" campaign', to which Orwell appended a response. On the People's Convention, see Angus Calder, *The People's War: Britain 1939–1945* (London: Jonathan Cape, 1969), chapter 5.
81. *Tribune*, 20 December 1940, in *CWGO* XII, pp. 309–12.
82. *Tribune*, 14 March 1941.
83. *Tribune*, 13 September 1940.
84. *Tribune*, 24 January 1941.
85. Postgate and Postgate, *Stomach for Dissent*, p. 231.
86. Foot, *Aneurin Bevan*, p. 350.
87. Campbell, *Nye Bevan and the Mirage of British Socialism*, p. 114.
88. *Tribune*, 18 September 1942, in *CWGO* XIV, pp. 42–5.
89. *Tribune*, 20 November 1942, in *CWGO* XIV, pp. 184–6.
90. 'Not Enough Money: A Sketch of George Gissing', *Tribune*, 2 April 1943, in *CWGO* XV, pp. 45–7; 'Review of *Order of the Day* by Thomas Mann', *Tribune*, 10 September 1943, in *CWGO* XV, pp. 242–4; 'Mark Twain – The Licensed Jester', *Tribune*, 26 November 1943, in *CWGO* XVI, pp. 5–8.
91. *Tribune*, 4 June 1943, in *CWGO* XV, pp. 125–6.
92. *Tribune*, 1 September 1944, p. 183 in this volume.
93. *Tribune*, 24 December 1943, p. 74 in this volume.

94. *Tribune*, 31 March 1944, p. 121 in this volume.
95. *Tribune*, 26 January 1945, p. 236 in this volume.
96. *Tribune*, 2 February 1945, p. 240 in this volume.
97. 'London Letter', *Partisan Review*, Winter 1944–45, in *CWGO* XVI, pp. 411–16.
98. Newsinger, *Orwell's Politics*, chapter 5.
99. 'London Letter', *Partisan Review*, Spring 1944, in *CWGO* XVI, pp. 64–70.
100. 'London Letter', *Partisan Review*, Fall 1944, in *CWGO* XVI, pp. 300–3.
101. 'London Letter', *Partisan Review*, Summer 1945, in *CWGO* XVII, pp. 161–5.
102. Crick, *George Orwell: A Life*, chapter 14.
103. Woodcock, *Crystal Spirit*, p. 16.
104. For Postgate, Kimche, Anderson and Fyvel, see '*Tribune* biographies', pp. 389–98 of this volume.

For Koestler, Comfort and Read, see note 16 above. For Borkenau, see note 17 above.

Tom Wintringham (1898–1949) was a writer and man of action. A member of the Communist Party from 1923 until 1938, he was commander of the British Batallion of the International Brigade in the Spanish civil war. He played a major role in the creation of the Home Guard after the outbreak of the Second World War and was a founder member of Common Wealth (see note 71 in the main text). He contributed to *Tribune* on several occasions in the 1940s. Orwell knew him from his time in the Home Guard. Hugh Purcell, *The Last English Revolutionary: Tom Wintringham 1898–1949* (London: Sutton, 2004) is an excellent biography.

Hugh (Humphrey) Slater (1905–58) was a writer and painter. A member of the CPGB from the early 1930s, he joined the International Brigade in Spain in 1936, serving as chief of operations. He left the CPGB in 1938 and with Wintringham helped set up the Home Guard in 1940, writing two key guides to guerrilla warfare against a German invasion of Britain and against German occupation of Europe. *Tribune* ran his articles on military strategy and tactics when Postgate was editor. He was editor of the journal *Polemic*, to which Orwell was a contributor, 1945–8.

Reginald Reynolds (1905–58) was a British journalist and author, the husband of the libertarian socialist journalist and novelist Ethel Mannin (1900–84). A Quaker pacifist, he became a personal friend of Orwell in the late 1930s through the Independent Labour Party. Despite his subsequent differences with Orwell over the war, they remained close friends, and they co-edited the collection *British Pamphleteers* (London: Allan Wingate, 1948).
105. David Astor (1912–2001) was the second son of the second Viscount Astor and his wife Nancy, the first woman to take her seat in the House of Commons. Educated at Eton and Oxford, he took little interest in the *Observer*, which had belonged to the family since 1911, until the outbreak of war. He then became increasingly involved, effectively taking over the direction of the paper from early 1942 (despite having a full-time army job). He became editor formally in 1948 and remained in post until 1976.
106. Malcolm Muggeridge (1903–90), the son of a left-wing Labour MP, was a journalist and author, in his later years best known as a presenter of religious television programmes and as a Christian (latterly Catholic) publicist. In the 1940s, however, his reputation rested on his

exposé as a foreign correspondent of the Ukrainian famine of 1932–3 (a story that his employer, the *Manchester Guardian*, refused to publish in full, leading to Muggeridge's departure from the paper) and his satirical writing, in particular *Winter in Moscow* (London: Eyre and Spottiswoode, 1934), a novel based on his time as a correspondent in Moscow, and *The Thirties* (London: Hamish Hamilton, 1940), a biting instant history of what W. H. Auden called 'a low dishonest decade'. Orwell reviewed *The Thirties* sympathetically for *New English Weekly* on 25 April 1940 and met Muggeridge soon afterwards. They became close personal friends. Muggeridge worked as an intelligence officer during the Second World War. He and the novelist Anthony Powell organised Orwell's funeral service in London. Muggeridge's memoir of Orwell, 'A Knight of the Woeful Countenance', appeared in Miriam Gross (ed.), *The World of George Orwell* (London: Weidenfeld and Nicolson, 1971).

A. J. Ayer (1910–89) was a philosopher. Educated at Eton and Oxford, he wrote his best-known work, *Language, Truth and Logic*, in his twenties. He too worked as an intelligence officer during the Second World War.

Ernest Hemingway (1899–1961) was an American novelist, author of *A Farewell to Arms* (1929) and *For Whom the Bell Tolls* (1940). He was in Paris in 1945 working as a war correspondent. Orwell, apparently worried that he was in danger of assassination by Soviet agents, borrowed a pistol from him.

107. Unpublished letter to *Tribune*, 26 June 1945, in *CWGO* XVII, pp. 193–4; 'Orwell and the Stinkers': a correspondence, *Tribune*, 29 June–27 July 1945, in *CWGO* XVII, pp. 201–4.

108. Letter to Herbert Read, 18 August 1945, in *CWGO* XVII, pp. 263–4.

109. A flavour of the atmosphere around the time of the 1945 election is given by Frederic Mullally in his account of how he took over from Kimche:

> Three months before the general election, when I was summoned to my first meeting with Nye, the venue was . . . The Ivy restaurant in Soho, favoured by the stars of show business, politics and journalism. Co-hosting the luncheon was G. R. Strauss, the wealthy Labour MP for North Lambeth, who had replaced Sir Stafford Cripps as the guarantor of *Tribune*'s overdrafts.
>
> We got down to business at once. A date for the general election would soon have to be decided by Winston Churchill. From that moment on, Nye would be totally caught up in the campaign, not just in his own constituency but in all those marginal divisions where the party's candidate might profit from politics' biggest crowd-puller after Churchill himself. Michael Foot, one of the pillars of *Tribune*, would be campaigning for the Plymouth seat. And Jon Kimche was leaving *Tribune* to devote himself to Israeli affairs. It would leave Evelyn Anderson as the only full-time editorial staff; but German-born Evelyn could neither write crisp copy nor sub-edit professionally; her expertise was in commissioning and vetting political writers on international affairs. Would I be willing, at least for the duration of the election campaign, to take over Jon Kimche's job as effective editor of the review, sharing with her the title of assistant editor? They could afford to pay me only 12 guineas a week, six of which would appear in the books as expenses, Strauss hastened to add, and therefore free of income tax.

> I took the job, initially for the run-up to polling day . . . and stayed with *Tribune* until November 1946.

Frederic Mullally, 'Fleet Street in the Forties', *British Journalism Review* (1999), vol. 10, no. 1.
110. Fyvel's review appeared on 24 August 1945, Symons's riposte a week later.
111. Cyril Connolly (1903–74) was a critic and editor. A contemporary of Orwell at St Cyprian's prep school and Eton, he went on to Oxford. He is best known today for his semi-autobiographical *The Enemies of Promise* (London: Routledge, 1938). He founded the literary magazine *Horizon* in 1939 and edited it until 1949. Orwell contributed several of his best-known essays to it, including 'Boys' Weeklies', 'The Art of Donald McGill' and 'Politics and the English Language'. See Michael Shelden, *Friends of Promise: Cyril Connolly and the World of* Horizon (London: Hamish Hamilton, 1989).
112. *Tribune*, 19 October 1945, p. 249 in this volume.
113. *Tribune*, 9 and 23 November 1945 and 18 January 1946; pp. 256, 259 and 280 in this volume, respectively.
114. *Tribune*, 7 and 14 December 1945 and 11 January 1946; pp. 262, 265 and 276 in this volume, respectively.
115. *Tribune*, 8 February and 3 May 1946; pp. 291 and 314 in this volume, respectively.
116. *Tribune*, 15 February and 12 April 1946; pp. 295 and 306 in this volume, respectively.
117. *Tribune*, 7 December 1945 and 25 January 1946; pp. 262 and 284 in this volume, respectively.
118. 'London Letter', *Partisan Review*, Summer 1946, in *CWGO* XIX, pp. 285–9.
119. *Tribune*, 3 August 1945.
120. See Jonathan Schneer, *Labour's Conscience: The Labour Left 1945–51* (London: Unwin Hyman, 1988).
121. *Tribune*, 1 March 1946.
122. *Tribune*, 23 November 1945 and 18 January 1946; pp. 259 and 280 in this volume, respectively.
123. See for example, 'The Prevention of Literature', *Polemic*, January 1946, in *CWGO* XVII, pp. 369–80; 'Second Thoughts on James Burnham', *Polemic*, May 1946, in *CWGO* XVIII, pp. 268–84; and 'London Letter', *Partisan Review*, Summer 1946, in *CWGO* XVIII, pp. 285–9.
124. Richard Crossman (1907–74) was a Labour politician and journalist. Educated at Winchester and Oxford, he became an Oxford classics fellow in 1931, joined the *New Statesman* as assistant editor in 1938 and served as a British government propagandist during the Second World War, returning to the *New Statesman* in 1945. He was Labour MP for Coventry East 1945–74, Minister of Housing 1964–6, leader of the House of Commons 1966–68 and health and social security secretary 1968–70. He then became editor of the *New Statesman* in 1970, a job he did disastrously for two years. His publications included *The God That Failed* (London: Hamish Hamilton, 1949), a book of essays by former communists describing how they became disillusioned with communism, among them Arthur Koestler and Stephen Spender, and (posthumously) *The Diaries of a Cabinet Minister* (London, Jonathan Cape, 1976). Anthony Howard, *Crossman: The Pursuit of Power* (London: Jonathan Cape, 1990) is the standard biography.

125. Ian Mikardo (1908–93) was Labour MP for Reading East 1945–59, Poplar 1964–74, Bethnal Green and Bow 1974–83 and Bow and Poplar 1983–87. He was a member of *Tribune*'s board from 1946, resigning over the paper's endorsement of NATO and its hard anti-Soviet line in May 1949. His autobiography is *Backbencher* (London: Weidenfeld and Nicolson, 1988).
126. Jenkins, *Bevanism: Labour's High Tide*, chapter 2.
127. *Tribune*, 17, 24 and 31 January and 7 February 1947, in *CWGO* XVIII, pp. 289–99.
128. *Tribune*, 17 January 1947.
129. *Tribune*, 17 January 1947.
130. *Tribune*, 7 February 1947.
131. Denis Healey (b. 1917) was international secretary of the Labour Party from 1945 to 1952. A member of the Communist Party as a student at Oxford, he joined Labour during the war. He returned from wartime service in the Royal Engineers to fight Pudsey and Otley unsuccessfully in the 1945 general election and joined the party's staff soon afterwards. *Cards on the Table* was the first of his major interventions in Labour's policy debates. It was followed by *Feet on the Ground* (1948), a polemic against European federalism, and *The Curtain Falls* (1951), a collection of essays on the communist suppression of democratic socialist parties in east central Europe. Healey was a *Tribune* contributor during the 1940s and a good friend of Evelyn Anderson. He was Labour MP for Leeds South East 1952–55 and Leeds South 1955–92, defence secretary 1964–70, Chancellor of the Exchequer 1974–9, Labour deputy leader 1980–3 and shadow foreign secretary 1980–7. His autobiography *The Time of My Life* (London: Michael Joseph, 1989) is the best of any postwar Labour politician. Edward Pearce, *Denis Healey: A Life in Our Times* (London: Little, Brown, 2002) is a readable biography.
132. *Tribune*, 13 June 1947.
133. *Tribune*, 20 June 1947.
134. 'In Defence of Comrade Zilliacus', letter intended for *Tribune* but not published, in *CWGO* XIX, pp. 181–4. Davison has this as written in August–September 1947.
135. 'Britain's Left-wing Press', *Progressive* (Madison, Wisconsin), June 1948, in *CWGO* XIX, pp. 294–8.
136. Richard Crossman and Michael Foot, *A Palestine Munich?* (London: Victor Gollancz, 1946). The story of the Labour left's embrace of Zionism in the 1940s is a fascinating one that deserves a book-length study.
137. 'London Letter', *Partisan Review*, Fall 1945, in *CWGO* XVII, pp. 244–9.
138. Letter to Julian Symons, 2 January 1948, in *CWGO* XIX, p. 237. Orwell went on:

> Crossman and his & the rest of that gang thought they saw an opening for themselves in squealing about foreign policy, which in the circumstances was bound to go badly, & so *Tribune* has been in the position of coming down on the side of the government whenever there is a major issue, eg. conscription, & at the same time trying to look fearfully left by raising an outcry about Greece etc. I really think I prefer the Zilliacus lot, since after all they do have a policy, ie. to appease Russia. I started writing an open letter to *Tribune* about this, but was taken ill before I finished it. I particularly hate that trick of sucking up to the left cliques by perpetually attacking America while relying on America to feed & protect us. I even

get letters from American university students asking why *Tribune* is always going for the USA & in such an ignorant way.

139. See for example 'Britain's Left-wing Press'; and 'The Labour Government after Three Years', *Commentary*, October 1948, in *CWGO* XIX, pp. 435–43.
140. *Tribune*, 17 June 1949.
141. *Tribune*, 27 January 1950.

As I Please 1

3 December 1943

Scene in a tobacconist's shop. Two American soldiers sprawling across the counter, one of them just sober enough to make unwanted love to the two young women who run the shop, the other at the stage known as 'fighting drunk'. Enter Orwell in search of matches. The pugnacious one makes an effort and stands upright.

Soldier: Wharrishay is, perfijious Albion. You heard that? Perfijious Albion. Never trust a Britisher. You can't trust the b--s.
Orwell: Can't trust them with what?
Soldier: Wharrishay is, down with Britain. Down with the British. You wanna do anything about that? Then you can -- well do it. (*Sticks his face out like a tomcat on a garden wall.*)
Tobacconist: He'll knock your block off if you don't shut up.
Soldier: Wharrishay is, down with Britain. (*Subsides across the counter again. The tobacconist lifts his head delicately out of the scales.*)

This kind of thing is not exceptional. Even if you steer clear of Piccadilly with its seething swarms of drunks and whores, it is difficult to go anywhere in London without having the feeling that Britain is now Occupied Territory. The general consensus of opinion seems to be that the only American soldiers with decent manners are the Negroes. On the other hand the Americans have their own justifiable complaints - in particular, they complain of the children who follow them night and day, cadging sweets.

Does this sort of thing matter? The answer is that it might matter at some moment when Anglo-American relations were in the balance, and when the still-powerful forces in this country which want an understanding with Japan were able to show their faces again. At such moments popular prejudice can count for a great deal. Before the war there was no popular anti-American feeling in this country. It all dates from the arrival of the American troops, and it is made vastly worse by the tacit agreement never to discuss it in print.

Seemingly it is our fixed policy in this war not to criticise our allies, nor to answer their criticisms of us. As a result things have happened which are capable of causing the worst kind of trouble sooner or later. An example is the agreement by which American troops in this country are not liable to British courts for offences against British subjects - practically 'extra-territorial rights'. Not one English person in ten knows of the existence of this agreement; the newspapers barely reported it and refrained from commenting on it. Nor have people been made to realise the extent of anti-British feeling in the United States. Drawing their picture of America from films carefully edited for the British market, they have no notion of the kind of thing that Americans are brought up to believe about us. Suddenly to discover, for instance, that the average American thinks the USA had more casualties than Britain in the last war comes as a shock, and the kind of shock that can cause a violent quarrel. Even such a fundamental difficulty as the fact that an American soldier's pay is five times that of a British soldier has never been properly ventilated. No sensible person wants to whip up Anglo-American jealousy. On the contrary, it is just because one does want a good relationship between the two countries that one wants plain speaking. Our official soft-soaping policy does us no good in America, while in this country it allows dangerous resentments to fester just below the surface.

* * *

Since 1935, when pamphleteering revived, I have been a steady collector of pamphlets, political, religious and what-not. To anyone who happens to come across it and has a shilling to spare I recommend *The 1946 MS* by Robin Maugham,[1] published by the War Facts Press. It is a good example of that small but growing school of literature, the non-party radical school. It purports to describe the establishment in Britain of a fascist dictatorship, starting in 1944 and headed by a successful general who is (I think) drawn from a living model. I found it interesting because it gives you the average middle-class man's conception of what fascism would be like, and more important, of the reasons why fascism might succeed. Its appearance (along with other similar pamphlets I have in my collection) shows how far that average middle-class man has travelled since 1939, when socialism still meant dividing the money up and what happened in Europe was none of our business.

* * *

Who wrote this?

> As we walked over the Drury Lane gratings of the cellars a most foul stench came up, and one in particular that I remember to this day. A man half-dressed pushed open a broken window beneath us, just as we passed by, and there issued such a blast of corruption, made up of gases bred by filth, air breathed and re-breathed a hundred times, charged with the odours of unnamable personal uncleanliness and disease, that

1. Robin Maugham (1916–81) became a novelist and playwright. His first and best-known novel, *The Servant* (London: Falcon Press, 1948) – later adapted by Harold Pinter for a film starring Dirk Bogarde – was massively controversial because of its explicit depiction of homosexual desire.

> I staggered to the gutter with a qualm which I could scarcely conquer . . . I did not know, until I came in actual contact with them, how far away the classes which lie at the bottom of great cities are from those above them; how completely they are inaccessible to motives which act upon ordinary human beings, and how deeply they are sunk beyond ray of sun or stars, immersed in the selfishness naturally begotten of their incessant struggle for existence and incessant warfare with society. It was an awful thought to me, ever present on those Sundays, and haunting me at other times; that men, women and children were living in brutish degradation, and that as they died others would take their place. Our civilisation seemed nothing but a thin film or crust lying over a bottomless pit and I often wondered whether some day the pit would not break up through it and destroy us all.

You would know, at any rate, that this comes from some nineteenth-century writer. Actually it is from a novel, *Mark Rutherford's Deliverance*. (Mark Rutherford, whose real name was Hale White, wrote this book as a pseudo-autobiography.)[2] Apart from the prose, you could recognise this as coming from the nineteenth century because of that description of the unendurable filth of the slums. The London slums of that day were like that, and all honest writers so described them. But even more characteristic is that notion of a whole block of the population being so degraded as to be beyond contact and beyond redemption.

Almost all nineteenth-century English writers are agreed upon this, even Dickens. A large part of the town working class, ruined by industrialism, are simply savages. Revolution is not a thing to be hoped for: it simply means the swamping of civilisation by the sub-human. In this novel (it is one of the best novels in English) Mark Rutherford describes the opening of a sort of mission or settlement near Drury Lane. Its object was 'gradually to attract Drury Lane to come and be saved'. Needless to say this was a failure. Drury Lane not only did not want to be saved in the religious sense, it didn't even want to be civilised. All that Mark Rutherford and his friend succeeded in doing, all that one could do, indeed, at that time, was to provide a sort of refuge for the few people of the neighbourhood who did not belong to their surroundings. The general masses were outside the pale.

Mark Rutherford was writing of the seventies, and in a footnote dated 1884 he remarks that 'socialism, nationalisation of the land and other projects' have now made their appearance, and may perhaps give a gleam of hope. Nevertheless, he assumes that the condition of the working class will grow worse and not better as time goes on. It was natural to believe this (even Marx seems to have believed it), because it was hard at that time to foresee the enormous increase in the productivity of labour. Actually, such an

2. William Hale White (1831–1913) was an Admiralty civil servant who doubled as a Nonconformist radical journalist and novelist.

improvement in the standard of living has taken place as Mark Rutherford and his contemporaries would have considered quite impossible.

The London slums are still bad enough, but they are nothing to those of the nineteenth century. Gone are the days when a single room used to be inhabited by four families, one in each corner, and when incest and infanticide were taken almost for granted. Above all, gone are the days when it seemed natural to write off a whole stratum of the population as irredeemable savages. The most snobbish Tory alive would not now write of the London working class as Mark Rutherford does. And Mark Rutherford – like Dickens, who shared his attitude – was a radical! Progress does happen, hard though it may be to believe it, in this age of concentration camps and big beautiful bombs.

George Orwell will write this column each week.

As I Please 2

10 December 1943

The recently issued special supplement to the *New Republic*[3] entitled *The Negro: His Future in America* is worth a reading, but it raises more problems than it discusses. The facts it reveals about the present treatment of Negroes in the USA are bad enough in all conscience. In spite of the quite obvious necessities of war, Negroes are still pushed out of skilled jobs, segregated and insulted in the army, assaulted by white policemen and discriminated against by white magistrates. In a number of the southern states they are disenfranchised by means of a poll tax. On the other hand, those of them who have votes are so fed up with the present administration that they are beginning to swing towards the Republican Party – that is, in effect, to give their support to big business. But all this is merely a single facet of the world-wide problem of colour. And what the authors of this supplement fail to point out is that that problem simply cannot be solved inside the capitalist system.

3. *The Negro: His Future in America* was published as a supplement to the American weekly the *New Republic* on 18 October 1943. The *New Republic* was in the 1930s and 1940s markedly pro-Soviet, but Orwell had contributed to it before and in 1946 agreed to send it carbons of his *Tribune* columns, explaining to Dwight Macdonald: 'I am well aware that the *NR* people are Stalino-liberals, but so long as they have no control over what I write, as they wouldn't under this arrangement, I rather like to have a foot in that camp.' The arrangement came to nothing, however.

One of the big unmentionable facts of politics is the differential standard of living. An English working-man spends on cigarettes about the same sum as an Indian peasant has for his entire income. It is not easy for socialists to admit this, or at any rate to emphasise it. If you want people to rebel against the existing system, you have got to show them that they are badly off, and it is doubtful tactics to start by telling an Englishman on the dole that in the eyes of an Indian coolie he would be next door to a millionaire. Almost complete silence reigns on this subject, at any rate at the European end, and it contributes to the lack of solidarity between white and coloured workers. Almost without knowing it – and perhaps without wanting to know it – the white worker exploits the coloured worker, and in revenge the coloured worker can be and is used against the white. Franco's Moors in Spain were only doing more dramatically the same thing as is done by half-starved Indians in Bombay mills or Japanese factory-girls sold into semi-slavery by their parents. As things are, Asia and Africa are simply a bottomless reserve of scab labour.

The coloured worker cannot be blamed for feeling no solidarity with his white comrades. The gap between their standard of living and his own is so vast that it makes any differences which may exist in the west seem negligible. In Asiatic eyes the European class struggle is a sham. The socialist movement has never gained a real foothold in Asia or Africa, or even among the American Negroes: it is everywhere side-tracked by nationalism and race-hatred . Hence the spectacle of thoughtful Negroes getting ready to vote for Dewey,[4] and Indian Congressmen preferring their own capitalists to the British Labour Party. There is no solution until the living-standards of the thousand million people who are not 'white' can be forced up to the same level as our own. But as this might mean temporarily lowering our own standards the subject is systematically avoided by left and right alike.

Is there anything that one can do about this, as an individual? One can at least remember that the colour problem exists. And there is one small precaution which is not much trouble, and which can perhaps do a little to mitigate the horrors of the colour war. That is to avoid using insulting nicknames. It is an astonishing thing that few journalists, even in the left-wing press, bother to find out which names are and which are not resented by members of other races. The word 'native', which makes any Asiatic boil with rage, and which has been dropped even by British officials in India these ten years past, is flung about all over the place. 'Negro' is habitually printed with a small n, a thing most Negroes resent. One's information about these matters needs to be kept up to date. I have just been carefully going through the proofs of a reprinted book of mine, cutting

4. Thomas E. Dewey (1902–71) was an American politician, governor of New York from 1943 to 1955 and twice (in 1944 and 1948) losing Republican candidate for the US presidency.

out the word 'Chinaman' wherever it occurred and substituting 'Chinese'. The book was written less than a dozen years ago, but in the intervening time 'Chinaman' has become a deadly insult. Even 'Mahomedan' is now beginning to be resented: one should say 'Muslim'. These things are childish, but then nationalism is childish. And after all we ourselves do not actually like being called 'Limeys' or 'Britishers'.

As I Please 3

17 December 1943

So many letters have arrived, attacking me for my remarks about the American soldiers in this country, that I must return to the subject.

Contrary to what most of my correspondents seem to think, I was not trying to make trouble between ourselves and our allies, nor am I consumed by hatred for the United States. I am much less anti-American than most English people are at this moment. What I say, and what I repeat, is that our policy of not criticising our allies, and not answering their criticism of us (we don't answer the Russians either, nor even the Chinese) is a mistake, and is likely to defeat its own object in the long run. And so far as Anglo-American relations go, there are three difficulties which badly need dragging into the open and which simply don't get mentioned in the British press.

1. *Anti-American feeling in Britain.* Before the war, anti-American feeling was a middle-class, and perhaps upper-class thing, resulting from imperialist and business jealousy and disguising itself as dislike of the American accent, etc. The working class, so far from being anti-American, were becoming rapidly Americanised in speech by means of the films and jazz songs. Now, in spite of what my correspondents may say, I can hear few good words for the Americans anywhere. This obviously results from the arrival of the American troops. It has been made worse by the fact that, for various reasons, the Mediterranean campaign had to be represented as an American show while most of the casualties had to be suffered by the British. (See Philip Jordan's remarks in his *Tunis Diary*.)[5] I am not saying that popular English prejudices are always justified: I am saying that they exist.

5. Philip Jordan (1902–51) was a British journalist who worked for the liberal *News Chronicle* between 1936 and 1940. Orwell reviewed *Jordan's Tunis Diary* (London: Collins, 1943) in the *Manchester Evening News* on 9 December 1943. Unknown to Orwell, he was the author of an unsympathetic anonymous review of *Homage to Catalonia* in the *Listener* on 25 May 1938.

2. *Anti-British feeling in America.* We ought to face the fact that large numbers of Americans are brought up to dislike and despise us. There is a large section of the press whose main accent is anti-British, and countless other papers which attack Britain in a more sporadic way. In addition there is a systematic guying of what are supposed to be British habits and manners on the stage and in comic strips and cheap magazines. The typical Englishman is represented as a chinless ass with a title, a monocle and a habit of saying 'Haw, haw'. This legend is believed in by relatively responsible Americans, for example by the veteran novelist Theodore Dreiser, who remarks in a public speech that 'the British are horse-riding aristocratic snobs'. (Forty-six million horse-riding snobs!) It is a commonplace on the American stage that the Englishman is almost never allowed to play a favourable role, any more than the Negro is allowed to appear as anything more than a comic. Yet right up to Pearl Harbor the American movie industry had an agreement with the Japanese government never to present a Japanese character in an unfavourable light!

   I am not blaming the Americans for all this. The anti-British press has powerful business forces behind it, besides ancient quarrels in many of which Britain was in the wrong. As for popular anti-British feeling, we partly bring it on ourselves by exporting our worst specimens. But what I do want to emphasise is that these anti-British currents in the USA are very strong, and that the British press has consistently failed to draw attention to them. There has never been in England anything that one could call an anti-American press: and since the war there has been a steady refusal to answer criticism and a careful censorship of the radio to cut out anything that the Americans might object to. As a result, many English people don't realise how they are regarded, and get a shock when they find out.

3. *Soldiers' pay.* It is now nearly two years since the first American troops reached this country, and I rarely see American and British soldiers together. Quite obviously the major cause of this is the difference of pay. You can't have really close and friendly relations with somebody whose income is five times your own. Financially, the whole American army is in the middle class. In the field this might not matter, but in the training period it makes it almost impossible for British and American soldiers to fraternise. If you don't want friendly relations between the British army and the American army, well and good. But if you do, you must either pay the British soldier ten shillings a day or make the American soldier bank the surplus of his pay in America. I don't profess to know which of these alternatives is the right one.

* * *

One way of feeling infallible is not to keep a diary. Looking back through the diary I kept in 1940 and 1941 I find that I was usually wrong when it was possible to be wrong. Yet I was not so wrong as the Military Experts. Experts of various schools were telling us in 1939 that the Maginot Line[6] was impregnable, and that the Russo-German Pact had put an end to Hitler's eastwards expansion; in early 1940 they were telling us that the days of tank warfare were over; in mid-1940 they were telling us that the Germans would invade Britain forthwith; in mid-1941 that the Red Army would fold up in six weeks; in December 1941, that Japan would collapse after ninety days; in July 1942, that Egypt was lost – and so on, more or less indefinitely.

Where now are the men who told us those things? Still on the job, drawing fat salaries. Instead of the unsinkable battleship we have the unsinkable Military Expert.

To be politically happy these days you need to have no more memory than an animal. The people who demonstrated most loudly against Mosley's[7] release were the leaders of the defunct People's Convention,[8] which at the time when Mosley was interned was running a 'stop the war' campaign barely distinguishable from Mosley's own. And I know myself of a ladies' knitting circle which was formed to knit comforts for the Finns, and which two years later – with no sense of incongruity – finished off various garments that had been left on its hands and sent them off to the Russians. Early in 1942 a friend of mine bought some fried fish done up in a piece of newspaper of 1940. On one side was an article proving that the Red Army was no good, and on the other a write-up of that gallant sailor and well-known Anglophile, Admiral Darlan.[9] But my favourite is the *Daily Express* leader which began, a few days after the USSR

6. The Maginot Line was a line of fortifications on the French border with Germany, named after the French defence minister André Maginot (1877–1932) and built between 1930 and 1940. When Germany attacked France in May 1940, it did so by sending its army through the Low Countries and the Ardennes forest north of the most fortified part of the line.

7. For Oswald Mosley, see Introduction, note 35.

8. For the People's Convention, see Introduction, note 80.

9. Admiral François Darlan (1881–1942) was commander of the French fleet in 1939–40 and then a key figure in Marshall Philippe Pétain's collaborationist Vichy regime. His Anglophobia (particularly after the British destroyed much of the French fleet in the Algerian port of Mers-el-Kébir in 1940) was notorious. Darlan was in Algiers when the Allies began landing troops in north-west Africa in November 1942 – and, seeing which way the wind was blowing, did a deal with the Americans, ordering a French ceasefire in return for their making him head of a French administration in north-west Africa. Darlan was assassinated on 24 December 1942, and there have been persistent claims that the killing, apparently the responsibility of a young French royalist acting alone, was actually an undercover British operation.

entered the war: 'This paper has always worked for good relations between Britain and Soviet Russia.'[10]

* * *

Books have gone up in price like everything else, but the other day I picked up a copy of Lemprière's *Classical Dictionary*, the *Who's Who* of the ancients, for only sixpence. Opening it at random, I came upon the biography of Laïs, the famous courtesan, daughter of the mistress of Alcibiades:

> She first began to sell her favours at Corinth for 10,000 drachmas, and the immense number of princes, noblemen, philosophers, orators and plebeians who courted her, bear witness to her personal charms . . . Demosthenes visited Corinth for the sake of Laïs, but informed by the courtesan that admittance to her bed was to be bought at the enormous sum of about £200 English money, the orator departed, and observed that he would not buy repentance at so dear a price . . . She ridiculed the austerity of philosophers, and the weakness of those who pretend to have gained a superiority over their passions, by observing that sages and philosophers were not above the rest of mankind, for she found them at her door as often as the rest of the Athenians.

There is more in the same vein. However, it ends on a good moral, for 'the other women, jealous of her charms, assassinated her in the temple of Venus about 340 BC'. That was 2,283 years ago. I wonder how many of the present denizens of *Who's Who* will seem worth reading about in AD 4226?

10. The *Daily Express*, owned by the maverick Tory press magnate Lord Beaverbrook (1879–1964) and the biggest-selling daily of the late 1930s and most of the 1940s, had in fact been virulently anti-Soviet right up to the point at which Germany attacked the USSR in 1941 - though Beaverbrook did subsequently campaign vigorously for the opening of a second front. See Anne Chisholm and Michael Davie, *Beaverbrook: A Life* (London: Hutchinson, 1992).

Can socialists be happy?

24 December 1943

Published under the pseudonym John Freeman

The thought of Christmas raises almost automatically the thought of Charles Dickens, and for two very good reasons. To begin with, Dickens is one of the few English writers who have actually written about Christmas. Christmas is the most popular of English festivals, and yet it has produced astonishingly little literature. There are the carols, mostly medieval in origin; there is a tiny handful of poems by Robert Bridges, T. S. Eliot, and some others, and there is Dickens; but there is very little else. Secondly, Dickens is remarkable, indeed almost unique, among modern writers in being able to give a convincing picture of happiness.

Dickens dealt successfully with Christmas twice in a chapter of *The Pickwick Papers* and in *A Christmas Carol*. The latter story was read to Lenin on his deathbed and according to his wife, he found its 'bourgeois sentimentality' completely intolerable. Now in a sense Lenin was right: but if he had been in better health he would perhaps have noticed that the story has interesting sociological implications. To begin with, however thick Dickens may lay on the paint, however disgusting the 'pathos' of Tiny Tim may be, the Cratchit family give the impression of enjoying themselves. They sound happy as, for instance, the citizens of William Morris's *News from Nowhere* don't sound happy. Moreover – and Dickens's understanding of this is one of the secrets of his power – their happiness derives mainly from contrast. They are in high spirits because for once in a way they have enough to eat. The wolf is at the door, but he is wagging his tail. The steam of the Christmas pudding drifts across a background of pawnshops and sweated labour, and in a double sense the ghost of Scrooge stands beside the dinner table. Bob Cratchit even wants to drink to Scrooge's health, which Mrs Cratchit rightly refuses. The Cratchits are able to enjoy Christmas precisely because it only comes once a year. Their happiness is convincing just because Christmas only comes once a year. Their happiness is convincing just because it is described as incomplete.

All efforts to describe permanent happiness, on the other hand, have been failures. Utopias (incidentally the coined word Utopia doesn't mean 'a good place', it means merely a 'non-existent place') have been common in literature of the past three or four hundred years but the 'favourable' ones are invariably unappetising, and usually lacking in vitality as well.

By far the best known modern Utopias are those of H. G. Wells.[11] Wells's vision of the future, implicit all through his early work and partly set forth in *Anticipations* and *A Modern Utopia*, is almost fully expressed in two books written in the early twenties, *The Dream* and *Men Like Gods*. Here you have a picture of the world as Wells would like to see it or thinks he would like to see it. It is a world whose keynotes are enlightened hedonism and scientific curiosity. All the evils and miseries we now suffer from have vanished. Ignorance, war, poverty, dirt, disease, frustration, hunger, fear, overwork, superstition all vanished. So expressed, it is impossible to deny that that is the kind of world we all hope for. We all want to abolish the things Wells wants to abolish. But is there anyone who actually wants to live in a Wellsian Utopia? On the contrary, not to live in a world like that, not to wake up in a hygienic garden suburb infested by naked schoolmarms, has actually become a conscious political motive. A book like *Brave New World* is an expression of the actual fear that modern man feels of the rationalised hedonistic society which it is within his power to create. A Catholic writer said recently that Utopias are now technically feasible and that in consequence how to avoid Utopia had become a serious problem. With the fascist movement in front of our eyes, we cannot write this off as merely a silly remark. For one of the sources of the fascist movement is the desire to avoid a too-rational and too-comfortable world.

All 'favourable' Utopias seem to be alike in postulating perfection while being unable to suggest happiness. *News from Nowhere* is a sort of goody-goody version of the Wellsian Utopia. Everyone is kindly and reasonable, all the upholstery comes from Liberty's, but the impression left behind is of a sort of watery melancholy. Lord Samuel's recent effort in the same direction, *An Unknown Country*, is even more dismal. The inhabitants of Bensalem (the word is borrowed from Francis Bacon) give the impression of looking on life as simply an evil to be got through with as little fuss as possible. All that their wisdom has brought them is permanent low spirits. But it is more impressive that Jonathan Swift, one of the greatest imaginative writers who have ever lived, is no more successful in constructing a 'favourable' Utopia than the others.

The earlier parts of *Gulliver's Travels* are probably the most devastating attack on human society that has ever been written. Every word of them is relevant today; in places

11. H. G. Wells (1866–1946) was one of Orwell's boyhood literary heroes, and Orwell was a consistent enthusiast for Wells's early novels, though he was less keen on the later ones and disagreed with many of Wells's political interventions. The pair met in 1940 through Fredric Warburg (1898–1982), who published them both, and thereafter maintained an uneasy relationship. They quarrelled in 1941 over a critical piece on Wells Orwell had written for *Horizon*, and in 1942 another critical Orwell piece prompted Wells to call Orwell 'you shit' in a letter. But Orwell remained a fan and wrote regularly on Wells, contributing a fine obituary to the *Manchester Evening News* on Wells's death.

they contain quite detailed prophecies of the political horrors of our own time. Where Swift fails, however, is in trying to describe a race of beings whom he does admire. In the last part, in contrast with the disgusting Yahoos, we are shown the noble Houyhnhnms, a race of intelligent horses who are free from human failings. Now these horses, for all their high character and unfailing common sense, are remarkably dreary creatures. Like the inhabitants of various other Utopias, they are chiefly concerned with avoiding fuss. They live uneventful, subdued, 'reasonable' lives, free not only from quarrels, disorder or insecurity of any kind, but also from 'passion', including physical love. They choose their mates on eugenic principles, avoid excesses of affection, and appear somewhat glad to die when their time comes. In the earlier parts of the book Swift has shown where man's folly and scoundrelism lead him: but take away the folly and scoundrelism, and all you are left with, apparently, is a tepid sort of existence, hardly worth leading.

Attempts at describing a definitely other-worldly happiness have been no more successful. Heaven is as great a flop as Utopia – though Hell, it is worth noting, occupies a respectable place in literature, and has often been described most minutely and convincingly.

It is a commonplace that the Christian Heaven, as usually portrayed, would attract nobody. Almost all Christian writers dealing with Heaven either say frankly that it is indescribable or conjure up a vague picture of gold, precious stones, and the endless singing of hymns. This has, it is true, inspired some of the best poems in the world:

Thy walls are of chalcedony,
Thy bulwarks diamonds square,
Thy gates are of right orient pearl
Exceeding rich and rare!

Or:

Holy, holy, holy, all the saints adore Thee
Casting down their golden crowns upon the glassy sea
Cherubim and seraphim falling down before Thee,
Thou wast and art, and evermore shalt be!

But what it could not do was to describe a condition in which the ordinary human being actively wanted to be. Many a revivalist minister, many a Jesuit priest (see, for instance, the terrific sermon in James Joyce's *Portrait of the Artist*) has frightened his congregation almost out of their skins with his word-pictures of Hell. But as soon as it comes to Heaven, there is a prompt falling-back on words like 'ecstasy' and 'bliss', with little attempt to say what they consist in. Perhaps the most vital bit of writing on this subject is the famous passage in which Tertullian explains that one of the chief joys of Heaven is watching the tortures of the damned.

The various pagan versions of Paradise are little better, if at all. One has the feeling it is always twilight in the Elysian fields. Olympus, where the gods lived, with their nectar and ambrosia, and their nymphs and Hebes, the 'immortal tarts' as D. H. Lawrence called them, might be a bit more homelike than the Christian Heaven, but you would not want to spend a long time there. As for the Muslim Paradise, with its 77 houris per man, all presumably clamouring for attention at the same moment, it is just a nightmare. Nor are the spiritualists, though constantly assuring us that 'all is bright and beautiful', able to describe any next-world activity which a thinking person would find endurable, let alone attractive.

It is the same with attempted descriptions of perfect happiness which are neither Utopian nor other-worldly, but merely sensual. They always give an impression of emptiness or vulgarity, or both. At the beginning of *La Pucelle* Voltaire describes the life of Charles IX with his mistress, Agnes Sorel. They were 'always happy', he says. And what did their happiness consist in? An endless round of feasting, drinking, hunting and love-making. Who would not sicken of such an existence after a few weeks? Rabelais describes the fortunate spirits who have a good time in the next world to console them for having had a bad time in this one. They sing a song which can be roughly translated: 'To leap, to dance, to play tricks, to drink the wine both white and red, and to do nothing all day long except count gold crowns' – how boring it sounds, after all! The emptiness of the whole notion of an everlasting 'good time' is shown up in Breughel's picture 'The Land of the Sluggard', where the three great lumps of fat lie asleep, head to head, with the boiled eggs and roast legs of pork coming up to be eaten of their own accord.

It would seem that human beings are not able to describe, nor perhaps to imagine, happiness except in terms of contrast. That is why the conception of Heaven or Utopia varies from age to age. In pre-industrial society Heaven was described as a place of endless rest, and as being paved with gold, because the experience of the average human being was overwork and poverty. The houris of the Muslim Paradise reflected a polygamous society where most of the women disappeared into the harems of the rich. But these pictures of 'eternal bliss' always failed because as the bliss became eternal (eternity being thought of as endless time), the contrast ceased to operate. Some of the conventions embedded in our literature first arose from physical conditions which have now ceased to exist. The cult of spring is an example. In the Middle Ages spring did not primarily mean swallows and wild flowers. It meant green vegetables, milk and fresh meat after several months of living on salt pork in smoky windowless huts. The spring songs were gay –

Do nothing but eat and make good cheer,
And thank Heaven for the merry year
When flesh is cheap and females dear,
And lusty lads roam here and there

So merrily,
And ever among so merrily!

because there was something to be so gay about. The winter was over, that was the great thing. Christmas itself, a pre-Christian festival, probably started because there had to be an occasional outburst of overeating and drinking to make a break in the unbearable northern winter.

The inability of mankind to imagine happiness except in the form of relief, either from effort or pain, presents socialists with a serious problem. Dickens can describe a poverty-stricken family tucking into a roast goose, and can make them appear happy; on the other hand, the inhabitants of perfect universes seem to have no spontaneous gaiety and are usually somewhat repulsive into the bargain. But clearly we are not aiming at the kind of world Dickens described, nor, probably, at any world he was capable of imagining. The socialist objective is not a society where everything comes right in the end, because kind old gentlemen give away turkeys. What are we aiming at, if not a society in which 'charity' would be unnecessary? We want a world where Scrooge, with his dividends, and Tiny Tim, with his tuberculous leg, would both be unthinkable. But does that mean we are aiming at some painless, effortless Utopia?

At the risk of saying something which the editors of *Tribune* may not endorse, I suggest that the real objective of socialism is not happiness. Happiness hitherto has been a by-product, and for all we know it may always remain so. The real objective of socialism is human brotherhood. This is widely felt to be the case, though it is not usually said, or not said loudly enough. Men use up their lives in heart-breaking political struggles, or get themselves killed in civil wars, or tortured in the secret prisons of the Gestapo, not in order to establish some central-heated, air-conditioned, strip-lighted Paradise, but because they want a world in which human beings love one another instead of swindling and murdering one another. And they want that world as a first step. Where they go from there is not so certain, and the attempt to foresee it in detail merely confuses the issue.

Socialist thought has to deal in prediction, but only in broad terms. One often has to aim at objectives which one can only very dimly see. At this moment, for instance, the world is at war and wants peace. Yet the world has no experience of peace, and never has had, unless the noble savage once existed. The world wants something which it is dimly aware could exist, but cannot accurately define. This Christmas Day, thousands of men will be bleeding to death in the Russian snows, or drowning in icy waters, or blowing one another to pieces on swampy islands of the Pacific; homeless children will be scrabbling for food among the wreckage of German cities. To make that kind of thing impossible is a good objective. But to say in detail what a peaceful world would be like is a different matter.

Nearly all creators of Utopia have resembled the man who has toothache, and therefore thinks happiness consists in not having toothache. They wanted to produce a perfect society by an endless continuation of something that had only been valuable because it was temporary. The wider course would be to say that there are certain lines along which humanity must move, the grand strategy is mapped out, but detailed prophecy is not our business. Whoever tries to imagine perfection simply reveals his own emptiness. This is the case even with a great writer like Swift, who can flay a bishop or a politician so neatly, but who, when he tries to create a superman, merely leaves one with the impression the very last he can have intended that the stinking Yahoos had in them more possibility of development than the enlightened Houyhnhnms.

As I Please 4

24 December 1943

Reading Michael Roberts's book on T. E. Hulme,[12] I was reminded once again of the dangerous mistake that the socialist movement makes in ignoring what one might call the neo-reactionary school of writers. There is a considerable number of these writers: they are intellectually distinguished, they are influential in a quiet way and their criticisms of the left are much more damaging than anything that issues from the Individualist League[13] or the Conservative Central Office.

T. E. Hulme was killed in the last war and left little completed work behind him, but the ideas that he had roughly formulated had great influence, especially on the numerous writers who were grouped round the *Criterion* in the twenties and thirties. Wyndham Lewis,[14] T. S. Eliot,[15] Aldous Huxley,[16] Malcolm Muggeridge,[17] Evelyn Waugh[18] and Graham Greene[19] all probably owe something to him. But more important

---

12. T. E. Hulme (1883–1917) was a literary critic and modernist poet who was killed in action on the western front during the First World War. He published little in his lifetime, but two collections of fragments edited by his friend Herbert Read (see Introduction, note 16) and published in 1924 and 1929 established a substantial posthumous reputation. Michael Roberts's biography, *T. E. Hulme*, was published in 1938 by Faber and Faber. Roberts (1902–48) is best known as an anthologist of poetry, in particular as editor of *The Faber Book of Modern Verse* (1936).
13. Orwell seems to be referring here to the Society of Individualists, which was set up in 1942 by Sir Ernest Benn (see note 66) and later became the Society for Individual Freedom.
14. Percy Wyndham Lewis (1882–1957) was an Anglo-American modernist writer and artist. Orwell knew his work well and admired his criticism and several of his novels – while at the same time being deeply suspicious of his authoritarian and anti-democratic politics. Lewis had been an apologist for Hitler in the early 1930s and backed Franco in the Spanish civil war. Lewis recanted on Hitler and Franco in the late 1930s, and Orwell believed that he would sooner or later embrace Stalinism. In 1946 in an article in *Partisan Review* Orwell reported wrongly – on the basis of hearsay – that he had actually done so.
15. For T. S. Eliot see Introduction, note 19.
16. Aldous Huxley (1894–1963) was a novelist. Orwell (whom he taught briefly at Eton) was dismissive of his pacifism: Orwell's remark about 'California brand especially' in this paragraph is a none-too-subtle dig at Huxley, who had emigrated to California in 1937. Orwell was also often disparaging about his novels.
17. For Malcolm Muggeridge see Introduction, note 106.
18. Evelyn Waugh (1903–66) was a novelist. Orwell had little time for his snobbery or Catholicism

than the extent of his personal influence is the general intellectual movement to which he belonged, a movement which could fairly be described as the revival of pessimism. Perhaps its best-known living exponent is Marshal Pétain.[20] But the new pessimism has queerer affiliations than that. It links up not only with Catholicism, conservatism and fascism, but also with pacifism (California brand especially), and anarchism. It is worth noting that T. E. Hulme, the upper-middle-class English conservative in a bowler hat, was an admirer and to some extent a follower of the anarcho-syndicalist, Georges Sorel.[21]

The thing that is common to all these people, whether it is Pétain mournfully preaching 'the discipline of defeat', or Sorel denouncing liberalism, or Berdyaev[22] shaking his head over the Russian revolution, or 'Beachcomber'[23] delivering side-kicks at Beveridge[24] in the *Express*, or Huxley advocating non-resistance behind the guns of the American Fleet, is their refusal to believe that human society can be fundamentally improved. Man is non-perfectible, merely political changes can effect nothing, progress is an illusion. The connexion between this belief and political reaction is, of course,

---

but admired him as a writer, describing him in notes he was planning to turn into an essay at the time of his death as 'as good a novelist as one can be . . . while holding untenable opinions'. They met twice.

19. Graham Greene (1904–91) was a novelist, short-story writer, playwright and journalist. Orwell distrusted his Catholicism and the closeness of his thinking to that of the Communist Party but admired several of his novels and liked him personally. They first met in summer 1944 through their mutual friend Michael Meyer (1921–2000). As director of the publishing house Eyre and Spottiswoode, Greene commissioned Orwell to write several introductions to new editions of old books, but only one was written (and that did not appear as planned).

20. Marshal Henri Philippe Pétain (1856–1951), who had become a French national hero for masterminding the defence of Verdun during the First World War, was the 'chief of state' of the Vichy regime in France from 1940 to 1944.

21. Georges Sorel (1847–1922) was a French political philosopher, best known as a revolutionary syndicalist in the first decade of the twentieth century (though he was subsequently a supporter of Charles Maurras's far-right Action Française movement and, in his seventies, an admirer of the Bolshevik revolution). His book *Reflections on Violence* (London: George Allen and Unwin, 1916), which develops his ideas about the necessity of motivating myths in politics (specifically the myth of the general strike), was translated into English by Hulme.

22. Nikolai Berdyaev (1874–1948) was a Russian theologian. A Marxist revolutionary in his youth, he discovered Orthodox Christianity in his thirties. Initially favoured by the Bolsheviks after their seizure of power in 1917 – he became professor of philosophy at Moscow University in 1920 – he was expelled from Russia in 1922 and in 1924 settled in Paris. He wrote prolifically both about religion and about the wrongs of communism.

23. J. B. Morton (1893–1979) wrote a column as 'Beachcomber' six times a week in the *Daily Express* from 1924 to 1965, when it went weekly until 1975. Orwell hated it.

24. William Beveridge (1879–1973) was a Liberal politician and academic. His 1942 report, *Social Insurance and Allied Services*, provided the blueprint for the post-1945 expansion of the welfare state.

obvious. Other-worldliness is the best alibi a rich man can have. 'Men cannot be made better by act of parliament; therefore I may as well go on drawing my dividends.' No one puts it quite so coarsely as that, but the thought of all these people is along those lines: even of those who, like Michael Roberts and Hulme himself, admit that a little, just a little, improvement in earthly society may be thinkable.

The danger of ignoring the neo-pessimists lies in the fact that up to a point they are right. So long as one thinks in short periods it is wise not to be hopeful about the future. Plans for human betterment do normally come unstuck, and the pessimist has many more opportunities of saying 'I told you so' than the optimist. By and large the prophets of doom have been righter than those who imagined that a real step forward would be achieved by universal education, female suffrage, the League of Nations, or what-not.

The real answer is to dissociate socialism from Utopianism. Nearly all neo-pessimist apologetics consist in putting up a man of straw and knocking him down again. The man of straw is called Human Perfectibility. Socialists are accused of believing that society can be - and indeed, after the establishment of socialism, will be - completely perfect; also that progress is inevitable. Debunking such beliefs is money for jam, of course.

The answer, which ought to be uttered more loudly than it usually is, is that socialism is not perfectionist, perhaps not even hedonistic. Socialists don't claim to be able to make the world perfect: they claim to be able to make it better. And any thinking socialist will concede to the Catholic that when economic injustice has been righted, the fundamental problem of man's place in the universe will still remain. But what the socialist does claim is that that problem cannot be dealt with while the average human being's preoccupations are necessarily economic. It is all summed up in Marx's saying that after socialism has arrived, human history can begin. Meanwhile the neo-pessimists are there, well entrenched in the press of every country in the world, and they have more influence and make more converts among the young than we sometimes care to admit.

* * *

From Philip Jordan's *Tunis Diary*:

> We discussed the future of Germany; and John [Strachey] said to an American present, 'You surely don't want a Carthaginian peace, do you?' Our American friend with great slowness but solemnity said, 'I don't recollect we've ever had much trouble from the Carthaginians since.' Which delighted me.

It doesn't delight me. One answer to the American might have been, 'No, but we've had a lot of trouble from the Romans.' But there is more to it than that. What the people who talk about a Carthaginian peace don't realise is that in our day such things are simply not practicable. Having defeated your enemy you have to choose (unless you want another war within a generation) between exterminating him and treating him generously. Conceivably the first alternative is desirable, but it isn't possible. It is quite true that Carthage was utterly destroyed, its buildings levelled to the ground, its inhabitants put to the sword. Such things were happening all the time in antiquity. But the populations involved were tiny. I wonder if that American knew how many people were found within the walls of Carthage when it was finally sacked? According to the nearest authority I can lay hands on, five thousand! What is the best way of killing off seventy million Germans? Rat poison? We might keep this in mind when 'Make Germany Pay' becomes a battle-cry again.

* * *

Attacking me in the *Weekly Review*[25] for attacking Douglas Reed,[26] Mr A. K. Chesterton[27] remarks: ' "My country – right or wrong" is a maxim which apparently has no place in Mr Orwell's philosophy.' He also states that 'all of us believe that

25. The *Weekly Review* started life as the *Eye-Witness*, founded in 1911 by the journalist Cecil Chesterton (1879–1918) and the Catholic polemicist and poet Hilaire Belloc (1870–1953) as a propaganda vehicle for distributism, a now forgotten movement that propounded a 'third way' between capitalism and socialism based on a revival of Christianity, family values, Medievalism and a more equitable distribution of private property. The paper became the *New Witness* in 1912 and was taken over by Cecil's brother, the critic and novelist G. K. Chesterton (1874–1936), best known today for his Father Brown stories, in 1916. He relaunched it as *G. K.'s Weekly* in 1925 and it became the *Weekly Review* when he died in 1936, the editorship passing to Belloc. By the 1940s, Belloc had given up writing after a stroke and the *Weekly Review* was being run by his son-in-law Reginald Jebb and the printer Hilary Pepler. The paper went monthly in 1948, becoming *The Register*, and expired soon after. Orwell's first published journalism appeared in *G. K.'s Weekly* on 29 December 1928.
26. Douglas Reed (1895–1976) was a journalist and author. A correspondent for the *Times* in Berlin and then Austria from the late 1920s, he left the paper in 1938 shortly after publishing a polemical book – part memoir, part analysis – denouncing Hitler and the appeasers, *Insanity Fair* (London: Jonathan Cape), an instant best-seller that was widely praised by the left despite its flagrant anti-Semitism. He then joined the *News Chronicle*. In 1940 he published an extraordinary encomium to the 'left' Nazi Otto Strasser, *Nemesis? The Story of Otto Strasser* (London: Jonathan Cape), and later in the war churned out several books urging greater exertion to defeat Germany, blaming Jews for undermining the British war effort. After the war he emigrated to South Africa, where he specialised in uncovering what he believed was a world Zionist conspiracy. Orwell reviewed Reed's *Lest We Regret* (London: Jonathan Cape, 1943) in the *Observer* on 7 November 1943.
27. A. K. Chesterton (1896–1973) was a major player on the British far right for forty years. An organiser and publicist for Oswald Mosley's British Union of Fascists, he split with Mosley in 1938 and, with William Joyce (later 'Lord Haw-Haw') and John Beckett, formed the Hitlerite National Socialist League. He was a member of the anti-Semitic Right Club in the early 1940s, founded the League of Empire Loyalists in 1954 and set up the National Front in 1967.

whatever her condition Britain must win this war, or for that matter any other war in which she is engaged'.

The operative phrase is *any other war*. There are plenty of us who would defend our own country, under no matter what government, if it seemed that we were in danger of actual invasion and conquest. But 'any war' is a different matter. How about the Boer war, for instance? There is a neat little bit of historical irony here. Mr A. K. Chesterton is the nephew of G. K. Chesterton, who courageously opposed the Boer war, and once remarked that 'My country, right or wrong' was on the same moral level as 'My mother, drunk or sober'.

* * *

When you have been watching bureaucrats at play, it is some consolation to reflect that the same kind of thing is probably happening in Germany. In general one can't test this, but sometimes the wireless gives a clue. A little while back I was listening to Berlin broadcasting in English, and the speaker spent some minutes in talking about the Indian nationalists – with whom, of course, the Nazis profess the keenest sympathy. I was interested to notice that all the Indian names were grossly mispronounced, worse even than would be done by the BBC. Ras Behari Bose,[28] for instance, was rendered as Rash Beery Bose. Yet the various Indians who also broadcast from Berlin must daily go in and out of the same building as the renegade Englishman who mispronounces their names. So much for German efficiency and also, of course, for Nazi interest in Indian nationalism.

As I Please 5

31 December 1943

Reading the discussions of 'war guilt' which reverberate in the correspondence columns of the newspapers, I note the surprise with which many people seem to discover that war is not crime. Hitler, it appears, has not done anything actionable. He has not raped

28. Ras Behari Bose (1880–1945) was an Indian nationalist revolutionary. In 1912, he was one of a group that attempted to blow up the Viceroy of India, Lord Harding. He evaded capture by the British authorities and made his way to Japan, where he settled. In 1942, with Japanese help, he founded the Indian National Army, which fought against the British during the Second World War.

anybody, nor carried off any pieces of loot with his own hands, nor personally flogged any prisoners, buried any wounded men alive, thrown any babies into the air and spitted them on his bayonet, dipped any nuns in petrol and touched them off with church tapers – in fact he has not done any of the things which enemy nationals are usually credited with doing in war-time. He has merely precipitated a world war which will perhaps have cost twenty million lives before it ends. And there is nothing illegal in that. How could there be, when legality implies authority and there is no authority with the power to transcend national frontiers?

At the recent trials in Kharkov some attempt was made to fix on Hitler, Himmler and the rest the responsibility for their subordinates' crimes, but the mere fact that this had to be done shows that Hitler's guilt is not self-evident. His crime, it is implied, was not to build up an army for the purpose of aggressive war, but to instruct that army to torture its prisoners. So far as it goes, the distinction between an atrocity and an act of war is valid. An atrocity means an act of terrorism which has no genuine military purpose. One must accept such distinctions if one accepts war at all, which in practice everyone does. Nevertheless, a world in which it is wrong to murder an individual civilian and right to drop a thousand tons of high explosive on a residential area does sometimes make me wonder whether this earth of ours is not a loony-bin made use of by some other planet.

* * *

As the 53 bus carries me to and fro I never, at any rate when it is light enough to see, pass the little church of St John, just across the road from Lord's, without a pang. It is a Regency church, one of the very few of the period, and when you pass that way it is well worth going inside to have a look at its friendly interior and read the resounding epitaphs of the East India nabobs who lie buried there. But its façade, one of the most charming in London, has been utterly ruined by a hideous war memorial which stands in front of it. That seems to be a fixed rule in London: whenever you do by some chance have a decent vista, block it up with the ugliest statue you can find. And, unfortunately, we have never been sufficiently short of bronze for these things to be melted down.

If you climb to the top of the hill in Greenwich Park, you can have the mild thrill of standing exactly on longitude 0°, and you can also examine the ugliest building in the world, Greenwich Observatory. Then look down the hill towards the Thames. Spread out below you are Wren's masterpiece, Greenwich Hospital (now the Naval College) and another exquisite classical building known as the Queen's House. The architects responsible for that shapeless sprawling muddle at the top of the hill had those other two buildings under their eyes while every brick was laid.

As Mr Osbert Sitwell[29] remarked at the time of the 'Baedeker raids'[30] – how simple-minded of the Germans to imagine that we British could be cowed by the destruction of our ancient monuments! As though any havoc of the German bombs could possibly equal the things we have done ourselves!

* * *

I see that Mr Bernard Shaw,[31] among others, wants to rewrite the second verse of the national anthem. Mr Shaw's version retains references to God and the King, but is vaguely internationalist in sentiment. This seems to me ridiculous. Not to have a national anthem would be logical. But if you do have one, its function must necessarily be to point out that we are Good and our enemies are Bad. Besides, Mr Shaw wants to cut out the only worth-while lines the anthem contains. All the brass instruments and big drums in the world cannot turn 'God Save the King' into a good tune, but on the very rare occasions when it is sung in full it does spring to life in the two lines:

Confound their politics,
Frustrate their knavish tricks!

And, in fact, I had always imagined that the second verse is habitually left out because of a vague suspicion on the part of the Tories that these lines refer to themselves.

* * *

Just about two years ago, as we filed past the menu board in the canteen, I said to the next person in the queue: 'A year from now you'll see "Rat Soup" on that board, and in 1943 it will be "Mock Rat Soup".' Events have proved me wrong (the war at sea has turned out

---

29. Osbert Sitwell (1892–1969) was a writer, best known today for a series of autobiographical books published between 1944 and 1950 but in 1943 famous for his poetry, essays and siblings – the poet and critic Edith Sitwell (1887–1964) and the critic Sacheverell Sitwell (1897–1988). Despite his political disagreements with Sitwell, Orwell tried to get him to review for *Tribune*, without success.

30. The 'Baedeker raids' were a series of German air raids in 1942 on British cities featured in Baedeker guide books, ordered by Hitler as reprisals for British air raids on Lübeck and Cologne. Exeter, Bath, Norwich, York and Canterbury were hit and nearly 1,700 civilians killed.

31. George Bernard Shaw (1856–1950) was an Irish dramatist, critic and political polemicist. Orwell admired him as a playwright and critic – he particularly liked Shaw's early plays, declaring in a radio broadcast in January 1943 that 'every one . . . is a masterpiece of technique, with never a false note or a wasted word' – but had no time for his politics. Shaw had been an admirer of Mussolini in the 1920s and was one of the most prominent Soviet fellow-travellers of the 1930s and 1940s. Orwell's description of Shaw in the notebook that he kept on Soviet fellow-travellers, 'reliably pro-Russian on all major issues', is precisely accurate.

better than was then foreseeable), but, once again, I can claim to have been less wrong than the full-time prophets. Turning up my copy of *Old Moore's Almanack*[32] for 1943, I find that the Germans sued for peace and were granted an armistice in June, and Japan surrendered in September. November finds us enjoying 'the blessings of peace and the complete removal of lighting conditions', while 'a reduction in taxation is highly appreciated'. It is like this all the way through.

Old Moore repeats this performance every year, without ever losing its popularity. Nor is it hard to see why. Its psychological approach is indicated by the advert, on the cover: 'Cosmo, famous Mystic, predicts VICTORY, PEACE, RECONSTRUCTION.' As long as Cosmo predicts that kind of thing he is safe for a hearing.

* * *

Another ninepenny acquisition: *Chronological Tablets, exhibiting every Remarkable Occurrence from the Creation of the World down to the Present Time*. Printed by J. D. Dewick, Aldersgate Street, in the year 1801.

With some interest I looked up the date of the creation of the world, and found it was in 4004 BC and 'is supposed to have taken place in the autumn'. Later in the book it is given more exactly as September 4004.

At the end there are a number of blank sheets in which the reader can carry on the chronicles for himself. Whoever possessed this book did not carry it very far, but one of the last entries is: 'Tuesday 4 May. Peace proclaimed here. General Illumination.' That was the Peace of Amiens.[33] This might warn us not to be too previous with our own illuminations when the armistice comes.

As I Please 6

7 January 1944

Looking through the photographs in the New Year honours list, I am struck (as usual) by the quite exceptional ugliness and vulgarity of the faces displayed there. It seems to be almost the rule that the kind of person who earns the right to call himself Lord Percy de

32. *Old Moore's Almanack* was founded by the physician and astrologer Francis Moore (1657–1715) and has been published since 1700.
33. The Treaty of Amiens of 1802 between Britain and France marked the end of the French revolutionary wars. But Britain and France were at war again a little more than a year later.

Falcontowers should look at best like an overfed publican and at worst like a tax-collector with a duodenal ulcer. But our country is not alone in this. Anyone who is a good hand with scissors and paste could compile an excellent book entitled *Our Rulers*, and consisting simply of published photographs of the great ones of the earth. The idea first occurred to me when I saw in *Picture Post*[34] some 'stills' of Beaverbrook delivering a speech and looking more like a monkey on a stick than you would think possible for anyone who was not doing it on purpose.

When you had got together your collection of fuehrers, actual and would-be, you would notice that several qualities recur throughout the list. To begin with, they are all old. In spite of the lip-service that is paid everywhere to youth, there is no such thing as a person in a truly commanding position who is less than fifty years old. Secondly, they are nearly all under-sized. A dictator taller than five feet six inches is a very great rarity. And, thirdly, there is this almost general and sometimes quite fantastic ugliness. The collection would contain photographs of Streicher[35] bursting a blood vessel, Japanese war-lords impersonating baboons, Mussolini with his scrubby dewlap, the chinless de Gaulle, the stumpy short-armed Churchill, Gandhi with his long sly nose and huge bat's ears, Tojo displaying thirty-two teeth with gold in every one of them. And opposite each, to make a contrast, there would be a photograph of an ordinary human being from the country concerned. Opposite Hitler a young sailor from a German submarine, opposite Tojo a Japanese peasant of the old type - and so on.

But to come back to the honours list. When you remember that nearly the whole of the rest of the world has dropped it, it does seem strange to see this flummery still continuing in England, a country in which the very notion of aristocracy perished hundreds of years ago. The race-difference on which aristocratic rule is usually founded had disappeared from England by the end of the Middle Ages, and the concept of 'blue

34. *Picture Post* was a weekly magazine, founded in 1938, which pioneered photojournalism in Britain. It was published by Edward G. Hulton (1906–88), the son of the newspaper publisher Edward Hulton (1869–1925), who had launched the *Daily Sketch* in 1909 and briefly owned the *Evening Standard*. *Picture Post* was edited from 1938 to 1940 by Stefan Lorent (1901–97) and from 1940 to 1950 by Tom Hopkinson (1905–90). Its political stance was left-wing, and it was a runaway commercial success: at the time Orwell was writing its weekly sale was approaching one million. The assistant editor of *Picture Post* from 1944 to 1950 was Ted Castle (1907–1979), husband of the Labour politician and former *Tribune* journalist Barbara Castle (née Betts). He was briefly made editor after Hopkinson was sacked by Hulton for running a story by James Cameron (with pictures by Bert Hardy) exposing maltreatment of Korean prisoners by American forces during the Korean war. See Tom Hopkinson, *Of This Our Time: A Journalist's Story 1905–1950* (London: Hutchinson, 1982). Hopkinson wrote a brief introduction to Orwell, *Writers and Their Work: George Orwell* (London: Longman, 1966).

35. Julius Streicher (1885–1946) was the publisher of the Nazi newspaper *Der Sturmer*.

blood' as something valuable in itself, and independent of money, was vanishing in the age of Elizabeth. Since then we have been a plutocracy plain and simple. Yet we still make spasmodic efforts to dress ourselves in the colours of medieval feudalism.

Think of the Heralds' Office solemnly faking pedigrees and inventing coats of arms with mermaids and unicorns couchant, regardant and what-not, for company directors in bowler hats and striped trousers! What I like best is the careful grading by which the honours are always dished out in direct proportion to the amount of mischief done – baronies for big business, baronetcies for fashionable surgeons, knighthoods for tame professors. But do these people imagine that by calling themselves lords, knights and so forth they somehow come to have something in common with the medieval aristocracy? Does Sir Walter Citrine,[36] say, feel himself to be rather the same kind of person as Childe Roland (Childe Citrine to the dark tower came!), or is Lord Nuffield[37] under the impression that we shall mistake him for a crusader in chain-armour?

However, this honours-list business has one severely practical aspect, and that is that a title is a first-class alias. Mr X can practically cancel his past by turning himself into Lord Y. Some of the ministerial appointments that have been made during this war would hardly have been possible without some such disguise. As Tom Paine put it: 'These people change their names so often that it is as hard to know them as it is to know thieves.'

* * *

I write this to the tune of an electric drill. They are drilling holes in the walls of a surface shelter, removing bricks at regular intervals. Why? Because the shelter is in danger of falling down and it is necessary to give it a cement facing.

It seems doubtful whether these surface shelters were ever of much use. They would give protection against splinters and blast, but not more than the walls of an ordinary house, and the only time I saw a bomb drop anywhere near one it sliced it off the ground as neatly as if it had been done with a knife. The real point is, however, that at the time when these shelters were built it was known that they would fall down in a year or two. Innumerable people pointed this out. But nothing happened; the slovenly building continued, and somebody scooped the contract. Sure enough, a year or two later, the prophets were justified. The mortar began to fall out of the walls, and it became

36. Walter Citrine (1887–1983) was general secretary of the Trades Union Congress from 1926 to 1946. He was knighted in 1935 and became Baron Citrine of Wembley in 1946, subsequently serving as chairman of the Central Electricity Authority for ten years.

37. Lord Nuffield (William Morris, 1877–1963) was a motor manufacturing entrepreneur. His Morris Motors, based in Oxford, was Britain's largest home-grown car-maker in the 1930s and 1940s. He became a baronet in 1929, a baron in 1934 and a viscount in 1938.

necessary to case the shelters in cement. Once again somebody – perhaps it was the same somebody – scooped the contract.

I do not know whether, in any part of the country, these shelters are actually used in air raids. In my part of London there has never been any question of using them; in fact, they are kept permanently locked lest they should be used for 'improper purposes'. There is one thing, however, that they might conceivably be useful for and that is as block-houses in street fighting. And on the whole they have been built in the poorer streets. It would amuse me if when the time came the higher-ups were unable to crush the populace because they had thoughtlessly provided them with thousands of machine-gun nests beforehand.

* * *

On page eighteen of this number there will be found an advertisement of the *Tribune* Short Story Competition. We hope for a large number of entries, and we hope that directly and indirectly the competition may help a little towards the rehabilitation of the short story in this country.

Few people would claim that the short story has been a successful art form in England during the past twenty years. American and Irish stories are perhaps a little better, but not much. One could explain the decline of the short story on sociological grounds, but such explanations are not altogether satisfactory, because, if true, they ought to apply equally to kindred forms of literature. Contemporary novels, for instance, are on average nowhere near so bad as contemporary short stories. There must also be technical causes, and I think I can suggest two of them.

The first is something that we cannot remedy in *Tribune* – the difficulty over length. Almost certainly the short story has suffered from the dwindled size of modern magazines. Nearly all the great English short stories of the past – and the same is true of many French stories, though perhaps less true of the Russians – would be far too long for publication in any ordinary modern periodical. But I think it is also true that the short story has suffered unnecessarily from the disappearance of the Victorian 'plot'. About the beginning of this century the convention of the 'surprise in the last chapter' fell out of fashion, and it was not sufficiently noticed that the eventless, non-dramatic kind of story is more effective when it is long than when it is short. A short story has to be a story. It cannot, to the same extent as the novel, depend upon 'atmosphere' and character-interest, because there is not enough space to build them up. A short story which does not convey any anecdote, any dramatic change, almost invariably ends on a note of weakness and pointlessness. What innumerable stories I have read which have kept me thinking almost up to the last line – 'Surely these preliminaries are leading to something? Surely something is going to happen?' – and then the invariable petering-out, to which the writer sometimes tries to give an air of profundity by means of a row of dots. I cannot help feeling that many short-story writers are inhibited by the notion that a 'plot' is hopelessly old-fashioned and therefore inadmissible.

I do not suggest that this is the only thing that is wrong with the contemporary short story. But after much reading of short stories this is the impression left upon my own mind, and I offer it as a hint which may be useful to intending contributors.

As I Please 7

14 January 1944

The old custom of binding up magazines and periodicals in book form seems to have gone out almost entirely, which is a pity, for a year's issue of even a very stupid magazine is more readable after a lapse of time than the majority of books. I do not believe I ever had a better bargain than the dozen volumes of the *Quarterly Review*, starting in 1809, which I once picked up for two shillings at a farmhouse auction; but a good sixpennyworth was a year's issue of the *Cornhill* when either Trollope or Thackeray, I forget which, was editing it, and another good buy was some odd volumes of the *Gentleman's Magazine* of the mid-sixties, at threepence each. I have also had some happy half-hours with *Chambers's Papers for the People*, which flourished in the fifties, the *Boy's Own Paper* in the days of the Boer war, the *Strand* in its great Sherlock Holmes days, and – a book I unfortunately only saw and didn't buy – a bound volume of the *Athenæum* in the early twenties, when Middleton Murry[38] was editing it, and T. S. Eliot, E. M. Forster and various others were making their first impact on the big public. I do not know why no one bothers to do this nowadays, for to get a year's issue of a magazine bound costs less than buying a novel, and you can even do the job yourself if you have a spare evening and the right materials.

---

38. John Middleton Murry (1889–1957) was a critic and editor, husband of the author Katherine Mansfield. After he left the *Athenæum*, he founded another literary magazine, the *Adelphi*, which during the late 1920s became a haven for non-communist left-wing writers, most of them sympathetic to the Independent Labour Party. During the early 1930s it was the main outlet Orwell (at first writing as Eric Blair) had for his essays. Two of Murry's co-editors on the *Adelphi*, Richard Rees (1900–70) and Max Plowman (1883–1941), became close friends of Orwell, as did the magazine's circulation manager, Jack Common (1903–68). Murry was editor of the pacifist weekly *Peace News* from 1940 to 1946 and corresponded with Orwell throughout the 1940s.

The great fascination of these old magazines is the completeness with which they 'date'. Absorbed in the affairs of the moment, they tell one about political fashions and tendencies which are hardly mentioned in the more general history books. It is interesting, for instance, to study in contemporary magazines the war scare of the early sixties, when it was assumed on all sides that Britain was about to be invaded, the Volunteers were formed, amateur strategists published maps showing the routes by which the French armies would converge on London, and peaceful citizens cowered in ditches while the bullets of the Rifle Clubs (the then equivalent of the Home Guard) ricocheted in all directions.

The mistake that nearly all British observers made at that time was not to notice that Germany was dangerous. The sole danger was supposed to come from France, which had shot its bolt as a military power and had in any case no reason for quarrelling with Britain. And I believe that casual readers in the future, dipping into our newspapers and magazines, will note a similar aberration in the turning-away from democracy and frank admiration for totalitarianism which overtook the British intelligentsia about 1940. Recently, turning up back numbers of *Horizon*,[39] I came upon a long article on James Burnham's *Managerial Revolution*,[40] in which Burnham's main thesis was accepted almost without examination. It represented, many people would have claimed, the most intelligent forecast of our time. And yet - founded as it really was on a belief in the invincibility of the German army - events have already blown it to pieces.

Shortly, Burnham's thesis is this. Laissez-faire capitalism is finished and socialism, at

39. *Horizon* was a literary magazine published from 1939 to 1949 and edited by Cyril Connolly (see Introduction, note 111). *Horizon*'s editorial assistant was Sonia Brownell (1918–80), who married Orwell just before his death. See Michael Shelden, *Friends of Promise: Cyril Connolly and the World of* Horizon (London: Hamish Hamilton, 1989) and Hilary Spurling, *The Girl from the Fiction Department: A Portrait of Sonia Orwell* (London: Hamish Hamilton, 2002).

40. James Burnham (1905–87) was an American political theorist and polemicist. A Trotskyist in the late 1930s, he and his mentor Max Shachtman (1904–72) left the orthodox Trotskyist American Socialist Workers Party in 1940, arguing that the Soviet Union was no longer a 'degenerate workers' state' (the orthodox Trotskyist analysis) but rather had become a new type of society, which they described as 'bureaucratic collectivist'. But Burnham soon left Shachtman behind too, abandoning revolutionary socialist politics for good and arguing in *The Managerial Revolution* (New York: John Day, 1941; London: Putnam, 1943) that the whole world would soon become a 'managerial' society. Burnham responded to this Orwell piece (and Orwell replied to him) in *Tribune* on 24 March 1944. Orwell returned to the book in his essay 'Second Thoughts on James Burnham', published in *Polemic* in May 1946 and also wrote about Burnham's *The Machiavellians* (London: Putnam, 1943) and *The Struggle for The World* (London: Jonathan Cape, 1947). Burnham became a major player in the American conservative intellectual milieu and is currently feted as a founding father of neo-conservatism. On Shachtman and Burnham see Peter Drucker, *Max Shachtman and His Left: A Socialist's Odyssey through the 'American Century'* (New York: Humanities Press, 1994).

any rate in this present period of history, is impossible. What is now happening is the appearance of a new ruling class, named by Burnham the 'managers'. These are represented in Germany and the USSR by the Nazis and Bolsheviks, and in the USA by the business executives. This new ruling class expropriates the capitalists, crushes the working-class movements and sets up a totalitarian society governed by the concept of efficiency. Britain is decadent and is bound to be rapidly conquered by Germany. After the conquest of Britain will come the attack on the USSR and Russia's 'military weakness' will cause her to 'fall apart to east and west'. You are then left with three great super-states, Germany, Japan and the USA, which divide the world between them, make ceaseless war upon one another, and keep the working class in permanent subjection.

Now, there is a great deal in what Burnham says. The fact that collectivism is not inherently democratic, that you do not do away with class rule by formally abolishing private property, is becoming clearer all the time. The tendency of the world to split up into several great power blocks is also clear enough, and the fact that each of these would probably be invincible has sinister possibilities. But the test of a political theory is its power to foretell the future, and Burnham's predictions were falsified almost as soon as made. Britain was not conquered, Russia turned out not to be militarily weak, and - a much more fundamental error - Germany did attack Russia while the war against Britain was still in progress. Burnham had declared this to be impossible, on the ground that the German and Russian régimes were essentially the same and would not quarrel until the struggle against old-style capitalism was finished.

Obviously these mistakes were partly due to wish-thinking. Hating both Britain and the USSR, Burnham (and many American intellectuals of similar outlook) wanted to see both these countries conquered, and was also unable to admit that there was an essential difference between Russia and Germany. But the basic error of this school of thought is its contempt for the common man. A totalitarian society, it is felt, must be stronger than a democratic one: the expert's opinion must be worth more than the ordinary man's. The German army had won the first battles: therefore it must win the last one. The great strength of democracy, its power of criticism, was ignored.

It would be absurd to claim that either Britain or the USA are true democracies, but in both countries public opinion can influence policy, and while making many minor mistakes it probably avoids the biggest ones. If the German common people had had any say in the conduct of the war it is very unlikely, for instance, that they would have attacked Russia while Britain was still in the field, and still more unlikely that they would have wantonly declared war on America six months later. It takes an expert to make mistakes as big as that. When one sees how the Nazi régime has succeeded in smashing itself to pieces within a dozen years it is difficult to believe in the survival value of totalitarianism. But I would not deny that the 'managerial' class might get control of our society, and that if they did they would lead us into some hellish places before they destroyed themselves. Where Burnham and his fellow-thinkers are wrong is in trying to spread the idea that totalitarianism is unavoidable, and that we must therefore do nothing to oppose it.

As I Please 8

21 January 1944

The dropping of the Forces programme and the rumours of large-scale commercial broadcasting after the war have once again set people talking about the BBC and its shortcomings.[41] We hope to publish in the not too remote future some articles on various aspects of broadcasting, but I would like to suggest here, just as something to think over, that the BBC is what it is because the public is not radio-conscious. People are vaguely aware that they don't like the BBC programmes, that along with some good stuff a lot of muck is broadcast, that the talks are mostly ballyhoo and that no subject of importance ever gets the honesty of discussion that it would get in even the most reactionary newspaper. But they make no effort to find out, either in general or particular terms, why the programmes are bad, or whether foreign programmes are any better, or what is or is not technically possible on the air. Even quite well-informed people seem completely ignorant of what goes on inside the BBC. When I was working in the BBC I was concerned solely with broadcasting English programmes to India. This did not save me from being constantly buttonholed by angry people who asked me whether I could not 'do something about' some item on the Home Programme which is like blaming a North Sea coastguard for something that happens in central Africa. A few months back there was a debate in the House of Commons in which our radio propaganda to America was criticised. Several MPs maintained that it was totally ineffective, which it is. But seemingly they knew this only by instinct. Not one of them was in a position to stand up and tell the House how much we spend every year in broadcasting to the USA, and how many listeners this secures us – facts which they could quite easily have found out.

---

41. The BBC had a monopoly on broadcasting on British soil from its foundation in 1922 until the launch of commercial television in 1955. There was no commercial radio broadcast from Britain until 1973.

When the BBC is attacked in the press, the attack is usually so ignorant that it is impossible to meet it. Some time ago I wrote to a well-known Irish writer, now living in England, asking him to broadcast. He sent me an indignant refusal, which incidentally revealed that he did not know (a) that there is a Broadcasting Corporation in India, (b) that Indians broadcast every day from London, and (c) that the BBC broadcasts in oriental languages. If people don't even know that much, of what use are their criticisms of the BBC likely to be? To quite a large extent the BBC is blamed for its virtues while its real faults are ignored. Everyone complains, for instance, about the Kensingtonian accent of BBC news-readers, which has been carefully selected not in order to cause annoyance in England, but because it is a 'neutral' accent which will be intelligible wherever English is spoken. Yet how many people are aware that millions of public money are squandered in broadcasting to countries where there is virtually no audience?

Here is a little catechism for amateur radio critics.

- You say you don't like the present programmes. Have you a clear idea of what kind of programmes you would like? If so, what steps have you taken towards securing them?
- In your opinion, are the BBC news bulletins truthful? Are they more or less truthful than those of other belligerent countries? Have you checked this by comparison?
- Have you any ideas about the possibilities of the radio play, the short story, the feature, the discussion? If so, have you bothered to find out which of your ideas are technically feasible?
- Do you think the BBC would benefit by competition? Give your opinion of commercial broadcasting.
- Who controls the BBC? Who pays for it? Who directs its policy? How does the censorship work?
- What do you know of BBC propaganda to foreign countries, hostile, friendly or neutral? How much does it cost? Is it effective? How would it compare with German propaganda? Add some notes on radio propaganda in general.

I could extend this considerably, but if even a hundred thousand people in England could give definite answers to the above questions it would be a big step forward.

* * *

A correspondent reproaches me with being 'negative' and 'always attacking things'. The fact is that we live in a time when causes for rejoicing are not numerous. But I like praising things, when there is anything to praise, and I would like here to write a few lines – they have to be retrospective, unfortunately – in praise of the Woolworth's rose.

In the good days when nothing in Woolworth's cost over sixpence, one of their best lines was their rose bushes. They were always very young plants, but they came into bloom in their second year, and I don't think I ever had one die on me. Their chief interest was that they were never, or very seldom, what they claimed to be on their labels. One that I bought for a Dorothy Perkins turned out to be a beautiful little white rose with a yellow heart, one of the finest ramblers I have ever seen. A polyantha rose labelled yellow turned out to be deep red. Another, bought for an Abertine, was like an Abertine, but more double, and gave astonishing masses of blossom. These roses had all the interest of a surprise packet, and there was always the chance that you might happen upon a new variety which you would have the right to name John Smith or something of that kind.

Last summer I passed the cottage where I used to live before the war.[42] The little white rose, no bigger than a boy's catapult when I put it in, had grown into a huge vigorous bush, the Abertine or near-Abertine was smothering half the fence in a cloud of pink blossom. I had planted both of those in 1936. And I thought, 'All that for sixpence!' I do not know how long a rose bush lives; I suppose ten years might be an average life. And throughout that time a rambler will be in full bloom for a month or six weeks each year, while a bush rose will be blooming, on and off, for at least four months. All that for sixpence – the price, before the war, of ten Players, or a pint and a half of mild, or a week's subscription to the *Daily Mail*,[43] or about twenty minutes of twice-breathed air in the movies!

42. The Stores at Wallington, Hertfordshire was leased by Orwell and his wife Eileen from 1937. They lived there until 1940 then rented it out to friends and family. Orwell could not bear to return there after Eileen's death in 1945 and gave up the lease in 1947. The rose was still there in summer 2005.

43. The *Daily Mail*, founded in 1896 by Alfred Harmsworth (later Lord Northcliffe), was the daily newspaper *Tribune* readers would have been least likely to subscribe to during the 1930s. Under the first Lord Rothermere (Harold Harmsworth, 1868–1940), who took it over on his brother Northcliffe's death in 1922, it had been responsible for publishing the Zinoviev letter in 1924 – a document, almost certainly a forgery, that Rothermere's *Mail* presented as implicating Ramsay MacDonald's first Labour government in subversion by Moscow. The Zinoviev letter was widely believed to have cost Labour the 1924 general election. In the early 1930s Rothermere lent support to Mosley and the British Union of Fascists and, although he was a supporter of rearmament, he kept up a convivial relationship with Hitler until the summer of 1939. For Northcliffe, see note 77. For Rothermere see Richard Cockett, *Twilight of Truth: Chamberlain and the Manipulation of the Press* (London: Weidenfeld and Nicolson, 1989) and Martin Pugh, *Hurrah for the Blackshirts!: Fascists and Fascism in Britain between the Wars* (London: Jonathan Cape, 2005).

As I Please 9

28 January 1944

I see that Mr Suresh Vaidya, an Indian journalist living in England, has been arrested for refusing military service. This is not the first case of its kind, and if it is the last it will probably be because no more Indians of military age are left to be victimised.

Everyone knows without being told them the juridical aspects of Mr Vaidya's case, and I have no wish to dwell on them. But I would like to draw attention to the common-sense aspect, which the British government so steadily refuses to consider. Putting aside the seamen who come and go, and the handful of troops who are still here, there might perhaps be two thousand Indians in this country, of all kinds and ages. By applying conscription to them you may raise a few score extra soldiers; and by coercing the minority who 'object' you may swell the British prison population by about a dozen. That is the net result from the military point of view.

But unfortunately that isn't all. By behaviour of this kind you antagonise the entire Indian community in Britain – for no Indian, whatever his views, admits that Britain had the right to declare war on India's behalf or has the right to impose compulsory service on Indians. Anything that happens in the Indian community here has prompt repercussions in India, and appreciable effects further afield. One Indian war resister victimised does us more harm than ten thousand British ones. It seems a high price to pay for the satisfaction the Blimps probably feel at having another 'red' in their clutches. I don't expect the Blimps to see Mr Vaidya's point of view. But they really might see, after all their experience, that making martyrs does not pay.

* * *

A correspondent has sent us a letter in defence of Ezra Pound, the American poet who transferred his allegiance to Mussolini some years before the war and has been a lively propagandist on the Rome radio. The substance of his claim is (a) that Pound did not sell himself simply for money, and (b) that when you get hold of a true poet you can afford to ignore his political opinions.

Now, of course, Pound did not sell himself solely for money. No writer ever does that. Anyone who wanted money before all else would choose some more paying profession. But I think it probable that Pound did sell himself partly for prestige, flattery and a professorship. He had a most venomous hatred for both Britain and the USA, where he felt that his talents had not been fully appreciated, and obviously believed that there was a conspiracy against him throughout the English-speaking countries. Then there were several ignominious episodes in which Pound's phony erudition was shown up, and which he no doubt found it hard to forgive. By the mid-thirties Pound was singing the praises of 'the Boss' (Mussolini) in a number of English papers, including Mosley's quarterly, *British Union* (to which Vidkun Quisling[44] was also a contributor). At the time of the Abyssinian war Pound was vociferously anti-Abyssinian. In 1938 or thereabouts the Italians gave him a chair at one of their universities, and some time after war broke out he took Italian citizenship.

Whether a poet, as such, is to be forgiven his political opinions is a different question. Obviously one mustn't say 'X agrees with me: therefore he is a good writer', and for the last ten years honest literary criticism has largely consisted in combating this outlook. Personally I admire several writers (Céline,[45] for instance) who have gone over to the fascists, and many others whose political outlook I strongly object to. But one has the right to expect ordinary decency of a poet. I never listened to Pound's broadcasts, but I often read them in the BBC monitoring reports, and they were intellectually and morally disgusting. Anti-Semitism, for instance, is simply not the doctrine of a grown-up person. People who go in for that kind of thing must take the consequences. But I do agree with our correspondent in hoping that the American authorities do not catch Pound and shoot him, as they have threatened to do. It would establish his reputation so thoroughly that it might be a good hundred years before anyone could determine dispassionately whether Pound's much-debated poems are any good or not.

* * *

The other night a barmaid informed me that if you pour beer into a damp glass it goes flat much more quickly. She added that to dip your moustache into your beer also turns it flat. I immediately accepted this without further inquiry; in fact, as soon as I got home I clipped my moustache, which I had forgotten to do for some days. Only later did it strike me that this was probably one of those superstitions which are able to keep alive because they have the air of being scientific truths. In my note-book I have a long list of fallacies which were taught to me in my childhood, in each case not as an old wives' tale but as a scientific fact. I can't give the whole list, but there are a few hardy favourites:

44. Vidkun Quisling (1887–1945) was a Norwegian fascist politician. He was Norwegian prime minister from 1942 to the end of the war.

45. Louis-Ferdinand Céline (1894–1961) was a French modernist novelist, best known for his *Voyage au bout de la nuit* (1932), translated as *Journey to the End of Night* (London: Chatto and Windus, 1934) and *Mort à crédit*, translated as *Death on the Instalment Plan* (London: Chatto and Windus, 1938). He was a virulent anti-Semite and supporter of the collaborationist Vichy regime in France.

That a swan can break your leg with a blow of its wing.
That if you cut yourself between the thumb and forefinger you get lockjaw.
That powdered glass is poisonous.
That if you wash your hands in the water eggs have been boiled in (why anyone should do this is a mystery) you will get warts.
That bulls become infuriated at the sight of red.
That sulphur in a dog's drinking water acts as a tonic.

And so on and so forth. Almost everyone carries some or other of these beliefs into adult life. I have met someone of over thirty who still retained the second of the beliefs I have listed above. As for the third, it is so widespread that in India, for instance, people are constantly trying to poison one another with powdered glass, with disappointing results.

* * *

I wish now that I had read *Basic English versus the Artificial Languages* before and not after reviewing the interesting little book in which Professor Lancelot Hogben[46] sets forth his own artificial language, *Interglossa*. For in that case I should have realised how comparatively chivalrous Professor Hogben had been towards the inventors of rival international languages. Controversies on serious subjects are often far from polite. Followers of the Stalinist–Trotskyist controversy will have observed that an unfriendly note tends to creep into it, and when the *Tablet* and the *Church Times* are having a go at one another the blows are not always above the belt. But for sheer dirtiness of fighting the feud between the inventors of various of the international languages would take a lot of beating.

Tribune may before long print one or more articles on Basic English.[47] If any language is ever adopted as a world-wide 'second' language it is immensely unlikely that it will be a manufactured one, and of the existing natural ones English has much the best chance, though not necessarily in the Basic form. Public opinion is beginning to wake up to the need for an international language, though fantastic misconceptions still exist. For example, many people imagine that the advocates of an international language aim at suppressing the natural languages, a thing no one has ever seriously suggested.

At present, in spite of the growing recognition of this need, the world is growing more and not less nationalistic in language. This is partly from conscious policy (about half a dozen of the existing languages are being pushed in an imperialistic way in various parts of the world), and partly owing to the dislocation caused by the war. And the

46. Lancelot Hogben (1895–1975) was a zoologist and geneticist.
47. Basic English is a simplified version of English, a first step for non-native speakers to learn the language, devised by Charles Ogden (1889–1957) in 1930. It has 850 key words.

difficulties of trade, travel and inter-communication between scientists, and the time-wasting labour of learning foreign languages, still continue. In my life I have learned seven foreign languages, including two dead ones, and out of those seven I retain only one, and that not brilliantly. This would be quite a normal case. A member of a small nationality, a Dane or a Dutchman, say, has to learn three foreign languages as a matter of course, if he wants to be educated at all. Clearly this position could be bettered, and the great difficulty is to decide which language is to be adopted as the international one. But there is going to be some ugly scrapping before that is settled, as anyone who has ever glanced into this subject knows.

As I Please 10

4 February 1944

When Sir Walter Raleigh was imprisoned in the Tower of London, he occupied himself with writing a history of the world. He had finished the first volume and was at work on the second when there was a scuffle between some workmen beneath the window of his cell, and one of the men was killed. In spite of diligent inquiries, and in spite of the fact that he had actually seen the thing happen, Sir Walter was never able to discover what the quarrel was about: whereupon, so it is said – and if the story is not true it certainly ought to be – he burned what he had written and abandoned his project.

This story has come into my head I do not know how many times during the past ten years, but always with the reflection that Raleigh was probably wrong. Allowing for all the difficulties of research at that date, and the special difficulty of conducting research in prison, he could probably have produced a world history which had some resemblance to the real course of events. Up to a fairly recent date, the major events recorded in the history books probably happened. It is probably true that the battle of Hastings was fought in 1066, that Columbus discovered America, that Henry VIII had six wives, and so on. A certain degree of truthfulness was possible so long as it was admitted that a fact may be true even if you don't like it. Even as late as the last war it was possible for the *Encyclopædia Britannica*, for instance, to compile its articles on the various campaigns partly from German sources. Some of the facts – the casualty figures, for instance – were regarded as neutral and in substance accepted by everybody. No such thing would be possible now. A Nazi and a non-Nazi version of the present war would have no resemblance to one another, and which of them finally gets into the history books will be decided not by evidential methods but on the battlefield.

During the Spanish civil war I found myself feeling very strongly that a true history of this war never would or could be written. Accurate figures, objective accounts of what was happening, simply did not exist. And if I felt that even in 1937, when the Spanish government was still in being, and the lies which the various Republican factions were telling about each other and about the enemy were relatively small ones, how does the case stand now? Even if Franco is overthrown, what kind of records will the future historian have to go upon? And if Franco or anyone at all resembling him remains in power, the history of the war will consist quite largely of 'facts' which millions of people now living know to be lies. One of these 'facts', for instance, is that there was a considerable Russian army in Spain. There exists the most abundant evidence that there was no such army. Yet if Franco remains in power, and if fascism in general survives, that Russian army will go into the history books and future schoolchildren will believe in it. So for practical purposes the lie will have become truth.

This kind of thing is happening all the time. Out of the millions of instances which must be available, I will choose one which happens to be verifiable. During part of 1941 and 1942, when the Luftwaffe was busy in Russia, the German radio regaled its home audience with stories of devastating air raids on London. Now, we are aware that those raids did not happen. But what use would our knowledge be if the Germans conquered Britain? For the purpose of a future historian, did those raids happen, or didn't they? The answer is: If Hitler survives, they happened, and if he falls they didn't happen. So with innumerable other events of the past ten or twenty years. Is the *Protocols of the Elders of Zion*[48] a genuine document? Did Trotsky plot with the Nazis? How many German aeroplanes were shot down in the Battle of Britain? Does Europe welcome the New Order? In no case do you get one answer which is universally accepted because it is true: in each case you get a number of totally incompatible answers, one of which is finally adopted as the result of a physical struggle. History is written by the winners.

In the last analysis our only claim to victory is that if we win the war we shall tell less lies about it than our adversaries. The really frightening thing about totalitarianism is not that it commits atrocities but that it attacks the concept of objective truth: it claims

48. *The Protocols of the Elders of Zion* is a notorious crude late nineteenth-century forgery that purports to comprise the minutes of meetings of Jewish leaders at a Zionist congress in Basle in 1897, at which they supposedly plotted to take over the world. Written by a Russian secret policeman from various sources and first published in a Russian newspaper in 1903, the document was circulated in Europe by anti-Bolshevik Russians after 1917 and was taken up enthusiastically by anti-Semites on the German right, among them Adolf Hitler, even though it had been exposed as a forgery (by Northcliffe's *Times* in London) as early as 1921. It is still circulated by neo-Nazis and Islamists.

to control the past as well as the future. In spite of all the lying and self-righteousness that war encourages, I do not honestly think it can be said that that habit of mind is growing in Britain. Taking one thing with another, I should say that the press is slightly freer than it was before the war. I know out of my own experience that you can print things now which you couldn't print ten years ago. War resisters have probably been less maltreated in this war than in the last one, and the expression of unpopular opinions in public is certainly safer. There is some hope, therefore, that the liberal habit of mind, which thinks of truth as something outside yourself, something to be discovered, and not as something you can make up as you go along, will survive. But I still don't envy the future historian's job. Is it not a strange commentary on our time that even the casualties in the present war cannot be estimated within several millions?

* * *

Announcing that the Board of Trade is about to remove the ban on turned-up trouser-ends, a tailor's advertisement hails this as 'a first instalment of the freedom for which we are fighting'.

If we were really fighting for turned-up trouser-ends, I should be inclined to be pro-Axis. Turn-ups have no function except to collect dust, and no virtue except that when you clean them out you occasionally find a sixpence there. But beneath that tailor's jubilant cry there lies another thought: that in a little while Germany will be finished, the war will be half over, rationing will be relaxed, and clothes snobbery will be in full swing again. I don't share that hope. The sooner we are able to stop food rationing the better I shall be pleased, but I would like to see clothes rationing continue till the moths have devoured the last dinner-jacket and even the undertakers have shed their top-hats. I would not mind seeing the whole nation in dyed battledress for five years if by that means one of the main breeding points of snobbery and envy could be eliminated. Clothes rationing was not conceived in a democratic spirit, but all the same it has had a democratising effect. If the poor are not much better dressed, at least the rich are shabbier. And since no real structural change is occurring in our society, the mechanical levelling process that results from sheer scarcity is better than nothing.

* * *

A copy of *The Ingoldsby Legends*[49] which someone gave me for Christmas, with illustrations by Cruikshank, set me wondering about the reasons for the decline in English comic draughtsmanship. The decline in comic verse is easier to explain. Barham himself, Hood,

49. *The Ingoldsby Legends* (1837) is a collection of myths, ghost stories and poems by Thomas Ingoldsby of Tappington Manor, a pseudonym of Richard Harris Barham (1788–1845).

Calverley, Thackeray, and other writers of the early and middle nineteenth century, could write good light verse, things in the style of

> Once, a happy child, I carolled
> On green lawns the whole day through,
> Not unpleasingly apparelled
> In a lightish suit of blue,

because on the whole, life - middle-class life - was carefree and one could go from birth to death with a boyish outlook. Except for an occasional thing like Clough's 'How pleasant it is to have money', or 'The Walrus and the Carpenter', English comic verse of the nineteenth century does not have any ideas in it. But with the draughtsmen it is just the other way about. The attraction of Leech, Cruikshank and a long line of them stretching back to Hogarth is in their intellectual brutality. *Punch* would not print Leech's illustrations to *Handley Cross* if they were new today. They are much too brutal: they even make the upper classes look as ugly as the working class! But they are funny, which *Punch* is not. How came it that we lost both our light-heartedness and our cruelty round about 1860? And why is it that now, when class-hatred is as fierce and political passion as near the surface as they were in the time of the Napoleonic wars, cartoonists who can express them are hardly to be found?

As I Please 11

11 February 1944

There are two journalistic activities that will always bring you a come-back. One is to attack the Catholics and the other is to defend the Jews. Recently I happened to review some books dealing with the persecution of the Jews in medieval and modern Europe. The review brought me the usual wad of anti-Semitic letters, which left me thinking for the thousandth time that this problem is being evaded even by the people whom it concerns most directly.

The disquieting thing about these letters is that they do not all come from lunatics. I don't greatly mind the person who believes in the *Protocols of the Elders of Zion*, nor even the discharged army officer who has been shabbily treated by the government and is infuriated by seeing 'aliens' given all the best jobs. But in addition to these types there is the small business or professional man who is firmly convinced that the Jews bring all their troubles upon themselves by underhand business methods and complete lack of public spirit. These people write reasonable, well-balanced letters, disclaim any belief in racialism, and back up everything they say with copious instances. They admit the existence of 'good Jews', and usually declare (Hitler says just the same in *Mein Kampf*) that they did not start out with any anti-Jewish feeling but have been forced into it simply by observing how Jews behave.

The weakness of the left-wing attitude towards anti-Semitism is to approach it from a rationalistic angle. Obviously the charges made against Jews are not true. They cannot be true, partly because they cancel out, partly because no one people could have such a monopoly of wickedness. But simply by pointing this out one gets no further. The official left-wing view of anti-Semitism is that it is something 'got up' by the ruling classes in order to divert attention away from the real evils of society. The Jews, in fact, are scapegoats. This is no doubt correct, but it is quite useless as an argument. One does not dispose of a belief by showing that it is irrational. Nor is it any use, in my experience, to talk about the persecution of the Jews in Germany. If a man has the slightest disposition towards anti-Semitism, such things bounce off his consciousness like peas off a steel helmet. The best argument of all, if rational arguments were ever of any use, would be to point out that the alleged crimes of the Jews are only possible because we live in a society which rewards crime. If all Jews are crooks, let us deal with them by so arranging our economic system that crooks cannot prosper. But what good is it to say that kind of thing to the man who believes as an article of faith that Jews dominate the black market, push their way to the front of queues and dodge military service?

We could do with a detailed inquiry into the causes of anti-Semitism, and it ought not to be vitiated in advance by the assumption that those causes are wholly economic. However true the 'scapegoat' theory may be in general terms, it does not explain why the Jews rather than some other minority group are picked on, nor does it make clear what they are a scapegoat for. A thing like the Dreyfus case,[50] for

50. The Dreyfus case was the long-running affair surrounding the conviction for treason in 1894 of an obscure captain in the French army, Alfred Dreyfus (1859–1935). Dreyfus was Jewish, and he was found guilty of passing military secrets on to Germany on the flimsiest of evidence. He was stripped of his military rank and jailed for life – but then a new chief of army intelligence re-examined the evidence and concluded that it showed that another officer who was still serving was guilty of espionage. The army's top brass refused to reopen the case, however, prompting the novelist Emile Zola to denounce the cover-up in his famous article 'J'accuse!' on the front page of the daily *L'Aurore* – for which he was found guilty of libelling the army, leading him to flee to England. In an atmosphere of growing polarisation between the Catholic, anti-Semitic *anti-Dreyfusard* right and the secularist *Dreyfusard* left, yet another officer was discovered to have forged documents to compromise Dreyfus. To cut a long story short, Dreyfus was pardoned in 1899 but had to wait until 1906 for the charges against him to be dropped and his rank restored.

instance, is not easily translated into economic terms. So far as Britain is concerned, the important things to find out are just what charges are made against the Jews, whether anti-Semitism is really on the increase (it may actually have decreased over the past thirty years), and to what extent it is aggravated by the influx of refugees since about 1938.

One not only ought not to assume that the causes of anti-Semitism are economic in a crude, direct way (unemployment, business jealousy, etc), one also ought not to assume that 'sensible' people are immune to it. It flourishes especially among literary men, for instance. Without even getting up from this table to consult a book I can think of passages in Villon, Shakespeare, Smollett, Thackeray, H. G. Wells, Aldous Huxley, T. S. Eliot and many another which would be called anti-Semitic if they had been written since Hitler came to power. Both Belloc and Chesterton flirted, or something more than flirted, with anti-Semitism, and other writers whom it is possible to respect have swallowed it more or less in its Nazi form. Clearly the neurosis lies very deep, and just what it is that people hate when they say that they hate a non-existent entity called 'the Jews' is still uncertain. And it is partly the fear of finding out how widespread anti-Semitism is that prevents it from being seriously investigated.

* * *

The following lines are quoted in Anthony Trollope's *Autobiography*:

> When Payne-Knight's *Taste* was issued on the town
> A few Greek verses in the text set down
> Were torn to pieces, mangled into hash,
> Hurled to the flames as execrable trash;
> In short, were butchered rather than dissected
> And several false quantities detected;
> Till, when the smoke had risen from the cinders
> It was discovered that – the lines were Pindar's!

Trollope does not make clear who is the author of these lines, and I should be very glad if any reader could let me know. But I also quote them for their own sake – that is, for the terrible warning to literary critics that they contain – and for the sake of drawing attention to Trollope's *Autobiography*, which is a most fascinating book, although or because it is largely concerned with money.

* * *

The dispute that has been going on in *Time and Tide* about Mr J. F. Horrabin's atlas of war geography[51] is a reminder that maps are tricky things, to be regarded with the same suspicion as photographs and statistics.

It is an interesting minor manifestation of nationalism that every nation colours itself red on the map. There is also a tendency to make yourself look bigger than you are, which is possible without actual forgery since every projection of the earth as a flat surface distorts some part or other. During the Empire Free Trade 'crusade'[52] there was a free distribution to schools of large coloured wall-maps which were made on a new projection and dwarfed the USSR while exaggerating the size of India and Africa. Then there are ethnological and political maps, a most rewarding material for propaganda. During the Spanish civil war, maps were pinned up in the Spanish villages which divided the world into socialist, democratic and fascist states. From these you could learn that India was a democracy, while Madagascar and Indo-China (this was the period of the Popular Front government in France) were labelled 'socialist'.

The war has probably done something towards improving our geography. People who five years ago thought that Croats rhymed with goats and drew only a very shadowy distinction between Minsk and Pinsk, could now tell you which sea the Volga flows into and indicate without much searching the whereabouts of Guadalcanal or Buthidaung. Hundreds of thousands, if not millions, of English people can nearly pronounce Dnepropetrovsk. But it takes a war to make map-reading popular. As late as the time of Wavell's Egyptian campaign I met a woman who thought that Italy was joined up with Africa, and in 1938, when I was leaving for Morocco, some of the people in my village – a very rustic village, certainly, but only fifty miles from London – asked whether it would

51. *Time and Tide* was a weekly founded in 1920 by Margaret Haig Thomas, Lady Rhondda (1883–1958), and edited by her from 1926 until her death. It expired in 1977. Orwell was an occasional contributor in the late 1930s, though his main outlet for journalism at this time was the *New English Weekly*, with which he fell out when it stuck to a pacifist position on the war. He was then ever present in *Time and Tide* as a reviewer (including a stint as drama critic) in 1940–1 before joining the BBC. Most of his work for *Time and Tide* is to be found in *Facing Unpleasant Facts 1937–1939* and *A Patriot after All 1940–1941*, volumes XI and XII respectively of Peter Davison's *The Complete Works of George Orwell* (London: Secker and Warburg, 1998).

52. 'Empire Free Trade' was the slogan used by Lord Beaverbrook, Canadian proprietor of the *Daily Express*, in his campaign (1929–31) for tariff protection for the British empire. In 1929, having failed to convert Stanley Baldwin, the Conservative leader, to the cause, he and Lord Rothermere, proprietor of the *Daily Mail*, created a United Empire Party to fight elections on the issue. It won one by-election, but Baldwin came back fighting, denouncing the press barons for wanting 'power without responsibility – the prerogative of the harlot throughout the ages', and the campaign fizzled out after the Tories defeated the UEP in the Westminster St George's by-election of 1931. Baldwin subsequently adopted a watered-down version of the Empire Free Trade programme. See Anne Chisholm and Michael Davie, *Beaverbrook: A Life* (London: Hutchinson, 1992).

be necessary to cross the sea to get there. If you ask any circle of people (I should particularly like to do this with the members of the House of Commons) to draw a map of Europe from memory, you get some surprising results. Any government which genuinely cared about education would see to it that a globe map, at present an expensive rarity, was accessible to every school child. Without some notion of which country is next to which, and which is the quickest route from one place to another, and where a ship can be bombed from shore, and where it can't, it is difficult to see what value the average citizen's views on foreign policy can have.

As I Please 12

18 February 1944

After the war there is going to be a severe housing shortage in this country, and we shall not overcome it unless we resort to prefabrication. If we stick to our traditional building methods the necessary houses will take decades to produce, and the discomfort and misery that this will lead to, the patching-up of blitzed premises and filthy slums, the rent rackets and overcrowding, are easy to foresee. So are the effects of a housing shortage on our already perilous birthrate. Meanwhile not only prefabrication, but any large, concerted effort at rehousing, has powerful vested interests working against it. The building societies, and the brick and cement trades, are directly involved, and the whole principle of private ownership in land is threatened. How could you rebuild London, for instance, on a sane plan without disregarding private property rights? But the people who traffic in bugs and basements are not going to come out into the open and say clearly what they are fighting for. By far their best card is the Englishman's sentimental but partly justified yearning for a 'home of his own'. They will play this card over and over again, and it is up to us to counter it before it takes effect.

To begin with, prefabrication does not mean – as people are already beginning to fear that it means – that we shall all be forced to live in ugly, cramped, flimsy and unhomelike chicken houses. The thing that ought to be pointed out in this connection is that existing English houses are for the most part very badly built. They are not built to withstand either heat or cold, they are lacking in cupboards, their water pipes are so placed as to ensure that they will burst every time there is a hard frost, and they have no convenient means of rubbish-disposal. All these problems, which a speculative builder will tell you are insoluble, are easily solved in various other countries. If we tackled our rehousing problem boldly we could get rid of discomforts which have come to be accepted like the weather, but are in fact quite unnecessary. We could get rid of 'blind back' houses, basements, geysers, filth-collecting gas stoves, offices where the light of day never penetrates, outdoor WCs, uncleanable stone sinks, and other miseries. We could put a bath in every house and install bells that actually ring, plugs that pull at the first attempt, waste-pipes that don't get blocked by a spoonful of tea-leaves. We could even, if we chose, make our rooms relatively easy to clean by streamlining them and making the corners curved instead of rectangular. But all this depends on our being able to build houses rapidly, by mass-production. Failing that, the housing shortage will be so desperate that we shall have to 'make do' with every mouse-ridden ruin that remains, and encourage the speculative builder to do his worst as well.

Secondly, the dislike of flats will somehow have to be exorcised. If people are going to live in big towns they must either live in flats or put up with overcrowding: there is no way out of that. A big block of flats, covering only an acre or two of ground, will contain as many people as live in a small country town, and give them as much room-space as they would have in houses. Rebuild London in big blocks of flats, and there could be light and air for everybody, and room for green spaces, allotments, playgrounds. People could live out of the noise of the traffic, children would not grow up in a world of bricks and dustbins, and historic buildings like St Paul's would be visible again instead of being swamped by seas of yellow brick.

Yet it is notorious that people, especially working-class people, don't like flats. They want a 'home of their own'. In a sense they are right, for it is true that in most blocks of working-class flats there isn't the privacy and freedom that you can get in a private house. They are not built to be noise-proof, the people who dwell in them are often burdened by nagging restrictions, and they are often quite unnecessarily uncomfortable. The first blocks built definitely as working-class flats did not even have baths. Even now they seldom have lifts, and they usually have stone stairs, which means that one lives in an endless clattering of boots. Much of this arises from the half-conscious conviction, so powerful in this country, that working-class people must not be made too comfortable. Deafening noise and irritating restrictions are not inherent in the nature of flats, and we ought to insist on that. For the feeling that four rooms are 'your own' if they are on the ground, and not 'your own' if they are in mid-air – and it is especially strong in women with children – is going to be a big obstacle in the way of replanning, even in areas where the Germans have already done the necessary clearance work.

* * *

A correspondent reproaches me for wanting to see clothes rationing continue until we are all equally shabby; though she adds that clothes rationing hasn't, in fact, had an equalising effect. I will quote an extract from her letter:

> I work in a very exclusive shop just off Bond Street . . . When I, shivering in my 25/- utility frock, serve these elegant creatures in sables, fur caps and fur-lined boots, who regard me uncomprehendingly when I say 'Good morning, it's very cold to-day, madam' (very stupid of me – after all, how should they know?), I do not wish to see them deprived of their lovely and warm attire, but rather that such attire was available to me, and for all . . . We should aim not at reducing the present highest standard of living, but at raising any and everything less than the highest. It is a malicious and mean-spirited attitude that wishes to drag Etonians and Harrovians from their fortunate positions of eminence and force them down the mines. Rather, in the present reshuffling of society we should seek to make these places accessible to all.

I answer, first of all, that although clothes rationing obviously bears hardest on those who don't possess large stocks of clothes already, it has had a certain equalising effect, because it has made people uneasy about appearing too smart. Certain garments, such as men's evening dress, have practically disappeared; also it is now considered permissible to wear almost any clothes for almost any job. But my original point was that if clothes rationing goes on long enough even wealthy people will have worn out their extra stocks of clothes, and we shall all be somewhere near equal.

But is it not the case that we ought always to aim at levelling 'up' and not levelling 'down'? I answer that in some cases you can't level 'up'. You can't give everyone a Rolls-Royce car. You can't even give everyone a fur coat, especially in war time. As to the statement that everyone ought to go to Eton or Harrow, it is meaningless. The whole value of those places, from the point of view of the people who go there, is their exclusiveness. And since certain luxuries – high-powered cars, for instance, fur coats, yachts, country houses and what-not – obviously can't be distributed to everybody, then it is better that nobody should have them. The rich lose almost as much by their wealth as the poor lose by their poverty. Doesn't my correspondent bring that out when she speaks of those ignorant rich women who cannot even imagine what a cold morning means to a person without an overcoat?

* * *

Another correspondent writes indignantly to know what I mean by saying that *Punch* is not funny.[53] Actually I exaggerated a little. Since 1918 I have seen three jokes in *Punch* that made me laugh. But – as I always tell puzzled foreign visitors who enquire about this

53. *Punch* was a weekly magazine published from 1841 to 1992 (and briefly revived by Mohammed al-Fayed in 1996–2002).

– *Punch* is not meant to be funny, it is meant to be reassuring. After all, where do you most frequently see it? In club lounges and in dentists' waiting rooms. In both places it has, and is meant to have, a soothing effect. You know in advance that it will never contain anything new. The jokes you were familiar with in your childhood will still be there, just the same as ever, like a circle of old friends. The nervous curate, the apoplectic colonel, the awkward recruit, the forgetful plumber – there they all are, unchangeable as the Pyramids. Glancing through those familiar pages, the clubman knows that his dividends are all right, the patient knows that the dentist will not really break his jaw. But as to being funny, that is a different matter. Jokes that are funny usually contain that un-English thing, an idea. The *New Yorker*, though it is overrated, is quite often funny. Thus a recent number has a picture of two German soldiers leading a huge ape into the orderly room on a chain. The officer is saying to them angrily, 'Can't you spell?' This seems to me funny. But it might take five seconds' thought to see the joke, and as it is an axiom of the middle class – at least the golf-playing, whisky-drinking, *Punch*-reading part of the middle class – that no decent person is capable of thought, jokes of that kind are barred from *Punch*.

As I Please 13

25 February 1944

A short story in the *Home Companion and Family Journal*, entitled 'Hullo, Sweetheart', recounts the adventures of a young girl named Lucy Fallows who worked on the switchboard of a long-distance telephone exchange. She had 'sacrificed her yearning to be in uniform' in order to take this job, but found it dull and uneventful. 'So many silly people seemed to use long-distance just to blether to each other . . . She felt fed up; she felt that she was a servant to selfish people,' and there was 'a cloud in her hazel eyes'. However, as you will readily guess, Lucy's job soon livened up, and before long she found herself in the middle of thrilling adventures which included the sinking of a U-boat, the capture of a German sabotage crew, and a long motor-ride with a handsome naval officer who had 'a crisp voice'. Such is life in the telephone exchange.

At the end of the story there is a little note: 'Any of our young readers themselves interested in the work of the Long Distance Telephone Exchange (such work as Lucy Fallows was doing) should apply to the Staff Controller, LTR, London, who will inform them as to the opportunities open.'

I do not know whether this is an advertisement likely to have much success. I should doubt whether even girls of the age aimed at would believe that capturing U-boats enters very largely into the lives of telephone operators. But I note with interest the direct correlation between a government recruiting advertisement and a piece of commercial fiction. Before the war the Admiralty, for instance, used to put its advertisements in the boys' adventure papers, which was a natural place to put them, but stories were not, so far as I know, written to order. Probably they are not definitely commissioned even now. It is more likely that the departments concerned keep their eye on the weekly papers (incidentally I like to think of some stripe-trousered personage in the GPO reading 'Hullo, Sweetheart' as part of his official duties) and push in an ad when any story seems likely to form an attractive bait. But from that to the actual commissioning of stories to be written round the ATS, Women's Land Army, or any other body in need of recruits, is only a short step. One can almost hear the tired, cultured voices from the MOI,[54] saying:

> Hullo! Hullo! Is that you, Tony? Oh, hullo. Look here, I've got another script for you, Tony, 'A Ticket to Paradise'. It's bus conductresses this time. They're not coming in. I believe the trousers don't fit, or something. Well, anyway, Peter says make it sexy, but kind of clean - you know. Nothing extra-marital. We want the stuff in by Tuesday. Fifteen thousand words. You can choose the hero. I rather favour the kind of outdoor man that dogs and kiddies all love - you know. Or very tall with a sensitive mouth, I don't mind, really. But pile on the sex, Peter says.

Something resembling this already happens with radio features and documentary films, but hitherto there has not been any very direct connexion between fiction and propaganda. That half-inch ad in the *Home Companion* seems to mark another small stage in the process of 'co-ordination' that is gradually happening to all the arts.

* * *

Looking through Chesterton's Introduction to *Hard Times* in the Everyman Edition (incidentally, Chesterton's Introductions to Dickens are about the best thing he ever wrote), I note the typically sweeping statement: 'There are no new ideas.' Chesterton is here claiming that the ideas which animated the French revolution were not new ones but simply a revival of doctrines which had flourished earlier and then been abandoned. But the claim that 'there is nothing new under the sun' is one of the stock arguments of intelligent reactionaries. Catholic apologists, in particular, use it almost automatically. Everything that you can say or think has been said or thought before. Every political

54. The Ministry of Information was the government's wartime propaganda arm, set up in 1939 and based in the University of London's Senate House for the duration of the Second World War. It was the model for Orwell's Ministry of Truth in *Nineteen Eighty-Four*.

theory from liberalism to Trotskyism can be shown to be a development of some heresy in the early church. Every system of philosophy springs ultimately from the Greeks. Every scientific theory (if we are to believe the popular Catholic press) was anticipated by Roger Bacon and others in the thirteenth century. Some Hindu thinkers go even further and claim that not merely the scientific theories, but the products of applied science as well, aeroplanes, radio and the whole bag of tricks, were known to the ancient Hindus, who afterwards dropped them as being unworthy of their attention.

It is not very difficult to see that this idea is rooted in the fear of progress. If there is nothing new under the sun, if the past in some shape or another always returns, then the future when it comes will be something familiar. At any rate what will never come – since it has never come before – is that hated, dreaded thing, a world of free and equal human beings. Particularly comforting to reactionary thinkers is the idea of a cyclical universe, in which the same chain of events happens over and over again. In such a universe every seeming advance towards democracy simply means that the coming age of tyranny and privilege is a bit nearer. This belief, obviously superstitious though it is, is widely held nowadays, and is common among fascists and near-fascists.

In fact, there *are* new ideas. The idea that an advanced civilisation need not rest on slavery is a relatively new idea, for instance: it is a good deal younger than the Christian religion. But even if Chesterton's dictum were true, it would only be true in the sense that a statue is contained in every block of stone. Ideas may not change, but emphasis shifts constantly. It could be claimed, for example, that the most important part of Marx's theory is contained in the saying: 'Where your treasure is, there will your heart be also.' But before Marx developed it, what force had that saying had? Who had paid any attention to it? Who had inferred from it – what it certainly implies – that laws, religions and moral codes are all a superstructure built over existing property relations? It was Christ, according to the Gospel, who uttered the text, but it was Marx who brought it to life. And ever since he did so the motives of politicians, priests, judges, moralists and millionaires have been under the deepest suspicion – which, of course, is why they hate him so much.

As I Please 14

3 March 1944

Some weeks ago a Catholic reader of *Tribune* wrote to protest against a review by Mr

Charles Hamblett. She objected to his remarks about St Teresa and about St Joseph of Copertino, the saint who once flew round a cathedral carrying a bishop on his back. I answered, defending Mr Hamblett, and got a still more indignant letter in return. This letter raises a number of very important points, and at least one of them seems to me to deserve discussion. The relevance of flying saints to the socialist movement may not at first sight be very clear, but I think I can show that the present nebulous state of Christian doctrine has serious implications which neither Christians nor socialists have faced.

The substance of my correspondent's letter is that it doesn't matter whether St Teresa and the rest of them flew through the air or not: what matters is that St Teresa's 'vision of the world changed the course of history'. I would concede this. Having lived in an oriental country I have developed a certain indifference to miracles, and I well know that having delusions, or even being an outright lunatic, is quite compatible with what is loosely called genius. William Blake, for instance, was a lunatic in my opinion. Joan of Arc was probably a lunatic. Newton believed in astrology, Strindberg believed in magic. However, the miracles of the saints are a minor matter. It also appears from my correspondent's letter that even the most central doctrines of the Christian religion don't have to be accepted in a literal sense. It doesn't matter, for instance, whether Jesus Christ ever existed. 'The figure of Christ (myth, or man, or god, it does not matter) so transcends all the rest that I only wish that everyone would look, before rejecting that version of life.' Christ, therefore, may be a myth, or he may have been merely a human being, or the account given of him in the Creeds may be true. So we arrive at this position: *Tribune* must not poke fun at the Christian religion, but the existence of Christ, which innumerable people have been burnt for denying, is a matter of indifference.

Now, is this orthodox Catholic doctrine? My impression is that it is not. I can think of passages in the writing of popular Catholic apologists such as Father Woodlock and Father Ronald Knox[55] in which it is stated in the clearest terms that Christian doctrine means what is appears to mean, and is not to be accepted in some wishy-washy metaphorical sense. Father Knox refers specifically to the idea that it doesn't matter whether Christ actually existed as a 'horrible' idea. But what my correspondent says would be echoed by many Catholic intellectuals. If you talk to a thoughtful Christian, Catholic or Anglican, you often find yourself laughed at for being so ignorant as to suppose that anyone ever took the doctrines of the church literally. These doctrines have, you are told, a quite other meaning which you are too crude to understand. Immortality

55. Father Francis Woodlock (1871–1940) was a Jesuit priest who wrote several popular books on Catholicism. Father Ronald Knox (1888–1957) was a Catholic priest and theologian who broadcast regularly on the BBC, wrote thrillers and translated the Bible.

of the soul doesn't 'mean' that you, John Smith, will remain conscious after you are dead. Resurrection of the body doesn't mean that John Smith's body will actually be resurrected – and so on and so on. Thus the Catholic intellectual is able, for controversial purposes, to play a sort of handy-pandy game, repeating the articles of the Creed in exactly the same terms as his forefathers, while defending himself from the charge of superstition by explaining that he is speaking in parables. Substantially his claim is that though he himself doesn't believe in any very definite way in life after death, there has been no change in Christian belief, since our ancestors didn't really believe in it either. Meanwhile a vitally important fact – that one of the props of western civilisation has been knocked away – is obscured.

I do not know whether, officially, there has been any alteration in Christian doctrine. Father Knox and my correspondent would seem to be in disagreement about this. But what I do know is that belief in survival after death – the individual survival of John Smith, still conscious of himself as John Smith – is enormously less widespread than it was. Even among professing Christians it is probably decaying: other people, as a rule, don't even entertain the possibility that it might be true. But our forefathers, so far as we know, did believe in it. Unless all that they wrote about it was intended to mislead us, they believed it in an exceedingly literal, concrete way. Life on earth, as they saw it, was simply a short period of preparation for an infinitely more important life beyond the grave. But that notion has disappeared, or is disappearing, and the consequences have not really been faced.

Western civilisation, unlike some oriental civilisations, was founded partly on the belief in individual immortality. If one looks at the Christian religion from the outside, this belief appears far more important than the belief in God. The western conception of good and evil is very difficult to separate from it. There is little doubt that the modern cult of power worship is bound up with the modern man's feeling that life here and now is the only life there is. If death ends everything, it becomes much harder to believe that you can be in the right, even if you are defeated. Statesmen, nations, theories, causes are judged almost inevitably by the test of material success. Supposing that one can separate the two phenomena, I would say that the decay of the belief in personal immortality has been as important as the rise of machine civilisation. Machine civilisation has terrible possibilities, as you probably reflected the other night when the ack-ack guns[56] started up: but the other thing has terrible possibilities too, and it cannot be said that the socialist movement has given much thought to them.

I do not want the belief in life after death to return, and in any case it is not likely to return. What I do point out is that its disappearance has left a big hole, and that we

56. Anti-aircraft guns.

ought to take notice of that fact. Reared for thousands of years on the notion that the individual survives, man has got to make a considerable psychological effort to get used to the notion that the individual perishes. He is not likely to salvage civilisation unless he can evolve a system of good and evil which is independent of heaven and hell. Marxism, indeed, does supply this, but it has never really been popularised. Most socialists are content to point out that once socialism has been established we shall be happier in a material sense, and to assume that all problems lapse when one's belly is full. But the truth is the opposite: when one's belly is empty, one's only problem is an empty belly. It is when we have got away from drudgery and exploitation that we shall really start wondering about man's destiny and the reason for his existence. One cannot have any worthwhile picture of the future unless one realises how much we have lost by the decay of Christianity. Few socialists seem to be aware of this. And the Catholic intellectuals who cling to the letter of the Creeds while reading into them meanings they were never meant to have, and who snigger at anyone simple enough to suppose that the fathers of the church meant what they said, are simply raising smoke-screens to conceal their own disbelief from themselves.

* * *

I have very great pleasure in welcoming the reappearance of the *Cornhill Magazine* after its four years' absence.[57] Apart from the articles - there is a good one on Mayakovsky by Maurice Bowra,[58] and another good one by Raymond Mortimer[59] on Brougham and Macaulay - there are some interesting notes by the editor on the earlier history of the *Cornhill*. One fact that these bring out is the size and wealth of the Victorian reading public, and the vast sums earned by literary men in those days. The first number of the *Cornhill* sold 120,000 copies. It paid Trollope £2,000 for a serial - he had demanded £3,000 - and commissioned another from George Eliot at £10,000. Except for the tiny few who managed to crash into the film world, these sums would be quite unthinkable

57. The *Cornhill Magazine*, which published fiction and poetry, was launched in 1860 and expired in 1975.

58. Maurice Bowra (1898–1971), warden of Wadham College, Oxford, was a classical scholar, poet, critic, bon viveur and wit. He was Oxford professor of poetry 1946–51 and vice-chancellor of Oxford University 1951–4.

59. Raymond Mortimer (1895–1980) was literary editor of the *New Statesman* 1935–47 and then chief reviewer for the *Sunday Times*. In 1937 he had turned down Orwell's review of Franz Borkenau's *The Spanish Cockpit* on the grounds that it was not actually a review - not knowing that his editor, Kingsley Martin, had already written to Orwell rejecting it on the grounds that 'it too far controverts the political policy of the paper'. Mortimer apologised profusely to Orwell when he found out about Martin's letter.

nowadays. You would have to be a top-notcher even to get into the £2,000 class. As for £10,000, to get that for a single book you would have to be someone like Edgar Rice Burroughs. A novel nowadays is considered to have done very well if it brings its author £500 – a sum which a successful lawyer can earn in a single day. The book ramp is not so new as 'Beachcomber' and other enemies of the literary race imagine.

As I Please 15

10 March 1944

Reading as nearly as possible simultaneously Mr Derrick Leon's *Life of Tolstoy*,[60] Miss Gladys Storey's book on Dickens,[61] Harry Levin's book on James Joyce,[62] and the autobiography (not yet published in this country) of Salvador Dali, the surrealist painter,[63] I was struck even more forcibly than usual by the advantage that an artist derives from being born into a relatively healthy society.

When I first read *War and Peace* I must have been twenty, an age at which one is not intimidated by long novels, and my sole quarrel with this book (three stout volumes – the length of perhaps four modern novels) was that it did not go on long enough. It seemed to me that Nicholas and Natasha Rostov, Pierre Bezukhov, Denisov and all the rest of them, were people about whom one would gladly go on reading for ever. The fact is that the minor Russian aristocracy of that date, with their boldness and simplicity, their countrified pleasures, their stormy love affairs and enormous families, were very charming people. Such a society could not possibly be called just or progressive. It was founded on serfdom, a fact that made Tolstoy uneasy even in his boyhood, and even the 'enlightened' aristocrat would have found it difficult to think of the peasant as the same

60. Derrick Leon (1908–44) was a novelist and biographer. As well as *Tolstoy: His Life and Work* (London: Routledge, 1944), he wrote biographies of Marcel Proust and John Ruskin.
61. Gladys Storey (1897–1964) was the daughter of the Victorian painter G. A. Storey and a friend of Dickens's daughter. Her *Dickens and Daughter* (London: Frederick Muller, 1939) revealed for the first time Dickens's secret relationship with the actress Nelly Ternan.
62. Harry Levin (1912–94) was an American literary critic. His *James Joyce: A Critical Introduction* (New York: New Directions, 1941) was the first major book on Joyce. Orwell reviewed it in the *Manchester Evening News* on 2 March 1944.
63. *The Secret Life of Salvador Dali* was published in New York by Dial Press in 1942, in a translation by Haakon M. Chevalier.

species of animal as himself. Tolstoy himself did not give up beating his servants till he was well on into adult life.

The landowner exercised a sort of *droit de seigneur* over the peasants on his estate. Tolstoy had at least one bastard, and his morganatic half-brother was the family coachman. And yet one cannot feel for these simple-minded, prolific Russians the same contempt as one feels for the sophisticated cosmopolitan scum who gave Dali his livelihood. Their saving grace is that they are rustics, they have never heard of benzedrine or gilded toenails, and though Tolstoy was later to repent of the sins of his youth more vociferously than most people, he must have known that he drew his strength - his creative power as well as the strength of his vast muscles - from that rude, healthy background where one shot woodcocks on the marshes and girls thought themselves lucky if they went to three dances in a year.

One of the big gaps in Dickens is that he writes nothing, even in a burlesque spirit, about country life. Of agriculture he does not even pretend to know anything. There are some farcical descriptions of shooting in the *Pickwick Papers*, but Dickens, as a middle-class radical, would be incapable of describing such amusements sympathetically. He sees field-sports as primarily an exercise in snobbishness, which they already were in the England of that date. The enclosures, industrialism, the vast differentiation of wealth, and the cult of the pheasant and the red deer had all combined to drive the mass of the English people off the land and make the hunting instinct, which is probably almost universal in human beings, seem merely a fetish of the aristocracy. Perhaps the best thing in *War and Peace* is the description of the wolf hunt. In the end it is the peasant's dog that outstrips those of the nobles and gets the wolf; and afterwards Natasha finds it quite natural to dance in the peasant's hut.

To see such scenes in England you would have had to go back a hundred or two hundred years, to a time when difference in status did not mean any very great difference in habits. Dickens's England was already dominated by the 'Trespassers will be prosecuted' board. When one thinks of the accepted left-wing attitude towards hunting, shooting and the like, it is queer to reflect that Lenin, Stalin and Trotsky were all of them keen sportsmen in their day. But then they belonged to a large empty country where there was no necessary connexion between sport and snobbishness, and the divorce between country and town was never complete. This society which almost any modern novelist has as his material is very much meaner, less comely and less carefree than Tolstoy's, and to grasp this has been one of the signs of talent. Joyce would have been falsifying the facts, if he had made the people in *Dubliners* less disgusting than they are. But the natural advantage lay with Tolstoy: for, other things being equal, who would not rather write about Pierre and Natasha than about furtive seductions in boarding-houses or drunken Catholic businessmen celebrating a 'retreat'?

* * *

In his book on Joyce Mr Harry Levin gives a few biographical details, but is unable to tell us much about Joyce's last year of life. All we know is that when the Nazis entered France he escaped over the border into Switzerland, to die about a year later in his old home in Zurich. Even the whereabouts of Joyce's children is not, it seems, known for certain.

The academic critics could not resist the opportunity to kick Joyce's corpse. *The Times* gave him a mean, cagey little obituary, and then - though *The Times* has never lacked space for letters about batting averages or the first cuckoo - refused to print the letter of protest that T. S. Eliot wrote. This was in accordance with the grand old English tradition that the dead must always be flattered unless they happen to be artists. Let a politician die, and his worst enemies will stand up on the floor of the House and utter pious lies in his honour, but a writer or artist must be sniffed at, at least if he is any good. The entire British press united to insult D. H. Lawrence ('pornographer' was the usual description) as soon as he was dead. But the snooty obituaries were merely what Joyce would have expected. The collapse of France, and the need to flee from the Gestapo like a common political suspect, were a different matter, and when the war is over it will be very interesting to find out what Joyce thought about it.

Joyce was a conscious exile from Anglo-Irish philistinism. Ireland would have none of him, England and America barely tolerated him. His books were refused publication, destroyed when in type by timid publishers, banned when they came out, pirated with the tacit connivance of the authorities, and, in any case, largely ignored until the publication of *Ulysses*. He had a genuine grievance, and was extremely conscious of it. But it was also his aim to be a 'pure' artist, 'above the battle' and indifferent to politics. He had written *Ulysses* in Switzerland, with an Austrian passport and a British pension, during the 1914–18 war, to which he paid as nearly as possible no attention. But the present war, as Joyce found out, is not of a kind to be ignored, and I think it must have left him reflecting that a political choice is necessary and that even stupidity is better than totalitarianism.

One thing that Hitler and his friends have demonstrated is what a relatively good time the intellectual has had during the past hundred years. After all, how does the persecution of Joyce, Lawrence, Whitman, Baudelaire, even Oscar Wilde, compare with the kind of thing that has been happening to liberal intellectuals all over Europe since Hitler came to power? Joyce left Ireland in disgust: he did not have to run for his life, as he did when the panzers rolled into Paris. The British government duly banned *Ulysses* when it appeared, but it took the ban off fifteen years later, and what is probably more important, it helped Joyce to stay alive while the book was written. And thereafter, thanks to the generosity of an anonymous admirer, Joyce was able to live a civilised life in Paris for nearly twenty years, working away at *Finnegans Wake* and surrounded by a circle of disciples, while industrious teams of experts translated *Ulysses* not only into various European languages but even into Japanese. Between 1900 and 1920 he had known hunger and neglect: but take it for all in all, his life would appear a pretty good one if one were viewing it from inside a German concentration camp.

What would the Nazis have done with Joyce if they could have laid hands on him? We don't know. They might even have made efforts to win him over and add him to their bag of 'converted' literary men. But he must have seen that they had not only broken up the society that he was used to, but were the deadly enemies of everything that he valued. The battle which he had wanted to be 'above' did, after all, concern him fairly directly, and I like to think that before the end he brought himself to utter some non-neutral comment on Hitler – and coming from Joyce it might be quite a stinger – which is lying in Zurich and will be accessible after the war.

As I Please 16

17 March 1944

With no power to put my decrees into operation, but with as much authority as most of the exile 'governments' now sheltering in various parts of the world, I pronounce sentence of death on the following words and expressions:

> Achilles' heel, jackboot, hydra-headed, ride roughshod over, stab in the back, petty-bourgeois, stinking corpse, liquidate, iron heel, blood-stained oppressor, cynical betrayal, lackey, flunkey, mad dog, jackal, hyena, blood-bath.

No doubt this list will have to be added to from time to time, but it will do to go on with. It contains a fair selection of the dead metaphors and ill-translated foreign phrases which have been current in Marxist literature for years past.

There are, of course, many other perversions of the English language besides this one. There is official English, or Stripetrouser, the language of white papers, parliamentary debates (in their more decorous moments) and BBC news bulletins. There are the scientists and the economists, with their instinctive preference for words like 'contraindicate' and 'deregionalisation'. There is American slang, which for all its attractiveness probably tends to impoverish the language in the long run. And there is the general slovenliness of modern English speech with its decadent vowel sounds (throughout the London area you have to use sign language to distinguish between 'threepence' and 'three-halfpence') and its tendency to make verbs and nouns interchangeable. But here I am concerned only with one kind of bad English, Marxist English, or Pamphletese, which can be studied in the *Daily Worker*, the *Labour Monthly*, *Plebs*, the *New Leader*, and similar papers.[64]

Many of the expressions used in political literature are simply euphemisms or rhetorical tricks. 'Liquidate' for instance (or 'eliminate') is a polite word for 'to kill', while 'realism' normally means 'dishonesty'. But Marxist phraseology is peculiar in that it consists largely of translations. Its characteristic vocabulary comes ultimately from German or Russian phrases which have been adopted in one country after another with no attempt to find suitable equivalents. Here, for instance, is a piece of Marxist writing – it happens to be an address delivered to the Allied armies by the citizens of Pantelleria.

---

64. The *Daily Worker* was the daily of the Communist Party of Great Britain. Launched in 1930, ten years after the CPGB was founded, the *Worker* became the *Morning Star* in 1966 and is still published, though not by the CPGB, which disbanded in 1991 and became Democratic Left, which in turn became the New Times Network in 1999 and is now the New Politics Network. The *Worker* was banned for subverting the war effort by Herbert Morrison, the Home Secretary, in January 1941 after the People's Convention (see Introduction, note 80). The ban was lifted only in August 1942. At the height of its circulation in the late 1940s, the *Worker* sold 100,000 copies a day. The best short history of the *Worker* is Kevin Morgan, 'The Communist Party and the *Daily Worker*', in Geoff Andrews, Nina Fishman and Kevin Morgan (eds), *Opening the Books: Essays on the Social and Cultural History of the British Communist Party* (London: Pluto Press, 1995).

Labour Monthly was formally independent of the CP but was effectively its theoretical journal, edited for all but the last seven years of its life – it lasted from 1921 to 1981 – by Rajani Palme Dutt (1896–1974), the party's chief ideologist, on whom see John Callaghan, *Rajani Palme Dutt: A Study in British Stalinism* (London: Lawrence and Wishart, 1997).

Plebs was the publication of the National Council of Labour Colleges. The NCLC was set up in 1922 as the successor to the Plebs League (a nationwide militant socialist rival to the Workers Educational Association) and the Central Labour College, both of which had their origins in student protests at Ruskin College, Oxford, in 1906–9 against the 'bourgeois' syllabus there. The NCLC, run by a coalition of CPers and independent Marxists (among the latter Raymond Postgate, later editor of *Tribune*), was a major player in the British left in the early 1920s but by the 1940s was twenty years past its peak and marginal. It did not breathe its last, however, until 1972.

The *New Leader* was the weekly of the Independent Labour Party, of which Orwell was briefly a member in the late 1930s. It was edited by Fenner Brockway (1888–1988) from 1931 to 1946. The ILP was by the mid-1940s in terminal decline. The largest organisation on the British left in the 1920s, it lost a vast swath of members when it decided to disaffiliate from the Labour Party in 1932, struggled to keep up with the Communist Party when the latter ditched its sectarian class-against-class rhetoric in the mid-1930s to campaign for anti-fascist unity, and then came close to collapse during the Second World War when it refused to rethink its pacifism.

The citizens of Pantelleria

> pay grateful homage to the Anglo-American forces for the promptness with which they have liberated them from the evil yoke of a megalomaniac and satanic régime which, not content with having sucked like a monstrous octopus the best energies of true Italians for twenty years, is now reducing Italy to a mass of ruins and misery for one motive - only the insane personal profit of its chiefs, who, under an ill-concealed mask of hollow, so-called patriotism, hide the basest passions, and, plotting together with the German pirates, hatch the lowest egoism and blackest treatment while all the time, with revolting cynicism, they tread on the blood of thousands of Italians.

This filthy stew of words is presumably a translation from the Italian, but the point is that one would not recognise it as such. It might be a translation from any other European language, or it might come straight out of the *Daily Worker*, so truly international is this style of writing. Its characteristic is the endless use of ready-made metaphors. In the same spirit, when Italian submarines were sinking the ships that took arms to Republican Spain, the *Daily Worker* urged the British Admiralty to 'sweep the mad dogs from the seas'. Clearly, people capable of using such phrases have ceased to remember that words have meanings.

A Russian friend tells me that the Russian language is richer than English in terms of abuse, so that Russian invective cannot always be accurately translated. Thus when Molotov referred to the Germans as 'cannibals', he was perhaps using some word which sounded natural in Russian, but to which 'cannibal' was only a rough approximation. But our local communists have taken over, from the defunct *Inprecor*[65] and similar sources, a whole series of these crudely translated phrases, and from force of habit have come to think of them as actual English expressions. The communist vocabulary of abuse (applied to fascists or socialists according to the 'line' of the moment) includes such terms as hyena, corpse, lackey, pirate, hangman, bloodsucker, mad dog, criminal, assassin. Whether at first, second or third hand, these are all translations, and by no means the kind of word that an English person naturally uses to express disapproval. The language of this kind is used with an astonishing indifference as to its meaning. Ask a journalist what a jackboot is, and you will find that he does not know. Yet he goes on talking about jack-boots. Or what is meant by 'to ride roughshod'? Very few people know that either. For that matter, in my experience, very few socialists know the meaning of the word 'proletariat'.

You can see a good example of Marxist language at its worst in the words 'lackey' and 'flunkey'. Pre-revolutionary Russia was still a feudal country in which hordes of idle men-

65. *Inprecor* - short for *International Press Correspondence*, under which title it was published for a time - was the official English-language publication of the Communist International (Comintern) from 1922 to 1938, when it was replaced by *World News and Views*.

servants were part of the social set-up; in that context 'lackey', as a word of abuse, had a meaning. In England, the social landscape is quite different. Except at public functions, the last time I saw a footman in livery was in 1921. And, in fact, in ordinary speech, the word 'flunkey' has been obsolete since the nineties, and the word 'lackey' for about a century. Yet they and other equally inappropriate words are dug up for pamphleteering purposes. The result is a style of writing that bears the same relation to writing real English as doing a jigsaw puzzle bears to painting a picture. It is just a question of fitting together a number of ready-made pieces. Just talk about hydra-headed jackboots riding roughshod over blood-stained hyenas, and you are all right. For confirmation of which, see almost any pamphlet issued by the Communist Party – or by any other political party, for that matter.

As I Please 17

24 March 1944

Of all the unanswered questions of our time, perhaps the most important is: 'What is fascism?'

One of the social survey organisations in America recently asked this question of a hundred different people, and got answers ranging from 'pure democracy' to 'pure diabolism'. In this country if you ask the average thinking person to define fascism, he usually answers by pointing to the German and Italian régimes. But this is very unsatisfactory, because even the major fascist states differ from one another a good deal in structure and ideology.

It is not easy, for instance, to fit Germany and Japan into the same framework, and it is even harder with some of the small states which are describable as fascist. It is usually assumed, for instance, that fascism is inherently warlike, that it thrives in an atmosphere of war hysteria and can only solve its economic problems by means of war preparation or foreign conquests. But clearly this is not true of, say, Portugal or the various south American dictatorships. Or again, anti-Semitism is supposed to be one of the distinguishing marks of fascism; but some fascist movements are not anti-Semitic. Learned controversies, reverberating for years on end in American magazines, have not even been able to determine whether or not fascism is a form of capitalism. But still, when we apply the term 'fascism' to Germany or Japan or Mussolini's Italy, we know broadly what we mean. It is in internal politics that this word has lost the last vestige of meaning. For if you examine the press you will find that there is almost no set of people – certainly no political party or organised body of any kind – which has not been denounced as fascist during the past ten years.

Here I am not speaking of the verbal use of the term 'fascist'. I am speaking of what I have seen in print. I have seen the words 'fascist in sympathy', or 'of fascist tendency', or just plain 'fascist', applied in all seriousness to the following bodies of people:

Conservatives: All Conservatives, appeasers or anti-appeasers, are held to be subjectively pro-fascist. British rule in India and the colonies is held to be indistinguishable from Nazism. Organisations of what one might call a patriotic and traditional type are labelled crypto-fascist or 'fascist-minded'. Examples are the Boy Scouts, the Metropolitan Police, MI5, the British Legion. Key phrase: 'The public schools are breeding-grounds of fascism.'

Socialists: Defenders of old-style capitalism (example, Sir Ernest Benn)[66] maintain that socialism and fascism are the same thing. Some Catholic journalists maintain that socialists have been the principal collaborators in the Nazi-occupied countries. The same accusation is made from a different angle by the Communist Party during its ultra-left phases. In the period 1930–35 the *Daily Worker* habitually referred to the Labour Party as the Labour fascists. This is echoed by other left extremists such as anarchists. Some Indian nationalists consider the British trade unions to be fascist organisations.

Communists: A considerable school of thought (examples, Rauschning,[67] Peter Drucker,[68] James Burnham,[69] F. A. Voigt)[70] refuses to recognise a difference between the

---

66. Sir Ernest Benn (1875–1954) was a publisher and a prolific propagandist for laissez-faire capitalism. His brother, William Wedgwood Benn, was father of Tony Benn, the Labour politician.
67. Hermann Rauschning (1887–1982) was a German conservative landowner who joined the Nazis but fled Germany in the mid-1930s. His books *Hitler Speaks* (London: Thornton Butterworth, 1939) and *Germany's Revolution of Destruction* (London: William Heinemann, 1939) were the first critical accounts of the Third Reich from an insider to appear in English, although the former has since been discredited.
68. Peter Drucker (1909–2005), best known today as a management theorist, was in the 1940s a journalist and polemicist. His book *The End of Economic Man: The Origins of Totalitarianism* (London: William Heinemann, 1939) is notable for its prediction of an alliance between Germany and Russia, although it got the details rather wrong. Orwell reviewed his *The Future of Industrial Man* (London: William Heinemann, 1943) in the *Manchester Evening News* on 3 January 1946.
69. For James Burnham, see note 40.
70. F. A. Voigt (1892–1957) was the *Manchester Guardian*'s diplomatic correspondent in the 1930s and one of the few journalists in the liberal or left-wing national press to oppose appeasement. Born in London of German parents, he worked as a propagandist for the British government during the Second World War. His book on the 1930s crisis, *Unto Caesar* (London: Constable, 1938), is notable as a precursor of 1950s theories of totalitarianism that emphasised the similarities of fascist and communist societies. He published his own anti-appeasement newsletter, the *Arrow*, from January to June 1939.

Nazi and Soviet régimes, and holds that all fascists and communists are aiming at approximately the same thing and are even to some extent the same people. Leaders in the *Times* (pre-war) have referred to the USSR as a 'fascist country'. Again from a different angle this is echoed by anarchists and Trotskyists.

Trotskyists: Communists charge the Trotskyists proper, i.e. Trotsky's own organisation, with being a crypto-fascist organisation in Nazi pay. This was widely believed on the left during the Popular Front period. In their ultra-right phases the communists tend to apply the same accusation to all factions to the left of themselves, e.g. Common Wealth[71] or the ILP.

Catholics: Outside its own ranks, the Catholic church is almost universally regarded as pro-fascist, both objectively and subjectively.

War resisters: Pacifists and others who are anti-war are frequently accused not only of making things easier for the Axis, but of becoming tinged with pro-fascist feeling.

Supporters of the war: War resisters usually base their case on the claim that British imperialism is worse than Nazism, and tend to apply the term 'fascist' to anyone who wishes for a military victory. The supporters of the People's Convention came near to claiming that willingness to resist a Nazi invasion was a sign of fascist sympathies. The Home Guard was denounced as a fascist organisation as soon as it appeared. In addition, the whole of the left tends to equate militarism with fascism. Politically conscious private soldiers nearly always refer to their officers as 'fascist-minded' or 'natural

---

71. Common Wealth was a left-wing political party set up in July 1942 through the merger of the 1941 Committee, led by the author and broadcaster J. B. Priestley (1894–1984), and the Forward March movement, led by the Christian socialist MP Richard Acland (1906–90), the scion of a West Country landowning family who had been elected for Barnstaple in 1935 as a Liberal.

Both the 1941 Committee and Forward March had been created to campaign for greater planning to increase the efficiency of the war effort, and Common Wealth adopted an austere ethical socialist stance, advocating a massive extension of planning and common ownership, constitutional reform and greater honesty in political life. Priestley soon withdrew from his leadership role in the new party, leaving Acland as the figurehead.

Although Labour and the Tories had agreed not to contest each other's seats in parliamentary by-elections for the duration of the war, Common Wealth ran against the Tories and won spectacular by-election victories at Eddisbury, Skipton and Chelmsford. It had great hopes of making a breakthrough in the 1945 general election but in the event won only one seat. Most Common Wealth members joined Labour.

Acland, who lost Barnstaple in 1945, was elected as Labour MP for Gravesend in 1947, resigning in 1955 (and unsuccessfully fighting a by-election) in protest at British development of the hydrogen bomb. Orwell wrote a largely sympathetic profile of Acland that was published anonymously in the *Observer* on 23 May 1943.

On Common Wealth, see Angus Calder, *The People's War: Britain 1939–1945* (London: Jonathan Cape, 1969), chapter 9.

fascists'. Battle-schools, spit and polish, saluting of officers are all considered conducive to fascism. Before the war, joining the Territorials was regarded as a sign of fascist tendencies. Conscription and a professional army are both denounced as fascist phenomena.

Nationalists: Nationalism is universally regarded as inherently fascist, but this is held only to apply to such national movements as the speaker happens to disapprove of. Arab nationalism, Polish nationalism, Finnish nationalism, the Indian Congress Party, the Muslim League, Zionism, and the IRA are all described as fascist but not by the same people.

It will be seen that, as used, the word 'fascism' is almost entirely meaningless. In conversation, of course, it is used even more wildly than in print. I have heard it applied to farmers, shopkeepers, Social Credit, corporal punishment, fox-hunting, bull-fighting, the 1922 Committee, the 1941 Committee, Kipling, Gandhi, Chiang Kai-Shek, homosexuality, Priestley's broadcasts, Youth Hostels, astrology, women, dogs and I do not know what else.

Yet underneath all this mess there does lie a kind of buried meaning. To begin with, it is clear that there are very great differences, some of them easy to point out and not easy to explain away, between the régimes called fascist and those called democratic. Secondly, if 'fascist' means 'in sympathy with Hitler', some of the accusations I have listed above are obviously very much more justified than others. Thirdly, even the people who recklessly fling the word 'fascist' in every direction attach at any rate an emotional significance to it. By 'fascism' they mean, roughly speaking, something cruel, unscrupulous, arrogant, obscurantist, anti-liberal and anti-working-class. Except for the relatively small number of fascist sympathisers, almost any English person would accept 'bully' as a synonym for 'fascist'. That is about as near to a definition as this much-abused word has come.

But fascism is also a political and economic system. Why, then, cannot we have a clear and generally accepted definition of it? Alas! we shall not get one – not yet, anyway. To say why would take too long, but basically it is because it is impossible to define fascism satisfactorily without making admissions which neither the fascists themselves, nor the Conservatives, nor socialists of any colour, are willing to make. All one can do for the moment is to use the word with a certain amount of circumspection and not, as is usually done, degrade it to the level of a swearword.

As I Please 18

31 March 1944

The other day I attended a press conference at which a newly arrived Frenchman, who was described as an 'eminent jurist' - he could not give his name or other specifications because of his family in France - set forth the French point of view on the recent execution of Pucheu.[72] I was surprised to note that he was distinctly on the defensive, and seemed to think that the shooting of Pucheu was a deed that would want a good deal of justification in British and American eyes. His main point was that Pucheu was not shot for political reasons, but for the ordinary crime of 'collaborating with the enemy', which has always been punishable by death under French law.

An American correspondent asked the question: 'Would collaborating with the enemy be equally a crime in the case of some petty official - an inspector of police, for example?' 'Absolutely the same,' answered the Frenchman. As he had just come from France he was presumably voicing French opinion, but one can assume that in practice only the most active collaborators will be put to death. Any really big-scale massacre, if it really happened, would be quite largely the punishment of the guilty by the guilty. For there is much evidence that large sections of the French population were more or less pro-German in 1940 and only changed their minds when they found out what the Germans were like.

I do not want people like Pucheu to escape, but a few very obscure quislings, including one or two Arabs, have been shot as well, and this whole business of taking vengeance on traitors and captured enemies raises questions which are strategic as well as moral. The point is that if we shoot too many of the small rats now we may have no stomach for dealing with the big ones when the time comes. It is difficult to believe that the fascist régimes can be thoroughly crushed without the killing of the responsible individuals, to the number of some hundreds or even thousands in each country. But it could well happen that all the truly guilty people will escape in the end, simply because public opinion has been sickened beforehand by hypocritical trials and cold-blooded executions.

72. Pierre Pucheu (1899–1944), disgraced former interior minister in the collaborationist French Vichy regime 1941–2, fled to north Africa with the intention of defecting to the Free French but was arrested, tried and found guilty of collaboration. De Gaulle refused to commute the death sentence despite the pleas of other defectors from Vichy. Pucheu's reception contrasted sharply with that of Admiral Darlan in 1942, who was welcomed by the Americans and given command of French north Africa before being assassinated by a French monarchist (see note 9).

In effect this was what happened in the last war. Who that was alive in those years does not remember the maniacal hatred of the Kaiser that was fostered in this country? Like Hitler in this war, he was supposed to be the cause of all our ills. No one doubted that he would be executed as soon as caught, and the only question was what method would be adopted. Magazine articles were written in which the rival merits of boiling in oil, drawing and quartering and breaking on the wheel were carefully examined. The Royal Academy exhibitions were full of allegorical pictures of incredible vulgarity, showing the Kaiser being thrown into Hell. And what came of it in the end? The Kaiser retired to Holland and (though he had been 'dying of cancer' in 1915) lived another twenty-two years, one of the richest men in Europe.

So also with all the other 'war criminals'. After all the threats and promises that had been made, no war criminals were tried: to be exact, a dozen people or so were put on trial, given sentences of imprisonment and soon released. And though, of course, the failure to crush the German military caste was due to the conscious policy of the Allied leaders, who were terrified of revolution in Germany, the revulsion of feeling in ordinary people helped to make it possible. They did not want revenge when it was in their power. The Belgian atrocities, Miss Cavell, the U-boat captains who had sunk passenger ships without warning and machine-gunned the survivors - somehow it was all forgotten. Ten million innocent men had been killed, and no one wanted to follow it up by killing a few thousand guilty ones.

Whether we do or don't shoot the fascists and quislings who happen to fall into our hands is probably not very important in itself. What is important is that revenge and 'punishment' should have no part in our policy or even in our day-dreams. Up to date, one of the mitigating features of this war is that in this country there has been very little hatred. There has been none of the nonsensical racialism that there was last time - no pretence that all Germans have faces like pigs, for instance. Even the word 'Hun' has not really popularised itself. The Germans in this country, mostly refugees, have not been well treated, but they have not been meanly persecuted as they were last time. In the last war it would have been very unsafe, for instance, to speak German in a London street. Wretched little German bakers and hairdressers had their shops sacked by the mob, German music fell out of favour, even the breed of dachshunds almost disappeared because no one wanted to have a 'German dog'. And the weak British attitude in the early period of German rearmament had a direct connexion with those follies of the war years.

Hatred is an impossible basis for policy, and curiously enough it can lead to over-softness as well as to over-toughness. In the war of 1914–18 the British people were whipped up into a hideous frenzy of hatred, they were fed on preposterous lies about crucified Belgian babies and German factories where corpses were made into margarine: and then as soon as the war stopped they suffered the natural revulsion, which was all the stronger because the troops came home, as British troops usually do, with a warm admiration for the enemy. The result was an exaggerated pro-German reaction which set in about 1920 and lasted till Hitler was well in the saddle. Throughout those years all 'enlightened' opinion (see any number of the *Daily Herald*[73] before 1929, for instance) held it as an article of faith that Germany bore no responsibility for the war. Treitschke, Bernhardi, the Pan-Germans, the 'nordic' myth, the open boasts about 'Der Tag' which the Germans had been making from 1900 onwards – all this went for nothing. The Versailles Treaty was the greatest infamy the world has ever seen: few people had even heard of Brest-Litovsk. All this was the price of that four years' orgy of lying and hatred.

Anyone who tried to awaken public opinion during the years of fascist aggression from 1933 onwards knows what the after-effects of that hate propaganda were like. 'Atrocities' had come to be looked on as synonymous with 'lies'. But the stories about the German concentration camps were atrocity stories: therefore they were lies – so reasoned the average man. The left-wingers who tried to make the public see that fascism was an unspeakable horror were fighting against their own propaganda of the past fifteen years.

73. The *Herald*, which grew out of a strike bulletin in 1912, was until 1922 a paper of the far left (during the First World War a weekly), edited from 1913 to 1922 by the charismatic pacifist socialist George Lansbury (1859–1940). Strapped for cash, Lansbury persuaded the Trades Union Congress to take it over in 1922 and it moved into the Labour mainstream, but it remained well to the left of the Labour leadership for the rest of the 1920s under the editorships of Hamilton Fyfe (1869–1951, editor 1922–6) and William Mellor (1888–1942, editor 1926–30, later the first editor of *Tribune*, on whom see *Tribune* biographies, p. 396 of this volume). In 1930, however, Ernest Bevin, the leader of the Transport and General Workers' Union and the key trade unionist on the *Daily Herald* board, persuaded Odhams Press to take a half-share of ownership of the paper and to assume its commercial direction. The *Herald* immediately took a much more market-oriented approach, relaunching and initiating a circulation war for sales against other popular papers by recruiting an army of canvassers to knock on doors offering insurance and gifts in return for subscriptions. It worked, in so far as the *Herald*'s circulation leapt from 800,000 in 1929 to two million in 1932, briefly making it the world's largest-circulation daily (until it was overtaken by Beaverbrook's *Daily Express*). But the pact with the capitalist devil had its price. Successive editors in the 1930s and 1940s – Will Stevenson (editor 1931–6), Francis Williams (1903–70, editor 1936–40, later press secretary for Clement Attlee at 10 Downing Street) and Percy Cudlipp (1905–62, editor 1940–53) – complained that Odhams, in the shape of Julius Elias (1873–1946), from 1937 Lord Southwood, had no concern for anything but the bottom line, ruthlessly pared editorial budgets and insisted on toning down anything that might put off advertisers, including (pre-1939) pessimistic stories on the international crisis. The TUC, meanwhile, took an interest in all aspects of the *Herald*'s editorial policy and suppressed stories that did not fit with the official Labour Party line. See Huw Richards, *The Bloody Circus: The* Daily Herald *and the Left* (London: Pluto Press, 1997) and Adrian Smith, 'The Fall and Fall of the Third *Daily Herald*, 1930–64', in Peter Catterall, Colin Seymour-Ure and Adrian Smith (eds), *Northcliffe's Legacy: Aspects of the British Popular Press 1896–1996* (Basingstoke: Macmillan, 2000).

That is why – though I would not save creatures like Pucheu even if I could – I am not happy when I see trials of 'war criminals', especially when they are very petty criminals and when witnesses are allowed to make inflammatory political speeches. Still less am I happy to see the left associating itself with schemes to partition Germany, enrol millions of Germans in forced-labour gangs and impose reparations which will make the Versailles reparations look like a bus fare. All these vindictive day-dreams, like those of 1914–18, will simply make it harder to have a realistic post-war policy. If you think now in terms of 'making Germany pay', you will quite likely find yourself praising Hitler in 1950. Results are what matter, and one of the results we want from this war is to be quite sure that Germany will not make war again. Whether this is best achieved by ruthlessness or generosity I am not certain: but I am quite certain that either of these will be more difficult if we allow ourselves to be influenced by hatred.

As I Please 19

7 April 1944

Sometimes, on top of a cupboard or at the bottom of a drawer, you come on a pre-war newspaper, and when you have got over your astonishment at its enormous size, you find yourself marvelling at its almost unbelievable stupidity. It happens that I have just come across a copy of the *Daily Mirror* of January 21st, 1936. One ought not, perhaps, to draw too many inferences from this one specimen, because the *Daily Mirror* was in those days our second silliest daily paper (the *Sketch* led, of course, as it still does),[74] and because this

74. The *Daily Mirror* (launched 1903) and the *Daily Sketch* (launched 1908) were in the mid-1930s the only British tabloid dailies – the rest of the national daily press was broadsheet – and both were shamelessly trivial, populist in tone and politically reactionary. (The *Mirror* was owned by Lord Rothermere, the *Sketch* by Lord Kemsley.) The *Sketch* stuck to its formula until its death in 1970 (though its name was changed to the *Daily Graphic* between 1946 and 1952), but the *Mirror* changed tack in the mid-1930s after Rothermere, convinced that it was going nowhere, decided to sell off his shares in it. Under the influence of Cecil King, Guy Bartholomew and Hugh Cudlipp, the paper adopted an even more sensationalist approach to news and, increasingly, a populist left-of-centre political position – and its circulation rocketed. By 1944, it was second only to Beaverbrook's *Express* in circulation, and its pro-Labour stance in the run-up to the 1945 general election is often cited as a reason Labour won such a massive landslide. On the *Mirror*, see Ruth Dudley Edwards, *Newspapermen: Hugh Cudlipp, Cecil Harmsworth King, and the Glory Days of Fleet Street* (London: Secker and Warburg, 2003), Maurice Edelman, *The Mirror: A Political History* (London: Hamish Hamilton, 1966) and Chris Horrie, *Tabloid Nation: From the Birth of the* Daily Mirror *to the Death of the Tabloid* (London: Andre Deutsch, 2004).

particular number contains the announcement of the death of George V. It is not, therefore, entirely typical. But still, it is worth analysing, as an extreme example of the kind of stuff that was fed to us in the between-war years. If you want to know why your house has been bombed, why your son is in Italy, why the income tax is ten shillings in the pound and the butter ration is only just visible without a microscope, here is part of the reason.

The paper consists of 28 pages. Of these the first 17 are devoted in their entirety to the dead King and the rest of the royal family. There is a history of the King's life, articles on his activities as statesman, family man, soldier, sailor, big and small game shot, motorist, broadcaster and what-not, with, of course, photographs innumerable. Except for one advertisement and one or two letters, you would not gather from these first 17 pages that any other topic could possibly interest the *Daily Mirror*'s readers. On page 18 there appears the first item unconnected with royalty. Needless to say this is the comic strip. Pages 18 to 23 inclusive are entirely given up to amusement guides, comic articles, and so forth. On page 24 some news begins to creep in, and you read of a highway robbery, a skating contest, and the forthcoming funeral of Rudyard Kipling. There are also some details about a snake at the zoo which is refusing its food. Then on page 26 comes the *Daily Mirror*'s sole reference to the real world, with the headline:

BOMBING PLEDGE BY DUCE
NO MORE ATTACKS ON RED CROSS

Underneath this, to the extent of about half a column, it is explained that il Duce 'deplores' the attacks on the Red Cross, which were not committed 'wilfully', and it is added that the League of Nations has just turned down Abyssinia's requests for assistance and refused to investigate the charges of Italian atrocities. Turning to more congenial topics the *Daily Mirror* then follows up with a selection of murders, accidental deaths and the secret wedding of Earl Russell. The last page of the paper is headed in huge letters: LONG LIVE KING EDWARD VIII, and contains a short biography and a highly idealised photograph of the man whom the Conservative Party were to sack like a butler a year later.

Among the topics not mentioned in this issue of the *Daily Mirror* are the unemployed (two or three millions of them at that date), Hitler, the progress of the Abyssinian war, the disturbed political situation in France, and the trouble already obviously blowing up in Spain. And though this is an extreme instance, nearly all newspapers of those days were more or less like that. No real information about current affairs was allowed into them if it could possibly be kept out. The world – so the readers of the gutter press were taught – was a cosy place dominated by royalty, crime, beauty-culture, sport, pornography and animals.

No one who makes the necessary comparisons can possibly doubt that our newspapers are far more intelligent than they were five years ago. Partly it is because they are so much smaller. There are only four pages or so to be filled, and the war news necessarily crowds out the rubbish. But there is also a far greater willingness to talk in a grown-up manner, to raise uncomfortable topics, to give the important news the big headlines, than there used to be, and this is bound up with the increased power of the journalist as against the advertiser. The unbearable silliness of English newspapers from about 1900 onward has had two main causes. One is that nearly the whole of the press is in the hands of a few big capitalists who are interested in the continuance of capitalism and therefore in preventing the public from learning to think: the other is that in peace time newspapers live off advertisements for consumption goods, building societies, cosmetics and the like, and are therefore interested in maintaining a 'sunshine mentality' which will induce people to spend money. Optimism is good for trade, and more trade means more advertisements. Therefore, don't let people know the facts about the political and economic situation; divert their attention to giant pandas, channel swimmers, royal weddings and other soothing topics. The first of these causes still operates, but the other has almost lapsed. It is now so easy to make a newspaper pay, and internal trade has dwindled so greatly, that the advertiser has temporarily lost his grip. At the same time there has been an increase in censorship and official interference, but this is not nearly so crippling and not nearly so conducive to sheer silliness. It is better to be controlled by bureaucrats than by common swindlers. In proof of which, compare the *Evening Standard*, the *Daily Mirror* or even the *Daily Mail* with the things they used to be.[75]

And yet the newspapers have not got back their prestige - on the contrary they have steadily lost prestige as against the wireless - partly because they have not yet lived down their pre-war follies, but partly also because all but a few of them retain their 'stunt' make-up and their habit of pretending that there is news when there is no news. Although far more willing than they used to be to raise serious issues, most of the papers remain completely reckless about details of fact. The belief that what is 'in the papers' must be true has been gradually evaporating ever since Northcliffe[76] set out to vulgarise

75. The *Evening Standard* was owned by Lord Beaverbrook, proprietor of the *Daily Express*. Beaverbrook was notoriously interventionist as a proprietor and the *Express* was in the vanguard of support for appeasement in the 1930s - it famously ran a front page declaring 'There will be no war' in summer 1939 - but he let the *Standard* take a very different line. His editors in the late 1930s and early 1940s - Percy Cudlipp, Reginald Thompson, Frank Owen and Michael Foot - were all left-wing opponents of appeasement. Foot was its editor at the time Orwell wrote this column.

76. Alfred Harmsworth (1865-1921) was the greatest of the press barons of the early twentieth century. He launched the *Daily Mail* in 1896 and the *Daily Mirror* in 1904, became Lord Northcliffe in 1905, and acquired the *Observer* the same year and the *Times* three years later. There are several biographies but the best is J. Lee Thompson, *Northcliffe: Press Baron in Politics 1865–1922* (London: John Murray, 2000).

journalism, and the war has not yet arrested the process. Many people frankly say that they take in such and such a paper because it is lively, but that they don't believe a word of what it says.

Meanwhile the BBC, so far as its news goes, has gained prestige since about 1940. 'I heard it on the wireless' is now almost equivalent to 'I know it must be true'. And throughout most of the world BBC news is looked on as more reliable than that of the other belligerent nations.

How far is this justified? So far as my own experience goes, the BBC is much more truthful, in a negative way, than the majority of newspapers, and has a much more responsible and dignified attitude towards news. It tells less direct lies, makes more effort to avoid mistakes, and – the thing the public probably values – keeps the news in better proportion. But none of this alters the fact that the decline in the prestige of the newspapers as against the radio is a disaster.

Radio is an inherently totalitarian thing, because it can only be operated by the government or by an enormous corporation, and in the nature of things it cannot give the news anywhere near so exhaustively as a newspaper. In the case of the BBC you have the additional fact that, though it doesn't tell deliberate lies, it simply avoids every awkward question. In even the most stupid or reactionary newspaper every subject can at least be raised, if only in the form of a letter. If you had nothing but the wireless to go upon, there would be some surprising gaps in your information. The press is of its nature a more liberal, more democratic thing, and the press lords who have dirtied its reputation, and the journalists who have more or less knowingly lent themselves to the process, have a lot to answer for.

As I Please 20

14 April 1944

The April issue of *Common Wealth* devotes several paragraphs to the problem of the falling British birthrate. A good deal of what it says is true, but it also lets drop the following remarks:

> The know-alls are quick to point to contraceptives, nutritional errors, infertility, selfishness, economic insecurity, etc, as basic causes of decline. But facts do not support them. In Nazi Germany, where contraceptives are illegal, the birthrate has reached a record low ebb, whereas in the Soviet Union, where there are no such

> restrictions, population is healthily on the up and up . . . Reproduction, as the Peckham experiment[77] has helped to prove, is stimulated in an environment marked by fellowship and cooperation . . . Once meaning and purpose are restored to life, the wheels of production are kept humming, and life is again an adventure instead of just an endurance, we shall hear no more of the baby shortage.

It is not fair to the public to treat all-important subjects in this slapdash way. To begin with, you would gather from the passage quoted above that Hitler lowered the German birthrate. On the contrary, he raised it to levels unheard-of during the Weimar Republic. Before the war it was above replacement level, for the first time in many years. The catastrophic drop in the German birthrate began in 1942, and must have been partly caused by so many German males being away from home. Figures cannot be available yet, but the Russian birthrate must also certainly have dropped over the same period.

You would also gather that the high Russian birthrate dates from the revolution. But it was also high in Czarist times. Nor is there any mention of the countries where the birthrate is highest of all, that is, India, China, and (only a little way behind) Japan. Would it be accurate to say, for instance, that a south Indian peasant's life is 'an adventure instead of just an endurance'?

The one thing that can be said with almost complete certainty on this subject is that a high birthrate goes with a low standard of living, and vice versa. There are few if any real exceptions to this. Otherwise the question is exceedingly complex. It is, all the same, vitally important to learn as much about it as we can, because there will be a calamitous drop in our own population unless the present trend is reversed within ten or, at most, twenty years. One ought not to assume, as some people do, that this is impossible, for such changes of trend have often happened before. The experts are proving now that our population will be only a few millions by the end of this century, but they were also proving in 1870 that by 1940 it would be 100 millions. To reach replacement level again, our birthrate would not have to take such a sensational upward turns as, for instance, the Turkish birthrate did after Mustapha Kemal took over. But the first necessity is to find out why populations rise and fall, and it is just as unscientific to assume that a high birthrate is a byproduct of socialism as to swallow everything that is said on the subject by childless Roman Catholic priests.

* * *

77. The 'Peckham experiment' was an innovative preventative health care centre in south-east London set up in 1935.

When I read of the goings-on in the House of Commons the week before last, I could not help being reminded of a little incident that I witnessed twenty years ago and more.

It was at a village cricket match. The captain of one side was the local squire who, besides being exceedingly rich, was a vain, childish man to whom the winning of this match seemed extremely important. Those playing on his side were all or nearly all his own tenants.

The squire's side were batting, and he himself was out and was sitting in the pavilion. One of the batsmen accidentally hit his own wicket at about the same moment as the ball entered the wicketkeeper's hands. 'That's not out,' said the squire promptly, and went on talking to the person beside him. The umpire, however, gave a verdict of 'out', and the batsman was half-way back to the pavilion before the squire realised what was happening. Suddenly he caught sight of the returning batsman, and his face turned several shades redder.

'What!' he cried, 'he's given him out? Nonsense! Of course he's not out!' And then, standing up, he cupped his hands and shouted to the umpire: 'Hi, what did you give that man out for? He wasn't out at all!' The batsman had halted. The umpire hesitated, then recalled the batsman to the wicket and the game went on. I was only a boy at the time, and this incident seemed to me about the most shocking thing I had ever seen. Now, so much do we coarsen with the passage of time, my reaction would merely be to inquire whether the umpire was the squire's tenant as well.

* * *

Attacking Mr C. A. Smith and myself in the *Malvern Torch* for various remarks about the Christian religion, Mr Sidney Dark grows very angry because I have suggested that the belief in personal immortality is decaying. 'I would wager,' he says, 'that if a Gallup poll were taken seventy-five per cent (of the British population) would confess to a vague belief in survival.' Writing elsewhere during the same week, Mr Dark puts it at eighty-five per cent.

Now, I find it very rare to meet anyone, of whatever background, who admits to believing in personal immortality. Still, I think it quite likely that if you asked everyone the question and put pencil and paper in his hands, a fairly large number (I am not so free with my percentages as Mr Dark) would admit the possibility that after death there might be 'something'. The point Mr Dark has missed is that the belief, such as it is, hasn't the actuality it had for our forefathers. Never, literally never in recent years, have I met anyone who gave me the impression of believing in the next world as firmly as he believed in the existence of, for instance, Australia. Belief in the next world does not influence conduct as it would if it were genuine. With that endless existence beyond death to look forward to, how trivial our lives here would seem! Most Christians profess to believe in Hell. Yet have you ever met a Christian who seemed as afraid of Hell as he was of cancer? Even very devout Christians will make jokes about Hell. They wouldn't make jokes about leprosy, or RAF pilots with their faces burnt away: the subject is too painful. Here there springs into my mind a little triolet by the late G. K. Chesterton:

It's a pity that Poppa has sold his soul,
It makes him sizzle at breakfast so.
The money was useful, but still on the whole
It's a pity that Poppa has sold his soul
When he might have held on like the Baron de Coal,
And not cleared out when the price was low.
It's a pity that Poppa has sold his soul,
It makes him sizzle at breakfast so.

Chesterton, a Catholic, would presumably have said that he believed in Hell. If his next-door neighbour had been burnt to death he would not have written a comic poem about it, yet he can make jokes about somebody being fried for millions of years. I say that such belief has no reality. It is a sham currency, like the money in Samuel Butler's Musical Banks.

As I Please 21

21 April 1944

In a letter published in this week's *Tribune*, someone attacks me rather violently for saying that the BBC is a better source of news than the daily papers, and is so regarded by the public. I have never, he suggests, heard ordinary working men shouting 'Turn that dope off!' when the news bulletin comes on.

On the contrary, I have heard this frequently. Still more frequently I have seen the customers in a pub go straight on with their darts, music and so forth without the slightest slackening of noise when the news bulletin began. But it was not my claim that anyone likes the BBC, or thinks it interesting, or grown-up, or democratic, or progressive. I said only that people regard it as a relatively sound source of news. Again and again I have known people, when they see some doubtful item of news, wait to have it confirmed by the radio before they believe it. Social surveys show the same thing – i.e. that as against the radio the prestige of newspapers has declined.

And I repeat what I said before – that in my experience the BBC is relatively truthful and, above all, has a responsible attitude towards news and does not disseminate lies simply because they are 'newsy'. Of course, untrue statements are constantly being broadcast and anyone can tell you of instances. But in most cases this is due to genuine error, and the BBC sins much more by simply avoiding anything controversial than by direct propaganda. And after all – a point not met by our correspondent – its reputation abroad is comparatively high. Ask any refugee from Europe which of the belligerent radios is considered to be the most truthful. So also in Asia. Even in India, where the population are so hostile that they will not listen to British propaganda and will hardly listen to a British entertainment programme, they listen to BBC news because they believe that it approximates to the truth.

Even if the BBC passes on the British official lies, it does make some effort to sift the others. Most of the newspapers, for instance, have continued to publish without any query as to their truthfulness the American claims to have sunk the entire Japanese fleet several times over. The BBC, to my knowledge, developed quite early on an attitude of suspicion towards this and certain other unreliable sources. On more than one occasion I have known a newspaper to print a piece of news – and news unfavourable to Britain – on no other authority than the German radio, because it was 'newsy' and made a good 'par'.

If you see something obviously untruthful in a newspaper and ring up to ask 'Where did you get that from?' you are usually put off with the formula: 'I'm afraid Mr So-and-So is not in the office.' If you persist, you generally find that the story has no basis whatever but that it looked like a good bit of news, so in it went. Except where libel is involved, the average journalist is astonished and even contemptuous if anyone bothers about accuracy with regard to names, dates, figures and other details. And any daily journalist will tell you that one of the most important secrets of his trade is the trick of making it appear that there is news when there is no news.

Towards the end of May 1940, newspaper posters were prohibited in order to save paper. Several newspapers, however, continued to display posters for some time afterwards. On inquiry it was found that they were using old ones. Such headlines as 'Panzer Divisions Hurled Back' or 'French Army Standing Firm' could be used over and over again. Then came the period when the paper-sellers supplied their own posters with a slate and a bit of chalk, and in their hands the poster became a comparatively sober and truthful thing. It referred to something that was actually in the paper you were going to buy, and it usually picked out the real news and not some piece of sensational nonsense. The paper-sellers, who frequently did not know which way round a capital S goes, had a better idea of what is news, and more sense of responsibility towards the public, than their millionaire employers.

Our correspondent considers that the public and the journalists rather than the proprietors are to blame for the silliness of English newspapers. You could not, he implies, make an intelligent newspaper pay because the public wants tripe. I am not certain whether this is so. For the time being most of the tripe has vanished and newspaper circulations have not declined. But I do agree - and I said so - that the journalists share the blame. In allowing their profession to be degraded they have largely acted with their eyes open, whereas, I suppose, to blame somebody like Northcliffe[77] for making money in the quickest way is like blaming a skunk for stinking.

* * *

One mystery about the English language is why, with the biggest vocabulary in existence, it has to be constantly borrowing foreign words and phrases. Where is the sense, for instance, of saying *cul de sac* when you mean blind alley? Other totally unnecessary French phrases are *joie de vivre, amour propre, reculer pour mieux sauter, raison d'être, vis-à-vis, tête-à-tête, au pied de la lettre, esprit de corps*. There are dozens more of them. Other needless borrowings come from Latin (though there is a case for 'i.e.' and 'e.g.', which are useful abbreviations), and since the war we have been much infested by German words, *Gleichschaltung, Lebensraum, Weltanschauung, Wehrmacht, Panzerdivisionen* and others being flung about with great freedom. In nearly every case an English equivalent already exists or could easily be improvised. There is also a tendency to take over American slang phrases without understanding their meaning. For example, the expression 'barking up the wrong tree' is fairly widely used, but inquiry shows that most people don't know its origin nor exactly what it means.

Sometimes it is necessary to take over a foreign word, but in that case we should anglicise its pronunciation, as our ancestors used to do. If we really need the word 'café' (we got on well enough with 'coffee house' for two hundred years), it should either be spelled 'caffay' or pronounced 'cayfe'. 'Garage' should be pronounced 'garridge'. For what point is there in littering our speech with fragments of foreign pronunciation, very tiresome to anyone who does not happen to have learned that particular language?

And why is it that most of us never use a word of English origin if we can find a manufactured Greek one? One sees a good example of this in the rapid disappearance of English flower names. What until twenty years ago was universally called a snapdragon is now called an antirrhinum, a word no one can spell without consulting a dictionary. Forget-me-nots are coming more and more to be called myosotis. Many other names, red-hot poker, mind-your-own-business, love-lies-bleeding, London pride, are disappearing in favour of colourless Greek names out of botany textbooks. I had better not continue too long on this subject, because last time I mentioned flowers in this column an indignant lady wrote in to say that flowers are bourgeois. But I don't think it a good augury for the future of the English language that 'marigold' should be dropped in favour of 'calendula', while the pleasant little Cheddar pink loses its name and becomes merely *Dianthus caesius*.

As I Please 22

28 April 1944

On the night in 1940 when the big ack-ack barrage was fired over London for the first time, I was in Piccadilly Circus when the guns opened up, and I fled into the Café Royal to take cover. Among the crowd inside a good-looking, well-made youth of about twenty-five was making somewhat of a nuisance of himself with a copy of *Peace News*,[78] which he was forcing upon the attention of everyone at the neighbouring tables. I got into conversation with him, and the conversation went something like this:

> *The youth*: I tell you, it'll all be over by Christmas. There's obviously going to be a compromise peace. I'm pinning my faith to Sir Samuel Hoare. It's degrading company to be in, I admit, but still Hoare is on our side. So long as Hoare's in Madrid, there's always hope of a sell-out.
>
> *Orwell*: What about all these preparations that they're making against invasion – the pill-boxes that they're building everywhere, the LDVs, and so forth?
>
> *The youth*: Oh, that merely means that they're getting ready to crush the working class when the Germans get here. I suppose some of them might be fools enough to try to resist, but Churchill and the Germans between them won't take long to settle them. Don't worry, it'll soon be over.

---

78. *Peace News* was the weekly newspaper of the Peace Pledge Union, the main British pacifist organisation during the Second World War. The PPU began in 1934 with the publication of a letter from Dick Sheppard (1880–1937), canon of St Paul's Cathedral, in the *Manchester Guardian* and other papers, inviting men to send him a postcard giving their undertaking to 'renounce war and never again to support another'. Within a few months, 30,000 had done so, and in 1935 Dr H. R. L. Sheppard's Peace Movement was launched at a meeting in the Albert Hall. It became the Peace Pledge Union the following year, and by 1937, when Sheppard died, it had collected 100,000 signatories. On pacifism during the Second World War, see Angus Calder, *The People's War: Britain 1939–1945* (London: Jonathan Cape, 1969), chapter 8. *Peace News* was edited during the war years by John Middleton Murry (see note 38). It is still published.

Orwell: Do you really want to see your children grow up Nazis?

The youth: Nonsense! You don't suppose the Germans are going to encourage fascism in this country, do you? They don't want to breed up a race of warriors to fight against them. Their object will be to turn us into slaves. They'll encourage every pacifist movement they can lay hands on. That's why I'm a pacifist. They'll encourage people like me.

Orwell: And shoot people like me?

The youth: That would be just too bad.

Orwell: But why are you so anxious to remain alive?

The youth: So that I can get on with my work, of course.

It had come out in the conversation that the youth was a painter – whether good or bad I do not know, but, at any rate, sincerely interested in painting and quite ready to face poverty in pursuit of it. As a painter, he would probably have been somewhat better off under a German occupation than a writer or journalist would be. But still, what he said contained a very dangerous fallacy, now very widespread in the countries where totalitarianism has not actually established itself.

The fallacy is to believe that under a dictatorial government you can be free *inside*. Quite a number of people console themselves with this thought, now that totalitarianism in one form or another is visibly on the up-grade in every part of the world. Out in the street the loudspeakers bellow, the flags flutter from the rooftops, the police with their tommy-guns prowl to and fro, the face of the Leader, four feet wide, glares from every hoarding; but up in the attics the secret enemies of the régime can record their thoughts in perfect freedom – that is the idea, more or less. And many people are under the impression that this is going on now in Germany and other dictatorial countries.

Why is this idea false? I pass over the fact that modern dictatorships don't, in fact, leave the loopholes that the old-fashioned despotisms did; and also the probable weakening of the *desire* for intellectual liberty owing to totalitarian methods of education. The greatest mistake is to imagine that the human being is an autonomous individual. The secret freedom which you can supposedly enjoy under a despotic government is nonsense, because your thoughts are never entirely your own. Philosophers, writers, artists, even scientists, not only need encouragement and an audience, they need constant stimulation from other people. It is almost impossible to think without talking. If Defoe had really lived on a desert island he could not have written *Robinson Crusoe*, nor would he have wanted to. Take away freedom of speech, and the creative faculties dry up. Had the Germans really got to England my acquaintance of the Café Royal would soon have found his painting deteriorating, even if the Gestapo had let him alone. And when the lid is taken off Europe, I believe one of the things that will surprise us will be to find how little worth-while writing of any kind – even such things as diaries, for instance – has been produced in secret under the dictators.

* * *

Mr Basil Henriques, chairman of the East London Juvenile Court, has just been letting himself go on the subject of the Modern Girl. English boys, he says, are 'just grand', but it is a different story with girls:

> One seldom comes across a really bad boy. The war seems to have affected girls more than boys . . . Children now went to the pictures several times a week and saw what they imagined was the high life of America, when actually it was a great libel on that country. They also suffer from the effects of listening through the microphone to wild raucous jitterbugging noises called music . . . Girls of 14 now dress and talk like those of 18 and 19, and put the same filth and muck on their faces.

I wonder whether Mr Henriques knows (a) that well before the other war it was already usual to attribute juvenile crime to the evil example of the cinematograph, and (b) that the Modern Girl has been just the same for quite two thousand years?

One of the big failures in human history has been the agelong attempt to stop women painting their faces. The philosophers of the Roman empire denounced the frivolity of the modern woman in almost the same terms as she is denounced today. In the fifteenth century the church denounced the damnable habit of plucking the eyebrows. The English puritans, the Bolsheviks and the Nazis all attempted to discourage cosmetics, without success. In Victorian England rouge was considered so disgraceful that it was usually sold under some other name, but it continued to be used.

Many styles of dress, from the Elizabethan ruff to the Edwardian hobble skirt, have been denounced from the pulpit, without effect. In the 1920s, when skirts were at their shortest, the Pope decreed that women improperly dressed were not to be admitted to Catholic churches; but somehow feminine fashions remained unaffected. Hitler's 'ideal woman', an exceedingly plain specimen in a mackintosh, was exhibited all over Germany and much of the rest of the world, but inspired few imitators. I prophesy that English girls will continue to 'put filth and muck on their faces' in spite of Mr Henriques. Even in jail, it is said, the female prisoners redden their lips with the dye from the Post Office mail bags.

Just why women use cosmetics is a different question, but it seems doubtful whether sex attraction is the main object. It is very unusual to meet a man who does not think painting your fingernails scarlet is a disgusting habit, but hundreds of thousands of women go on doing it all the same. Meanwhile it might console Mr Henriques to know that though make-up persists, it is far less elaborate than it used to be in the days when

Victorian beauties had their faces 'enamelled', or when it was usual to alter the contour of your cheeks by means of 'plumpers', as described in Swift's poem, 'On a Beautiful Young Nymph Going to Bed'.

As I Please 23

5 May 1944

For anyone who wants a good laugh I recommend a book which was published about a dozen years ago, but which I only recently succeeded in getting hold of. This is I. A. Richards's *Practical Criticism*.[79]

Although mostly concerned with the general principles of literary criticism, it also describes an experiment that Mr Richards made with, or one should perhaps say on, his English students at Cambridge. Various volunteers, not actually students but presumably interested in English literature, also took part. Thirteen poems were presented to them, and they were asked to criticise them. The authorship of the poems was not revealed, and none of them was well enough known to be recognised at sight by the average reader. You are getting, therefore, specimens of literary criticism not complicated by snobbishness of the ordinary kind.

One ought not to be too superior, and there is no need to be, because the book is so arranged that you can try the experiment on yourself. The poems, unsigned, are all together at the end, and the authors' names are on a fold-over page which you need not look at till afterwards. I will say at once that I only spotted the authorship of two, one of which I knew already, and though I could date most of the others within a few decades, I made two bad bloomers, in one case attributing to Shelley a poem written in the nineteen-twenties. But still, some of the comments recorded by Dr Richards are startling. They go to show that many people who would describe themselves as lovers of poetry have no more notion of distinguishing between a good poem and a bad one than a dog has of arithmetic.

For example, a piece of completely spurious bombast by Alfred Noyes gets quite a lot of praise. One critic compares it to Keats. A sentimental ballad from *Rough Rhymes of a Padre*, by 'Woodbine Willie', also gets quite a good press. On the other hand, a

79. Ivor Armstrong Richards (1893–1979) was a literary critic and a proponent of Basic English (see note 47).

magnificent sonnet by John Donne gets a distinctly chilly reception. Dr Richards records only three favourable criticisms and about a dozen cold or hostile ones. One writer says contemptuously that the poem 'would make a good hymn', while another remarks, 'I can find no other reaction except disgust.' Donne was at that time at the top of his reputation and no doubt most of the people taking part in this experiment would have fallen on their faces at his name. D. H. Lawrence's poem 'The Piano' gets many sneers, though it is praised by a minority. So also with a short poem by Gerard Manley Hopkins. 'The worst poem I have ever read,' declares one writer, while another's criticism is simply 'Pish-posh!'

However, before blaming these youthful students for their bad judgment, let it be remembered that when some time ago somebody published a not very convincing fake of an eighteenth-century diary, the aged critic, Sir Edmund Gosse, librarian of the House of Lords, fell for it immediately. And there was also the case of the Parisian art critics, of I forget which 'school', who went into rhapsodies over a picture which was afterwards discovered to have been painted by a donkey with a paint-brush tied to its tail.

* * *

Under the heading 'We Are Destroying Birds that Save Us', the *News Chronicle*[80] notes that 'beneficial birds suffer from human ignorance. There is senseless persecution of the kestrel and barn owl. No two species of birds do better work for us.'

Unfortunately it isn't even from ignorance. Most of the birds of prey are killed off for the sake of that enemy of England, the pheasant. Unlike the partridge, the pheasant does not thrive in England, and apart from the neglected woodlands and the vicious game laws that it has been responsible for, all birds or animals that are suspected of eating its eggs or chicks are systematically wiped out. Before the war, near my village in Hertfordshire, I used to pass a stretch of fence where the gamekeeper kept his 'larder'. Dangling from the wires were the corpses of stoats, weasels, rats, hedgehogs, jays, owls, kestrels and sparrow-hawks. Except for the rats and perhaps the jays, all of these creatures are beneficial to agriculture. The stoats keep down the rabbits, the weasels eat mice, and so do the kestrels and sparrow-hawks, while the owls eat rats as well. It has been calculated that a barn owl destroys between 1,000 and 2,000 rats and mice in a year. Yet it has to be killed off for the sake of this useless bird which Rudyard Kipling correctly described as 'lord of many a shire'.

---

80. The *News Chronicle* was a popular Liberal daily, created in 1930 by the merger of the *Daily News* and the *Daily Chronicle*. Orwell was very ambivalent about it: it had been soft on the Chamberlain government's policy of appeasement in the 1930s and hosted some of the most shameless fellow-travellers with Stalinism both before and during the Second World War, but it also carried some of the best foreign correspondents. It struggled in the 1950s and was sold to the *Daily Mail* and closed in 1960.

* * *

We had to postpone announcing the results of the short story competition, but we are publishing the winning story next week. The runners-up will appear, I hope, in the two subsequent weeks.

I will set forth my opinions about the English short story another week, but I will say at once that of the five or six hundred stories that were sent in, the great majority were, in my judgment, very bad. A fairly large number of competitors, more than I had expected, had a story to tell, but too many of them simply gave the bare bones of the story, making it into an anecdote, without character interest and usually written in a slovenly way. Others sent in entries which were written with more distinction, but had no interest or development in them - being, in fact, sketches and not stories. A dismayingly large number dealt with Utopias, or took place in Heaven, or brought in ghosts or magic or something of that kind. I do admit, however, that it is not easy to write a story which is about real people, and in which something happens, within the compass of 1,800 words, and I do not believe there is much hope of English short stories improving till our magazines again swell to Victorian size.

As I Please 24

12 May 1944

Reading recently a batch of rather shallowly optimistic 'progressive' books, I was struck by the automatic way in which people go on repeating certain phrases which were fashionable before 1914. Two great favourites are 'the abolition of distance' and 'the disappearance of frontiers'. I do not know how often I have met with the statements that 'the aeroplane and the radio have abolished distance' and 'all parts of the world are now interdependent'.

Actually, the effect of modern inventions has been to increase nationalism, to make travel enormously more difficult, to cut down the means of communication between one country and another, and to make the various parts of the world less, not more dependent on one another for food and manufactured goods. This is not the result of the war. The same tendencies had been at work ever since 1918, though they were intensified after the world depression.

Take simply the instance of travel. In the nineteenth century some parts of the world were unexplored, but there was almost no restriction on travel. Up to 1914 you did not need a passport for any country except Russia. The European emigrant, if he could scrape together a few pounds for the passage, simply set sail for America or Australia, and when he got there no questions were asked. In the eighteenth century it had been quite normal and safe to travel in a country with which your own country was at war.

In our own time, however, travel has been becoming steadily more difficult. It is worth listing the parts of the world which were already inaccessible before the war started.

First of all, the whole of central Asia. Except perhaps for a very few tried communists, no foreigner has entered Soviet Asia for many years past. Tibet, thanks to Anglo-Russian jealousy, has been a closed country since about 1912. Sinkiang, theoretically part of China, was equally un-get-atable. Then the whole of the Japanese empire, except Japan itself, was practically barred to foreigners. Even India has been none too accessible since 1918. Passports were often refused even to British subjects – sometimes even to Indians!

Even in Europe the limits of travel were constantly narrowing. Except for a short visit it was very difficult to enter Britain, as many a wretched anti-fascist refugee discovered. Visas for the USSR were issued very grudgingly from about 1935 onwards. All the fascist countries were barred to anyone with a known anti-fascist record. Various areas could only be crossed if you undertook not to get out of the train. And along all the frontiers were barbed wire, machine-guns and prowling sentries, frequently wearing gas-masks.

As to migration, it had practically dried up since the nineteen-twenties. All the countries of the New World did their best to keep the immigrant out unless he brought considerable sums of money with him. Japanese and Chinese immigration into the Americas had been completely stopped. Europe's Jews had to stay and be slaughtered because there was nowhere for them to go, whereas in the case of the Czarist pogroms forty years earlier they had been able to flee in all directions. How, in the face of all this, anyone can say that modern methods of travel promote intercommunication between different countries defeats me.

Intellectual contacts have also been diminishing for a long time past. It is nonsense to say that the radio puts people in touch with foreign countries. If anything, it does the opposite. No ordinary person ever listens in to a foreign radio; but if in any country large numbers of people show signs of doing so, the government prevents it either by ferocious penalties, or by confiscating short-wave sets, or by setting up jamming stations. The result is that each national radio is a sort of totalitarian world of its own, braying propaganda night and day to people who can listen to nothing else. Meanwhile, literature grows less and less international. Most totalitarian countries bar foreign newspapers and let in only a small number of foreign books, which they subject to careful censorship and sometimes issue in garbled versions. Letters going from one country to another are habitually tampered with on the way. And in many countries, over the past dozen years, history books have been rewritten in far more nationalistic terms than before, so that children may grow up with as false a picture as possible of the world outside.

The trend towards economic self-sufficiency ('autarchy') which has been going on since about 1930 and has been intensified by the war, may or may not be reversible. The industrialisation of countries like India and South America increases their purchasing power and therefore ought, in theory, to help world trade. But what is not grasped by those who say cheerfully that 'all parts of the world are interdependent' is that they don't any longer have to be interdependent. In an age when wool can be made out of milk and rubber out of oil, when wheat can be grown almost on the Arctic Circle, when atebrin will do instead of quinine and vitamin C tablets are a tolerable substitute for fruit, imports don't matter very greatly. Any big area can seal itself off much more completely than in the days when Napoleon's Grand Army, in spite of the embargo, marched to Moscow wearing British overcoats. So long as the world tendency is towards nationalism and totalitarianism, scientific progress simply helps it along.

* * *

Here are some current prices. Small Swiss-made alarm clock, price before the war, 5/- or 10/-: present price, £3 15s. Second-hand portable typewriter, price before the war, £12 new: present price, £30. Small, very bad quality coconut fibre scrubbing-brush, price before the war, 3d: present price 1/9d. Gas lighter, price before the war, about 1/-: present price, 5/9d.

I could quote other similar prices. It is worth noticing that, for instance, the clock mentioned above must have been manufactured before the war at the old price. But, on the whole, the worst racket seems to be in second-hand goods – for instance, chairs, tables, clothes, watches, prams, bicycles and bed linen. On inquiry, I find that there is now a law against overcharging on second-hand goods. This comforts me a great deal, just as it must comfort the 18b-ers[81] to hear about *habeas corpus*, or Indian coolies to learn that all British subjects are equal before the law.

* * *

In Hooper's *Campaign of Sedan*[82] there is an account of the interview in which General de Wympffen tried to obtain the best possible terms for the defeated French army. 'It is to

81. The '18b-ers' were those interned without trial in 1939 and 1940 under Defence Regulation 18b because they were suspected of having Nazi sympathies.
82. George Hooper's *The Campaign of Sedan: The Downfall of the Second Empire* (London: George Bell, 1887) tells the story of the crucial action in the 1870 Franco-Prussian war.

your interest,' he said, 'from a political standpoint, to grant us honourable conditions . . . A peace based on conditions which would flatter the amour-propre of the army would be durable, whereas rigorous measures would awaken bad passions, and, perhaps, bring on an endless war between France and Prussia.'

Here Bismarck, the Iron Chancellor, chipped in, and his words are recorded from his memoirs:

> I said to him that we might build on the gratitude of a prince, but certainly not on the gratitude of a people – least of all on the gratitude of the French. That in France neither institutions nor circumstances were enduring; that governments and dynasties were constantly changing, and one need not carry out what the other had bound itself to do . . . As things stood it would be folly if we did not make full use of our success.

The modern cult of 'realism' is generally held to have started with Bismarck. That imbecile speech was considered magnificently 'realistic' then, and so it would be now. Yet what Wympffen said, though he was only trying to bargain for terms, was perfectly true. If the Germans had behaved with ordinary generosity (i.e. by the standards of the time) it might have been impossible to whip up the revanchiste spirit in France. What would Bismarck have said if he had been told that harsh terms now would mean a terrible defeat forty-eight years later? There is not much doubt of the answer: he would have said that the terms ought to have been harsher still. Such is 'realism' – and on the same principle, when the medicine makes the patient sick, the doctor responds by doubling the dose.

As I Please 25

19 May 1944

Miss Vera Brittain's pamphlet, *Seed of Chaos*, is an eloquent attack on indiscriminate or 'obliteration' bombing.[83] 'Owing to the RAF raids,' she says, 'thousands of helpless and

83. Vera Brittain (1893–1970) was a feminist pacifist writer. She is best known today for her autobiographical books *Testament of Youth* (London: Victor Gollancz, 1933), *Testament of Friendship* (London: Macmillan, 1940) and *Testament of Experience* (London: Victor Gollancz, 1957) but was also an accomplished novelist. She responded to Orwell in *Tribune* on 23 June 1944 and he replied in turn.

innocent people in German, Italian and German-occupied cities are being subjected to agonising forms of death and injury comparable to the worst tortures of the Middle Ages.' Various well-known opponents of bombing, such as General Franco and Major-General Fuller, are brought out in support of this. Miss Brittain is not, however, taking the pacifist standpoint. She is willing and anxious to win the war, apparently. She merely wishes us to stick to 'legitimate' methods of war and abandon civilian bombing, which she fears will blacken our reputation in the eyes of posterity. Her pamphlet is issued by the Bombing Restriction Committee, which has issued others with similar titles.

Now, no one in his senses regards bombing, or any other operation of war, with anything but disgust. On the other hand, no decent person cares tuppence for the opinion of posterity. And there is something very distasteful in accepting war as an instrument and at the same time wanting to dodge responsibility for its more obviously barbarous features. Pacifism is a tenable position; provided that you are willing to take the consequences. But all talk of 'limiting' or 'humanising' war is sheer humbug, based on the fact that the average human being never bothers to examine catchwords.

The catchwords used in this connexion are 'killing civilians', 'massacre of women and children' and 'destruction of our cultural heritage'. It is tacitly assumed that air bombing does more of this kind of thing than ground warfare.

When you look a bit closer, the first question that strikes you is: Why is it worse to kill civilians than soldiers? Obviously one must not kill children if it is in any way avoidable, but it is only in propaganda pamphlets that every bomb drops on a school or an orphanage. A bomb kills a cross-section of the population; but not quite a representative selection, because the children and expectant mothers are usually the first to be evacuated, and some of the young men will be away in the army. Probably a disproportionately large number of bomb victims will be middle-aged. (Up to date, German bombs have killed between six and seven thousand children in this country. This is, I believe, less than the number killed in road accidents in the same period.) On the other hand, 'normal' or 'legitimate' warfare picks out and slaughters all the healthiest and bravest of the young male population. Every time a German submarine goes to the bottom about fifty young men of fine physique and good nerves are suffocated. Yet people who would hold up their hands at the very words 'civilian bombing' will repeat with satisfaction such phrases as 'We are winning the Battle of the Atlantic'. Heaven knows how many people our blitz on Germany and the occupied countries has killed and will kill, but you can be quite certain it will never come anywhere near the slaughter that has happened on the Russian front.

War is not avoidable at this stage of history, and since it has to happen it does not seem to me a bad thing that others should be killed besides young men. I wrote in 1937: 'Sometimes it is a comfort to me to think that the aeroplane is altering the conditions of war. Perhaps when the next great war comes we may see that sight unprecedented in all history, a jingo with a bullet hole in him.' We haven't yet seen that (it is perhaps a contradiction in terms), but at any rate the suffering of this war has been shared out more evenly than the last one was. The immunity of the civilian, one of the things that have made war possible, has been shattered. Unlike Miss Brittain, I don't regret that. I can't feel that war is 'humanised' by being confined to the slaughter of the young and becomes 'barbarous' when the old get killed as well.

As to international agreements to 'limit' war, they are never kept when it pays to break them. Long before the last war the nations had agreed not to use gas, but they used it all the same. This time they have refrained, merely because gas is comparatively ineffective in a war of movement, while its use against civilian populations would be sure to provoke reprisals in kind. Against an enemy who can't hit back, e.g. the Abyssinians, it is used readily enough. War is of its nature barbarous, it is better to admit that. If we see ourselves as the savages we are, some improvement is possible, or at least thinkable.

* * *

A specimen of *Tribune*'s correspondence:

TO THE JEW-PAID EDITOR,
TRIBUNE,
LONDON.
JEWS IN THE POLISH ARMY
YOU ARE CONSTANTLY ATTACKING OUR GALLANT POLISH ALLY BECAUSE THEY KNOW HOW TO TREAT THE JEW PEST. THEY ALSO KNOW HOW TO TREAT ALL JEW-PAID EDITORS AND COMMUNIST PAPERS. WE KNOW YOU ARE IN THE PAY OF THE YIDS AND SOVIETS.

YOU ARE A FRIEND OF THE ENEMIES OF BRITAIN! THE DAY OF RECKONING IS AT HAND. BEWARE. ALL JEW PIGS WILL BE EXTERMINATED THE HITLER WAY - THE ONLY WAY TO GET RID OF THE YIDS.
PERISH JUDAH.

Typed on a Remington typewriter (postmark SW), and, what is to my mind an interesting detail, this is a carbon copy.

Anyone acquainted with the type will know that no assurance, no demonstration, no proof of the most solid kind would ever convince the writer of this that *Tribune* is not a communist paper and not in the pay of the Soviet government. One very curious characteristic of fascists - I am speaking of amateur fascists: I assume that the Gestapo are cleverer - is their failure to recognise that the parties of the left are distinct from one another and by no means aiming at the same thing. It is always assumed that they are all one gang, whatever the outward appearances may be. In the first number of Mosley's

British Union Quarterly, which I have by me (incidentally, it contains an article by no less a person than Major Vidkun Quisling), I note that even Wyndham Lewis[84] speaks of Stalin and Trotsky as though they were equivalent persons. Arnold Lunn,[85] in his *Spanish Rehearsal*, actually seems to suggest that Trotsky started the Fourth International on Stalin's instructions.

In just the same way, very few communists, in my experience, will believe that the Trotskyists are not in the pay of Hitler. I have sometimes tried the experiment of pointing out that if the Trotskyists were in the pay of Hitler, or of anybody, they would occasionally have some money. But it is no use, it doesn't register. So also with the belief in the machinations of the Jews, or the belief, widespread among Indian nationalists, that all Englishmen, of whatever political colour, are in secret conspiracy with one another. The belief in the Freemasons as a revolutionary organisation is the strangest of all. In this country it would be just as reasonable to believe such a thing of the Buffaloes.[86] Less than a generation ago, if not now, there were Catholic nuns who believed that at Masonic gatherings the Devil appeared in person, wearing full evening dress with a hole in the trousers for his tail to come through. In one form or another this kind of thing seems to attack nearly everybody, apparently answering to some obscure psychological need of our time.

As I Please 26

26 May 1944

I was talking the other day to a young American soldier, who told me – as quite a number of others have done – that anti-British feeling is completely general in the American army. He had only recently landed in this country, and as he came off the boat he asked the military policeman on the dock, 'How's England?'

'The girls here walk out with niggers,' answered the MP. 'They call them American Indians.'

---

84. For Wyndham Lewis, see note 14.

85. Arnold Lunn (1888–1974) was a famous skier and mountaineer who became a right-wing Catholic polemicist. *Spanish Rehearsal* (London: Hutchinson, 1937), his pro-Franco book on Spain, was savaged by Orwell in *Time and Tide* on 11 December 1937.

86. The Royal Antediluvian Order of Buffaloes was and is a quasi-Masonic order founded in the nineteenth century, with a membership largely consisting of businessmen.

That was the salient fact about England, from the MP's point of view. At the same time my friend told me that anti-British feeling is not violent and there is no very clearly defined cause of complaint. A good deal of it is probably a rationalisation of the discomfort most people feel at being away from home. But the whole subject of anti-British feeling in the United States badly needs investigation. Like anti-Semitism, it is given a whole series of contradictory explanations, and again like anti-Semitism, it is probably a psychological substitute for something else. What else is the question that needs investigating.

Meanwhile, there is one department of Anglo-American relations that seems to be going well. It was announced some months ago that no less than 20,000 English girls had already married American soldiers and sailors, and the number will have increased since. Some of these girls are being educated for their life in a new country at the 'Schools for Brides of US Servicemen' organised by the American Red Cross. Here they are taught practical details about American manners, customs and traditions - and also, perhaps, cured of the widespread illusion that every American owns a motor car and every American house contains a bathroom, a refrigerator and an electric washing-machine.

* * *

The May number of the *Matrimonial Post and Fashionable Marriage Advertiser* contains advertisements from 191 men seeking brides and over 200 women seeking husbands. Advertisements of this type have been running in a whole series of magazines since the sixties or earlier, and they are nearly always very much alike. For example:

> Bachelor, age 25, height 6ft 1in., slim, fond of horticulture, animals, children, cinema, etc, would like to meet lady, age 27 to 35, with love of flowers, nature, children, must be tall, medium build, Church of England.

The general run of them are just like that, though occasionally a more unusual note is struck. For instance:

> I'm 29, single, 5ft 10in., English, large build, kind, quiet, varied intellectual interests, firm moral background (registered unconditionally as absolute CO), progressive, creative, literary inclinations. A dealer in rare stamps, income variable but quite adequate. Strong swimmer, cyclist, slight stammer occasionally. Looking for the following rarity, amiable, adaptable, educated girl, easy on eye and ear, under 30, secretary type or similar, mentally adventurous, immune to mercenary and social incentives, bright sense of genuine humour, a reliable working partner. Capital unimportant, character vital.

The thing that is and always has been striking in these advertisements is that nearly all the applicants are remarkably eligible. It is not only that most of them are broad-minded, intelligent, home-loving, musical, loyal, sincere and affectionate, with a keen sense of humour and, in the case of women, a good figure: in the majority of cases they are financially OK as well. When you consider how fatally easy it is to get married, you would not imagine that a 36-year-old bachelor, 'dark hair, fair complexion, slim build, height 6 ft, well educated and of considerate, jolly and intelligent disposition, income £1,000 per annum and capital', would need to find himself a bride through the columns of a newspaper. And ditto with 'Adventurous young woman, left-wing opinions, modern outlook' with 'fairly full but shapely figure, medium colour curly hair, grey-blue eyes, fair skin, natural colouring, health exceptionally good, interested in music, art, literature, cinema, theatre, fond of walking, cycling, tennis, skating and rowing'. Why does such a paragon have to advertise?

It should be noted that the *Matrimonial Post* is entirely above-board and checks up carefully on its advertisers.

What these things really demonstrate is the atrocious loneliness of people living in big towns. People meet for work and then scatter to widely separated homes. Anywhere in inner London it is probably exceptional to know even the names of the people who live next door.

Years ago I lodged for a while in the Portobello Road. This is hardly a fashionable quarter, but the landlady had been lady's maid to some woman of title and had a good opinion of herself. One day something went wrong with the front door and my landlady, her husband and myself were all locked out of the house. It was evident that we should have to get in by an upper window, and as there was a jobbing builder next door I suggested borrowing a ladder from him. My landlady looked somewhat uncomfortable.

'I wouldn't like to do that,' she said finally. 'You see we don't know him. We've been here fourteen years, and we've always taken care not to know the people on either side of us. It wouldn't do, not in a neighbourhood like this. If you once begin talking to them they get familiar, you see.'

So we had to borrow a ladder from a relative of her husband's, and carry it nearly a mile with great labour and discomfort.

As I Please 27

2 June 1944

An extract from the Italian radio, about the middle of 1942, describing life in London:

> Five shillings were given for one egg yesterday, and one pound sterling for a kilogram of potatoes. Rice has disappeared, even from the black market, and peas have become the prerogative of millionaires. There is no sugar on the market, although small quantities are still to be found at prohibitive prices.

One day there will be a big, careful, scientific inquiry into the extent to which propaganda is believed. For instance, what is the effect of an item like the one above, which is fairly typical of the fascist radio? Any Italian who took it seriously would have to assume that Britain was due to collapse within a few weeks. When the collapse failed to happen, one would expect him to lose confidence in the authorities who had deceived him. But it is not certain that that is the reaction. For quite long periods, at any rate, people can remain undisturbed by obvious lies, either because they simply forget what is said from day to day or because they are under such a constant propaganda bombardment that they become anaesthetised to the whole business.

It seems clear that it pays to tell the truth when things are going badly, but it is by no means certain that it pays to be consistent in your propaganda. British propaganda is a good deal hampered by its efforts not to be self-contradictory. It is almost impossible, for instance, to discuss the colour question in a way that will please both the Boers and the Indians. The Germans are not troubled by a little thing like that. They just tell everyone what they think he will want to hear, assuming, probably rightly, that no one is interested in anyone else's problems. On occasion their various radio stations have even attacked one another.

One which aimed at middle-class fascists used sometimes to warn its listeners against the pseudo-left Worker's Challenge, on the ground that the latter was 'financed by Moscow'.

Another thing that that inquiry, if it ever takes place, will have to deal with is the magical properties of names. Nearly all human beings feel that a thing becomes different if you call it by a different name. Thus when the Spanish civil war broke out the BBC produced the name 'Insurgents' for Franco's followers. This covered the fact that they were rebels while making rebellion sound respectable. During the Abyssinian war Haile Selassie was called the Emperor by his friends and the Negus by his enemies. Catholics strongly resent being called Roman Catholics. The Trotskyists call themselves Bolshevik-Leninists but are refused this name by their opponents. Countries which have liberated themselves from a foreign conqueror or gone through a nationalist revolution almost invariably change their names, and some countries have a whole series of names, each with a different implication. Thus the USSR is called Russia or USSR (neutral or for short), Soviet Russia (friendly) and Soviet Union (very friendly). And it is a curious fact that of the six names by which our own country is called, the only one that does not tread on somebody or other's toes is the archaic and slightly ridiculous name 'Albion'.

* * *

Wading through the entries for the short story competition, I was struck once again by the disability that English short stories suffer in being all cut to a uniform length. The great short stories of the past are of all lengths from perhaps 1,500 words to 20,000. Most of Maupassant's stories, for instance, are very short, but his two masterpieces, 'Boule de Suif' and 'La Maison de Madame Tellier', are decidedly long. Poe's stories vary similarly. D. H. Lawrence's 'England, My England', Joyce's 'The Dead', Conrad's 'Youth', and many stories by Henry James, would probably be considered too long for any modern English periodical. So, certainly, would a story like Mérimée's 'Carmen'. This belongs to the class of 'long short' stories which have almost died out in this country, because there is no place for them. They are too long for the magazines and too short to be published as books. You can, of course, publish a book containing several short stories, but this is not often done because at normal times these books never sell.

It would almost certainly help to rehabilitate the short story if we could get back to the bulky nineteenth-century magazine, which had room in it for stories of almost any length. But the trouble is that in modern England monthly and quarterly magazines of any intellectual pretensions don't pay. Even the *Criterion*, perhaps the best literary paper we have ever had, lost money for sixteen years before expiring.[87]

Why? Because people were not willing to fork out the seven and sixpence that it cost. People won't pay that much for a mere magazine. But why then will they pay the same sum for a novel, which is no bulkier than the *Criterion*, and much less worth keeping? Because they don't pay for the novel directly. The average person never buys a new book, except perhaps a Penguin. But he does, without knowing it, buy quite a lot of books by paying twopence into lending libraries. If you could take a literary magazine out of the library just as you take a book, these magazines would become commercial propositions and would be able to enlarge their bulk as well as paying their contributors better. It is book-borrowing and not book-buying that keeps authors and publishers alive, and there seems no good reason why the lending library system should not be extended to magazines. Restore the monthly magazine - or make the weekly paper about a quarter of an inch fatter - and you might be able to restore the short story. And incidentally the book review, which for lack of elbow room has dwindled to a perfunctory summary, might become a work of art again, as it was in the days of the *Edinburgh* and the *Quarterly*.

* * *

87. The *Criterion* was founded and edited by T. S. Eliot. It was published quarterly from 1922 to 1939.

After reading the *Matrimonial Post* last week I looked in the Penguin Herodotus for a passage I vaguely remembered about the marriage customs of the Babylonians. Here it is:

> Once a year in each village the maidens of an age to marry were collected altogether into one place, while the men stood round them in a circle. Then a herald called up the damsels one by one and offered them for sale. He began with the most beautiful. When she was sold for no small sum of money, he offered for sale the one who came next to her in beauty . . . The custom was that when the herald had gone through the whole number of the beautiful damsels, he should then call up the ugliest and offer her to the men, asking who would agree to take her with the smallest marriage portion. And the man who offered to take the smallest sum had her assigned to him. The marriage portions were furnished by the money paid for the beautiful damsels, and thus the fairer maidens portioned out the uglier.

This custom seems to have worked very well and Herodotus is full of enthusiasm for it. He adds, however, that, like other good customs, it was already going out round about 450 BC.

As I Please 28

9 June 1944

Arthur Koestler's recent article in *Tribune*[88] set me wondering whether the book racket will start up again in its old vigour after the war, when paper is plentiful and there are other things to spend your money on.

Publishers have got to live, like anyone else, and you cannot blame them for advertising their wares, but the truly shameful feature of literary life before the war was the blurring of the distinction between advertisement and criticism. A number of the so-called reviewers, and especially the best-known ones, were simply blurb writers. The 'screaming' advertisement started some time in the 1920s, and as the competition to take up as much space and use as many superlatives as possible became fiercer, publishers' advertisements grew to be an important source of revenue to a number of papers. The literary pages of several well-known papers were practically owned by a handful of publishers, who had their quislings planted in all the important jobs. These wretches churned forth their praise – 'masterpiece', 'brilliant', 'unforgettable' and so forth – like so many mechanical pianos. A book coming from the right publishers could be absolutely certain not only of favourable

88. For Arthur Koestler, see Introduction, note 16. The article referred to here was one giving advice on the reliability of book reviewers, published on 28 April 1944.

reviews, but of being placed on the 'recommended' list which industrious book borrowers would cut out and take to the library the next day.

If you published books at several different houses you soon learned how strong the pressure of advertisement was. A book coming from a big publisher, who habitually spent large sums on advertisement, might get fifty or seventy-five reviews: a book from a small publisher might get only twenty. I knew of one case where a theological publisher, for some reason, took it into his head to publish a novel. He spent a great deal of money on advertising it. It got exactly four reviews in the whole of England, and the only full-length one was in a motoring paper, which seized the opportunity to point out that the part of the country described in the novel would be a good place for a motoring tour. This man was not in the racket, his advertisements were not likely to become a regular source of revenue to the literary papers, and so they just ignored him.

Even reputable literary papers could not afford to disregard their advertisers altogether. It was quite usual to send a book to a reviewer with some such formula as, 'Review this book if it seems any good. If not, send it back. We don't think it's worthwhile to print simply damning reviews.'

Naturally, a person to whom the guinea or so that he gets for the review means next week's rent is not going to send the book back. He can be counted on to find something to praise, whatever his private opinion of the book may be.

In America even the pretence that hack reviewers read the books they are paid to criticise has been partially abandoned. Publishers, or some publishers, send out with review copies a short synopsis telling the reviewer what to say. Once, in the case of a novel of my own, they misspelt the name of one of the characters. The same misspelling turned up in review after review. The so-called critics had not even glanced into the book - which, nevertheless, most of them were boosting to the skies.

* * *

A phrase much used in political circles in this country is 'playing into the hands of'. It is a sort of charm or incantation to silence uncomfortable truths. When you are told that by saying this, that or the other you are 'playing into the hands of' some sinister enemy, you know that it is your duty to shut up immediately.

For example, if you say anything damaging about British imperialism, you are playing into the hands of Dr Goebbels. If you criticise Stalin you are playing into the hands of the *Tablet* and the *Daily Telegraph*. If you criticise Chiang Kai-Shek you are playing into the hands of Wang Ching-Wei[89] - and so on, indefinitely.

---

89. Wang Ching-Wei (1883-1944) was head of state of the Japanese-sponsored puppet government in China from 1940 to 1944.

Objectively this charge is often true. It is always difficult to attack one party to a dispute without temporarily helping the other. Some of Gandhi's remarks have been very useful to the Japanese. The extreme Tories will seize on anything anti-Russian, and don't necessarily mind if it comes from Trotskyist instead of right-wing sources. The American imperialists, advancing to the attack behind a smoke-screen of novelists, are always on the look-out for any disreputable detail about the British empire. And if you write anything truthful about the London slums, you are liable to hear it repeated on the Nazi radio a week later. But what, then, are you expected to do? Pretend there are no slums?

Everyone who has ever had anything to do with publicity or propaganda can think of occasions when he was urged to tell lies about some vitally important matter, because to tell the truth would give ammunition to the enemy. During the Spanish civil war, for instance, the dissensions on the government side were never properly thrashed out in the left-wing press, although they involved fundamental points of principle. To discuss the struggle between the communists and the anarchists, you were told, would simply give the *Daily Mail* the chance to say that the Reds were all murdering one another. The only result was that the left-wing cause as a whole was weakened. The *Daily Mail* may have missed a few horror stories because people held their tongues, but some all-important lessons were not learned, and we are suffering from the fact to this day.

As I Please 29

16 June 1944

Several times, by word of mouth and in writing, I have been asked why I do not make use of this column for an onslaught on *The Brains Trust*.[90] 'For Christ's sake take a crack at Joad,' one reader put it. Now, I would not deny that *The Brains Trust* is a very dismal thing. I am objectively anti-*Brains Trust*, in the sense that I always switch off any radio from which it begins to emerge. The phony pretence that the whole thing is spontaneous and

90. *The Brains Trust* was a BBC radio programme, broadcast from 1941, in which 'highbrow' panellists answered listeners' questions. Its three original members, who appeared every week, were the philosopher C. E. M. Joad (1891–1951), the biologist Julian Huxley (1887–1975) and Commander A. B. Campbell, a retired naval officer. Two guest 'Brains' joined them each week. The panel was expanded in autumn 1942 after a summer break to nine regulars and by 1943 had a regular audience of more than ten million every week. See Angus Calder, *The People's War: Britain 1939–1945* (London: Jonathan Cape, 1969), chapter 6.

uncensored, the steady avoidance of any serious topic and concentration on questions of the 'Why do children's ears stick out' type, the muscular-curate heartiness of the question-master, the frequently irritating voices, and the thought of incompetent amateur broadcasters being paid ten or fifteen shillings a minute to say 'Er—er—er', are very hard to bear. But I cannot feel the same indignation against this programme as many of my acquaintances seem to do, and it is worth explaining why.

By this time the big public is probably growing rather tired of *The Brains Trust*, but over a long period it was a genuinely popular programme. It was listened to not only in England, but in various other parts of the world, and its technique has been adopted by countless discussion groups in the forces and civil defence. It was an idea that 'took on', as the saying goes. And it is not difficult to see why. By the standards of newspaper and radio discussion prevailing in this country up to about 1940, *The Brains Trust* was a great step forward. It did at least make some show of aiming at free speech and at intellectual seriousness, and though latterly it has had to keep silent about 'politics and religion', you could pick up from it interesting facts about birds' nest soup or the habits of porpoises, scraps of history and a smattering of philosophy. It was less obviously frivolous than the average radio programme. By and large it stood for enlightenment, and that was why millions of listeners welcomed it, at any rate for a year or two.

It was also why the Blimps loathed it, and still do. *The Brains Trust* is the object of endless attacks by right-wing intellectuals of the G. M. Young-A. P. Herbert[91] type (also Mr Douglas Reed),[92] and when a rival brains trust under a squad of clergymen was set up, all the Blimps went about saying how much better it was than Joad and company. These people see *The Brains Trust* as a symbol of freedom of thought, and they realise that, however silly its programmes may be in themselves, their tendency is to start people thinking. You or I, perhaps, would not think of the BBC as a dangerously subversive organisation, but that is how it is regarded in some quarters, and there are perpetual attempts to interfere with its programmes. To a certain extent a man may be known by his enemies, and the dislike with which all right-thinking people have regarded *The Brains Trust* - and also the whole idea of discussion groups, public or private - from the very start, is a sign that there must be something good in it. That is why I feel no strong impulse to take a crack at Dr Joad, who gets his fair share of cracks anyway. I say rather: just think what *The Brains Trust* would have been like if its permanent members had been

91. G. M. Young (1882-1959) was a Tory historian and polemicist, best known for his work on Victorian England. A. P. Herbert (1890-1971) was a writer, humorist (as a contributor to *Punch*) and politician, Independent MP for Oxford University from 1935 to 1950, when the university seats were abolished.

92. For Douglas Reed, see note 26.

(as they might so well have been) Lord Elton, Mr Harold Nicolson and Mr Alfred Noyes.[93]

* * *

The squabble in the House about *Your MP*,[94] was perhaps less disgusting than it might have been, since after all Brendan Bracken did announce that he was not going to ban the book for export; but it was a bad symptom all the same. Mr Beverley Baxter is not the most effective of the many guns now firing in the counter-attack of the Conservative Party – indeed he is less like a gun than a home-made mortar with a strong tendency to blow up – but it is significant that he should have the impudence to make the remarks he did.[95] He wanted the book banned on the ground (a) that the author had been in prison, (b) that it was 'scurrilous,' and (c) that it 'might disturb our relations with Russia'. Of these, (a) is a simple appeal to prejudice, while (b) and (c) boil down to saying that the book is a reminder of what the record of the Conservative Party has actually been. I have my own quarrel with books like *Your MP*, but at least this book is almost entirely a compilation of admitted facts, all of them easily verifiable. A great deal of it could be dug out of Hansard, which is available to anyone who can pay the sixpence a day. But, as Mr Baxter realises, *Your MP* will be read by tens of thousands who would never think of looking into Hansard or even into *Who's Who*. Therefore, ban the book from export, and if possible discredit it in this country as well. It will never do to let people know who our Conservative MPs are, what shares they own, how they have voted on crucially important issues, and what they said about Hitler before we went to war with

93. Godfrey Elton (1892–1973) was an Oxford historian, Christian publicist and political ally of Ramsay MacDonald, who ennobled him as Baron Elton of Headington. Sir Harold Nicholson (1886–1968), a diplomat turned journalist and politician, was another associate of MacDonald (he sat as MP for his National Labour Party for Leicester West 1935–45) and was a junior Ministry of Information minister from 1940 to 1945. His diaries are one of the key sources for British political history in the 1930s and 1940s. Alfred Noyes (1880–1958) was a traditionalist poet and Catholic apologist.

94. *Your MP* by 'Gracchus' (London: Victor Gollancz, 1944) listed the voting records of MPs on such matters as appeasement, rearmament and the Beveridge report. 'Gracchus' was the pen name of the left-wing military strategist, journalist and activist Tom Wintringham (see Introduction, note 104).

95. Brendan Bracken (1901–58) was a journalist and Conservative politician, MP for Paddington North 1929–45 and Bournemouth East and Christchurch 1945–51. He was Minister of Information from 1941 to 1945 and then briefly First Lord of the Admiralty. Arthur Beverley Baxter (1891–1964) was a journalist and Conservative politician, editor of the *Daily Express* 1929–33 and MP for Wood Green 1935–50 and Enfield Southgate 1950–64. Both were key allies of Beaverbrook and considered likely to be at the core of the Tories' campaign in any forthcoming general election. They were the targets of Michael Foot's polemic *Brendan and Beverley* (London: Victor Gollancz, 1944).

him. Heaven knows the Conservative Party have enough reason for wanting to keep their record dark. But a couple of years ago they did not have the nerve to say so, and there lies the difference.

Also, Brendan Bracken in his reply said that the book contained a 'venomous attack' on Sir Arnold Wilson[96] who 'with the greatest gallantry gave his life for his country', the implication being that Sir Arnold Wilson's death in action made it improper to criticise him.

Sir Arnold Wilson was a brave and honourable man. When the policy he had supported came to ruin he was ready to face the consequences. In spite of his age he insisted on joining the RAF, and was killed in battle. I can think of plenty of other public figures who have behaved less well. But what has that to do with his pre-war record, which was mischievous in the extreme? His newspaper, the *Hitchin Mercury*, was a frankly pro-fascist paper and buttered up the Nazi régime almost to the last. Are we supposed to believe that if a man dies well his previous actions cease to have results?

* * *

One cannot buy magazines from abroad nowadays, but I recommend anyone who has a friend in New York to try and cadge a copy of *Politics*, the new monthly magazine, edited by the Marxist literary critic, Dwight Macdonald.[97] I don't agree with the policy of this

96. Sir Arnold Wilson (1884–1940) was a Conservative politician, MP for Hitchin 1933–40. An ultra-Chamberlainite who was arguing for concessions to Hitler until well after war broke out – see his book *More Thoughts and Talks* (London: Right Book Club, 1939) – he volunteered for the RAF, became an air gunner and was killed in action.

97. Dwight Macdonald (1906–82) was an American journalist and critic. Briefly a fellow-traveller of the Communist Party of the USA in the mid-1930s, he (like many of his fellow left intellectuals in New York) lost his faith after the Moscow show trials, joining the literary and political magazine *Partisan Review* as an editor when its founders, William Phillips and Philip Rahv, both former communist literati, relaunched it as anti-Stalinist in 1937. Macdonald became a convinced Trotskyist around this time, but sided with Max Shachtman and James Burnham (see note 40) in their 1940 split with the orthodox Trotskyists over the nature of the Soviet Union; and in 1943 he broke with Philips and Rahv over their support for the war, setting up *Politics* as a rival to *Partisan Review* in 1944. *Politics* lasted until 1949, increasingly adopting a despairing anarchist-pacifist tone. Orwell wrote a quarterly 'London Letter' for *Partisan Review* from 1941 to 1945 and occasional pieces after that. He contributed only two articles to *Politics* but kept up a regular correspondence with Macdonald and considered him a friend despite their political differences. During the 1950s Macdonald, describing himself as a 'conservative anarchist', became a hardline Congress for Cultural Freedom cold-warrior, working as a staff writer for the *New Yorker* and film critic of *Esquire*, but in the 1960s he was notably supportive of the American New Left and a fierce opponent of the Vietnam war. Michael Wreszin's *A Rebel in Defense of Tradition* (New York: Basic Books, 1994) is an excellent biography.

paper, which is anti-war (not from a pacifist angle), but I admire its combination of highbrow political analysis with intelligent literary criticism. It is sad to have to admit it, but we have no monthly or quarterly magazines in England to come up to the American ones – for there are several others of rather the same stamp as *Politics*. We are still haunted by a half-conscious idea that to have aesthetic sensibilities you must be a Tory. But of course the present superiority of American magazines is partly due to the war. Politically, the paper in this country most nearly corresponding to *Politics* would be, I suppose, the *New Leader*. You have only to compare the get-up, the style of writing, the range of subjects and the intellectual level of the two papers, to see what it means to live in a country where there are still leisure and woodpulp.

As I Please 30

23 June 1944

The week before last *Tribune* printed a centenary article on Gerard Manley Hopkins, and it was only after this that the chance of running across an April number of the *American Nation* reminded me that 1944 is also the centenary of a much better-known writer – Anatole France.[98]

When Anatole France died, twenty years ago, his reputation suffered one of those sudden slumps to which highbrow writers who have lived long enough to become popular are especially liable. In France, according to the charming French custom, vicious personal attacks were made upon him while he lay dying and when he was freshly dead. A particularly venomous one was written by Pierre Drieu la Rochelle, afterwards to become a collaborator of the Nazis. In England, also, it was discovered that Anatole France was no good. A few years later than this a young man attached to a weekly paper (I met him afterwards in Paris and found that he could not buy a tram ticket without assistance) solemnly assured me that Anatole France 'wrote very bad French'. France was, it seemed, a vulgar, spurious and derivative writer whom everyone could now 'see through'. Round about the same time, similar discoveries were being made about Bernard Shaw and Lytton Strachey: but curiously enough all three writers have remained very readable, while most of their detractors are forgotten.

How far the revulsion against Anatole France was genuinely literary I do not know.

98. Anatole France (1844–1924) was a French writer and critic.

Certainly he had been overpraised, and one must at times get tired of a writer so mannered and so indefatigably pornographic. But it is unquestionable that he was attacked partly from political motives. He may or may not have been a great writer, but he was one of the symbolic figures in the politico-literary dogfight which has been raging for a hundred years or more. The clericals and reactionaries hated him in just the same way as they hated Zola. Anatole France had championed Dreyfus, which needed considerable courage, he had debunked Joan of Arc, he had written a comic history of France; above all, he had lost no opportunity of poking fun at the church. He was everything that the clericals and revanchistes, the people who first preached that the Boche must never be allowed to recover and afterwards sucked the blacking off Hitler's boots, most detested.

I do not know whether Anatole France's most characteristic books, for instance, *La Rôtisserie de la reine Pédauque*, are worth rereading at this date. Whatever is in them is really in Voltaire. But it is a different story with the four novels dealing with Monsieur Bergeret. Besides being extremely amusing these give a most valuable picture of French society in the nineties and the background of the Dreyfus case. There is also 'Crainquebille', one of the best short stories I have ever read, and incidentally a devastating attack on 'law and order'.

But though Anatole France could speak up for the working class in a story like 'Crainquebille', and though cheap editions of his works were advertised in communist papers, one ought not really to class him as a socialist. He was willing to work for socialism, even to deliver lectures on it in draughty halls, and he knew that it was both necessary and inevitable, but it is doubtful whether he subjectively wanted it. The world, he once said, would get about as much relief from the coming of socialism as a sick man gets from turning over in bed. In a crisis he was ready to identify himself with the working class, but the thought of a Utopian future depressed him, as can be seen from his book, *La Pierre blanche*. There is an even deeper pessimism on *Les Dieux ont soif*, his novel about the French revolution. Temperamentally he was not a socialist but a radical. At this date that is probably the rarer animal of the two, and it is his radicalism, his passion for liberty and intellectual honesty, that give their special colour to the four novels about Monsieur Bergeret.

* * *

I have never understood why the *News Chronicle*, whose politics are certainly a very pale pink – about the colour of shrimp paste, I should say, but still pink – allows the professional Roman Catholic 'Timothy Shy' (D. B. Wyndham Lewis)[99] to do daily

99. D. B. Wyndham Lewis (1891–1963) was a British writer and humorist. He was the first 'Beachcomber' in the *Daily Express* from 1919 to 1924 before handing over to J. B. Morton (see note 23).

sabotage in his comic column. In Lord Beaverbrook's *Express* his fellow-Catholic 'Beachcomber' (J. B. Morton) is, of course, more at home.

Looking back over the twenty years or so that these two have been on the job, it would be difficult to find a reactionary cause that they have not championed – Pilsudski, Mussolini, appeasement, flogging, Franco, literary censorship; between them they have found good words for everything that any decent person instinctively objects to. They have conducted endless propaganda against socialism, the League of Nations and scientific research. They have kept up a campaign of abuse against every writer worth reading, from Joyce onwards. They were viciously anti-German until Hitler appeared, when their anti-Germanism cooled off in a remarkable manner. At this moment, needless to say, the especial target of their hatred is Beveridge.

It is a mistake to regard these two as comics pure and simple. Every word they write is intended as Catholic propaganda, and some at least of their co-religionists think very highly of their work in this direction. Their general 'line' will be familiar to anyone who has read Chesterton and kindred writers. Its essential note is denigration of England and of the Protestant countries generally. From the Catholic point of view this is necessary. A Catholic, at least an apologist, feels that he must claim superiority for the Catholic countries, and for the Middle Ages as against the present, just as a communist feels that he must in all circumstances support the USSR. Hence the endless jibing of 'Beachcomber' and 'Timothy Shy' at every English institution – tea, cricket, Wordsworth, Charlie Chaplin, kindness to animals, Nelson, Cromwell and what-not. Hence also Timothy Shy's attempts to rewrite English history and the snarls of hatred that escape him when he thinks of the defeat of the Spanish Armada. (How it sticks in his gizzard, that Spanish Armada! As though anyone cared, at this date!) Hence, even, the endless jeering at novelists, the novel being essentially a post-Reformation form of literature at which on the whole Catholics have not excelled.

From either a literary or a political point of view these two are simply the leavings on Chesterton's plate. Chesterton's vision of life was false in some ways, and he was hampered by enormous ignorance, but at least he had courage. He was ready to attack the rich and powerful, and he damaged his career by doing so. But it is the peculiarity of both 'Beachcomber' and 'Timothy Shy' that they take no risks with their own popularity. Their strategy is always indirect. Thus, if you want to attack the principle of freedom of speech, do it by sneering at *The Brains Trust*, as if it were a typical example. Dr Joad[100] won't retaliate! Even their deepest convictions go into cold storage when they become dangerous. Earlier in the war, when it was safe to do so, 'Beachcomber' wrote viciously anti-Russian pamphlets, but no anti-Russian remarks appear in his column these days.

100. For C. E. M. Joad, see note 90.

They will again, however, if popular pro-Russian feeling dies down. I shall be interested to see whether either 'Beachcomber' or 'Timothy Shy' reacts to these remarks of mine. If so, it will be the first recorded instance of either of them attacking anyone likely to hit back.

As I Please 31

30 June 1944

I notice that apart from the widespread complaint that the German pilotless planes 'seem so unnatural' (a bomb dropped by a live airman is quite natural, apparently), some journalists are denouncing them as barbarous, inhumane, and 'an indiscriminate attack on civilians'.

After what we have been doing to the Germans over the past two years, this seems a bit thick, but it is the normal human response to every new weapon. Poison gas, the machine-gun, the submarine, gunpowder, and even the crossbow were similarly denounced in their day. Every weapon seems unfair until you have adopted it yourself. But I would not deny that the pilotless plane, flying bomb, or whatever its correct name may be, is an exceptionally unpleasant thing, because, unlike most other projectiles, it gives you time to think. What is your first reaction when you hear that droning, zooming noise? Inevitably, it is a hope that the noise won't stop. You want to hear the bomb pass safely overhead and die away into the distance before the engine cuts out. In other words, you are hoping that it will fall on somebody else. So also when you dodge a shell or an ordinary bomb - but in that case you have only about five seconds to take cover and no time to speculate on the bottomless selfishness of the human being.

* * *

It cannot be altogether an accident that nationalists of the more extreme and romantic kind tend not to belong to the nation that they idealise. Leaders who base their appeal on *la patrie*, or 'the fatherland', are sometimes outright foreigners, or else come from the border countries of great empires. Obvious examples are Hitler, an Austrian, and Napoleon, a Corsican, but there are many others. The man who may be said to have been the founder of British jingoism was Disraeli, a Spanish Jew, and it was Lord Beaverbrook, a Canadian, who tried to induce the unwilling English to describe themselves as Britons. The British empire was largely built up by Irishmen and Scotsmen, and our most obstinate nationalists and imperialists have frequently been Ulstermen. Even Churchill, the leading exponent of romantic patriotism in our own day, is half an American. But not merely the men of action, but even the theorists of nationalism are frequently foreigners. Pan-Germanism, for instance, from which the Nazis later took many of their ideas, was largely the product of men who were not Germans: for instance, Houston Chamberlain, an Englishman, and Gobineau, a Frenchman. Rudyard Kipling was an Englishman, but of a rather doubtful kind. He came from an unusual Anglo-Indian background (his father was curator of the Bombay Museum), he had spent his early childhood in India, and he was of small stature and very dark complexion which caused him to be wrongly suspected of having Asiatic blood. I have always held that if we ever have a Hitler in this country he will be, perhaps, an Ulsterman, a South African, a Maltese, a Eurasian, or perhaps an American – but, at any rate, not an Englishman.

* * *

Two samples of the English language:

1. Elizabethan English:

> While the pages are at their banqueting, I keep their mules, and to someone I cut the stirrup-leather of the mounting side, till it hangs by a thin strap or thread, that when the great puff-guts of the counsellor or some other hath taken his swing to get up, he may fall flat on his side like a porker, and so furnish the spectators with more than a hundred francs' worth of laughter. But I laugh yet further, to think how at his homecoming the master-page is to be swinged like green rye, which makes me not to repent what I have bestowed in feasting them.
>
> (Thomas Urquhart: Translation of Rabelais.)

2. Modern American:

> The phase of detachment may be isolated from its political context and in the division of labour become an end in itself. Those who restrict themselves to work only such segments of intellectual endeavour may attempt to generalise them, making them the basis for political and personal orientation. Then the key problem is held to arise from the fact that social science lags behind physical science and technology, and political and social problems are a result of this deficiency and lag. Such a position is inadequate.
>
> (American highbrow magazine.)

* * *

Six million books, it is said, perished in the blitz of 1940, including a thousand irreplaceable titles. Most of them were probably no loss, but it is dismaying to find how many standard works are now completely out of print. Paper is forthcoming for the most ghastly tripe, as you can see by glancing into any bookshop window, while all the reprint editions, such as the Everyman Library, have huge gaps in their lists. Even so well-known a work of reference as Webster's dictionary is no longer obtainable unless you run across a copy second-hand. About a year ago I had to do a broadcast on Jack London.[101] When I started to collect the material I found that those of his books that I most wanted had vanished so completely that even the London Library could not produce them. To get hold of them I should have had to go to the British Museum reading-room, which in these days is not at all easy of access. And this seems to me a disaster, for Jack London is one of those border-line writers whose works might be forgotten altogether unless somebody takes the trouble to revive them. Even *The Iron Heel* was distinctly a rarity for some years, and was only reprinted because Hitler's rise to power made it topical.

He is remembered chiefly by *The Iron Heel*, and – in totally different circles – by books like *White Fang* and *The Call of the Wild*, in which he exploited a typically Anglo-Saxon sentimentality about animals. But there were also *The People of the Abyss*, his book about the London slums, *The Road*, which gives a wonderful picture of the American hoboes, and *The Jacket*, which is valuable for its prison scenes. And above all there are his short stories. When he is in a certain vein – it is chiefly when he is dealing with American city life – Jack London is one of the best short-story writers the English-speaking peoples have had. There is a story called 'Just Meat', about two burglars who get away with a big haul, and then simultaneously poison one another with strychnine, which sticks very vividly in my memory. 'Love of Life', the last story that was read to Lenin when he was dying, is another wonderful story, and so is 'A Piece of Steak', which describes the last battle of a worn-out prizefighter. These and other similar stories benefit by the strong streak of brutality that London had in his nature. It was this also that gave him a subjective understanding of fascism which socialists do not usually have, and which made *The Iron Heel* in some ways a true prophecy.

Or am I overrating those short stories? I may be, for it is many years since I have set eyes on them. Two of those I have named above were included in a book called *When God Laughs*. So far as I can discover this book has simply ceased to exist, and if anyone has a copy to sell I should be glad to hear of it.

---

101. Jack London (1876–1916) was an American writer, man of action and socialist. Orwell was a great enthusiast for his work.

As I Please 32

7 July 1944

When the Caliph Omar destroyed the libraries of Alexandria he is supposed to have kept the public baths warm for eighteen days with burning manuscripts, and great numbers of tragedies by Euripides and others are said to have perished, quite irrevocably. I remember that when I read about this as a boy it simply filled me with enthusiastic approval. It was so many less words to look up in the dictionary – that was how I saw it. For, though I am only forty-one, I am old enough to have been educated at a time when Latin and Greek were only escapable with great difficulty, while 'English' was hardly regarded as a school subject at all.

Classical education is going down the drain at last, but even now there must be far more adults who have been flogged through the entire extant works of Aeschylus, Sophocles, Euripides, Aristophanes, Vergil, Horace and various other Latin and Greek authors than have read the English masterpieces of the eighteenth century. People pay lip service to Fielding and the rest of them, of course, but they don't read them, as you can discover by making a few inquiries among your friends. How many people have ever read *Tom Jones*, for instance? Not so many have even read the later books of *Gulliver's Travels*. *Robinson Crusoe* has a sort of popularity in nursery versions, but the book as a whole is so little known that few people are even aware that the second part (the journey through Tartary) exists. Smollett, I imagine, is the least read of all. The central plot of Shaw's play, *Pygmalion*, is lifted out of *Peregrine Pickle*, and I believe that no one has ever pointed this out in print, which suggests that few people can have read the book. But what is strangest of all is that Smollett, so far as I know, has never been boosted by the Scottish nationalists, who are so careful to claim Byron for their own. Yet Smollett, besides being one of the best novelists the English-speaking races have produced, was a Scotsman, and proclaimed it openly at a time when being so was anything but helpful to one's career.

* * *

Life in the civilised world. (The family are at tea.)

Zoom-zoom-zoom!

'Is there an alert on?'

'No, it's all clear.'

'I thought there was an alert on.'

Zoom-zoom-zoom!

'There's another of those things coming!'

'It's all right, it's miles away.'

Zoom-zoom-ZOOM!

'Look out, here it comes! Under the table, quick!'

Zoom-zoom-zoom!

'It's all right, it's getting fainter.'

Zoom-zoom-ZOOM!

'It's coming back!'

'They seem to kind of circle round and come back again. They've got something on their tails that makes them do it. Like a torpedo.'

ZOOM-ZOOM-ZOOM!

'Christ! It's bang overhead!'

Dead silence.

'Now get right underneath. Keep your head well down. What a mercy baby isn't here!'

'Look at the cat! He's frightened too.'

'Of course animals know. They can feel the vibrations.'

BOOM!

'It's all right, I told you it was miles away.' (Tea continues.)

* * *

I see that Lord Winterton,[102] writing in the *Evening Standard*, speaks of the 'remarkable reticence (by no means entirely imposed by rule or regulation) which parliament and press alike have displayed in this war to avoid endangering national security' and adds that it has 'earned the admiration of the civilised world'.

It is not only in war-time that the British press observes this voluntary reticence. One of the most extraordinary things about England is that there is almost no official censorship, and yet nothing that is actually offensive to the governing class gets into print, at least in any place where large numbers of people are likely to read it. If it is 'not done' to mention something or other, it just doesn't get mentioned. The position is summed up in the lines by (I think) Hilaire Belloc:[103]

You cannot hope to bribe or twist
Thank God! the British journalist.
But seeing what the man will do
unbribed, there's no occasion to.

---

102. Lord Winterton (1888–1962) was a Tory politician, an MP from 1904 to 1951 and briefly a member of the Cabinet in the late 1930s.

103. In fact, the lines are by Humbert Wolfe (1885–1940).

No bribes, no threats, no penalties – just a nod and a wink and the thing is done. A well-known example was the business of the abdication.[104] Weeks before the scandal officially broke, tens or hundreds of thousands of people had heard all about Mrs Simpson, and yet not a word got into the press, not even into the *Daily Worker*, although the American and European papers were having the time of their lives with the story. Yet I believe there was no definite official ban: just an official 'request' and a general agreement that to break the news prematurely 'would not do'. And I can think of other instances of good news stories failing to see the light although there would have been no penalty for printing them.

Nowadays this kind of veiled censorship even extends to books. The MOI[105] does not, of course, dictate a party line or issue an *index expurgatorius*.[106] It merely 'advises'. Publishers take manuscripts to the MOI and the MOI 'suggests' that this or that is undesirable, or premature, or 'would serve no good purpose'. And though there is no definite prohibition, no clear statement that this or that must not be printed, official policy is never flouted. Circus dogs jump when the trainer cracks his whip, but the really well-trained dog is the one that turns his somersault when there is no whip. And that is the state we have reached in this country thanks to three hundred years of living together without a civil war.

* * *

Here is a little problem sometimes used as an intelligence test.

A man walked four miles due south from his house and shot a bear. He then walked two miles due west, then walked another four miles due north and was back at his home again. What was the colour of the bear?[107]

The interesting point is that – so far as my own observations go – men usually see the answer to this problem and women do not.

104. On the death of George V in January 1936, his eldest son assumed the throne as Edward VIII. He was having an affair with a married American woman, Wallis Simpson, who divorced her husband in October that year with the intention of marrying the King. Neither the Church of England nor the political establishment was prepared to accept the marriage. The British press knew precisely what was going on but reported nothing until Edward's abdication had been all but sealed.

105. For the Ministry of Information, see note 54.

106. The list of books banned by the Roman Catholic church. The first was issued in 1557.

107. The answer, not given by Orwell until 28 July, is white: the man lived at the North Pole and the bear must therefore be a polar bear.

As I Please 33

14 July 1944

I have received a number of letters, some of them quite violent ones, attacking me for my remarks on Miss Vera Brittain's anti-bombing pamphlet. There are two points that seem to need further comment.

First of all there is the charge, which is becoming quite a common one, that 'we started it', i.e. that Britain was the first country to practise systematic bombing of civilians. How anyone can make this claim, with the history of the past dozen years in mind, is almost beyond me. The first act in the present war – some hours, if I remember rightly, before any declaration of war passed – was the German bombing of Warsaw. The Germans bombed and shelled the city so intensively that, according to the Poles, at one time 700 fires were raging simultaneously. They made a film of the destruction of Warsaw, which they entitled *Baptism of Fire* and sent all round the world with the object of terrorising neutrals.

Several years earlier than this the Condor Legion, sent to Spain by Hitler, had bombed one Spanish city after another. The 'silent raids' on Barcelona in 1938 killed several thousand people in a couple of days. Earlier than this the Italians had bombed entirely defenceless Abyssinians and boasted of their exploits as something screamingly funny. Bruno Mussolini[108] wrote newspaper articles in which he described bombed Abyssinians 'bursting open like a rose', which, he said, was 'most amusing'. And the Japanese ever since 1931, and intensively since 1937, have been bombing crowded Chinese cities where there are not even any ARP arrangements, let alone any AA guns or fighter aircraft.[109]

I am not arguing that two blacks make a white, nor that Britain's record is a particularly good one. In a number of 'little wars' from about 1920 onwards the RAF has dropped its bombs on Afghans, Indians and Arabs who had little or no power of hitting back. But it is simply untruthful to say that large-scale bombing of crowded town areas, with the object of causing panic, is a British invention. It was the fascist states who started this practice, and so long as the air war went in their favour they avowed their aims quite clearly.

108. Bruno Mussolini was the aviator son of the Italian dictator, Benito Mussolini. He died in an air accident in 1941 at the age of twenty-three.

109. ARP: Air Raid Protection. AA: anti-aircraft.

The other thing that needs dealing with is the parrot cry 'killing women and children'. I pointed out before, but evidently it needs repeating, that it is probably somewhat better to kill a cross-section of the population than to kill only the young men. If the figures published by the Germans are true, and we have really killed 1,200,000 civilians in our raids, that loss of life has probably harmed the German race somewhat less than a corresponding loss on the Russian front or in Africa and Italy.

Any nation at war will do its best to protect its children, and the number of children killed in raids probably does not correspond to their percentage of the general population. Women cannot be protected to the same extent, but the outcry against killing women, if you accept killing at all, is sheer sentimentality. Why is it worse to kill a woman than a man? The argument usually advanced is that in killing women you are killing the breeders, whereas men can be more easily spared. But this is a fallacy based on the notion that human beings can be bred like animals. The idea behind it is that since one man is capable of fertilising a very large number of women, just as a prize ram fertilises thousands of ewes, the loss of male lives is comparatively unimportant. Human beings, however, are not cattle. When the slaughter caused by a war leaves a surplus of women, the enormous majority of those women bear no children. Male lives are very nearly as important, biologically, as female ones.

In the last war the British empire lost nearly a million men killed, of whom about three-quarters came from these islands. Most of them will have been under thirty. If all those young men had had only one child each we should now have an extra 750,000 people round about the age of twenty. France, which lost much more heavily, never recovered from the slaughter of the last war, and it is doubtful whether Britain has fully recovered, either. We can't yet calculate the casualties of the present war, but the last one killed between ten and twenty million young men. Had it been conducted, as the next one will perhaps be, with flying bombs, rockets and other long-range weapons which kill old and young, healthy and unhealthy, male and female impartially, it would probably have damaged European civilisation somewhat less than it did.

Contrary to what some of my correspondents seem to think, I have no enthusiasm for air raids, either ours or the enemy's. Like a lot of other people in this country, I am growing definitely tired of bombs. But I do object to the hypocrisy of accepting force as an instrument while squealing against this or that individual weapon, or of denouncing war while wanting to preserve the kind of society that makes war inevitable.

* * *

I note in my diary for 1940 an expectation that commercial advertisements will have disappeared from the walls within a year. This seemed likely enough at the time, and a year or even two years later the disappearance seemed to be actually happening, though more slowly than I had expected. Advertisements were shrinking both in numbers and size, and the announcements of the various ministries were more and more taking their place both on the walls and in the newspapers. Judging from this symptom alone, one would have said that commercialism was definitely on the downgrade.

In the last two years, however, the commercial ad, in all its silliness and snobbishness, has made a steady come-back. In recent years I consider that the most offensive of all British advertisements are the ones for Rose's lime juice, with their 'young squire' motif and their P. G. Wodehouse dialogue.

'I fear you do not see me at my best this morning, Jenkins. There were jollifications last night. Your young master looked upon the wine when it was red and also upon the whisky when it was yellow. To use the vulgar phrase, I have a thick head. What do you think the doctor would prescribe, Jenkins?'

'If I might make so bold, sir, a glass of soda water with a dash of Rose's lime juice would probably have the desired effect.'

'Go to it, Jenkins! You were always my guide, philosopher and friend,' etc, etc, etc.

When you reflect that this advertisement appears, for instance, in every theatre programme, so that every theatre-goer is at any rate assumed to have a secret fantasy life in which he thinks of himself as a young man of fashion with faithful old retainers, the prospect of any drastic social change recedes perceptibly.

There are also the hair-tonic adverts which tell you how Daphne got promotion in the WAAFS thanks to the neatness and glossiness of her hair. But these are misleading as well as whorish, for I seldom or never pass a group of officers in the WAAFS, ATS or WRENS[110] without having cause to reflect that at any rate, promotion in the women's service has nothing to do with looks.

As I Please 34

21 July 1944

I have just found my copy of Samuel Butler's *Note-Books*, the full edition of the first series,

110. WAAFs: members of the Women's Auxiliary Air Force, the women's section of the RAF. ATS: Auxiliary Territorial Service, the women's section of the Army. WRENS: members of the Women's Royal Naval Service.

111. Samuel Butler (1835–1902) was a novelist and critic, best known today for his autobiographical novel *The Way of All Flesh*, published posthumously in 1903.

published by Jonathan Cape in 1921.[111] It is twenty years old and none the better for having gone through several rainy seasons in Burma, but at any rate it exists, which is all to the good, for this is another of those well-known books which have now ceased to be procurable. Cape's later produced an abridged version in the Traveller's Library, but it is an unsatisfactory abridgement, and the second series which was published about 1934 does not contain much that is of value. It is in the first series that you will find the story of Butler's interview with a Turkish official at the Dardanelles, the description of his method of buying new-laid eggs and his endeavours to photograph a seasick bishop, and other similar trifles which in a way are worth more than his major works.

Butler's main ideas now seem either to be unimportant, or to suffer from wrong emphasis. Biologists apart, who now cares whether the Darwinian theory of evolution, or the Lamarckian version which Butler supported, is the correct one? The whole question of evolution seems less momentous than it did, because, unlike the Victorians, we do not feel that to be descended from animals is degrading to human dignity. On the other hand, Butler often makes a mere joke out of something that now seems to us vitally important. For example:

> The principal varieties and sub-varieties of the human race are not now to be looked for among the Negroes, the Circassians, the Malays or the American aborigines, but among the rich and the poor. The difference in physical organisation between these two species of man is far greater than that between the so-called types of humanity. The rich man can go from (New Zealand) to England whenever he feels inclined. The legs of the other are by an invisible fatality prevented from carrying him beyond certain narrow limits. Neither rich nor poor can yet see the philosophy of the thing, or admit that he who can tack a portion of one of the P & O boats on to his identity is a much more highly organised being than he who cannot.

There are innumerable similar passages in Butler's work. You could easily interpret them in a Marxist sense, but the point is that Butler himself does not do so. Finally his outlook is that of a conservative, in spite of his successful assaults on Christian belief and the institution of the family. Poverty is degrading: therefore, take care not to be poor – that is his reaction. Hence the improbable and unsatisfying ending of *The Way of All Flesh*, which contrasts so strangely with the realism of the earlier parts.

Yet Butler's books have worn well, far better than those of more earnest contemporaries like Meredith and Carlyle,[112] partly because he never lost the power to use

112. George Meredith (1828–1909) was a novelist, now best known for his comic novel *The Egoist* (London: Kegan Paul, 1879). Thomas Carlyle (1795–1881) was a Scottish historian and essayist, now best known for *The French Revolution: A History* (London: Chapman and Hall, 1837) and a book of lectures, *On Heroes, Hero-Worship, and The Heroic in History* (London: Chapman and Hall, 1841).

his eyes and to be pleased by small things, partly because in the narrow technical sense he wrote so well. When one compares Butler's prose with the contortions of Meredith or the affectations of Stevenson, one sees what a tremendous advantage is gained simply by not trying to be clever. Butler's own ideas on the subject are worth quoting:

> I never knew a writer yet who took the smallest pains with his style and was at the same time readable. Plato's having had seventy shies at one sentence is quite enough to explain to me why I dislike him. A man may, and ought to, take a great deal of pains to write clearly, tersely and euphoniously: he will write many a sentence three or four times over – to do much more than this is worse than not rewriting at all: he will be at great pains to see that he does not repeat himself, to arrange his matter in the way that shall best enable the reader to master it, to cut out superfluous words and, even more, to eschew irrelevant matter: but in each case he will be thinking not of his own style but of his reader's convenience . . . I should like to put it on record that I never took the smallest pains with my style, have never thought about it, and do not know or want to know whether it is a style at all or whether it is not, as I believe and hope, just common, simple straightforwardness. I cannot conceive how any man can take thought for his style without loss to himself and his readers.

Butler adds characteristically, however, that he has made considerable efforts to improve his handwriting.

* * *

An argument that socialists ought to be prepared to meet, since it is brought up constantly both by Christian apologists and by neo-pessimists such as James Burnham, is the alleged immutability of 'human nature'. Socialists are accused – I think without justification – of assuming that man is perfectible, and it is then pointed out that human history is in fact one long tale of greed, robbery and oppression. Man, it is said, will always try to get the better of his neighbour, he will always hog as much property as possible for himself and his family. Man is of his nature sinful, and cannot be made virtuous by act of parliament. Therefore, though economic exploitation can be controlled to some extent, the classless society is for ever impossible.

The proper answer, it seems to me, is that this argument belongs to the Stone Age. It presupposes that material goods will always be desperately scarce. The power hunger of human beings does indeed present a serious problem, but there is no reason for thinking that the greed for mere wealth is a permanent human characteristic. We are selfish in economic matters because we all live in terror of poverty. But when a commodity is not scarce, no one tries to grab more than his fair share of it. No one tries to make a corner in air, for instance. The millionaire as well as the beggar is content with just so much air as he can breathe. Or, again, water. In this country we are not troubled by lack of water.

If anything we have too much of it, especially on bank holidays. As a result water hardly enters into our consciousness. Yet in dried-up countries like north Africa, what jealousies, what hatreds, what appalling crimes the lack of water can cause! So also with any other kind of goods. If they were made plentiful, as they so easily might be, there is no reason to think that the supposed acquisitive instincts of the human being could not be bred out in a couple of generations. And after all, if human nature never changes, why is it that we not only don't practise cannibalism any longer, but don't even want to?

* * *

Another brain-tickler.

A businessman was in the habit of going home by a suburban train which left London at seven-thirty. One evening the night-watchman, who had just come on duty, stopped him and said: 'Excuse me, sir, but I'd advise you not to go by your usual train tonight. I dreamed last night that the train was smashed up and half the people in it were killed. Maybe you'll think I'm superstitious, but it was all so vivid that I can't help thinking it was meant as a warning.'

The businessman was sufficiently impressed to wait and take a later train. When he opened the newspaper the next morning he saw that, sure enough, the train had been wrecked and many people killed. That evening he sent for the night-watchman and said to him: 'I want to thank you for your warning yesterday. I consider that you saved my life, and in return I should like to make you a present of thirty pounds. In addition, I have to inform you that you are sacked. Take a week's notice from today.'

This was an ungrateful act, but the businessman was strictly within his rights. Why?[113]

As I Please 35

28 July 1944

Some years ago, in the course of an article about boys' weekly papers, I made some passing remarks about women's papers – I mean the twopenny ones of the type of *Peg's Paper*, often called 'love books'. This brought me, among much other correspondence, a

113. Orwell did not give the answer to this teaser, but it is that the night-watchman must have been sleeping on duty.

long letter from a woman who had contributed to and worked for the *Lucky Star*, the *Golden Star*, *Peg's Paper*, *Secrets*, the *Oracle*, and a number of kindred papers. Her main point was that I had been wrong in saying that these papers aim at creating wealth fantasy. Their stories are 'in no sense Cinderella stories' and do not exploit the 'she married her boss' motif. My correspondent adds:

> Unemployment is mentioned – quite frequently . . . The dole and the trade union are certainly never mentioned. The latter may be influenced by the fact that the largest publishers of these women's magazines are a non-union house. One is never allowed to criticise the system, or to show up the class struggle for what it really is, and the word socialist is never mentioned – all this is perfectly true. But it might be interesting to add that class feeling is not altogether absent. The rich are often shown as mean, and as cruel and crooked money-makers. The rich and idle beau is nearly always planning marriage without a ring, and the lass is rescued by her strong, hard-working garage hand. Men with cars are generally 'bad' and men in well-cut expensive suits are nearly always crooks. The ideal of most of these stories is not an income worthy of a bank manager's wife, but a life that is 'good'. A life with an upright, kind husband, however poor, with babies and a 'little cottage'. The stories are conditioned to show that the meagre life is not so bad really, as you are at least honest and happy, and that riches bring trouble and false friends. The poor are given moral values to aspire to as something within their reach.

There are many comments I could make here, but I choose to take up the point of the moral superiority of the poor being combined with the non-mention of trade unions and socialism. There is no doubt that this is deliberate policy. In one woman's paper I actually read a story dealing with a strike in a coal mine, and even in that connexion trade unionism was not mentioned. When the USSR entered the war one of these papers promptly cashed in with a serial entitled 'Her Soviet Lover', but we may be sure that Marxism did not enter into it very largely.

The fact is that this business about the moral superiority of the poor is one of the deadliest forms of escapism the ruling class have evolved. You may be downtrodden and swindled, but in the eyes of God you are superior to your oppressors, and by means of films and magazines you can enjoy a fantasy existence in which you constantly triumph over the people who defeat you in real life. In any form of art designed to appeal to large numbers of people, it is an almost unheard-of thing for a rich man to get the better of a poor man. The rich man is usually 'bad', and his machinations are invariably frustrated. 'Good poor man defeats bad rich man' is an accepted formula, whereas if it were the other way about we should feel that there was something very wrong somewhere. This is as noticeable in films as in the cheap magazines, and it was perhaps most noticeable of all in the old silent films, which travelled from country to country and had to appeal to a very varied audience. The vast majority of the people who will see a film are poor, and so it is politic to make a poor man the hero. Film magnates, press lords and the like amass quite a lot of their wealth by pointing out that wealth is wicked.

The formula 'good poor man defeats bad rich man' is simply a subtler version of 'pie in the sky'. It is a sublimation of the class struggle. So long as you can dream of yourself as a 'strong, hard-working garage hand' giving some moneyed crook a sock on the jaw, the real facts can be forgotten. That is a cleverer dodge than wealth fantasy. But, curiously enough, reality does enter into these women's magazines, not through the stories but through the correspondence columns, especially in those papers that give free medical advice. Here you can read harrowing tales of 'bad legs' and haemorrhoids, written by middle-aged women who give themselves such pseudonyms as 'A Sufferer', 'Mother of Nine' and 'Always Constipated'. To compare these letters with the love stories that lie cheek by jowl with them is to see how vast a part mere day-dreaming plays in modern life.

* * *

I have just been reading Arthur Koestler's novel *The Gladiators*, which describes the slave rebellion under Spartacus, about 70 BC. It is not one of his best books, and, in any case, any novel describing a slave rebellion in antiquity suffers by having to stand comparison with *Salammbô*, Flaubert's great novel about the revolt of the Carthaginian mercenaries. But it reminded me of how tiny is the number of slaves of whom anything whatever is known. I myself know the names of just three slaves - Spartacus himself, the fabulous Aesop, who is supposed to have been a slave, and the philosopher Epictetus, who was one of those learned slaves whom the Roman plutocrats liked to have among their retinue. All the others are not even names. We don't, for instance - or at least I don't - know the name of a single one of the myriads of human beings who built the pyramids. Spartacus, I suppose, is much the most widely known slave there ever was. For five thousand years or more civilisation rested upon slavery. Yet when even so much as the name of a slave survives, it is because he did not obey the injunction 'resist not evil', but raised violent rebellion. I think there is a moral in this for pacifists.

* * *

In spite of the appalling overcrowding of the trains (sixteen people in a carriage designed for ten is fairly normal nowadays), I note that the distinction between first and third class is definitely coming back. Earlier in the war it almost lapsed for a while. If you were crowded out of the third class you went as a matter of course into the first, and no questions were asked. Now you are invariably made to pay the difference in fare - at least, if you sit down - even though it would have been quite impossible to find a place anywhere else in the train. (You can, I believe, travel in a first-class carriage with a third-class ticket if you choose to stand up the whole way.) A few years ago the railway companies would hardly have dared to enforce this distinction. By such small symptoms (another, by the way, is that evening suits are beginning to come out of their moth balls) you can judge how confident the higher-ups are and how insolent they feel it safe to be.

* * *

We published last week part of a very truculent letter about the anti-war poem entitled 'The Little Apocalypse of Obadiah Hornbrook',[114] with the comment, 'I am surprised that you publish it.' Other letters and private comments took the same line.

I do not, any more than our correspondent, agree with 'Obadiah Hornbrook', but that is not a sufficient reason for not publishing what he writes. Every paper has a policy, and in its political sections it will press that policy, more or less to the exclusion of all others. To do anything else would be stupid. But the literary end of a paper is another matter. Even there, of course, no paper will give space to direct attacks on the things it stands for. We wouldn't print an article in praise of anti-Semitism, for instance. But granted the necessary minimum of agreement, literary merit is the only thing that matters.

Besides, if this war is about anything at all, it is a war in favour of freedom of thought. I should be the last to claim that we are morally superior to our enemies, and there is quite a strong case for saying that British imperialism is actually worse than Nazism. But there does remain the difference, not to be explained away, that in Britain you are relatively free to say and print what you like. Even in the blackest patches of the British empire, in India, say, there is very much more freedom of expression than in a totalitarian country. I want that to remain true, and by sometimes giving a hearing to unpopular opinions, I think we help it to do so.

As I Please 36

4 August 1944

Apropos of saturation bombing, a correspondent who disagreed with me very strongly added that he was by no means a pacifist. He recognised, he said, that 'the Hun had got to be beaten'. He merely objected to the barbarous methods that we are now using.

114. The poem was written by Alex Comfort, for whom see Introduction, note 16.

Now, it seems to me that you do less harm by dropping bombs on people than by calling them 'Huns'. Obviously one does not want to inflict death and wounds if it can he avoided, but I cannot feel that mere killing is all-important. We shall all be dead in less than a hundred years, and most of us by the sordid horror known as 'natural death'. The truly evil thing is to act in such a way that peaceful life becomes impossible. War damages the fabric of civilisation not by the destruction it causes (the net effect of a war may even be to increase the productive capacity of the world as a whole), nor even by the slaughter of human beings, but by stimulating hatred and dishonesty. By shooting at your enemy you are not in the deepest sense wronging him. But by hating him, by inventing lies about him and bringing children up to believe them, by clamouring for unjust peace terms which make further wars inevitable, you are striking not at one perishable generation, but at humanity itself.

It is a matter of observation that the people least infected by war hysteria are the fighting soldiers. Of all people they are the least inclined to hate the enemy, to swallow lying propaganda or to demand a vindictive peace. Nearly all soldiers – and this applies even to professional soldiers in peace time – have a sane attitude towards war. They realise that it is disgusting, and that it may often be necessary. This is harder for a civilian, because the soldier's detached attitude is partly due to sheer exhaustion, to the sobering effects of danger, and to continuous friction with his own military machine. The safe and well-fed civilian has more surplus emotion, and he is apt to use it up in hating somebody or other – the enemy if he is a patriot, his own side if he is a pacifist. But the war mentality is something that can be struggled against and overcome, just as the fear of bullets can be overcome. The trouble is that neither the Peace Pledge Union nor the Never Again Society[115] know the war mentality when they see it. Meanwhile, the fact that in this war offensive nicknames like 'Hun' have not caught on with the big public seems to me a good omen.

What has always seemed to me one of the most shocking deeds of the last war was one that did not aim at killing anyone – on the contrary, it probably saved a great many lives. Before launching their big attack at Caporetto,[116] the Germans flooded the Italian army with faked socialist propaganda leaflets in which it was alleged that the German soldiers were ready to shoot their officers and fraternise with their Italian comrades, etc, etc. Numbers of Italians were taken in, came over to fraternise with the Germans, and were made prisoner – and, I believe, jeered at for their simple-mindedness. I have heard this defended as a highly intelligent and humane way of making war – which it is, if your

115. For the Peace Pledge Union, see note 78.

116. The battle of Caporetto in autumn 1917 was a humiliating defeat for Italy in the latter stages of the First World War by combined German and Austro-Hungarian forces.

sole aim is to save as many skins as possible. And yet a trick like that damages the very roots of human solidarity in a way that no mere act of violence could do.

* * *

I see that the railings are returning – only wooden ones, it is true, but still railings – in one London square after another. So the lawful denizens of the squares can make use of their treasured keys again, and the children of the poor can be kept out.

When the railings round the parks and squares were removed, the object was partly to accumulate scrap-iron, but the removal was also felt to be a democratic gesture. Many more green spaces were now open to the public, and you could stay in the parks till all hours instead of being hounded out at closing times by grim-faced keepers. It was also discovered that these railings were not only unnecessary but hideously ugly. The parks were improved out of recognition by being laid open, acquiring a friendly, almost rural look that they had never had before. And had the railings vanished permanently, another improvement would probably have followed. The dreary shrubberies of laurel and privet – plants not suited to England and always dusty, at any rate in London – would probably have been grubbed up and replaced by flower beds. Like the railings, they were merely put there to keep the populace out. However, the higher-ups managed to avert this reform, like so many others, and everywhere the wooden palisades are going up, regardless of the wastage of labour and timber.

When I was in the Home Guard we used to say that the bad sign would be when flogging was introduced. That has not happened yet, I believe, but all minor social symptoms point in the same direction. The worst sign of all – and I should expect this to happen almost immediately if the Tories win the general election – will be the reappearance in the London streets of top-hats not worn by either undertakers or bank messengers.

* * *

We hope to review before long – and meanwhile I take the opportunity of drawing attention to it – an unusual book called *Branch Street*, by Marie Paneth.[117] The author is or was a voluntary worker at a children's club, and her book reveals the almost savage conditions in which some London children still grow up. It is not quite clear, however, whether these conditions are to any extent worse as a result of the war. I should like to read – I suppose some such thing must exist somewhere, but I don't know of it – an

117. Marie Paneth was an Australian-born sociologist and social worker. Her *Branch Street: A Sociological Study* (London: George Allen and Unwin, 1944), an exposé of slum conditions in London, was reviewed by Orwell in the *Observer* on 13 August 1944.

authoritative account of the effect of the war on children. Hundreds of thousands of town children have been evacuated to country districts, many have had their schooling interrupted for months at a time, others have had terrifying experiences with bombs (earlier in the war a little girl of eight, evacuated to a Hertfordshire village, assured me that she had been bombed out seven times), others have been sleeping in Tube shelters, sometimes for a year or so at a stretch. I would like to know to what extent the town children have adapted themselves to country life – whether they have grown interested in birds and animals, or whether they simply pine to be back among the picture houses – and whether there has been any significant increase in juvenile crime. The children described by Mrs Paneth sound almost like the gangs of 'wild children' who were a by-product of the Russian revolution.

* * *

Back in the eighteenth century, when the India muslins were one of the wonders of the world, an Indian king sent envoys to the court of Louis XV to negotiate a trade agreement. He was aware that in Europe women wield great political influence, and the envoys brought with them a bale of costly muslins, which they had been instructed to present to Louis's mistress. Unfortunately their information was not up to date: Louis's not very stable affections had veered, and the muslins were presented to a mistress who had already been discarded. The mission was a failure, and the envoys were decapitated when they got home.

I don't know whether this story has a moral, but when I see the kind of people that our Foreign Office likes to get together with, I am often reminded of it.

As I Please 37

11 August 1944

A few days ago a west African wrote to inform us that a certain London dance hall had recently erected a 'colour bar', presumably in order to please the American soldiers who formed an important part of its clientele. Telephone conversations with the management of the dance hall brought us the answers: (a) that the 'colour bar' had been cancelled, and (b) that it had never been imposed in the first place; but I think one can take it that our informant's charge had some kind of basis. There have been other similar incidents recently. For instance, during last week a case in a magistrate's court brought out the fact that a West Indian Negro working in this country had been refused admission to a place of entertainment when he was wearing Home Guard uniform. And there have been many instances of Indians, Negroes and others being turned away from hotels on the ground that 'we don't take coloured people'.

It is immensely important to be vigilant against this kind of thing, and to make as much public fuss as possible whenever it happens. For this is one of those matters in which making a fuss can achieve something. There is no kind of legal disability against coloured people in this country, and, what is more, there is very little popular colour feeling. (This is not due to any inherent virtue in the British people, as our behaviour in India shows. It is due to the fact that in Britain itself there is no colour problem.)

The trouble always arises in the same way. A hotel, restaurant or what-not is frequented by people who have money to spend who object to mixing with Indians or Negroes. They tell the proprietor that unless he imposes a colour bar they will go elsewhere. They may be a very small minority, and the proprietor may not be in agreement with them, but it is difficult for him to lose good customers; so he imposes the colour bar. This kind of thing cannot happen when public opinion is on the alert and disagreeable publicity is given to any establishment where coloured people are insulted. Anyone who knows of a provable instance of colour discrimination ought always to expose it. Otherwise the tiny percentage of colour-snobs who exist among us can make endless mischief, and the British people are given a bad name which, as a whole, they do not deserve.

In the 1920s, when American tourists were as much a part of the scenery of Paris as tobacco kiosks and tin urinals, the beginnings of a colour bar began to appear even in France. The Americans spend money like water, and restaurant proprietors and the like could not afford to disregard them. One evening, at a dance in a very well-known café some Americans objected to the presence of a Negro who was there with an Egyptian woman. After making some feeble protests, the proprietor gave in, and the Negro was turned out.

Next morning there was a terrible hullabaloo and the café proprietor was hauled up before a minister of the government and threatened with prosecution. It had turned out that the offended Negro was the ambassador of Haiti. People of that kind can usually get satisfaction, but most of us do not have the good fortune to be ambassadors, and the ordinary Indian, Negro or Chinese can only be protected against petty insult if other ordinary people are willing to exert themselves on his behalf.

* * *

Readers of this week's *Tribune* will notice that Mr Reginald Reynolds,[118] reviewing *What*

118. For Reginald Reynolds, see Introduction, note 104.

the German Needs, repeats and appears to believe a story about British troops advancing to the attack behind the cover of civilian hostages. His authority for it is a casual undated reference to the *News Chronicle*.

Now, this business of advancing behind a screen of civilian hostages is a very old favourite in the history of war propaganda. The Germans were accused of doing it in 1914, and again in 1940. But would Mr Reynolds believe it if it were told about Germans? I very much doubt it. He would at once reject it as an 'atrocity story', which it is. As it happens, his quoted authority, the *News Chronicle*, reported last week from the Normandy front another time-honoured atrocity – dipping women in petrol and setting fire to them. (This has been a steady favourite in the wars of the last thirty years. Ideally the women should be nuns. The *News Chronicle* made them schoolmistresses, which is perhaps the next best thing.) I feel pretty certain that Mr Reynolds would reject that one too. It is only when these tales are told about our own side that they become, from the point of view of a war-resister, true or at any rate credible; just as for a Blimp they only become true when told about the enemy.

I doubt whether the war-resister's attitude is any better than the Blimp's, and in essentials I don't even think it is different. During recent years many pacifists and other war-resisters have assured me that all the tales of Nazi atrocities – the concentration camps, the gas vans, the rubber truncheons, the castor oil and all the rest of it – are simply lies emanating from the British government. Or, alternatively, they are not lies, but then we do exactly the same ourselves. All that is said about the enemy is 'war propaganda', and war propaganda, as we know from the experience of 1914–18, is invariably untruthful.

God knows there was enough lying in 1914–18, but I do urge that this time there is a radical difference. For it is not the case this time that the atrocity stories have only appeared since the war started. On the contrary, there were far more of them during the period 1933–39. During that time the whole civilised world looked on in horror at the things that were done in the fascist countries. Nor did these stories emanate from the British government, or from any government.

It was everywhere the socialists and communists who believed them and circulated them. The concentration camps, the pogroms and all the rest of it were believed in by the whole of the European left, including the majority of pacifists. They were also believed in by the hundreds of thousands of refugees who fled from the fascist countries. If it is true now, therefore, that the tales of Nazi outrages are all lies, we have to accept one of two things. Either (a) between the years 1933–39 some tens of millions of socialists and some hundreds of thousands of refugees suffered a mass hallucination about concentration camps, or (b) atrocities happen in peace time, but stop as soon as war breaks out.

I submit that both of these are incredible, and that the case against the Nazis must be substantially true. Nazism is a quite exceptionally evil thing, and it has been responsible for outrages quite unparalleled in recent times. It is definitely worse than British imperialism, which has plenty of crimes of its own to answer for. Not to accept this seems to me merely unrealistic.

There is a point at which incredulity becomes credulity. 'The Duke of Bedford,' a young pacifist writes to me, 'knows – I assure you that this is so – that Hitler is a good man, and he would like to have a talk with him in order to bring out what is best in him.' I suggest on the contrary that Hitler is not a good man, and that there is a large body of evidence to support this. I don't know, of course, whether the Duke of Bedford[119] is correctly reported. But if he is, then I see no significant difference between his outlook and that of any fat-headed *Daily Telegraph* reader who cries out against doodlebugs while not caring a damn for the starvation of millions of Indians.

As I Please 38

18 August 1944

Apropos of my remarks on the railings round London squares, a correspondent writes: 'Are the squares to which you refer public or private properties? If private, I suggest that your comments in plain language advocate nothing less than theft, and should be classed as such.'

If giving the land of England back to the people of England is theft, I am quite happy to call it theft. In his zeal to defend private property, my correspondent does not stop to consider how the so-called owners of the land got hold of it. They simply seized it by force, afterwards hiring lawyers to provide them with title-deeds. In the case of the enclosure of the common lands, which was going on from about 1600 to 1850, the land-grabbers did not even have the excuse of being foreign conquerors; they were quite frankly taking the heritage of their own countrymen, upon no sort of pretext except that they had the power to do so.

Except for the few surviving commons, the high roads, the lands of the National

119. The Duke of Bedford (Hastings Russell, 1888–1953, Marquis of Tavistock until 1940) was a right-wing pacifist. Founder and funder of the far-right British People's Party in the late 1930s, he became chairman of the defeatist British Council for a Christian Settlement in Europe in 1939. He revived the BPP after war.

Trust, a certain number of parks, and the sea shore below high-tide mark, every square inch of England is 'owned' by a few thousand families. These people are just about as useful as so many tapeworms. It is desirable that people should own their own dwelling houses, and it is probably desirable that a farmer should own as much land as he can actually farm. But the ground-landlord in a town area has no function and no excuse for existence. He is merely a person who has found out a way of milking the public while giving nothing in return. He causes rents to be higher, he makes town planning more difficult, and he excludes children from green spaces: that is literally all that he does, except to draw his income. The removal of the railings in the squares was a first step against him. It was a very small step, and yet an appreciable one, as the present move to restore the railings shows. For three years or so the squares lay open, and their sacred turf was trodden by the feet of working-class children, a sight to make dividend-drawers gnash their false teeth. If that is theft, all I can say is, so much the better for theft.

* * *

I note that once again there is serious talk of trying to attract tourists to this country after the war. This, it is said, will bring in a welcome trickle of foreign currency. But it is quite safe to prophesy that the attempt will be a failure. Apart from the many other difficulties, our licensing laws and the artificial price of drink are quite enough to keep foreigners away. Why should people who are used to paying sixpence for a bottle of wine visit a country where a pint of beer costs a shilling? But even these prices are less dismaying to foreigners than the lunatic laws which permit you to buy a glass of beer at half past ten while forbidding you to buy it at twenty-five past, and which have done their best to turn the pubs into mere boozing-shops by excluding children from them.

How downtrodden we are in comparison with most other peoples is shown by the fact that even people who are far from being 'temperance' don't seriously imagine that our licensing laws could be altered. Whenever I suggest that pubs might be allowed to open in the afternoon, or to stay open till midnight, I always get the same answer: 'The first people to object would be the publicans. They don't want to have to stay open twelve hours a day.' People assume, you see, that opening hours, whether long or short, must be regulated by the law, even for one-man businesses. In France, and in various other countries, a café proprietor opens or shuts just as it suits him. He can keep open the whole twenty-four hours if he wants to; and, on the other hand, if he feels like shutting his café and going away for a week, he can do that too. In England we have had no such liberty for about a hundred years, and people are hardly able to imagine it.

England is a country that ought to be able to attract tourists. It has much beautiful scenery, an equable climate, innumerable attractive villages and medieval churches, good beer, and foodstuffs of excellent natural taste. If you could walk where you chose instead of being fenced in by barbed wire and 'Trespassers will be prosecuted' boards, if speculative builders had not been allowed to ruin every pleasant view within ten miles of a big town, if you could get a drink when you wanted it at a normal price, if an eatable meal in a country inn were a normal experience, and if Sunday were not artificially made into a day of misery, then foreign visitors might be expected to come here. But if those things were true England would no longer be England, and I fancy that we shall have to find some way of acquiring foreign currency that is more in accord with our national character.

* * *

In spite of my campaign against the jackboot - in which I am not operating single-handed - I notice that jackboots are as common as ever in the columns of the newspapers. Even in the leading articles in the *Evening Standard*, I have come upon several of them lately. But I am still without any clear information as to what a jackboot is. It is a kind of boot that you put on when you want to behave tyrannically: that is as much as anyone seems to know.

Others besides myself have noted that war, when it gets into the leading articles, is apt to be waged with remarkably old-fashioned weapons. Planes and tanks do make occasional appearances, but as soon as an heroic attitude has to be struck, the only armaments mentioned are the sword ('We shall not sheathe the sword until', etc, etc), the spear, the shield, the buckler, the trident, the chariot and the clarion. All of these are hopelessly out of date (the chariot, for instance, has not been in effective use since about AD 50), and even the purpose of some of them has been forgotten. What is a buckler, for instance? One school of thought holds that it is a small round shield, but another school believes it to be a kind of belt. A clarion, I believe, is a trumpet, but most people imagine that a 'clarion call' merely means a loud noise.

One of the early Mass Observation[120] reports, dealing with the coronation of George VI, pointed out that what are called 'national occasions', always seem to cause a lapse into archaic language. The 'ship of state', for instance, when it makes one of its official

120. Mass Observation was a pioneering survey of social attitudes, founded in 1937 in response to the abdication crisis of 1936, which had shocked many on the left by revealing the high regard in which the monarchy was held by most Britons. Founded by Tom Harrisson (1911-76), an anthropologist, Charles Madge (1912-96), a poet and artist, and Humphrey Jennings (1906-50), an artist, writer and film-maker, Mass Observation employed teams of observers to record people's behaviour and conversation. It made its name with a survey of working-class life in Bolton and Blackpool ('Worktown') in 1937-40 and during the war years more-or-less systematically recorded civilian attitudes to the war. See Angus Calder, *The People's War: Britain 1939-1945* (London: Jonathan Cape, 1969).

appearances, has a prow and a helm instead of having a bow and a wheel, like modern ships. So far as it is applied to war, the motive for using this kind of language is probably a desire for euphemism. 'We will not sheathe the sword' sounds a lot more gentlemanly than 'We will keep on dropping block-busters', though in effect it means the same.

* * *

One argument for Basic English[121] is that by existing side by side with Standard English it can act as a sort of corrective to the oratory of statesmen and publicists. High-sounding phrases, when translated into Basic, are often deflated in a surprising way. For example, I presented to a Basic expert the sentence, 'He little knew the fate that lay in store for him' – to be told that in Basic this would become 'He was far from certain what was going to happen'. It sounds decidedly less impressive, but it means the same. In Basic, I am told, you cannot make a meaningless statement without its being apparent that it is meaningless – which is quite enough to explain why so many schoolmasters, editors, politicians and literary critics object to it.

As I Please 39

25 August 1944

A certain amount of material dealing with Burma and the Burma campaign has been passed on to me by the India-Burma Association, which is an unofficial body representing the European communities in those countries, and standing for a 'moderate' policy based on the Cripps proposals.[122]

The India-Burma Association complains with justice that Burma has been extraordinarily ill-served in the way of publicity. Not only has the general public no interest in Burma, in spite of its obvious importance from many points of view, but the authorities have not even succeeded in producing an attractive booklet which would tell

121. For Basic English, see note 47.

122. For Sir Stafford Cripps see *Tribune* biographies, pp. 390–1 of this volume. The 'Cripps proposals' to which Orwell refers were made during his mission to India in spring 1942. They were for India to be given substantial self-government and Dominion status within the British empire, with Britain retaining responsibility for India's defence and foreign policy. The Cripps plan was scuppered by a combination of the hostility of Churchill and others, who thought it went too far, and the opposition of Indian nationalists, who didn't think it went far enough.

people what the problems of Burma are and how they are related to our own. Newspaper reports of the fighting in Burma, from 1942 onwards, have been consistently uninformative, especially from a political point of view. As soon as the Japanese attack began the newspapers and the BBC adopted the practice of referring to all the inhabitants of Burma as 'Burmans', even applying this name to the quite distinct and semi-savage peoples of the far north. This is not only about as accurate as calling a Swede an Italian, but masks the fact that the Japanese find their support mostly among the Burmese proper, the minorities being largely pro-British. In the present campaign, when prisoners are taken, the newspaper reports never state whether they are Japanese or whether they are Burmese and Indian partisans - a point of very great importance.

Almost all the books that have been published about the campaign of 1942 are misleading. I know what I am talking about, because I have had most of them to review. They have either been written by American journalists with no background knowledge and a considerable anti-British bias, or by British officials who are on the defensive and anxious to cover up everything discreditable. Actually, the British officials and military men have been blamed for much that was not their fault, and the view of the Burma campaign held by left-wingers in this country was almost as distorted as that held by the Blimps. But this trouble arises because there is no official effort to publicise the truth. For to my knowledge manuscripts do exist which give valuable information, but which, for commercial reasons, cannot find publishers.

I can give three examples. In 1942 a young Burman who had been a member of the Thakin (extreme nationalist) party and had intrigued with the Japanese fled to India, having changed his mind about the Japanese when he saw what their rule was like. He wrote a short book which was published in India under the title of *What Happened in Burma* and which was obviously authentic in the main. The Indian government in its negligent way sent exactly two copies to England. I tried to induce various publishers to reissue it, but failed every time: they all gave the same reason - it was not worth wasting paper on a subject which the big public was not interested in. Later a Major Enriquez, who had published various travel books dealing with Burma, brought to England a diary covering the Burma campaign and the retreat into India. It was an extremely revealing - in places a disgracefully revealing - document, but it suffered the same fate as the other book. At the moment I am reading another manuscript which gives valuable background material about Burma's history, its economic conditions, its systems of land tenure, and so forth. But I would bet a small sum that it won't be published either, at any rate until the paper shortage lets up.

If paper and money are not forthcoming for books of this kind - books which may spill a lot of beans but do help to counteract the lies put about by Axis sympathisers - then the government must not be surprised if the public knows nothing about Burma and cares less. And what applies to Burma applies to scores of other important but neglected subjects.

Meanwhile here is a suggestion. Whenever a document appears which is not commercially saleable but which is likely to be useful to future historians, it should be submitted to a committee set up by, for instance, the British Museum. If they consider it historically valuable they should have the power to print a few copies and store them for the use of scholars. At present a manuscript rejected by the commercial publishers almost always ends up in the dustbin. How many possible correctives to accepted lies must have perished in this way!

* * *

At a time when muck floods the bookshops while good books go out of print, I was rather glad to see recently that one or two of Leonard Merrick's novels have been re-issued in a cheap edition.

Leonard Merrick[123] is a writer who seems to me never to have quite had his due. He was not trying to be anything but a popular writer, he has many of the characteristic faults of the pre-1914 period, and he takes almost for granted the middle-class values of that time. But his books are not only sincere, they have the fascination that belongs to all books which deal with the difficulty of earning a living. The most characteristic of them are about struggling artists, usually actors, but Art with a big A hardly enters: everything centres round the ghastly effort to pay the rent and remain 'respectable' at the same time. Ever since reading Leonard Merrick, the horrors of a travelling actor's life – the Sunday journeys and draughty ill-lit theatres, the catcalling audiences, the theatrical lodgings presided over by 'Ma', the white china chamberpot and the permanent smell of fried fish, the sordid rivalries and love affairs, the swindling manager who disappears with all the takings in the middle of the tour – have had their own special corner in my mind.

To anyone who wants to try Leonard Merrick, I would say: lay off the Paris books, which are William J. Locke-ish and tiresome, and read either *The Man Who Was Good*, *The House of Lynch* or *The Position of Peggy Harper*. In a different vein, but also worth reading, is *The Worldlings*.

* * *

123. Leonard Merrick (1864–1939) was a novelist. In 1945, Orwell was commissioned by Graham Greene, then working for the publisher Eyre and Spottiswoode, to write an introduction for a proposed reissue of Merrick's *The Position of Peggy Harper*. Orwell wrote it but the edition did not appear. See *CWGO* XVIII, pp. 216–9.

I wish some botanist among my readers would give me a clear ruling about the name of the weed with a pink flower which grows so profusely on blitzed sites.

I was brought up to call this plant willowherb. Another similar but distinct plant, which grows in marshy places, I was taught to call rosebay or French willow. But I notice that Sir William Beach Thomas, writing in the *Observer*, calls the plant on the blitzed sites rosebay willowherb, thus combining the two names. The only wildflower book I have consulted gives no help. Other people who have referred to the plant seem to use all three names interchangeably. I should like the point cleared up, if only for the satisfaction of knowing whether a nature correspondent of fifty years' standing can be wrong.

As I Please 40[124]

1 September 1944

It is not my primary job to discuss the details of contemporary politics, but this week there is something that cries out to be said. Since, it seems, nobody else will do so, I want to protest against the mean and cowardly attitude adopted by the British press towards the recent rising in Warsaw.[125] As soon as the news of the rising broke, the *News Chronicle* and kindred papers adopted a markedly disapproving attitude. One was left with the general impression that the Poles deserved to have their bottoms smacked for doing what all the Allied wirelesses had been urging them to do for years past, and that they would not be given and did not deserve to be given any help from outside. A few papers tentatively suggested that arms and supplies might be dropped by the Anglo-Americans, a thousand miles away: no one, so far as I know, suggested that this might be done by the Russians, perhaps twenty miles away. The *New Statesman*, in its issue of 18 August, even went so far as to doubt whether appreciable help could be given from the air in such

124. This was probably the most controversial column Orwell wrote for *Tribune*: for the next three weeks its pages were filled with responses. See *CWGO* XVIII, pp. 366–76.

125. The Polish Home Army (Armia Krajowa) rose in Warsaw against the occupying Germans on 1 August 1944, holding out heroically for two months. Although the Red Army had reached the river Vistula, just to the east of Warsaw, it responded to the uprising by ceasing its offensive against the Germans, and Stalin refused to supply the insurgents or even to allow British and American planes that had flown from Italy and dropped arms to land in Soviet-held territory. The most comprehensive account in English is Norman Davies, *Rising '44: The Battle for Warsaw* (London: Macmillan, 2003).

circumstances. All or nearly all the papers of the left were full of blame for the émigré London government which had 'prematurely' ordered its followers to rise when the Red Army was at the gates. This line of thought is adequately set forth in a letter to last week's *Tribune* from Mr G. Barraclough. He makes the following specific charges:

1. The Warsaw rising was 'not a spontaneous popular rising', but was 'begun on orders from the *soi-disant* Polish government in London'.
2. The order to rise was given 'without consultation with either the British or Soviet governments', and 'no attempt was made to co-ordinate the rising with Allied action'.
3. The Polish resistance movement is no more united round the London government than the Greek resistance movement is united round King George of the Hellenes. (This is further emphasised by frequent use of the words *émigré, soi-disant*, etc, applied to the London government.)
4. The London government precipitated the rising in order to be in possession of Warsaw when the Russians arrived, because in that case 'the bargaining position of the émigré government would be improved'. The London government, we are told, 'is ready to betray the Polish people's cause to bolster up its own tenure of precarious office', with much more to the same effect.

No shadow of proof is offered for any of these charges, though 1 and 2 are of a kind that could be verified and may well be true. My own guess is that 2 is true and 1 partly true. The third charge makes nonsense of the first two. If the London government is not accepted by the mass of the people in Warsaw, why should they raise a desperate insurrection on its orders? By blaming Sosnkowski[126] and the rest for the rising, you are automatically assuming that it is to them that the Polish people looks for guidance. This obvious contradiction has been repeated in paper after paper, without, so far as I know, a single person having the honesty to point it out. As for the use of such expressions as émigré, it is simply a rhetorical trick. If the London Poles are émigrés, so are the Polish National Committee of Liberation, besides the 'free' governments of all the occupied countries. Why does one become an émigré by emigrating to London and not by emigrating to Moscow?

Charge No 4 is morally on a par with the *Osservatore Romano*'s suggestion that the Russians held up their attack on Warsaw in order to get as many Polish resisters as possible killed off. It is the unproved and unprovable assertion of a mere propagandist who has no wish to establish the truth, but is simply out to do as much dirt on his

126. General Kazimierz Sosnkowski (1885–1969) was commander-in-chief of the Polish armed forces in the west between 1943 and 1944.

opponent as possible. And all that I have read about this matter in the press – except for some very obscure papers and some remarks in *Tribune*, the *Economist* and the *Evening Standard* – is on the same level as Mr Barraclough's letter.

Now, I know nothing of Polish affairs, and even if I had the power to do so I would not intervene in the struggle between the London Polish government and the Moscow National Committee of Liberation. What I am concerned with is the attitude of the British intelligentsia, who cannot raise between them one single voice to question what they believe to be Russian policy, no matter what turn it takes, and in this case have had the unheard-of meanness to hint that our bombers ought not to be sent to the aid of our comrades fighting in Warsaw. The enormous majority of left-wingers who swallow the policy put out by the *News Chronicle*, etc, know no more about Poland than I do. All they know is that the Russians object to the London government and have set up a rival organisation, and so far as they are concerned that settles the matter. If tomorrow Stalin were to drop the Committee of Liberation and recognise the London government, the whole British intelligentsia would flock after him like a troop of parrots. Their attitude towards Russian foreign policy is not 'Is this policy right or wrong?' but 'This is Russian policy: how can we make it appear right?' And this attitude is defended, if at all, solely on grounds of power. The Russians are powerful in eastern Europe, we are not: therefore we must not oppose them. This involves the principle, of its nature alien to socialism, that you must not protest against an evil which you cannot prevent.

I cannot discuss here why it is that the British intelligentsia, with few exceptions, have developed a nationalistic loyalty towards the USSR and are dishonestly uncritical of its policies. In any case, I have discussed it elsewhere. But I would like to close with two considerations which are worth thinking over.

First of all, a message to English left-wing journalists and intellectuals generally: 'Do remember that dishonesty and cowardice always have to be paid for. Don't imagine that for years on end you can make yourself the boot-licking propagandist of the Soviet régime, or any other régime, and then suddenly return to mental decency. Once a whore, always a whore.'

Secondly, a wider consideration. Nothing is more important in the world today than Anglo-Russian friendship and co-operation, and that will not be attained without plain speaking. The best way to come to an agreement with a foreign nation is not to refrain from criticising its policies, even to the extent of leaving your own people in the dark about them. At present, so slavish is the attitude of nearly the whole British press that ordinary people have very little idea of what is happening, and may well be committed to policies which they will repudiate in five years' time. In a shadowy sort of way we have been told that the Russian peace terms are a super-Versailles, with partition of Germany, astronomical reparations, and forced labour on a huge scale. These proposals go practically uncriticised, while in much of the left-wing press hack writers are even hired to extol them. The result is that the average man has no notion of the enormity of what is proposed. I don't know whether, when the time comes, the Russians will really want to put such terms into operation. My guess is that they won't. But what I do know is that if any such thing were done, the British and probably the American public would never support it when the passion of war had died down. Any flagrantly unjust peace settlement will simply have the result, as it did last time, of making the British people unreasonably sympathetic with the victims. Anglo-Russian friendship depends upon there being a policy which both countries can agree upon, and this is impossible without free discussion and genuine criticism now. There can be no real alliance on the basis of 'Stalin is always right'. The first step towards a real alliance is the dropping of illusions.

Finally, a word to the people who will write me letters about this. May I once again draw attention to the title of this column and remind everyone that the editors of *Tribune* are not necessarily in agreement with all that I say, but are putting into practice their belief in freedom of speech?

[This column was written some days before the appearance of Vernon Bartlett's article in the *News Chronicle* of 29 August,[127] which gives at any rate a hint of disagreement with the policy prevailing throughout the press.]

As I Please 41

8 September 1944

For a book of thirty-two pages, Sir Osbert Sitwell's *A Letter to My Son* contains a quite

127. Vernon Bartlett (1894–1983) was a journalist and politician. Invalided out of the army during the First World War, he worked for the *Daily Mail*, Reuters and the *Times* before becoming director of the London office of the League of Nations in 1922. He became a regular broadcaster on the BBC while doing this job, but in 1933 he was forced to resign from the BBC for making pro-German remarks and joined the *News Chronicle* as a diplomatic correspondent. Any sympathy Bartlett had for Hitler's antagonism towards the Versailles settlement soon evaporated, however, and he became a staunch opponent of appeasement. In 1938, he won the Bridgwater by-election as an anti-appeasement independent with Labour and Liberal backing – the sole success of the anti-Tory Popular Front – and held the seat until 1950. He worked as a British propagandist during the Second World War, broadcasting regularly on the BBC and serving briefly as British press attaché in Moscow in 1941. He left the *News Chronicle* in 1954 and moved to Singapore, working as a correspondent for the *Manchester Guardian* until the early 1960s.

astonishing quantity of invective.[128] I imagine that it is the invective, or rather the eminence of the people it is directed against, that has led Sir Osbert to change his publisher. But in among passages that are sometimes unfair and occasionally frivolous, he manages to say some penetrating things about the position of the artist in a modern centralised society. Here, for instance, are some excerpts:

> The true artist has always had to fight, but it is, and will be, a more ferocious struggle for you, and the artists of your generation, than ever before. The working man, this time, will be better looked after, he will be flattered by the press and bribed with Beveridge schemes, because he possesses a plurality of votes. But who will care for you and your fate, who will trouble to defend the cause of the young writer, painter, sculptor, musician? And what inspiration will you be offered when theatre, ballet, concert-hall lie in ruins, and, owing to the break in training, there are no great executant artists for several decades? Above all, do not underestimate the amount and intensity of genuine ill-will that people will feel for you; not the working man, for though not highly educated he has a mild respect for the arts and no preconceived notions, not the few remaining patricians, but the vast army between, the fat middle classes and the little men. And here I must make special mention of the civil servant as enemy . . . At the best, you will be ground down between the small but powerful authoritarian minority of art directors, museum racketeers, the chic, giggling modistes who write on art and literature, publishers, journalists and dons (who will, to do them justice, try to help you, if you will write as they tell you) – and the enormous remainder who would not mind, who would indeed be pleased, if they saw you starve. For we English are unique in that, albeit an art-producing nation, we are not an art-loving one. In the past the arts depended on a small number of very rich patrons. The enclave they formed has never been re-established. The very name 'art-lover' stinks . . . The privileges you hold today, then, as an artist, are those of Ishmael, the hand of every man is against you. Remember, therefore, that outcasts must never be afraid.

These are not my views. They are the views of an intelligent conservative who underrates the virtues of democracy and attributes to feudalism certain advantages which really belong to capitalism. It is a mistake, for instance, to yearn after an aristocratic patron. The patron could be just as hard a master as the BBC, and he did not pay your salary so regularly. François Villon had, I suppose, as rough a time as any poet in our own day, and the literary man starving in a garret was one of the characteristic figures of the eighteenth century. At best, in an age of patronage you had to waste time and talent on revolting flatteries, as Shakespeare did. Indeed, if one thinks of the artist as an Ishmael, an autonomous individual who owes nothing to society, then the golden age of the artist was the age of capitalism. He had then escaped from the patron and not yet been

128. For Osbert Sitwell, see note 29.

captured by the bureaucrat. He could – at any rate a writer, a musician, an actor, and perhaps even a painter could – make his living off the big public, who were uncertain of what they wanted and would to a great extent take what they were given. Indeed, for about a hundred years it was possible to make your livelihood by openly insulting the public, as the careers of, say Flaubert, Tolstoy, D. H. Lawrence, and even Dickens, show.

But all the same there is much in what Sir Osbert Sitwell says. Laissez-faire capitalism is passing away, and the independent status of the artist must necessarily disappear with it. He must become either a spare-time amateur or an official. When you see what has happened to the arts in the totalitarian countries, and when you see the same thing happening here in a more veiled way through the MOI, the BBC and the film companies – organisations which not only buy up promising young writers and geld them and set them to work like cab-horses, but manage to rob literary creation of its individual character and turn it into a sort of conveyor-belt process – the prospects are not encouraging. Yet it remains true that capitalism, which in many ways was kind to the artist and the intellectual generally, is doomed and is not worth saving anyway. So you arrive at these two antithetical facts: (1) society cannot be arranged for the benefit of artists; (2) without artists civilisation perishes. I have never yet seen this dilemma solved (there must be a solution), and it is not often that it is honestly discussed.

* * *

I have before me an exceptionally disgusting photograph, from the *Star*[129] of 29 August, of two partially undressed women, with shaven heads and with swastikas painted on their faces, being led through the streets of Paris amid grinning onlookers. The *Star* – not that I am picking on the *Star*, for most of the press has behaved likewise – reproduces this photograph with seeming approval.

I don't blame the French for doing this kind of thing. They have had four years of suffering, and I can partially imagine how they feel towards the collaborators. But it is a different matter when newspapers in this country try to persuade their readers that shaving women's heads is a nice thing to do. As soon as I saw this *Star* photograph, I thought, 'Where have I seen something like this before?' Then I remembered. Just about ten years ago, when the Nazi régime was beginning to get into its stride, very similar pictures of humiliated Jews being led through the streets of German cities were exhibited in the British press – but with this difference, that on that occasion we were not expected to approve.

---

129. The *Star* was a liberal London evening newspaper, a stablemate of the *News Chronicle*. It is not to be confused with the *Daily Star*, launched in 1978 by Express Newspapers to use surplus print capacity in Manchester and currently (2006) the most down-market tabloid daily.

Recently another newspaper published photographs of the dangling corpses of Germans hanged by the Russians in Kharkov, and carefully informed its readers that these executions had been filmed and that the public would shortly be able to witness them at the news theatres. (Were children admitted, I wonder?)

There is a saying of Nietzsche which I have quoted before (not in this column, I think), but which is worth quoting again: 'He who fights too long against dragons becomes a dragon himself: and if thou gaze too long into the abyss, the abyss will gaze into thee.'

'Too long', in this context, should perhaps be taken as meaning 'after the dragon is beaten'.

* * *

The correspondents who wrote in answer to my query about the weed which grows on blitzed sites are too numerous to thank individually, but I would like to thank them collectively. The upshot is that Sir William Beach Thomas was right. The plant is called rosebay willowherb. The name of the other plant I referred to is not completely certain, but as there are, it seems, nine kinds of willowherb, this must be one of them. As a piece of information which may be useful at a time when whisky costs twenty-seven shillings a bottle, I pass on the statement of one of my correspondents that 'an infusion of the whole plant is extremely intoxicating'. If anyone is brave enough to try this, I shall be interested to learn the results.

As I Please 42

15 September 1944

About the end of 1936, as I was passing through Paris on the way to Spain, I had to visit somebody at an address I did not know, and I thought that the quickest way of getting there would probably be to take a taxi. The taxi-driver did not know the address either. However, we drove up the street and asked the nearest policeman, whereupon it turned out that the address I was looking for was only about a hundred yards away. So I had taken the taxi-driver off the rank for a fare which in English money was about threepence.

The taxi-driver was furiously angry. He began accusing me, in a roaring voice and with the maximum of offensiveness, of having 'done it on purpose'. I protested that I had not known where the place was, and that I obviously would not have taken a taxi if I had known. 'You knew very well!' he yelled back at me. He was an old, grey, thick-set man, with ragged grey moustaches and a face of quite unusual malignity. In the end I lost my temper, and, my command of French coming back to me in my rage, I shouted at him, 'You think you're too old for me to smash your face in. Don't be too sure!' He backed up against the taxi, snarling and full of fight, in spite of his sixty years.

Then the moment came to pay. I had taken out a ten-franc note. 'I've no change,' he yelled as soon as he saw the money. 'Go and change it for yourself!'

'Where can I get change?'

'How should I know? That's your business.'

So I had to cross the street, find a tobacconist's shop and get change. When I came back I gave the taxi-driver the exact fare, telling him that after his behaviour I saw no reason for giving him anything extra; and after exchanging a few more insults we parted.

This sordid squabble left me at the moment violently angry, and a little later saddened and disgusted. 'Why do people have to behave like that?' I thought.

But that night I left for Spain. The train, a slow one, was packed with Czechs, Germans, Frenchmen, all bound on the same mission. Up and down the train you could hear one phrase repeated over and over again, in the accents of all the languages of Europe – *là-bas* (down there). My third-class carriage was full of very young, fair-haired, underfed Germans in suits of incredible shoddiness – the first ersatz cloth I had seen – who rushed out at every stopping-place to buy bottles of cheap wine and later fell asleep in a sort of pyramid on the floor of the carriage. About half-way down France the ordinary passengers dropped off. There might still be a few nondescript journalists like myself, but the train was practically a troop train, and the countryside knew it. In the morning, as we crawled across southern France, every peasant working in the fields turned round, stood solemnly upright and gave the anti-fascist salute. They were like a guard of honour, greeting the train mile after mile.

As I watched this, the behaviour of the old taxi-driver gradually fell into perspective. I saw now what had made him so unnecessarily offensive. This was 1936, the year of the great strikes, and the Blum government was still in office. The wave of revolutionary feeling which had swept across France had affected people like taxi-drivers as well as factory workers. With my English accent I had appeared to him as a symbol of the idle, patronising foreign tourists who had done their best to turn France into something midway between a museum and a brothel. In his eyes an English tourist meant a bourgeois. He was getting a bit of his own back on the parasites who were normally his employers. And it struck me that the motives of the polyglot army that filled the train, and of the peasants with raised fists out there in the fields, and my own motive in going to Spain, and the motive of the old taxi-driver in insulting me, were at bottom all the same.

* * *

The official statement on the doodlebug,[130] even taken together with Churchill's earlier statement, is not very revealing, because no clear figures have been given of the number of people affected. All we are told is that on average something under thirty bombs have hit London daily. My own estimate, based simply on such 'incidents' as I have witnessed, is that on average every doodlebug hitting London makes thirty houses uninhabitable, and that anything up to five thousand people have been rendered homeless daily. At that rate between a quarter and half a million people will have been blitzed out of their homes in the last three months.

It is said that good billiard-players chalk their cues before making a stroke, and bad players afterwards. In the same way, we should have got on splendidly in this war if we had prepared for each type of blitz before and not after it happened. Shortly before the outbreak of war an official, returning from some conference with other officials in London, told me that the authorities were prepared for air-raid casualties of the order of 200,000 in the first week. Enormous supplies of collapsible cardboard coffins had been laid in, and mass graves were being dug. There were also special preparations for a great increase in mental disorders. As it turned out the casualties were comparatively few, while mental disorders, I believe, actually declined. On the other hand, the authorities had failed to foresee that blitzed people would be homeless and would need food, clothes, shelter, and money. They had also, while foreseeing the incendiary bomb, failed to realise that you would need an alternative water supply if the mains were burst by bombs.

By 1942 we were all set for the blitz of 1940. Shelter facilities had been increased, and London was dotted with water tanks which would have saved its historic buildings if only they had been in existence when the fires were happening. And then along came the doodlebug, which, instead of blowing three or four houses out of existence, makes a large number uninhabitable, while leaving their interiors more or less intact. Hence another unforeseen headache – storage of furniture. The furniture from a doodlebugged house is nearly always salvaged, but finding places to put it in, and labour to move it, has been almost too much for the local authorities. In general it has to be dumped in derelict and unguarded houses, where such of it as is not looted is ruined by damp.

The most significant figures in Duncan Sandys's speech were those dealing with the

---

130. The 'doodlebug' or 'buzz bomb', properly speaking the V-1, was a German jet-propelled cruise missile first deployed in June 1944. In the first couple of months of their use, nearly 7,000 were seen over Britain, more than half of which were destroyed by fighters, guns or barrage balloons. But more than 2,300 made it to the London area, killing more than 5,000 people. See Angus Calder, *The People's War: Britain 1939–1945* (London: Jonathan Cape, 1969), chapter 9.

Allied counter-measures.[131] He stated, for instance, that whereas the Germans shot off 8,000 doodlebugs, or something under 8,000 tons of high explosive, we dropped 100,000 tons of bombs on the bases, besides losing 450 aeroplanes and shooting off hundreds of thousands or millions of AA shells. One can only make rough calculations at this date, but it looks as though the doodlebug may have a big future before it in forthcoming wars. Before writing it off as a flop, it is worth remembering that artillery scored only a partial success at the battle of Crécy.[132]

As I Please 43

6 October 1944

By permission of a correspondent, I quote passages from a letter of instruction which she recently received from a well-known school of journalism. I should explain that when she undertook her 'course' the instructor asked her to supply the necessary minimum of information about her background and experience, and then told her to write a couple of specimen essays on some subject interesting to her. Being a miner's wife, she chose to write about coal-mining. Here is the reply she got from someone calling himself the 'assistant director of studies'. I shall have to quote from it at some length:

> I have read your two exercises with care and interest. You should have a good deal to write about: but do be careful of getting a bee in your bonnet. Miners are not the only men who have a hard time. How about young naval officers, earning less than a skilled miner – who must spend three or four years from home and family, in ice or the tropics? How about the many retired folks on a tiny pension or allowance, whose previous £2 or £3 have been reduced by half by the income tax. We all make sacrifices in this war – and the so-called upper classes are being hard hit indeed.
>
> Instead of writing propaganda for socialist newspapers you will do better to describe – for the housewives – what life is like in a mining village. Do not go out of your way to be hostile to owners and managers – who are ordinary fellow creatures –

131. Duncan Sandys (1908–87), son-in-law of Winston Churchill, was a Conservative politician, MP for Norwood 1935–45 and Streatham 1950–74. A junior minister during the Second World War, in late 1944 he chaired a War Cabinet committee on defence against German flying bombs and rockets.

132. The battle of Crécy (1346) was an early battle of the Hundred Years War between England and France, the first occasion on which English longbowmen triumphed over French armoured knights.

> but, if you must air a grievance, do so tolerantly, and fit it in with your plot or theme.
>
> Many of your readers will be people who are not in the least inclined to regard employers as slave drivers and capitalist villains of society . . . Write simply and naturally, without any attempt at long words or sentences. Remember that your task is to entertain. No reader will bother after a hard day's work to read a list of somebody else's woes. Keep a strict eye on your inclination to write about the 'wrongs' of mining. There are millions of people who will not forget that miners did strike while our sons and husbands were fighting the Germans. Where would the miners be if the troops had refused to fight? I mention this to help you keep a sense of perspective. I advise you against writing very controversial things. They are hard to sell. A plain account of mining life will stand a far better chance . . . The average reader is willing to read facts about other ways of life – but unless he is a fool or knave, he will not listen to one-sided propaganda. So forget your grievances, and tell us something of how you manage in a typical mining village. One of the women's magazines will, I'm sure, consider a housewife's article on that subject.

My correspondent, who, it seems, had agreed in advance to pay £11 for this course, sent the letter on to me with the query: Did I think that her instructor was trying to influence her to give her writings an acceptable political slant? Was an attempt being made to talk her out of writing like a socialist?

I do think so, of course, but the implications of this letter are worse than that. This is not a subtle capitalist plot to dope the workers. The writer of that slovenly letter is not a sinister plotter, but simply an ass (a female ass, I should say by the style) upon whom years of bombing and privation have made no impression. What it demonstrates is the unconquerable, weed-like vitality of pre-war habits of mind. The writer assumes, it will be seen, that the only purpose of journalism is to tickle money out of the pockets of tired businessmen, and that the best way of doing this is to avoid telling unpleasant truths about present-day society. The reading public, so he (or she) reasons, don't like being made to think: therefore don't make them think. You are after the big dough, and no other consideration enters.

Anyone who has had anything to do with 'courses' in freelance journalism, or has ever come as near to them as studying the now-defunct *Writer* and the *Writers' and Artists' Yearbook*, will recognise the tone of that letter. 'Remember that your task is to entertain,' 'No reader will bother after a hard day's work to read a list of somebody else's woes,' and 'I advise you against writing very controversial things. They are hard to sell.' I pass over the fact that even from a commercial point of view such advice is misleading. What is significant is the assumption that nothing ever changes, that the public always will be and always must be the same mob of nit-wits wanting only to be doped, and that no sane person would sit down behind a typewriter with any other object than to produce saleable drivel.

When I started writing, about fifteen years ago, various people – who, however, didn't succeed in getting £11 out of me in return – gave me advice almost identical with what I have quoted above. Then too, it seemed, the public did not want to hear about 'unpleasant' things like unemployment, and articles on 'controversial' subjects were 'hard to sell'. The dreary sub-world of the freelance journalist, the world of furnished bed-sitting rooms, hired typewriters and self-addressed envelopes, was entirely dominated by the theory that 'your task is to entertain'. But at that time there was some excuse. To begin with there was widespread unemployment, and every newspaper and magazine was besieged by hordes of amateurs struggling frantically to earn odd guineas; and in addition the press was incomparably sillier than it is now and there was some truth in the claim that editors would not print 'gloomy' contributions. If you looked on writing as simply and solely a way of making money, then cheer-up stuff was probably the best line. What is depressing is to see that for the -- school of journalism the world has stood still. The bombs have achieved nothing. And, indeed, when I read that letter I had the same feeling that the pre-war world is back upon us as I had a little while ago when, through the window of some chambers in the Temple, I watched somebody – with great care and evident pleasure in the process – polishing a top-hat.

* * *

It is superfluous to say that long railway journeys are not pleasant in these days, and for a good deal of the discomfort that people have to suffer, the railway companies are not to blame. It is not their fault that there is an enormous to-and-fro of civilian traffic at a time when the armed forces are monopolising most of the rolling stock, nor that an English railway carriage is built with the seeming object of wasting as much space as possible. But journeys which often entail standing for six or eight hours in a crowded corridor could be made less intolerable by a few reforms.

To begin with, the first class nonsense should be scrapped once and for all. Secondly, any woman carrying a baby should have a priority right to a seat. Thirdly, waiting rooms should be left open at night. Fourthly, if timetables cannot be adhered to, porters and other officials should be in possession of correct information, and not, as at present, tell you that you will have to change when you won't, and vice versa. Also – a thing that is bad enough in peace time but is even worse at this moment – why is it that there is no cheap way of moving luggage across a big town? What do you do if you have to move a heavy trunk from Paddington to Camden Town? You take a taxi. And suppose you can't afford a taxi, what do you do then? Presumably you borrow a hand-cart, or balance the trunk on a perambulator. Why are there not cheap luggage-vans, just as there are buses for human passengers? Or why not make it possible to carry luggage on the Underground?

This evening, as King's Cross discharged another horde of returned evacuees, I saw a man and woman, obviously worn out by a long journey, trying to board a bus. The woman carried a squalling baby and clutched a child of about six by the other hand; the man was carrying a broken suitcase tied with rope and the elder child's cot. They were refused by one bus after another. Of course, no bus could take a cot on board. How could it be expected to? But, on the other hand, how were those people to get home? It ended by the woman boarding a bus with the two children, while the man trailed off carrying the cot. For all I know he had a five-mile walk ahead of him.

In war-time one must expect this kind of thing. But the point is that if those people had made the same journey, similarly loaded, in peace time, their predicament would have been just the same. For:

> The rain it raineth every day
> Upon the just and unjust feller,
> But more upon the just because
> The unjust has the just's umbrella.

Our society is not only so arranged that if you have money you can buy luxuries with it. After all, that is what money is for. It is also so arranged that if you don't have money you pay for it at every hour of the day with petty humiliations and totally unnecessary discomforts - such as, for instance, walking home with a suitcase cutting your fingers off when a mere half-crown would get you there in five minutes.

As I Please 44

13 October 1944

Sir Osbert Sitwell's little book, and my remarks on it, brought in an unusually large amount of correspondence, and some of the points that were raised seem to need further comment.

One correspondent solved the whole problem by asserting that society can get along perfectly well without artists. It can also get along without scientists, engineers, doctors, bricklayers or road-menders - for the time being. It can even get along without sowing next year's harvest, provided it is understood that everyone is going to starve to death in about twelve months' time.

This notion, which is fairly widespread and has been encouraged by people who should know better, simply restates the problem in a new form. What the artist does is not immediately and obviously necessary in the same way as what the milkman or the coalminer does. Except in the ideal society which has not yet arrived, or in very chaotic and prosperous ages like the one that is just ending, this means in practice that the artist must have some kind of patron – a ruling class, the church, the state, or a political party. And the question 'Which is best?' normally means 'Which interferes least?'

Several correspondents pointed out that one solution is for the artist to have an alternative means of livelihood. 'It is quite feasible,' says Mr P. Philips Price, 'to write and devote oneself to socialism whilst accepting the patronage of the BBC, MOI,[133] Rank[134] or CEMA[135] . . . the only way out is some minor form of prostitution, part time.' The difficulty here is that the practice of writing or any other art takes up a lot of time and energy. Moreover, the kind of job that a writer gets in war-time, if he is not in the forces (or even if he is – for there is always PR),[136] usually has something to do with propaganda. But this is itself a kind of writing. To compose a propaganda pamphlet or a radio feature needs just as much work as to write something you believe in, with the difference that the finished product is worthless. I could give a whole list of writers of promise or performance who are now being squeezed dry like oranges in some official job or other. It is true that in most cases it is voluntary. They want the war to be won, and they know that everyone must sacrifice something. But still the result is the same. They will come out of the war with nothing to show for their labours and with not even the stored-up experience that the soldier gets in return for his physical suffering.

If a writer is to have an alternative profession, it is much better that it should have nothing to do with writing. A particularly successful holder of two jobs was Trollope, who produced two thousand words between seven and nine o'clock every morning before leaving for his work at the Post Office. But Trollope was an exceptional man, and as he also hunted three days a week and was usually playing whist till midnight, I suspect that he did not overwork himself in his official duties.

Other correspondents pointed out that in a genuinely socialist society the distinction between the artist and the ordinary man would vanish. Very likely, but then no such society yet exists. Others rightly claimed that state patronage is a better guarantee against starvation than private patronage, but seemed to me too ready to disregard the

133. For the Ministry of Information, see note 54.

134. The Rank Organisation, named after its owner, J. Arthur Rank (1888–1972), dominated the British film industry, owning studios, newsreels, production companies, a distribution arm and more than 650 cinemas.

135. CEMA was the Committee for the Encouragement of Music and the Arts, the forerunner of the Arts Council, chaired by John Maynard Keynes.

136. Public relations.

censorship that this implies. The usual line was that it is better for the artist to be a responsible member of a community than an anarchic individualist. The issue, however, is not between irresponsible 'self-expression' and discipline; it is between truth and lies.

Artists don't so much object to aesthetic discipline. Architects will design theatres or churches equally readily, writers will switch from the three-volume novel to the one-volume, or from the play to the film, according to the demand. But the point is that this is a political age. A writer inevitably writes – and less directly this applies to all the arts – about contemporary events, and his impulse is to tell what he believes to be the truth. But no government, no big organisation, will pay for the truth. To take a crude example: can you imagine the British government commissioning E. M. Forster to write *A Passage to India*? He could only write it because he was not dependent on state aid. Multiply that instance by a million, and you see the danger that is involved – not, indeed, in a centralised economy as such, but in our going forward into a collectivist age without remembering that the price of liberty is eternal vigilance.

* * *

Recently I was told the following story, and I have every reason to believe that it is true.

Among the German prisoners captured in France there are a certain number of Russians. Some time back two were captured who did not speak Russian or any other language that was known either to their captors or their fellow prisoners. They could, in fact, only converse with one another. A professor of Slavonic languages, brought down from Oxford, could make nothing of what they were saying. Then it happened that a sergeant who had served on the frontiers of India overheard them talking and recognised their language, which he was able to speak a little. It was Tibetan! After some questioning, he managed to get their story out of them.

Some years earlier they had strayed over the frontier into the Soviet Union and had been conscripted into a labour battalion, afterwards being sent to western Russia when the war with Germany broke out. They were taken prisoner by the Germans and sent to north Africa; later they were sent to France, then exchanged into a fighting unit when the second front opened, and taken prisoner by the British. All this time they had been able to speak to nobody but one another, and had no notion of what was happening or who was fighting whom.

It would round the story off neatly if they were now conscripted into the British army and sent to fight the Japanese, ending up somewhere in central Asia, quite close to their native village, but still very much puzzled as to what it is all about.

* * *

An Indian journalist sends me a cutting of an interview he had with Bernard Shaw. Shaw says one or two sensible things and does state that the Congress leaders ought not to have been arrested, but on the whole it is a disgusting exhibition. Here are some samples:

> Q: Supposing you were a national leader of India, how would you have dealt with the British? What would have been your methods to achieve Indian independence?
> A: Please do not suppose a situation that can never happen. The achievement of Indian independence is not my business.
> Q: What do you think is the most effective way of getting the British out of India? What should the Indian people do?
> A: Make them superfluous by doing their work better. Or assimilate them by cross-fertilisation. British babies do not thrive in India.

What kind of answers are those to give to people who are labouring under a huge and justified grievance? Shaw also refuses to send birthday greetings to Gandhi, on the ground that this is a practice he never follows, and advises the Indian people not to bother if Britain repudiates the huge credit balance which India has piled up in this country during the war. I wonder what impression this interview would give to some young Indian student who has been a couple of years in jail and has dimly heard of Bernard Shaw as one of Britain's leading 'progressive' thinkers? Is it surprising if even very level-headed Indians are liable to a recurrent suspicion that 'all Englishmen are the same'?

As I Please 45

20 October 1944

Reading recently a book on Brigadier-General Wingate,[137] who was killed early this year in Burma, I was interested to note that Wingate's 'Chindits', who marched across Upper Burma in 1943, were wearing not the usual clumsy and conspicuous pith helmets, but slouch hats like those worn in the Gurkha regiments. This sounds a very small point, but it is of considerable social significance, and twenty or even ten years ago it would have been impossible. Nearly everyone, including nearly any doctor, would have predicted that large numbers of these men would perish of sunstroke.

Till recently the European in India had an essentially superstitious attitude towards heat apoplexy, or sunstroke as it is usually called. It was supposed to be something

137. Orde Wingate (1903–44) was a British military commander in the Second World War, the army's foremost specialist in guerrilla warfare.

dangerous to Europeans but not to Asiatics. When I was in Burma I was assured that the Indian sun, even at its coolest, had a peculiar deadliness which could only be warded off by wearing a helmet of cork or pith. 'Natives', their skulls being thicker, had no need of these helmets, but for a European even a double felt hat was not a reliable protection.

But why should the sun in Burma, even on a positively chilly day, be deadlier than in England? Because we were nearer to the equator and the rays of the sun were more perpendicular. This astonished me, for obviously the rays of the sun are only perpendicular round about noon. How about the early morning, when the sun is creeping over the horizon and the rays are parallel with the earth? It is exactly then, I was told, that they are at their most dangerous. But how about the rainy season, when one frequently does not see the sun for days at a time? Then of all times, the old-stagers told me, you should cling to your topi. (The pith helmet is called a 'topi', which is Hindustani for 'hat'.) The deadly rays filter through the envelope of cloud just the same, and on a dull day you are in danger of forgetting it. Take your topi off in the open for one moment, even for one moment, and you may be a dead man. Some people, not content with cork and pith, believed in the mysterious virtues of red flannel and had little patches of it sewn into their shirts over the top vertebra. The Eurasian community, anxious to emphasise their white ancestry, used at that time to wear topis even larger and thicker than those of the British.

My own disbelief in all this dated from the day when my topi was blown off my head and carried away down a stream, leaving me to march bareheaded all day without ill effects. But I soon noticed other facts that conflicted with the prevailing belief. To begin with some Europeans (for instance sailors working in the rigging of ships) did habitually go bareheaded in the sun. Again, when cases of sunstroke occurred (for they do occur), they did not seem to be traceable to any occasion when the victim had taken his hat off. They happened to Asiatics as well as to Europeans, and were said to be commonest among stokers on coal-burning ships, who were subjected to fierce heat but not to sunshine. The final blow was the discovery that the topi, supposedly the only protection against the Indian sun, is quite a recent invention. The early Europeans in India knew nothing of it. In short, the whole thing was bunkum.

But why should the British in India have built up this superstition about sunstroke? Because an endless emphasis on the differences between the 'natives' and yourself is one of the necessary props of imperialism. You can only rule over a subject race, especially when you are in a small minority, if you honestly believe yourself to be racially superior, and it helps towards this if you can believe that the subject race is biologically different. There were quite a number of ways in which Europeans in India used to believe, without any evidence, that Asiatic bodies differed from their own. Even quite considerable anatomical differences were supposed to exist. But this nonsense about Europeans being subject to sunstroke and Orientals not, was the most cherished superstition of all. The thin skull was the mark of racial superiority, and the pith topi was a sort of emblem of imperialism.

That is why it seems to me a sign of the changing times that Wingate's men, British, Indians and Burmese alike, set forth in ordinary felt hats. They suffered from dysentery, malaria, leeches, lice, snakes and Japanese, but I do not think any cases of sunstroke were recorded. And above all, there seems to have been no official protest and no feeling that the abandonment of the topi was a subtle blow at white prestige.

* * *

In Mr Stanley Unwin's recent pamphlet, *Publishing in Peace and War*, some interesting facts are given about the quantities of paper allotted by the government for various purposes. Here are the present figures:

Newspapers	250,000 tons
H. M. Stationery Office	100,000
Periodicals (nearly)	50,000
Books	22,000

A particularly interesting detail is that out of the 100,000 tons allotted to the Stationery Office, the War Office gets no less than 25,000 tons, or more than the whole book trade put together.

I haven't personally witnessed, but I can imagine, the kind of wastage of paper that goes on in the War Office and the various ministries. I know what happens in the BBC. Would you credit, for instance, that of every radio programme that goes out on the air, even the inconceivable rubbish of cross-talk comedians, at least six copies are typed – sometimes as many as fifteen copies? For years past all this trash has been filed somewhere or other in enormous archives. At the same time paper for books is so short that even the most hackneyed 'classic' is liable to be out of print, many schools are short of text-books, new writers get no chance to start and even established writers have to expect a gap of a year or two years between finishing a book and seeing it published. And incidentally the export trade in English books has been largely swallowed up by America.

This part of Mr Unwin's pamphlet is a depressing story. He writes with justified anger of the contemptuous attitude towards books shown by one government department after another. But in fact the English as a whole, though somewhat better in this respect than the Americans, have not much reverence for books. It is in the small countries, such as Finland and Holland, that the book consumption per head is largest. Is it not rather humiliating to be told that a few years before the war a remote town like Reykjavik had a better display of British books than any English town of comparable size?

As I Please 46

27 October 1944

Reading, a week or two ago, Mr C. S. Lewis's recently-published book, *Beyond Personality* (it is a series of reprinted broadcasts on theology),[138] I learned from the blurb on the dust jacket that a critic who should, and indeed does, know better had likened an earlier book, *The Screwtape Letters*, to *The Pilgrim's Progress*. 'I do not hesitate to compare Mr Lewis's achievement with *Pilgrim's Progress*' were his quoted words. Here is a sample, entirely representative, from the later book:

> Well, even on the human level, you know, there are two kinds of pretending. There's a bad kind, where the pretence is instead of the real thing, as when a man pretends he's going to help you instead of really helping you. But there's also a good kind, where the pretence leads up to the real thing. When you're not feeling particularly friendly but know you ought to be, the best thing you can do, very often, is to put on a friendly manner and behave as if you were a much nicer chap than you actually are. And in a few minutes, as we've all noticed. you will be really feeling friendlier than you were. Very often the only way to get a quality is to start behaving as if you had it already. That's why children's games are so important. They're always pretending to be grown-ups - playing soldiers, playing shop. But all the time they are hardening their muscles and sharpening their wits, so that the pretence of being grown-ups helps them in earnest.

The book is like this all the way through, and I think most of us would hesitate a long time before equating Mr Lewis with Bunyan. One must make some allowance for the fact that these essays are reprinted broadcasts, but even on the air it is not really necessary to insult your hearers with homey little asides like 'you know' and 'mind you', or Edwardian slang like 'awfully', 'jolly well', 'specially' for 'especially', 'awful cheek' and so forth. The idea, of course, is to persuade the suspicious reader, or listener, that one can be a Christian and a 'jolly good chap' at the same time. I don't imagine that the attempt would have much success, and in any case the cotton wool with which the BBC stuffs its speakers' mouths makes any real discussion of theological problems impossible, even from an orthodox angle. But Mr Lewis's vogue at this moment, the time allowed to him on the air and the exaggerated praise he has received, are bad symptoms and worth noticing.

138. C. S. Lewis (1893–1961), best known today for his *Chronicles of Narnia* children's books, published in the 1950s, owed his reputation in the 1940s to his vigorous Christian apologetics in fictional and polemical writing.

Students of popular religious apologetics will notice early in the book a side-kick at 'all these people who turn up every few years with some patent simplified religion of their own', and various hints that unbelief is 'out of date', 'old-fashioned' and so forth. And they will remember Ronald Knox saying much the same thing fifteen years ago, and R. H. Benson twenty or thirty years before that, and they will know in which pigeon-hole Mr Lewis should be placed.[139]

A kind of book that has been endemic in England for quite sixty years is the silly-clever religious book, which goes on the principle not of threatening the unbeliever with Hell, but of showing him up as an illogical ass, incapable of clear thought and unaware that everything he says has been said and refuted before. This school of literature started, I think, with W. H. Mallock's *New Republic*, which must have been written about 1880, and it has had a long line of practitioners - R. H. Benson, Chesterton, Father Knox, 'Beachcomber' and others, most of them Catholics, but some, like Dr Cyril Alington and (I suspect) Mr Lewis himself, Anglicans.[140] The line of attack is always the same. Every heresy has been uttered before (with the implication that it has also been refuted before); and theology is only understood by theologians (with the implication that you should leave your thinking to the priests). Along these lines one can, of course, have a lot of clean fun by 'correcting loose thinking' and pointing out that so-and-so is only saying what Pelagius said in AD 400 (or whenever it was), and has in any case used the word transubstantiation in the wrong sense. The special targets of these people have been T. H. Huxley, H. G. Wells, Bertrand Russell, Professor Joad, and others who are associated in the popular mind with science and rationalism. They have never had much difficulty in demolishing them - though I notice that most of the demolished ones are still there, while some of the Christian apologists themselves begin to look rather faded.

One reason for the extravagant boosting that these people always get in the press is that their political affiliations are invariably reactionary. Some of them were frank admirers of fascism as long as it was safe to be so. That is why I draw attention to Mr C. S. Lewis and his chummy little wireless talks, of which no doubt there will be more. They are not really so unpolitical as they are meant to look. Indeed they are an out-flanking movement in the big counter-attack against the left which Lord Elton, A. P. Herbert, G. M. Young, Alfred Noyes and various others have been conducting for two years past.[141]

---

139. R. H. Benson (1871-1914) was a Catholic priest and novelist. He was the son of the Archbishop of Canterbury, E. W. Benson, and his conversion to Catholicism in 1903 caused a sensation. For Father Ronald Knox, see note 55.

140. The Rev Cyril Allington (1872-1955) was headmaster of Eton when Orwell was a pupil, becoming dean of Durham Cathedral in the early 1930s. For G. K. Chesterton, see note 25, for 'Beachcomber' note 23.

141. For Lord Elton, see note 93, for A. P. Herbert and G. M. Young note 91, for Alfred Noyes note 93.

* * *

I notice that in his new book, *Adam and Eve*, Mr Middleton Murry instances the agitation against Mosley's release from internment as a sign of the growth of totalitarianism, or the totalitarian habit of mind, in this country. The common people, he says, still detest totalitarianism: but he adds in a later footnote that the Mosley business has shaken this opinion somewhat. I wonder whether he is right.

On the face of it, the demonstrations against Mosley's release were a very bad sign. In effect people were agitating against *habeas corpus*. In 1940 it was a perfectly proper action to intern Mosley, and in my opinion it would have been quite proper to shoot him if the Germans had set foot in Britain. When it is a question of national existence, no government can stand on the letter of the law: otherwise a potential quisling has only to avoid committing any indictable offence, and he can remain at liberty, ready to go over to the enemy and act as their gauleiter as soon as they arrive. But by 1943 the situation was totally different. The chance of a serious German invasion had passed, and Mosley (though possibly he may make a come-back at some future date – I won't prophesy about that) was merely a ridiculous failed politician with varicose veins. To continue imprisoning him without trial was an infringement of every principle we are supposedly fighting for.

But there was also strong popular feeling against Mosley's release, and not, I think, for reasons so sinister as Mr Murry implies. The comment one most frequently heard was 'They've only done it because he's a rich man', which was a simplified way of saying 'Class privilege is on the up-grade again'. It is a commonplace that the political advance we seemed to make in 1940 has been gradually filched away from us again. But though the ordinary man sees this happening, he is curiously unable to combat it: there seems to be nowhere to take hold. In a way, politics has stopped. There has been no general election, the elector is conscious of being unable to influence his MP, parliament has no control over the government. You may not like the way things are going, but what exactly can you do about it? There is no concrete act against which you can plausibly protest.

But now and again something happens which is obviously symptomatic of the general trend – something round which existing discontents can crystallise. 'Lock up Mosley' was a good rallying cry. Mosley, in fact, was a symbol, as Beveridge still is and as Cripps was in 1942. I don't believe Mr Murry need bother about the implications of this incident. In spite of all that has happened, the failure of any genuinely totalitarian outlook to gain ground among the ordinary people of this country is one of the most surprising and encouraging phenomena of the war.

As I Please 47

3 November 1944

Penguin Books have now started publishing books in French, very nicely got up, at half-a-crown each. Among those to appear shortly is the latest instalment of André Gide's *Journal*, which covers a year of the German occupation. As I glanced through an old favourite, Anatole France's *Les Dieux ont soif* (it is a novel about the Reign of Terror during the French revolution), the thought occurred to me: what a remarkable anthology one could make of pieces of writing describing executions! There must be hundreds of them scattered through literature, and – for a reason I think I can guess – they must be far better written on average than battle pieces.

Among the examples I remember at the moment are Thackeray's description of the hanging of Courvoisier, the crucifixion of the gladiators in *Salammbô*, the final scene of *A Tale of Two Cities*, a piece from a letter or diary of Byron's, describing a guillotining, and the beheading of two Scottish noblemen after the 1745 rebellion, described by, I think, Horace Walpole. There is a very fine chapter describing a guillotining in Arnold Bennett's *Old Wives' Tale*, and a horrible one in one of Zola's novels (the one about the Sacré Coeur). Then there is Jack London's short story, 'The Chinago', Plato's account of the death of Socrates – but one could extend the list indefinitely. There must also be a great number of specimens in verse, for instance the old hanging ballads, to which Kipling's 'Danny Beever' probably owes something.

The thing that I think very striking is that no one, or no one I can remember, ever writes of an execution with approval. The dominant note is always horror. Society, apparently, cannot get along without capital punishment – for there are some people whom it is simply not safe to leave alive – and yet there is no one, when the pinch comes, who feels it right to kill another human being in cold blood. I watched a man hanged once.[142] There was no question that everybody concerned knew this to be a dreadful, unnatural action. I believe it is always the same – the whole jail, warders and prisoners alike, is upset when there is an execution. It is probably the fact that capital punishment is accepted as necessary, and yet instinctively felt to be wrong, that gives so many descriptions of executions their tragic atmosphere. They are mostly written by people who have actually watched an execution and feel it to be a terrible and only partly comprehensible experience which they want to record;

142. Related in his essay 'A Hanging' (1931).

whereas battle literature is largely written by people who have never heard a gun go off and think of a battle as a sort of football match in which nobody gets hurt.

Perhaps it was a bit previous to say that no one writes of an execution with approval, when one thinks of the way our newspapers have been smacking their chops over the bumping-off of wretched quislings in France and elsewhere. I recall, in one paper, a whole series of photos showing the execution of Caruso, the ex-chief of the Rome police. You saw the huge, fat body being straddled across a chair with his back to the firing squad, then the cloud of smoke issuing from the rifle barrels and the body slumping sideways. The editor who saw fit to publish this thought it a pleasant titbit, I suppose, but then he had not had to watch the actual deed. I think I can imagine the feelings of the man who took the photographs, and of the firing squad.

* * *

To the lovers of useless knowledge (and I know there are a lot of them, from the number of letters I always get when I raise any question of this kind) I present a curious little problem arising out of the recent Pelican, *Shakespeare's England.* A writer named Fynes Morrison, touring England in 1607, describes melons as growing freely. Andrew Marvell, in a very well-known poem written about fifty years later, also refers to melons. Both references make it appear that the melons grew in the open, and indeed they must have done so if they grew at all. The hot-bed was a recent invention in 1600, and glass-houses, if they existed, must have been a very great rarity. I imagine it would be quite impossible to grow a melon in the open in England nowadays. They are hard enough to grow under glass, whence their price. Fynes Morrison also speaks of grapes growing in large enough quantities to make wine. Is it possible that our climate has changed radically in the last three hundred years? Or was the so-called melon actually a pumpkin?

* * *

As from November 10th, *Tribune* intends to replan its book reviews. The present policy of trying to give every book a review of about a column is felt to be unsatisfactory, because with the small space at our disposal we cannot keep up to date, and the more important books frequently do not get the detailed treatment they deserve. The best solution seems to be to make some reviews shorter and others longer.

Daniel George's novel reviews will not be affected, but for the rest we intend to have about nine very short notices – a sort of guide to the current books – and one very long one, probably of about 1,500 words. This will allow us to cover rather more books than at present and keep more nearly up to date, but it will have the added advantage that serious books can be seriously treated. In every week there is at least one book that deserves a full-length review, even if its importance is only indirect.

From years of experience as a book reviewer I should say that the rock-bottom minimum in which you can both summarise and criticise a book is 800 words. But a book review is seldom of much value as a piece of writing if it is under 1,000 words. The generally higher standard of criticism in monthly and quarterly magazines is partly due to the fact that the reviewers are less pinched for space. In the old days of the *Edinburgh* and the *Quarterly*, a hundred years ago, a reviewer often had fifteen pages to play with!

If this policy does not work out well we shall scrap it, but we shall give it several months' trial. Our aim is to produce leading reviews which thoroughly criticise the chosen book and at the same time are worth-while articles in themselves. Apart from people who already write fairly frequently for *Tribune*, we have collected a first-rate team of reviewers, including Herbert Read, Stephen Spender, Franz Borkenau, Hugh Kingsmill, Michael Roberts, Mulk Raj Anand, Arturo Barea, Arthur Koestler and several others.[143]

As I Please 48

17 November 1944

Some weeks ago, in the course of some remarks on schools of journalism, I carelessly described the magazine the *Writer* as being 'defunct'. As a result I have received a severe letter from its proprietors, who enclose a copy of the November issue of the *Writer* and call on me to withdraw my statement.

I withdraw it readily. The *Writer* is still alive and seems to be much the same as ever, though it has changed its format since I knew it. And I think this specimen copy is worth examining for the light it throws on schools of journalism and the whole business of extracting fees from struggling freelance journalists.

The articles are of the usual type, 'Plotting Technique' (fifteenth instalment) by

143. Arturo Barea (1897–1957) was a Spanish writer and broadcaster. The head of the foreign press and censorship bureau of the Republican Government in Madrid during the Spanish civil war, he was forced to leave Spain in 1938 and eventually found his way to Britain. He worked for the BBC during the war, and contributed articles to *Horizon, London Forum* and the *Times Literary Supplement*. Orwell reviewed the first volume of his autobiography, *The Forge* (London: Faber and Faber, 1941), in *Time and Tide* and *Horizon*, and the third *The Clash* (London: Faber and Faber, 1946), in the *Observer*.

For Read, Spender, Anand and Koestler, see Introduction, note 16. For Borkenau, Kingsmill and Roberts, see Introduction, note 17.

William A. Bagley, etc, but I am more interested in the advertisements, which take up more than a quarter of the space. The majority of them are from people who profess to be able to teach you how to make money out of writing. A surprising number undertake to supply you with ready-made plots. Here are a few specimens:

> Plotting without tears. Learn my way. The simplest method ever. Money returned if dissatisfied. 5s post free.
> Inexhaustible plotting method for women's press, 5s 3d. Gives real mastery. Ten days' approval.
> PLOTS. Our plots are set out in sequence all ready for write-up, with lengths for each sequence. No remoulding necessary – just the requisite clothing of words. All types supplied.
> PLOTS: in vivid scenes. With striking opening lines for actual use in story. Specimen conversation, including authentic dialect . . . Short-short, 5s. Short story, 6s 6d. Long-complete (with tense, breathless 'curtains') 5s 6d. Radio plays, 10s 6d. Serial, novel, novelette (chapter by chapter, appropriate prefix, prose or poetical quotations if desired) 15s 6d–1gn.

There are many others. Somebody called Mr Martin Walter claims to have reduced story-construction to an exact science and eventually evolved the Plot Formula according to which his own stories and those of his students throughout the world are constructed. . . Whether you aspire to write the 'literary' story or the popular story, or to produce stories for any existing market, remember that Mr Walter's Formula alone tells you just what a 'plot' is and how to produce one. The Formula only costs you a guinea, it appears. Then there are the 'Fleet Street journalists' who are prepared to revise your manuscripts for you at 2s 6d per thousand words. Nor are the poets forgotten:

> GREETINGS
> Are you poets neglecting the great post-war demand for sentiments?
> Do you specialise and do you know what is needed?
> Aida Reuben's famous Greeting Card Course is available to approved students willing to work hard. Her book Sentiment and Greeting Card Publishers, published at 3s 6d, may be obtained from, etc, etc.

I do not wish to say anything offensive, but to anyone who is inclined to respond to the sort of advertisement quoted above, I offer this consideration. If these people really know how to make money out of writing, why aren't they just doing it instead of peddling their secret at 5s a time? Apart from any other consideration, they would be raising up hordes of competitors for themselves. This number of the *Writer* contains about thirty advertisements of this stamp, and the *Writer* itself, besides giving advice in its articles, also runs its own literary bureau in which manuscripts are 'criticised by acknowledged experts' at so much a thousand words. If each of these various teachers had even ten successful pupils a week, they would between them be letting loose on to the market some fifteen thousand successful writers per annum!

Also, isn't it rather curious that the 'Fleet Street journalists', 'established authors' and 'well-known novelists' who either run these courses or write the testimonials for them are not named – or, when named, are seldom or never people whose published work you have seen anywhere. If Bernard Shaw or J. B. Priestley offered to teach you how to make money out of writing, you might feel that there was something in it. But who would buy a bottle of hair-restorer from a bald man?

If the *Writer* wants some more free publicity it shall have it, but I dare say this will do to go on with.

* * *

One favourite way of falsifying history nowadays is to alter dates. Maurice Thorez,[144] the French communist, has been amnestied by the French government (he was under sentence for deserting from the army). Apropos of this, one London newspaper remarks that Thorez 'will now be able to return from Moscow, where he has been living in exile for the last six years'.

On the contrary, he has been in Moscow for at most five years, as the editor of this newspaper is well aware. Thorez, who for several years past has been proclaiming his anxiety to defend France against the Germans, was called up at the outbreak of war in 1939, and failed to make an appearance. Some time later he turned up in Moscow.

But why the alteration of date? In order to make it appear that Thorez deserted, if he did desert, a year before the war and not after the fighting had started. This is merely one act in the general effort to whitewash the behaviour of the French and other communists during the period of the Russo-German pact. I could name other similar falsifications in recent years. Sometimes you can give an event a quite different colour by switching its date only a few weeks. But it doesn't matter so long as we all keep our eyes open and see to it that the lies do not creep out of the newspapers and into the history books.

* * *

A correspondent who lacks the competing instinct has sent a copy of *Principles or Prejudices*, a sixpenny pamphlet by Kenneth Pickthorn,[145] the Conservative MP, with the advice (underlined in red ink): 'Burn when read.'

I wouldn't think of burning it. It has gone straight into my archives. But I agree that

144. Maurice Thorez (1900–64) was general secretary of the French Communist Party 1930–64. A hard-line Stalinist, he deserted from the French army in 1940 and spent the war in Moscow.
145. Kenneth Pickthorn (1892–1975) was Conservative MP for Cambridge University 1935–50.

it is a disgusting piece of work, and that this whole series of pamphlets (the Signpost Booklets, by such authors as G. M. Young, Douglas Woodruff and Captain L. D. Gammans)[146] is a bad symptom. Mr Pickthorn is one of the more intelligent of the younger Tory MPs ('younger' in political circles means under sixty), and in this pamphlet he is trying to present Toryism in a homely and democratic light while casting misleading little smacks at the left. Look at this, for instance, for a misrepresentation of the theory of Marxism:

> Not one of the persons who say that economic factors govern the world believes it about himself. If Karl Marx had been more economically than politically interested he could have done better for himself than by accepting the kindnesses of the capitalist Engels and occasionally selling articles to American newspapers.

Aimed at ignorant people, this is meant to imply that Marxism regards individual acquisitiveness as the motive force in history. Marx not only did not say this, he said almost the opposite of it. Much of the pamphlet is an attack on the notion of internationalism, and is backed up by such remarks as: 'No British statesman should feel himself authorised to spend British blood for the promotion of something superior to British interests.' Fortunately, Mr Pickthorn writes too badly to have a very wide appeal, but some of the other pamphleteers in this series are leveller. The Tory Party used always to be known as 'the stupid party'. But the publicists of this group have a fair selection of brains among them, and when Tories grow intelligent it is time to feel for your watch and count your small change.

As I Please 49

24 November 1944

There have been innumerable complaints lately about the rudeness of shopkeepers. People say, I think with truth, that shopkeepers appear to take a sadistic pleasure in telling you that they don't stock the thing you ask for. To go in search of some really rare object, such as a comb or a tin of boot polish, is a miserable experience. It means trailing from shop to shop and getting a series of curt or actually hostile negatives. But even the

146. Douglas Woodruff (1897–1978) was editor of the *Tablet*, the Catholic weekly, 1936–67. Captain L. D. Gammans (1895–1957), formerly a colonial administrator in Malaya, was Conservative MP for Hornsey 1941–57.

routine business of buying the rations and the bread is made as difficult as possible for busy people. How is a woman to do her household shopping if she is working till six every day while most of the shops shut at five? She can only do it by fighting round crowded counters during her lunch hour. But it is the snubs that they get when they ask for some article which is in short supply that people dread most. Many shopkeepers seem to regard the customer as a kind of mendicant and to feel that they are conferring a favour on him by selling him anything. And there are other justified grievances - for instance, the shameless overcharging on uncontrolled goods such as second-hand furniture, and the irritating trick, now very common, of displaying in the window goods which are not on sale.

But before blaming the shopkeeper for all this, there are several things one ought to remember. To begin with, irritability and bad manners are on the increase everywhere. You have only to observe the behaviour of normally long-suffering people like bus conductors to realise this. It is a neurosis produced by the war. But, in addition, many small independent shopkeepers (in my experience you are treated far more politely in big shops) are people with a well-founded grievance against society. Some of them are in effect the ill-paid employees of wholesale firms, others are being slowly crushed by the competition of the chain stores, and they are often treated with the greatest inconsiderateness by the local authorities. Sometimes a rehousing scheme will rob a shopkeeper of half his customers at one swoop. In war-time this may happen even more drastically owing to bombing and the call-up. And war has other special irritations for the shopkeeper. Rationing puts a great deal of extra work on to grocers, butchers, etc and it is very exasperating to be asked all day long for articles which you have not got.

But after all, the main fact is that at normal times both the shop assistant and the independent shopkeepers are downtrodden. They live to the tune of 'the customer is always right'. In peace time, in capitalist society, everyone is trying to sell goods which there is never enough money to buy, whereas in war-time money is plentiful and goods scarce. Matches, razor blades, torch batteries, alarm clocks and teats for babies' feeding bottles are precious rarities, and the man who possesses them is a powerful being, to be approached cap in hand. I don't think one can blame the shopkeeper for getting a bit of his own back, when the situation is temporarily reversed. But I do agree that the behaviour of some of them is disgusting, and that when one is treated with more than normal haughtiness it is a duty to the rest of the public not to go to that shop again.

* * *

Examining recently a copy of *Old Moore's Almanack*,[147] I was reminded of the fun I used

147. For *Old Moore's Almanack*, see note 32.

to extract in my boyhood from answering advertisements. Increase your height, earn five pounds a week in your spare time, drink habit conquered in three days, electric belts, bust-developers and cures for obesity, insomnia, bunions, backache, red noses, stammering, blushing, piles, bad legs, flat feet and baldness - all the old favourites were there or nearly all. Some of these advertisements have remained totally unchanged for at least thirty years.

You cannot, I imagine, get much benefit from any of these nostrums, but you can have a lot of fun by answering the advertisements and then, when you have drawn them out and made them waste a lot of stamps in sending successive wads of testimonials, suddenly leaving them cold. Many years ago I answered an advertisement from Winifred Grace Hartland (the advertisement used to carry a photograph of her - a radiant woman with a sylph-like figure), who undertook to cure obesity. In replying to my letter she assumed that I was a woman - this surprised me at the time, though I realise now that the dupes of these advertisements are almost all female. She urged me to come and see her at once. 'Do come,' she wrote, 'before ordering your summer frocks, as after taking my course your figure will have altered out of recognition.' She was particularly insistent that I should make a personal visit, and gave an address somewhere in the London Docks. This went on for a long time, during which the fee gradually sank from two guineas to half a crown, and then I brought the matter to an end by writing to say that I had been cured of my obesity by a rival agency.

Years later I came across a copy of the cautionary list which *Truth*[148] used to issue from time to time in order to warn the public against swindlers. It revealed that there was no such person as Winifred Grace Hartland, this swindle being run by two American crooks named Harry Sweet and Dave Little. It is curious that they should have been so anxious for a personal visit, and indeed I have since wondered whether Harry Sweet and Dave Little were actually engaged in shipping consignments of fat women to the harems of Istanbul.

* * *

Everyone has a list of books which he is 'always meaning to read', and now and again one gets round to reading one of them. One that I recently crossed off my list was George

148. *Truth* was a right-wing magazine run by Sir Joseph Ball, a former MI5 officer who was the first director of the Conservative Research Department (from 1930), the founder and director of the National Publicity Bureau (the National government's propaganda organisation, set up in 1935) and a close friend of Neville Chamberlain. Ball and his associates acquired the magazine in 1936 to act as a propaganda vehicle for Chamberlain, and after Chamberlain's fall it became rabidly anti-American, anti-Soviet and anti-semitic. It expired in 1955. See Richard Cockett, *Twilight of Truth: Chamberlain and the Manipulation of the Press* (London: Weidenfeld and Nicholson, 1989).

Bourne's *Memoirs of a Surrey Labourer.*[149] I was slightly disappointed with it, because, though it is a true story, Bettesworth, the man it is about, was not quite an ordinary labourer. He had been a farm worker, but had become a jobbing gardener, and his relation with George Bourne was that of servant and master. Nevertheless there is some remarkable detail in it, and it gives a true picture of the cruel, sordid end with which a lifetime of heavy work on the land is often rewarded. The book was written more than thirty years ago, but things have not changed fundamentally. Immediately before the war, in my own village in Hertfordshire, two old men were ending their days in much the same bare misery as George Bourne describes.

Another book I recently read, or rather re-read, was *The Follies and Frauds of Spiritualism*, issued about twenty years ago by the Rationalist Press Association.[150] This is probably not an easy book to get hold of, but I can equally recommend Mr Bechhofer Roberts's book on the same subject.[151] An interesting fact that these and similar books bring out is the number of scientists who have been taken in by spiritualism. The list includes Sir William Crookes, Wallace the biologist, Lombroso, Flammarion the astronomer (he afterwards changed his mind, however), Sir Oliver Lodge, and a whole string of German and Italian professors. These people are not, perhaps, the top-notchers of the scientific world, but you do not find, for instance, poets in comparable numbers falling a prey to the mediums. Elizabeth Barrett Browning is supposed to have been taken in by the famous medium Home, but Browning himself saw through him at a glance and wrote a scarifying poem about him ('Sludge the Medium'). Significantly, the people who are never converted to spiritualism are conjurors.

As I Please 50

1 December 1944

V-2 (I am told that you can now mention it in print so long as you just call it V-2 and

149. George Bourne was the pen name of George Sturt (1863–1927). *Memoirs of a Surrey Labourer* was first published in 1907.
150. Walter Mann, *The Follies and Frauds of Spiritualism* (London: Watts, 1919). The Rationalist Press Association was founded in 1899. It still produces the excellent *New Humanist* magazine every two months. For its history see Bill Cooke, *The Blasphemy Depot: A Hundred Years of the Rationalist Press Association* (London: RPA, 2003).
151. C. E. Bechhofer Roberts, *The Truth about Spiritualism* (London: Eyre and Spottiswoode, 1932).

don't describe it too minutely) supplies another instance of the contrariness of human nature.[152] People are complaining of the sudden unexpected wallop with which these things go off. 'It wouldn't be so bad if you got a bit of warning' is the usual formula. There is even a tendency to talk nostalgically of the days of the V-1.[153] The good old doodlebug did at least give you time to get under the table, etc, etc. Whereas, in fact, when the doodlebugs were actually dropping, the usual subject of complaint was the uncomfortable waiting period before they went off. Some people are never satisfied. Personally, I am no lover of the V-2, especially at this moment when the house still seems to be rocking from a recent explosion, but what depresses me about these things is the way they set people talking about the next war. Every time one goes off I hear gloomy references to 'next time', and the reflection: 'I suppose they'll be able to shoot them across the Atlantic by that time.' But if you ask who will be fighting whom when this universally expected war breaks out, you get no clear answer. It is just war in the abstract – the notion that human beings could ever behave sanely having apparently faded out of many people's memories.

* * *

Maurice Baring, in his book on Russian literature, which was published in 1907 and must have been the means of introducing many people in this country to the great Russian novelists, remarks that English books were always popular in Russia. Among other favourites he mentions *The Diary of a Nobody* (which, by the way, is reprinted by the Everyman Library, if you can run across a copy).[154]

I have always wondered what on earth *The Diary of a Nobody* could be like in a Russian translation, and indeed I have faintly suspected that the Russians may have enjoyed it because when translated it was just like Chekhov. But in a way it would be a very good book to read if you wanted to get a picture of English life, even though it was written in the eighties and has an intensely strong smell of that period. Charles Pooter is a true Englishman both in native gentleness and his impenetrable stupidity. The interesting thing, however, is to follow this book up to its origins. What does it ultimately derive from? Almost certainly, I think, from Don Quixote, of which, indeed, it is a sort of modern anglicised version. Pooter is a high-minded, even adventurous man, constantly

152. The V-2 rocket was a German ballistic missile deployed from autumn 1944 and used against targets in France, Belgium and Holland as well as Britain. More than 1,100 of them were observed over Britain and they killed more than 2,000 people, mostly in London. See Angus Calder, *The People's War: Britain 1939–1945* (London: Jonathan Cape, 1969), chapter 9.

153. For the V-1, see note 130.

154. *The Diary of a Nobody* by George and Weedon Grossmith was first published in 1892.

suffering disasters brought upon him by his own folly, and surrounded by a whole tribe of Sancho Panzas. But apart from the comparative mildness of the things that befall him, one can see in the endings of the two books the enormous difference between the age of Cervantes and our own.

In the end the Grossmiths have to take pity on poor Pooter. Everything, or nearly everything, comes right, and at the last there is a tinge of sentimentality which does not quite fit in with the rest of the book. The fact is that, in spite of the way we actually behave, we cannot any longer feel that the infliction of pain is merely funny. Nietzsche remarks somewhere that the pathos of Don Quixote may well be a modern discovery. Quite likely Cervantes didn't mean Don Quixote to seem pathetic - perhaps he just meant him to be funny and intended it as a screaming joke when the poor old man has half his teeth knocked out by a sling-stone. However this may be with Don Quixote, I am fairly certain that it is true of Falstaff. Except possibly for the final scene in *Henry V*, there is nothing to show that Shakespeare sees Falstaff as a pathetic as well as a comic figure. He is just a punching-bag for fortune, a sort of Billy Bunter with a gift for language. The thing that seems saddest to us is Falstaff's helpless dependence on his odious patron, Prince Harry, whom John Masefield aptly described as a 'disgusting beefy brute'. There is no sign, or at any rate, no clear sign, that Shakespeare sees anything pathetic or degrading in such a relationship.

* * *

Say what you like, things do change. A few years ago I was walking across Hungerford Bridge with a lady aged about sixty or perhaps less. The tide was out, and as we looked down at the beds of filthy, almost liquid mud, she remarked: 'When I was a little girl we used to throw pennies to the mudlarks down there.'

I was intrigued and asked what mudlarks were. She explained that in those days professional beggars, known as mudlarks, used to sit under the bridge waiting for people to throw them pennies. The pennies would bury themselves deep in the mud, and the mudlarks would plunge in head first and recover them. It was considered a most amusing spectacle.

Is there anyone who would degrade himself in that way nowadays? And how many people are there who would get a kick out of watching it?

* * *

Shortly before his assassination, Trotsky had completed a life of Stalin. One may assume that it was not an altogether unbiased book, but obviously a biography of Stalin by Trotsky - or, for that matter, a biography of Trotsky by Stalin - would be a winner from a selling point of view. A very well-known American firm of publishers were to issue it.

The book had been printed and - this is the point that I have been waiting to verify before mentioning this matter in my notes - the review copies had been sent out when the USA entered the war. The book was immediately withdrawn, and the reviewers were asked to co-operate in 'avoiding any comment whatever regarding the biography and its postponement'.

They have co-operated remarkably well. The affair has gone almost unmentioned in the American press and, as far as I know, entirely unmentioned in the British press, although the facts were well known and obviously worth a paragraph or two.

Since the American entry into the war made the USA and the USSR allies, I think that to withdraw the book was an understandable if not particularly admirable deed. What is disgusting is the general willingness to suppress all mention of it. A little while back I attended a meeting of the PEN Club,[155] which was held to celebrate the tercentenary of *Areopagitica*, Milton's famous tract on the freedom of the press. There were countless speeches emphasising the importance of preserving intellectual liberty, even in war-time. If I remember rightly, Milton's phrase about the special sin of 'murdering' a book was printed on the PEN leaflet for the occasion. But I heard no reference to this particular murder, the facts of which were no doubt known to plenty of people there.

* * *

Here is another little brain-tickler. The following often-quoted passage comes from Act V of Shakespeare's tragedy, *Timon of Athens*:

> Come not to me again, but say to Athens,
> Timon hath made his everlasting mansion
> Upon the beachèd verge of the salt flood
> Who once a day with his embossed froth
> The turbulent surge shall cover.

This passage contains three errors. What are they?

155. The PEN Club was the British section of PEN International, set up in 1921 to promote co-operation among writers and the defence of literature with John Galsworthy as its first president. Its president in 1944 was the novelist Margaret Storm Jameson, a *Tribune* contributor.

As I Please 51

8 December 1944

For years past I have been an industrious collector of pamphlets, and a fairly steady reader of political literature of all kinds. The thing that strikes me more and more – and it strikes a lot of other people, too – is the extraordinary viciousness and dishonesty of political controversy in our time. I don't mean merely that controversies are acrimonious. They ought to be that when they are on serious subjects. I mean that almost nobody seems to feel that an opponent deserves a fair hearing or that the objective truth matters as long as you can score a neat debating point. When I look through my collection of pamphlets – conservative, communist, Catholic, Trotskyist, pacifist, anarchist or what-have-you – it seems to me that almost all of them have the same mental atmosphere, though the points of emphasis vary. Nobody is searching for the truth, everybody is putting forward a 'case' with complete disregard for fairness or accuracy, and the most plainly obvious facts can be ignored by those who don't want to see them. The same propaganda tricks are to be found almost everywhere. It would take many pages of this paper merely to classify them, but here I draw attention to one very widespread controversial habit – disregard of an opponent's motives. The key-word here is 'objectively'.

We are told that it is only people's objective actions that matter, and their subjective feelings are of no importance. Thus pacifists, by obstructing the war effort, are 'objectively' aiding the Nazis; and therefore the fact that they may be personally hostile to fascism is irrelevant. I have been guilty of saying this myself more than once. The same argument is applied to Trotskyism. Trotskyists are often credited, at any rate by communists, with being active and conscious agents of Hitler; but when you point out the many and obvious reasons why this is unlikely to be true, the 'objectively' line of talk is brought forward again. To criticise the Soviet Union helps Hitler: therefore 'Trotskyism is fascism'. And when this has been established, the accusation of conscious treachery is usually repeated.

This is not only dishonest; it also carries a severe penalty with it. If you disregard people's motives, it becomes much harder to foresee their actions. For there are occasions when even the most misguided person can see the results of what he is doing. Here is a crude but quite possible illustration. A pacifist is working in some job which gives him access to important military information, and is approached by a German secret agent. In those circumstances his subjective feelings do make a difference. If he is subjectively pro-Nazi he will sell his country, and if he isn't, he won't. And situations essentially similar though less dramatic are constantly arising.

In my opinion a few pacifists are inwardly pro-Nazi, and extremist left-wing parties will inevitably contain fascist spies. The important thing is to discover which individuals are honest and which are not, and the usual blanket accusation merely makes this more difficult. The atmosphere of hatred in which controversy is conducted blinds people to considerations of this kind. To admit that an opponent might be both honest and intelligent is felt to be intolerable. It is more immediately satisfying to shout that he is a fool or a scoundrel, or both, than to find out what he is really like. It is this habit of mind, among other things, that has made political prediction in our time so remarkably unsuccessful.

* * *

The following leaflet (printed) was passed to an acquaintance of mine in a pub:

> LONG LIVE THE IRISH!
> The first American soldier to kill a Jap was Mike Murphy.
> The first American pilot to sink a Jap battleship was Colin Kelly.
> The first American family to lose five sons in one action and have a naval vessel named after them were the Sullivans.
> The first American to shoot a Jap plane was Dutch O'Hara.
> The first coastguardsman to spot a German spy was John Conlan.
> The first American soldier to be decorated by the President was Pat Powers.
> The first American admiral to be killed leading his ship into battle was Dan Callahan.
> The first American son-of-a-bitch to get four new tyres from the Ration Board was Abie Goldstein.

The origin of this thing might just possibly be Irish, but it is much likelier to be American. There is nothing to indicate where it was printed, but it probably comes from the printing-shop of some American organisation in this country. If any further manifestos of the same kind turn up, I shall be interested to hear of them.

* * *

This number of *Tribune* includes a long letter from Mr Martin Walter, controller of the British Institute of Fiction-Writing Science Ltd, in which he complains that I have traduced him. He says (a) that he did not claim to have reduced fiction-writing to an exact science, (b) that numbers of successful writers have been produced by his teaching methods, and (c) he asks whether *Tribune* accepts advertisements that it believes to be fraudulent.

With regard to (a): 'It is claimed by this Institute that these problems [of fiction-writing] have been solved by Martin Walter, who, convinced of the truth of the hypothesis that every art is a science at heart, analyzed over 5,000 stories and eventually evolved the Plot Formula according to which all his own stories and those of his students throughout the world are constructed.' 'I had established that the nature of the 'plot' is strictly scientific.' Statements of this type are scattered throughout Mr Walter's booklets and advertisements. If this is not a claim to have reduced fiction-writing to an exact science, what the devil is it?

With regard to (b): Who are these successful writers whom Mr Walter has launched upon the world? Let us hear their names, and the names of their published works, and then we shall know where we are.

With regard to (c): A periodical ought not to accept advertisements which have the appearance of being fraudulent, but it cannot sift everything beforehand. What is to be done, for instance, about publishers' advertisements, in which it is invariably claimed that every single book named is of the highest possible value? What is most important in this connexion is that a periodical should not let its editorial columns be influenced by its advertisements. *Tribune* has been very careful not to do that – it has not done it in the case of Mr Walter himself, for instance.

It may interest Mr Walter to know that I should never have referred to him if he had not accompanied the advertisement he inserted some time ago with some free copies of his booklets (including the Plot Formula), and the suggestion that I might like to mention them in my column. It was this that drew my attention to him. Now I have given him his mention, and he does not seem to like it.

* * *

Answer to last week's problem. The three errors are:

(a) The 'who' should be 'whom'.
(b) Timon was buried below the high-tide mark. The sea would cover him twice a day, not once, as there are always two high tides within the twenty-four hours.
(c) It wouldn't cover him at all, as there is no perceptible tide in the Mediterranean.

As I Please 52

29 December 1944

I am indebted to an article by Mr Dwight Macdonald[156] in the September number of *Politics*, the New York monthly, for some extracts from a book entitled *Kill – or Get Killed, a Manual of Hand-to-Hand Fighting* by Major Rex Applegate.

This book, a semi-official American publication, not only gives extensive information about knifing, strangling, and the various horrors that come under the heading of 'unarmed combat', but describes the battle-schools in which soldiers are trained for house-to-house fighting. Here are some sample directions:

> . . . Before entering the tunnel, the coach exposes dummy A and the student uses the knife on it while the student is proceeding from target No. 1 to target No. 4, the 'Gestapo torture scene' or the 'Italian cursing' sequence is played over the loudspeaker . . . Target No. 9 is in darkness, and as the student enters this compartment the 'Jap rape' sequence is used . . . While the coach is reloading the student's pistol, the 'Get that American son-of-a-bitch' sequence is used. As the coach and student pass through the curtain into the next compartment, they are confronted by a dummy which has a knife stuck in its back, and represents a dead body. This dummy is illuminated by a green light and is not to be fired at by the student, although practically all of them do.

Mr Macdonald comments:

> There is one rather interesting problem in operating the course. Although the writer never states so directly, it would seem there is danger that the student's inhibitions will be broken down so thoroughly that he will shoot or stab the coach who accompanies him . . . The coach is advised to keep himself in a position to grab the student's gun arm 'at any instant'; after the three dummies along the course have been stabbed, 'the knife is taken away from the student to prevent accidents'; and finally: 'There is no place on the course where total darkness prevails while instructor is near student.'

I believe the similar battle-courses in the British army have now been discontinued or toned down, but it is worth remembering that something like this is inevitable if one wants military efficiency. No ideology, no consciousness of having 'something to fight

156. For Dwight Macdonald, see note 97.

for', is fully a substitute for it. This deliberate brutalising of millions of human beings is part of the price of society in its present form. The Japanese, incidentally, have been experts at this kind of thing for hundreds of years. In the old days the sons of aristocrats used to be taken at a very early age to witness executions, and if any boy showed the slightest sign of nausea he was promptly made to swallow large quantities of rice stained the colour of blood.

* * *

The English common people are not great lovers of military glory, and I have pointed out elsewhere that when a battle poem wins really wide popularity, it usually deals with a disaster and not a victory. But the other day, when I repeated this in some connexion, there came into my head the once popular song – it might be popular again if one of the gramophone companies would bother to record it – 'Admiral Benbow'. This rather jingoistic ballad seems to contradict my theory, but I believe it may have owed some of its popularity to the fact that it had a class-war angle which was understood at the time.

Admiral Benbow, when going into action against the French, was suddenly deserted by his subordinate captains and left to fight against heavy odds. As the ballad puts it:

Said Kirby unto Wade, 'We will run, we will run,'
Said Kirby unto Wade, 'We will run;
For I value no disgrace
Nor the losing of my place,
But the enemy I won't face,
Nor his guns, nor his guns.'

So Benbow was left to fight single-handed and, though victorious, he himself was killed. There is a gory but possibly authentic description of his death:

Brave Benbow lost his legs, by chain shot, by chain shot,
Brave Benbow lost his legs, by chain shot;
Brave Benbow lost his legs
And all on his stumps he begs,
'Fight on, my English lads,
'Tis our lot, 'tis our lot.'
The surgeon dressed his wounds, Benbow cries, Benbow cries,
The surgeon dressed his wounds, Benbow cries;
'Let a cradle now in haste
On the quarter-deck be placed,
That the enemy I may face
Till I die, till I die.'

The point is that Benbow was an ordinary seaman who had risen from the ranks. He had started off as a cabin boy. And his captains are supposed to have fled from the action because they did not want to see so plebeian a commander win a victory. I wonder whether it was this tradition that made Benbow into a popular hero and caused his name to be commemorated not only in the ballad but on the signs of innumerable public houses?

I believe no recording of this song exists, but – as I discovered when I was broadcasting and wanted to use similar pieces as five-minute fill-ups – it is only one of a long list of old popular songs and folk songs which have not been recorded. Until recently, at any rate, I believe there was not even a record of 'Tom Bowling' or of 'Greensleeves', i.e. the words as well as the music. Others that I failed to get hold of were 'A Cottage Well Thatched with Straw', 'Green Grow the Rushes, O', 'Blow Away the Morning Dew', and 'Come Lasses and Lads'. Other well-known songs are recorded in mutilated versions, and usually sung by professional singers with such a stale perfunctoriness that you seem to smell the whisky and cigarette smoke coming off the record. The collection of recorded carols is also very poor. You can't, I believe, get hold of 'Minstrels and maid', or 'Like Silver Lamps in a Distant Shrine', or 'Dives and Lazarus', or other old favourites. On the other hand, if you want a record of 'Roll Out the Barrel', 'Boomps-a-Daisy', etc, you would find quite a number of different renderings to choose from.

* * *

A correspondent in *Tribune* of 15 December expresses his 'horror and disgust' at hearing that Indian troops had been used against the Greeks, and compared this to the action of Franco in using Moorish troops against the Spanish Republic.

It seems to me important that this ancient red herring should not be dragged across the trail. To begin with, the Indian troops are not strictly comparable to Franco's Moors. The reactionary Moorish chieftains, bearing rather the same relationship to Franco as the Indian princes do to the British Conservative Party, sent their men to Spain with the conscious aim of crushing democracy. The Indian troops are mercenaries, serving the British from family tradition or for the sake of a job, though latterly a proportion of them have probably begun to think of themselves as an Indian army, nucleus of the armed forces of a future independent India. It is not likely that their presence in Athens had any political significance. Probably it was merely that they happened to be the nearest troops available.

But in addition, it is of the highest importance that socialists should have no truck with colour prejudice. On a number of occasions – the Ruhr occupation of 1923 and the Spanish civil war, for instance – the cry 'using coloured troops' has been raised as though it were somehow worse to be shot up by Indians or Negroes than by Europeans. Our crime in Greece is to have interfered in Greek internal affairs at all: the colour of the troops who carry out the orders is irrelevant. In the case of the Ruhr occupation, it was perhaps justifiable to protest against the use of Senegalese troops, because the Germans probably felt this an added humiliation, and the French may have used black troops for that very reason. But such feelings are not universal in Europe, and I doubt whether there is anywhere any prejudice against Indian troops, who are conspicuously well-behaved.

Our correspondent might have made the point that in an affair of this kind it is particularly mean to make use of politically ignorant colonial troops who don't understand in what a dirty job they're being mixed up. But at least don't let us insult the Indians by suggesting that their presence in Athens is somehow more offensive than that of the British.

Books and the people: a new year message

5 January 1945

For some months past we have intended to make some kind of explanatory statement about *Tribune*'s literary policy, present and future, and the first week of the new year seems a suitable time to do it.

Regular readers of *Tribune* will have noted that during recent months we have printed short stories only intermittently, we have printed less verse than we used to do, and we have altered our system of reviewing, giving a full-length review each week to only one book, and 200-word 'shorts' to all the others. The new system of reviewing seems to be giving general satisfaction. By means of it we can cover – including the books in Daniel George's column[157] – anything up to fifteen books a week, and thus can keep more or less abreast of the current output, which was quite impossible before. We can also in this way make some mention of cheap reprints and even a certain number of pamphlets and periodicals. From time to time we are charged by our readers with concentrating on books which the average person cannot afford to buy, but anyone who chooses to look back through our columns will see that Penguins and other very cheap publications have had their fair share of notice.

The gradual dropping of short stories is deliberate. In future we shall probably abandon short stories almost completely, though we shall not refuse a *good* short story when we happen to get one. We shall also from time to time, as we have done once or twice already, print detachable excerpts from old books. This seems to us a useful thing to do at a time like the present, when so many standard books are unobtainable.

It was only unwillingly that we decided on the dropping of short stories, but the quality of the stories sent in to me makes them, in much more than nine cases out of ten, simply not worth ink and paper. For long past there has been a volume of justified complaints from readers that *Tribune*'s stories were 'always so gloomy'. The trouble, as anyone who had my job would quickly appreciate, is that one almost never nowadays sees a story with any serious literary pretensions that is *not* gloomy. The reasons for this are many and complex, but I think literary fashion is

157. Daniel George Bunting (1890–1967) was an essayist and poet. He reviewed for *Tribune* until well into the 1950s.

one of them. A 'happy ending', or indeed any admission that anything is right with the world anywhere, seems to be as out of date as Dundreary whiskers,[158] and it hardly seems worth diffusing gloom from the final pages of the paper unless exceptional literary distinction goes with it. Many readers have told me, in writing and by word of mouth, how tired they are of the kind of story that begins 'Marjorie's husband was to be hanged on Tuesday, and the children were starving', or 'For seven years no ray of sunlight had penetrated the dusty room where William Grocock, a retired insurance agent, lay dying of cancer'; but I don't fancy they are more tired of them than I am myself, who have to work my way through round about twenty such stories every week.

By printing less stories we shall have more room for essays and articles on literary or general (i.e. not directly political) subjects. But upon all those readers who complain that we do not have enough articles on music, or painting, or the drama, or radio, or modern educational methods, or psychoanalysis, or what-not, I urge one important consideration: that we have very little space. In most weeks we have well under five pages at our disposal, and we have already been driven into smaller print for the short reviews. It is principally lack of space that has prevented us from undertaking any notes on radio, gramophone records and music generally. We could not do it regularly, and therefore should not be able to keep sufficiently up to date. Nor can we notice concerts, exhibitions, etc, because these occur only in one place, usually London, and *Tribune*'s readers are spread all over the country.

So far I have been dealing with details. But a more general defence, or at least explanation, of our literary policy is needed, because there are certain criticisms of an adverse kind that come up in varying forms over and over again. Our critics are divisible into two main schools. It would be manifestly impossible to satisfy both, and in practice, I should say, impossible to satisfy either.

The first school accuses us of being lowbrow, vulgar, ignorant, obsessed with politics, hostile to the arts, dominated by back-scratching cliques and anxious to prevent talented young writers from getting a hearing. The other school accuses us of being highbrow, arty, bourgeois, indifferent to politics and constantly wasting space on material that can be of no interest to a working man and of no direct use to the socialist movement. Both points need meeting, because between them they express a difficulty that is inherent in running any paper that is not a pure propaganda sheet.

Against the first school, we point out that *Tribune* reaches a large, heterogeneous left-wing audience and cannot be turned into a sort of trade paper for young poets, or a tilting-ground on which rival gangs of Surrealists, Apocalyptics and what-not can fight

158. What would now be called mutton-chop sideburns, very fashionable in the 1870s and 1970s.

out their battles.[159] We can assume that our public is intelligent, but not that its primary interests are literary or artistic, and still less that all of our readers have been educated in the same way and will know the same jokes and recognise the same allusions. The smaller literary magazines tend to develop a sort of family atmosphere - and, at the risk of offending a contributor now and then, we have made efforts to prevent that kind of thing from being imported into *Tribune*. We never, for instance, review books written in foreign languages, and we try to cut out avoidable foreign quotations and obscure literary allusions. Nor will we print anything that is verbally unintelligible. I have had several angry letters because of this, but I refuse to be responsible for printing anything that I do not understand. If can't understand it, the chances are that many of our readers will not be able to either. As to the charge that we are dominated by cliques (contributions sometimes arrive with a sarcastic inquiry as to whether 'someone outside the clique' may put a word in), a quick glance through our back numbers would easily disprove it. The number of our contributors is much larger than is usual in a paper of these dimensions, and many of them are people whose work has hardly appeared elsewhere.

The other school of critics presents a more serious difficulty. Any socialist paper which has a literary section is attacked from time to time by the person who says: 'What is the use of all this literary stuff? Does it bring socialism any nearer? If not, drop it. Surely our task should be to work for socialism and not waste our time on bourgeois literature?' There are various quick answers to this person (he is easily quelled, for instance, by pointing out that Marx wrote some excellent criticism of Shakespeare), but nevertheless he has a case. Here it is, put in an extreme form by a correspondent in last week's issue:

> May I ask if the book reviews in your paper contribute largely (if at all) to its upkeep? If not, why is so much precious space taken up each week with descriptions of books which (I guess) few of your readers buy?
>
> As a socialist, my aim in life is to destroy Toryism.
>
> For this purpose I require all the ammunition I can get, and I look to *Tribune* as the main source of supply. You may reply that some of the books would be useful for that purpose, but I think it would be a very small percentage, and in any case I have neither the money nor the time to read them.

159. In fact, *Tribune* didn't completely avoid engaging in the infighting of fractious modernist groups. The contributors to its literary pages included several prominent members of the English Group of Surrealists as well as a number of New Apocalyptics - a group of poets who took their name from the 1940 anthology *The New Apocalypse* (London: Fortune Press), edited by J. F. Hendry (1912-86) and Henry Treece (1911-66) - and there were several occasions on which disagreements among them flared up on the letters pages.

This correspondent, by the way, like many others who write in the same vein, is under the misconception that in order to read books you have to buy them. Actually you could read most of the books mentioned in *Tribune* without ever buying a book from one year's end to the other. What else are libraries for - not merely Boots, Smith's, etc, but the public libraries at which anyone who numbers a householder among his acquaintances can get three tickets without any charge whatever? But our correspondent also assumes (a) that a socialist needs no recreations, and (b) that books are of no use to the socialist movement unless they consist of direct propaganda. It is this viewpoint that we tacitly challenge when, for instance, we use up a whole column on a poem, or print a popularisation of some little-known dead writer, or give a good review to a book written by a conservative.

Even the most unpolitical book, even an outright reactionary book, can be of use to the socialist movement if it provides reliable information or forces people to think. But we also assume that books are not to be regarded simply as propaganda, that literature exists in its own right - and that a large number of our readers are interested in it. This involves, unavoidably, a slight divergence between the political and the literary sections of the paper. Obviously we cannot print contributions that grossly violate *Tribune*'s policy. Even in the name of free speech a socialist paper cannot, for instance, throw open its columns to anti-Semitic propaganda. But it is only in this negative sense that any pressure is put upon contributors to the literary end of the paper. Looking through the list of our contributors, I find among them Catholics, communists, Trotskyists, anarchists, pacifists, left-wing Conservatives, and Labour Party supporters of all colours. All of them knew, of course, what kind of paper they were writing for and what topics were best left alone, but I think it is true to say that none of them has ever been asked to modify what he had written on the ground that it was 'not policy'.

This is particularly important in the case of book reviews, in which it is often difficult for the reviewer to avoid indicating his own opinions. To my knowledge, some periodicals coerce their reviewers into following the political line of the paper, even when they have to falsify their own opinions to do so.[160] *Tribune* has never done this. We hold that the reviewer's job is to say what he thinks of the book he is dealing with, and not what we think our readers ought to think. And if, as a result, unorthodox opinions are expressed from time to time - even, on occasion, opinions that contradict some editorial

160. Orwell's most notorious experience of this was with the *New Statesman*, which in 1937 infamously refused on political grounds to publish his review of Franz Borkenau's *The Spanish Cockpit* (see note 59). But he had more recently had a review of Harold Laski's *Faith, Reason and Civilisation* (London: Victor Gollancz, 1944) spiked by the *Manchester Evening News* (in March 1944) and one of C. S. Lewis's *Beyond Personality* (London: Geoffrey Bles, 1944) spiked by the *Observer* (in October 1944).

statement at the other end of the paper - we believe that our readers are tough enough to stand a certain amount of diversity. We hold that the most perverse human being is more interesting than the most orthodox gramophone record. And though, in this section of the paper, our main aim is to talk about books as books, we believe that anyone who upholds the freedom of the intellect, in this age of lies and regimentation, is not serving the cause of socialism so badly either.

As I Please 53

5 January 1945

I have just been looking through a bound volume of the *Quarterly Review*[161] for the year 1810, which was, I think, the second year of the *Quarterly Review*'s existence.

1810 was not quite the blackest period, from the British point of view, of the Napoleonic war, but it was nearly the blackest. It perhaps corresponded to 1941 in the present war. Britain was completely isolated, its commerce barred from every European port by the Berlin decrees.[162] Italy, Spain, Prussia, Denmark, Switzerland and the Low Countries had all been subjugated. Austria was in alliance with France. Russia was also in an uneasy agreement with France, but it was known that Napoleon intended to invade Russia shortly. The United States, though not yet in the war, was openly hostile to Britain. There was no visible cause for hope, except the revolt in Spain, which had once again given Britain a foothold on the continent and opened the South American countries to British trade. It is therefore interesting to observe the tone of voice in which the *Quarterly Review* – a conservative paper which emphatically supported the war – speaks about France and about Napoleon at this desperate moment.

Here is the *Quarterly* on the alleged war-making propensities of the French people. It is reviewing a pamphlet by a Mr Walsh, an American who had just returned from France:

> We doubt the continued action of those military propensities which Mr Walsh ascribes to the French people. Without at all questioning the lively picture which he has drawn of the exultation excited amongst the squalid and famished inhabitants of Paris at the intelligence of every fresh triumph of their armies, we may venture to observe that such exultation is, everywhere, the usual concomitant of such events; that the gratification of national vanity is something, and that the festivities which victory brings with it may afford a pleasing dissipation to wretches who are perfectly free from any feelings of ambition. Our belief indeed is, that those feelings are, at present, nearly confined to the breast of the great conqueror; and that amongst his subjects, we may almost say among his officers and armies, the universal wish is for PEACE.

---

161. The *Quarterly Review* was published from 1809 to 1922.
162. The Berlin decree of 1806 was the first in a series promulgated by Napoleon that set up an economic blockade of Britain known as the Continental System.

Compare this with the utterances of Lord Vansittart,[163] or, indeed, of the great part of the press. The same article contains several tributes to the military genius of Napoleon. But the thing I find most impressive is that this year's issue of the *Quarterly* contains numerous reviews of recently published French books - and they are careful, serious reviews, not different in tone from the rest of its articles. There is, for instance, an article of about 9,000 words on the publication of the French scientific body known as the Société d'Arcueil. The French scientists, Gay-Lussac, Laplace and the rest of them, are treated with the utmost respect, and given their 'Monsieur' every time. From reading this article it would be impossible to discover that there was a war on.

Can you imagine current German books being reviewed in the British press during the present war? No, I don't think you can. I do not, indeed, remember hearing the name of a single book published in Germany throughout the war. And if a contemporary German book did get mentioned in the press, it would almost certainly be misrepresented in some way. Looking through the reviews of French books in the *Quarterly*, I note that only when they are on directly political subjects does any propaganda creep in, and even then it is extremely mild by our standards. As for art, literature and science, their international character is taken for granted. And yet, I suppose, Britain was fighting for existence in the Napoleonic war just as surely as in this one, and relative to the populations involved the war was not much less bloody or exhausting . . .

* * *

When Burma comes into the centre of the news again, somebody could do a useful job by evolving a sensible way of spelling Burmese place names. What is the average newspaper-reader to make of names like Tuangdwingyi, Myaungmya and Nyaungbeinzeik?

When the Japs invaded Burma at the beginning of 1942, efforts were made to get correct pronunciation of Burmese names on the radio. The BBC announcers took no notice and went merrily ahead, mispronouncing every name that could be mispronounced. Since then the newspapers have made matters a little worse by supplying their own pronunciations, which are generally wrong.

At present, Burmese names are spelt by transliterating the Burmese characters as nearly as possible. This is a very bad system unless one knows the Burmese alphabet. How is the average person to know that in a Burmese name e spells ay, ai spells eye, gy spells j, ky spells ch, and so on? It should be quite easy to evolve a better system, and the

163. Lord Vansittart (1881-1957), former permanent under-secretary at the Foreign Office (1930-8) and chief diplomatic adviser to the government (1938-41), was the chief British proponent of a punitive peace settlement with Germany.

British public, which can now make quite a good stab at pronouncing Dnepropetrovsk, could also learn to pronounce Kyaukse and Kungyangon if it were taught how.

* * *

I have been rereading with some interest *The Fairchild Family*, which was written in 1813 and was for fifty years or more a standard book for children.[164] Unfortunately I only possess the first volume, but even that, in its unexpurgated state – for various pretty-pretty versions, with all the real meat cut out, have been issued in recent years – is enough of a curiosity.

The tone of the book is sufficiently indicated by the sentence: 'Papa,' said Lucy (Lucy was aged nine, by the way), 'may we say some verses about mankind having bad hearts?' And, of course, Papa is only too willing, and out come the verses, all correctly memorised. Or here is Mrs Fairchild, telling the children how when she herself was a child she disobeyed orders by picking cherries in company with the servant girl:

> Nanny was given up to her mother to be flogged; and I was shut up in the dark room, where I was to be kept several days upon bread and water. At the end of three days my aunts sent for me, and talked to me for a long time.
>
> 'You broke the Fourth Commandment,' said my Aunt Penelope, 'which is, "Remember the Sabbath day to keep it holy": and you broke the Fifth, which is, "Honour your parents" . . . You broke the Eighth, too, which is, "Thou shalt not steal".' 'Besides,' said my Aunt Grace, 'the shame and disgrace of climbing trees in such low company, after all the care and pains we have taken with you, and the delicate manner in which we have reared you.'

The whole book is in this vein, with a long prayer at the end of every chapter, and innumerable hymns and verses from the Bible interspersed through the text. But its chief feature is the fearful visitations from Heaven which fall upon the children whenever they misbehave themselves. If they swing in the swing without leave they fall out and break several teeth: if they forget to say their prayers they fall into the trough of pig-swill; the theft of a few damsons is punished by an attack of pneumonia and narrow escape from death. On one occasion Mr Fairchild catches his children quarrelling. After the usual flogging, he takes them for a long walk to see the rotting body of a murderer hanging on a gibbet – the result, as he points out, of a quarrel between two brothers.

A curious and interesting feature of the book is that the Fairchild children, reared upon these stern principles, seem to be rather exceptionally untrustworthy. As soon as

164. Mary Sherwood's *History of the Fairchild Family – or the Child's Manual: Being a Collection of Stories Calculated to Shew the Importance and Effects of a Religious Education* (London: Hatchard, 1818) was a children's bestseller throughout the nineteenth century.

their parents' backs are turned they invariably misbehave themselves, which suggests that flogging and bread and water are not a very satisfactory treatment after all. It is worth recording, by the way, that the author, Mrs Sherwood, brought up several children, and at any rate they did not actually die under her ministrations.

As I Please 54

12 January 1945

Some time back a correspondent wrote to ask whether I had seen the exhibition of waxworks, showing German atrocities, which has been on show in London for a year or more. It is advertised outside with such captions as: HORRORS OF THE CONCENTRATION CAMP. COME INSIDE AND SEE REAL NAZI TORTURES. FLOGGING, CRUCIFIXION, GAS CHAMBERS, ETC. CHILDREN'S AMUSEMENT SECTION NO EXTRA CHARGE.

I did go and see this exhibition a long time ago, and I would like to warn prospective visitors that it is most disappointing. To begin with many of the figures are not life-size, and I suspect that some of them are not even real waxworks, but merely dressmakers' dummies with new heads attached. And secondly, the tortures are not nearly so fearful as you are led to expect by the posters outside. The whole exhibition is grubby, unlifelike and depressing. But the exhibitors are, I suppose, doing their best, and the captions are interesting in the complete frankness of their appeal to sadism and masochism. Before the war, if you were a devotee of all-in wrestling, or wrote letters to your MP to protest against the abolition of flogging, or haunted secondhand bookshops in search of such books as *The Pleasures of the Torture Chamber*, you laid yourself open to very unpleasant suspicions. Moreover, you were probably aware of your own motives and somewhat ashamed of them. Now, however, you can wallow in the most disgusting descriptions of torture and massacre, not only without any sensation of guilt, but with the feeling that you are performing a praiseworthy political action.

I am not suggesting that the stories about Nazi atrocities are untrue. To a great extent I think they are true. These horrors certainly happened in German concentration camps before the war, and there is no reason why they should have stopped since. But they are played up largely because they give the newspapers a pretext for pornography. This morning's papers are splashing the official British army report on Nazi atrocities. They are careful to inform you that naked women were flogged, sometimes spotlighting this detail by means of a headline. The journalists responsible know very well what they are doing. They know that innumerable people get a sadistic kick out of thinking about torture, especially the torture of women, and they are cashing in on this widespread neurosis. No qualms need be felt, because these deeds are committed by the enemy, and the enjoyment that one gets out of them can be disguised as disapproval. And one can get a very similar kick out of barbarous actions committed by one's own side so long as they are thought of as the just punishment of evil-doers.

We have not actually got to the point of Roman gladiatorial shows yet, but we could do so if the necessary pretext were supplied. If, for instance, it were announced that the leading war criminals were to be eaten by lions or trampled to death by elephants in the Wembley Stadium, I fancy that the spectacle would be quite well attended.

* * *

I invite attention to an article entitled 'The Truth about Mihailovich?' (the author of it also writes for *Tribune*, by the way) in the current *World Review*.[165] It deals with the campaign in the British press and the BBC to brand Mihailovich as a German agent.

Yugoslav politics are very complicated and I make no pretence of being an expert on them. For all I know it was entirely right on the part of Britain as well as the USSR to drop Mihailovich and support Tito. But what interests me is the readiness, once this decision had been taken, of reputable British newspapers to connive at what amounted to forgery in order to discredit the man whom they had been backing a few months earlier. There is no doubt that this happened. The author of the article gives details of one out of a number of instances in which material facts were suppressed in the most impudent way. Presented with very strong evidence to show that Mihailovich was not a German agent, the majority of our newspapers simply refused to print it, while repeating the charges of treachery just as before.

Very similar things happened during the Spanish civil war. Then, anarchists, Trotskyists and others who opposed Franco, but also opposed the official political line of the Spanish Republican government, were accused of being traitors in fascist pay. Various British newspapers sympathetic to the Republic took up this charge and repeated it with picturesque exaggerations of their own, at the same time refusing to print any kind of reply, even in letter form. They had the excuse that the Spanish Republic was fighting for its life and that to discuss its internecine troubles too frankly

165. Draža Mihailović (1893–1946) was the leader of the Serbian nationalist *chetniks*, rivals and bitter enemies of Tito's communist partisans. By 1944, Mihailović had lost Allied support. He continued fighting against both the Germans and the partisans and was captured, tried and executed by the Titoites. *World Review* was published by Edward Hulton, publisher of *Picture Post*, as a side project.

was to give a handle to the pro-fascist press in this country. Still, they did confuse the issues and make entirely unfounded accusations against innocent people. And, then as now, if you protested you got the answer, first, that the charges were true, and secondly, that perhaps they weren't true but that these people were politically undesirable and deserved what they got.

I recognise the force of this argument. In fighting against fascism you cannot always be bound by the Marquess of Queensberry rules, and sometimes a lie is almost unavoidable. There are always unscrupulous opponents on the look-out for damaging admissions, and on some questions the truth is so complex that a plain statement of the facts simply misleads the general public. Still, I think it could be shown from the history of the past twenty years that totalitarian methods of controversy – falsification of history, personal libel, refusal of a fair hearing to opponents, and so forth – have on the whole worked against the interests of the left.

A lie is a boomerang, and sometimes it comes back surprisingly soon. During the Spanish civil war one left-wing paper employed a certain journalist[166] to 'write up' the charges against the Spanish Trotskyists, which he did with considerable unscrupulousness. It was impossible to answer him, at any rate in the columns of this particular paper. Less than three years later this man was being hired by another paper to do the worst kind of 'anti-Red' propaganda during the Russian war against Finland. And I suppose that the anti-Russian lies which he told in 1940 carried all the more weight because the pro-Russian lies which he was telling in 1937 had not been exposed.

* * *

166. Almost certainly John Langdon-Davies (1897–1971), who reported for the *News Chronicle* on the Spanish civil war, including the May Days in Barcelona in 1937, which were also witnessed by Orwell and recounted in *Homage to Catalonia*. Langdon-Davies was very much an orthodox leftist in the 1930s, an enthusiast for a Popular Front against fascism among socialists, communists and liberals (and between the democracies and the Soviet Union). His *News Chronicle* account of the fighting in Barcelona in May 1937 reflected that of the communists: there had been 'a frustrated putsch by the "Trotskyist" POUM, working through their controlled organisations, "Friends of Durruti" and Libertarian Youth'. Orwell took issue with Langdon-Davies's account in *Homage to Catalonia*, pointing out that the Friends of Durruti and Libertarian Youth had nothing to do with the POUM and claiming that Langdon-Davies had simply repeated communist propaganda. In return, Langdon-Davies wrote an unsympathetic review of Orwell's book in the communist *Daily Worker*. Langdon-Davies subsequently lost all sympathy for the CP, and his book about the Soviet invasion of Finland and 'Winter war' of 1939–40, *Finland: The First Total War* (London: Routledge, 1940), is notably pro-Finnish and anti-Russian – though whether it amounts to 'the worst kind of "anti-Red" propaganda' is a moot point: its account of the military campaign is substantially accurate.

In the same number of *World Review* I note that Mr Edward Hulton[167] remarks rather disapprovingly that 'the small city of Athens possesses far more daily newspapers than London'. All I can say is, good luck to Athens! It is only when there are large numbers of newspapers, expressing all tendencies, that there is some chance of getting at the truth. Counting evenings, London has only twelve daily papers, and they cover the whole of the south of England and penetrate as far north as Glasgow. When they all decide to tell the same lie, there is no minority press to act as a check. In pre-war France the press was largely venal and scurrilous, but you could dig more news out of it than out of the British press, because every political fraction had its paper and every viewpoint got a hearing. I shall be surprised if Athens keeps its multiplicity of newspapers under the kind of government that we apparently intend to impose.

As I Please 55

19 January 1945

Last week Henri Béraud, the French journalist, was sentenced to death – later commuted to life imprisonment – for collaboration with the Germans.[168] Béraud used to contribute to the fascist weekly paper *Gringoire*, which in its later years had become the most disgusting rag it is possible to imagine. I have seldom been so angered by anything in the press as by its cartoon when the wretched Spanish refugees streamed into France with Italian aeroplanes machine-gunning them all the way. The Spaniards were pictured as a procession of villainous-looking men, each pushing a hand-cart piled with jewellery and bags of gold. *Gringoire* kept up an almost continuous outcry for the suppression of the French Communist Party, but it was equally fierce against even the mildest politicians of the left. One can get an idea of the moral level at which it conducted political controversy from the fact that it once published a cartoon showing Léon Blum[169] in bed with his own sister. Its advertisement columns were full of ads for

167. For Edward Hulton, see note 34.

168. Henri Béraud (1885–1958) was one of the most notorious French anti-Semitic and fascist publicists of the 1930s and 1940s. The winner of the Prix Goncourt in 1922 for his novel *Le Vitriol de lune* (Paris: Albin Michel, 1921), he was editor of the far-right weekly *Gringoire* (named after a character in Victor Hugo's *The Hunchback of Notre Dame*) from the mid-1930s.

169. Leon Blum (1872–1950) was leader of the French socialists and prime minister in the French Popular Front government 1936–7. He was Jewish.

clairvoyants and books of pornography. This piece of rubbish was said to have a circulation of 500,000.

At the time of the Abyssinian war Béraud wrote a violent pro-Italian article in which he proclaimed 'I hate England', and gave his reasons for doing so. It is significant that it was mostly people of this type, who had made no secret of their fascist sympathies for years beforehand, that the Germans had to make use of for press propaganda in France. A year or two ago Mr Raymond Mortimer published an article on the activity of French writers during the war, and there have been several similar articles in American magazines. When one pieces these together, it becomes clear that the French literary intelligentsia has behaved extremely well under the German occupation. I wish I could feel certain that the English literary intelligentsia as a whole would have behaved equally well if we had had the Nazis here. But it is true that if Britain had also been overrun, the situation would have been hopeless and the temptation to accept the New Order very much stronger.

* * *

I think I owe a small apology to the twentieth century. Apropos of my remarks about the *Quarterly Review* for 1810 – in which I pointed out that French books could get favourable reviews in England at the height of the war with France – two correspondents have written to tell me that during the present war German scientific publications have had fair treatment in the scientific press in this country. So perhaps we aren't such barbarians after all.

But I still feel that our ancestors were better at remaining sane in war-time than we are. If you ever have to walk from Fleet Street to the Embankment, it is worth going into the office of the *Observer* and having a look at something that is preserved in the waiting-room. It is a framed page from the *Observer* (which is one of our oldest newspapers) for a certain day in June, 1815. In appearance it is very like a modern newspaper, though slightly worse printed, and with only five columns on the page. The largest letters used are not much more than a quarter of an inch high. The first column is given up to 'Court and Society', then follows several columns of advertisements, mostly of rooms to let. Half-way down the last column is a headline SANGUINARY BATTLE IN FLANDERS. COMPLETE DEFEAT OF THE CORSICAN UPRISING. This is the first news of Waterloo!

* * *

'Today there are only eighty people in the United Kingdom, with net incomes of over six thousand pounds a year.' (Mr Quintin Hogg MP, in his pamphlet *The Times We Live In*.)

There are also about eighty ways in the English and American languages of expressing incredulity – for example, *garn, come off it, you bet, sez you, oh yeah, not half, I don't think, less of it* or *and the pudding*! But I think *and then you wake up* is the exactly suitable answer to a remark like the one quoted above.

* * *

Recently I read the biography of Edgar Wallace[170] which was written by Margaret Lane some years ago. It is a real 'log cabin to White House' story, and by implication a frightful commentary on our age. Starting off with every possible disadvantage – an illegitimate child, brought up by very poor foster-parents in a slum street – Wallace worked his way up by sheer ability, enterprise and hard work. His output was enormous. In his later years he was turning out eight books a year, besides plays, radio scripts and much journalism. He thought nothing of composing a full-length book in less than a week. He took no exercise, worked behind a glass screen in a super-heated room, smoked incessantly and drank vast quantities of sweetened tea. He died of diabetes at the age of fifty-seven.

It is clear from some of his more ambitious books that Wallace did in some sense take his work seriously, but his main aim was to make money, and he made it. Towards the end of his life he was earning round about £50,000 a year. But it was all fairy gold. Besides losing money by financing theatres and keeping strings of race-horses which seldom won, Wallace spent fantastic sums on his various houses, where he kept a staff of twenty servants. When he died very suddenly in Hollywood, it was found that his debts amounted to £140,000, while his liquid assets were practically nil. However, the sales of his books were so vast that his royalties amounted to £26,000 in the two years following his death.

The curious thing is that this utterly wasted life – a life of sitting almost continuously in a stuffy room and covering acres of paper with slightly pernicious nonsense – is what is called, or would have been called a few years ago, 'an inspiring story'. Wallace did what all the 'get on or get out' books, from Smiles's *Self Help* onwards, have told you to do. And the world gave him the kind of rewards he would have asked for, after his death as well as in life. When his body was brought home,

> He was carried on board the *Berengaria* . . . They laid a Union Jack over him, and covered him with flowers. He lay alone in the empty saloon under his burden of wreaths, and no journey that he had ever taken had been made in such quiet dignity and state. When the ship crept into Southampton Water her flag was flying at half-mast, and the flags of Southampton slipped gently down to salute him. The bells of Fleet Street tolled, and Wyndham's was dark.

170. Edgar Wallace (1875–1932) was a massively successful English popular novelist, playwright and journalist, probably best known today for his credit on the film *King Kong* – though in fact he did not work on the screenplay, providing only the scenario before he died.

All that and £50,000 a year as well! They also gave Wallace a plaque on the wall at Ludgate Circus. It is queer to think that London could commemorate Wallace in Fleet Street and Barrie in Kensington Gardens, but has never yet got round to giving Blake a monument in Lambeth.

As I Please 56

26 January 1945

The other night I attended a mass meeting of an organisation called the League for European Freedom.[171] Although officially an all-party organisation - there was one Labour MP on the platform - it is, I think it is safe to say, dominated by the anti-Russian wing of the Tory Party.

I am all in favour of European freedom, but I feel happier when it is coupled with freedom elsewhere - in India, for example. The people on the platform were concerned with the Russian actions in Poland, the Baltic countries, etc, and the scrapping of the principles of the Atlantic Charter that those actions imply. More than half of what they said was justified, but curiously enough they were almost as anxious to defend our own coercion of Greece as to condemn the Russian coercion of Poland. Victor Raikes,[172] the Tory MP, who is an able and outspoken reactionary, made a speech which I should have considered a good one if it had referred only to Poland and Yugoslavia. But after dealing with those two countries he went on to speak about Greece, and then suddenly black became white, and white black. There was no booing, no interjections from the quite large audience - and none there, apparently, who could see that the forcing of quisling governments upon unwilling peoples is equally undesirable whoever does it.

It is very hard to believe that people like this are really interested in political liberty as such. They are merely concerned because Britain did not get a big enough cut in the sordid bargain that appears to have been driven at Tehran. After the meeting I talked with a journalist whose contacts among influential people are much more extensive than

171. The League for European Freedom, founded by the Duchess of Atholl (see note 173), was a right-wing anti-Soviet campaign. Its Scottish offshoot, the Scottish League for European Freedom, was used by MI6 to recruit east European exiles into its ranks in the late 1940s.

172. Victor Raikes (1901-86) was Conservative MP for South East Essex 1931-45, Liverpool Wavertree 1945-50 and Liverpool Garston 1950-7. He was chairman of the Monday Club, the far-right anti-immigration Tory pressure group, in the 1970s.

mine. He said he thought it probable that British policy will shortly take a violent anti-Russian swing, and that it would be quite easy to manipulate public opinion in that direction if necessary. For a number of reasons I don't believe he was right, but if he did turn out to be right, then ultimately it is our fault and not that of our adversaries.

No one expects the Tory Party and its press to spread enlightenment. The trouble is that for years past it has been just as impossible to extract a grown-up picture of foreign politics from the left-wing press either. When it comes to such issues as Poland, the Baltic countries, Yugoslavia or Greece, what difference is there between the russophile press and the extreme Tory press? The one is simply the other standing on its head. The *News Chronicle* gives the big headlines to the fighting in Greece but tucks away the news that 'force has had to be used' against the Polish Home Army in small print at the bottom of a column. The *Daily Worker* disapproves of dictatorship in Athens, the *Catholic Herald* disapproves of dictatorship in Belgrade. There is no one who is able to say - at least, no one who has the chance to say in a newspaper of big circulation - that this whole dirty game of spheres of influence, quislings, purges, deportation, one-party elections and hundred per cent plebiscites is morally the same whether it is done by ourselves, the Russians or the Nazis. Even in the case of such frank returns to barbarism as the use of hostages, disapproval is only felt when it happens to be the enemy and not ourselves who is doing it.

And with what result? Well, one result is that it becomes much easier to mislead public opinion. The Tories are able to precipitate scandals when they want to partly because on certain subjects the left refuses to talk in a grown-up manner. An example was the Russo-Finnish war of 1940. I do not defend the Russian action in Finland, but it was not especially wicked. It was merely the same kind of thing as we ourselves did when we seized Madagascar. The public could be shocked by it, and indeed could be worked up into a dangerous fury about it, because for years they had been falsely taught that Russian foreign policy was morally different from that of other countries. And it struck me as I listened to Mr Raikes the other night that if the Tories do choose to start spilling the beans about the Lublin Committee, Marshal Tito and kindred subjects, there will be - thanks to prolonged self-censorship on the left - plenty of beans for them to spill.

But political dishonesty has its comic side. Presiding over that meeting of the League for European Freedom was no less a person than the Duchess of Atholl.[173] It is only

173. Katherine Stewart-Murray, Duchess of Atholl (1874–1960), had an unusual political journey. Elected as Conservative MP for West Perth and Kinross in 1923, she made a name for herself as a mainstream Tory as a junior education minister from 1924 to 1929 and as an opponent of Indian independence and Soviet communism (on which she published a largely accurate book on the effects of forced collectivisation of the peasantry, *The Conscription of a People*, in 1930). During the 1930s, however, the rise of Hitler and the Francoist rebellion in Spain propelled her into alliance

about seven years since the Duchess – 'the Red Duchess' as she was affectionately nicknamed – was the pet of the *Daily Worker* and lent the considerable weight of her authority to every lie that the communists happened to be uttering at the moment. Now she is fighting against the monster that she helped to create. I am sure that neither she nor her communist ex-friends see any moral in this.

* * *

I want to correct an error that I made in this column last week. It seems that there is a plaque to William Blake, and that it is somewhere near St George's church in Lambeth. I had looked for one in that area and had failed to find it. My apologies to the LCC.

* * *

If one cares about the preservation of the English language, a point one often has to decide is whether it is worth putting up a struggle when a word changes its meaning.

Some words are beyond redemption. One could not, I imagine, restore 'impertinent' to its original meaning, or 'journal', or 'decimate'. But how about the use of 'infer' for 'imply' ('He didn't actually say I was a liar, but he inferred it'), which has been gaining ground for some years? Ought one to protest against it? And ought one to acquiesce when certain words have their meanings arbitrarily narrowed? Examples are 'immoral' (nearly always taken as meaning sexually immoral), and 'criticise' (always taken as meaning criticise unfavourably). It is astonishing what numbers of words have come to have a purely sexual significance, partly owing to the need of the newspapers for euphemisms. Constant use of such phrases as 'intimacy took place twice' has practically nulled the original meaning of 'intimacy', and quite a dozen other words have been perverted in the same way.

---

with the left. She visited Spain in 1937 and campaigned for the Republic, publishing a book, *Searchlight on Spain* (Harmondsworth: Penguin, 1938), reviewed by Orwell briefly and sympathetically in *Time and Tide* (16 July 1938) and more critically in *New English Weekly* (21 July 1938). At the end of 1938 she resigned her seat in protest at the Munich agreement, forcing a by-election that she fought and narrowly lost as an independent. Orwell never took her altogether seriously. In *Homage to Catalonia* he wrote:

> The Duchess of Atholl writes, I notice (*Sunday Express*, 17 October 1937): 'I was in Valencia, Madrid, and Barcelona ... perfect order prevailed in all three towns without any display of force. All the hotels in which I stayed were not only "normal" and "decent", but extremely comfortable, in spite of the shortage of butter and coffee.'
>
> It is a peculiarity of English travellers that they do not really believe in the existence of anything outside the smart hotels. I hope they found some butter for the Duchess of Atholl.

Obviously this kind of thing ought to be prevented if possible, but it is uncertain whether one can achieve anything by struggling against the current usage. The coming and going of words is a mysterious process whose rules we do not understand. In 1940 the word 'wallop', meaning mild beer, suddenly became current all over London. I had never heard it until that date, but it seems that it was not a new word, but had been peculiar to one quarter of London. Then it suddenly spread all over the place, and now it appears to have died out again. Words can also revive, for no very clear reason, after lying dormant for hundreds of years: for example the word 'car', which had never had any currency in England except in highflown classical poetry, but was resurrected about 1900 to describe the newly invented automobile.

Possibly, therefore, the degradation which is certainly happening to our language is a process which one cannot arrest by conscious action. But I would like to see the attempt made. And as a start I would like to see a few dozen journalists declare war on some obviously bad usage – for example, the disgusting verb 'to contact', or the American habit of tying an unnecessary preposition on to every verb – and see whether they could kill it by their concerted efforts.

As I Please 57

2 February 1945

I have just been rereading, with great interest, an old favourite of my boyhood, *The Green Curve* by 'Ole Luk-Oie'. 'Ole Luk-Oie' was the pseudonym of Major Swinton[174] (afterwards General Swinton), who was, I believe, one of the rather numerous people credited with the invention of the tank. The stories in this book, written about 1908, are the forecasts of an intelligent professional soldier who had learned the lessons of the Boer war and the Russo-Japanese war, and it is interesting to compare them with what actually happened a few years later.

One story, written as early as 1907 (at which date no aeroplane had actually risen off the ground for more than a few seconds), describes an air raid. The aeroplanes carry eight-pounder bombs! Another story, written in the same year, deals with a German invasion of England, and I was particularly interested to notice that in this story the

174. Major-General Sir Ernest Swinton (1868–1951) was a soldier, author and intellectual, the professor of military history at Oxford University 1925–39. *The Green Curve* was published in 1909.

Germans are already nicknamed 'Huns'. I had been inclined to attribute the use of the word 'Hun', for Germans, to Kipling, who certainly used it in the poem that he published during the first week of the last war.

In spite of the efforts of several newspapers, 'Hun' has never caught on in this war, but we have plenty of other offensive nicknames. Someone could write a valuable monograph on the use of question-begging names and epithets, and their effect in obscuring political controversies. It would bring out the curious fact that if you simply accept and apply to yourself a name intended as an insult, it may end by losing its insulting character. This appears to be happening to 'Trotskyist', which is already dangerously close to being a compliment. So also with 'conchy' during the last war. Another example is 'Britisher'. This word was used for years as a term of opprobrium in the anglophobe American press. Later on, Northcliffe and others, looking round for some substitute for 'Englishman' which should have an imperialistic and jingoistic flavour, found 'Britisher' ready to hand, and took it over. Since then the word has had an aura of gutter patriotism, and the kind of person who tells you that 'what these natives need is a firm hand' also tells you that he is 'proud to be a Britisher' – which is about equivalent to a Chinese nationalist describing himself as a 'chink'.

* * *

A leaflet recently received from the Friends' Peace Committee[175] states that if the current scheme to remove all Poles from the areas to be taken over by the USSR, and, in compensation, all Germans from the portions of Germany to be taken over by Poland, is put into operation, 'this will involve the transfer of not less than seven million people'.

Some estimates, I believe, put it higher than this, but let us assume it to be seven millions. This is equivalent to uprooting and transplanting the entire population of Australia, or the combined populations of Scotland and Ireland. I am no expert on transport or housing, and I would like to hear from somebody better qualified a rough estimate (a) of how many wagons and locomotives, running for how long, would be involved in transporting those seven million people, plus their livestock, farm machinery and household goods; or, alternatively, (b) of how many of them are going to die of starvation and exposure if they are simply shipped off without their livestock, etc.

I fancy the answer to (a) would show that this enormous crime cannot actually be carried through, though it might be started, with confusion, suffering and the sowing of irreconcilable hatreds as the result. Meanwhile, the British people should be made to understand, with as much concrete detail as possible, what kind of policies their statesmen are committing them to.

175. The Friends Peace Committee was the Quakers' pacifist publishing arm.

* * *

A not-too-distant explosion shakes the house, the windows rattle in their sockets, and in the next room the 1964 class[176] wakes up and lets out a yell or two. Each time this happens I find myself thinking, 'Is it possible that human beings can continue with this lunacy very much longer?' You know the answer, of course. Indeed, the difficulty nowadays is to find anyone who thinks that there will not be another war in the fairly near future.

Germany, I suppose, will be defeated this year, and when Germany is out of the way Japan will not be able to stand up to the combined power of Britain and the USA. Then there will be a peace of exhaustion, with only minor and unofficial wars raging all over the place, and perhaps this so-called peace may last for decades. But after that, by the way the world is actually shaping, it may well be that war will become permanent. Already, quite visibly and more or less with the acquiescence of all of us, the world is splitting up into the two or three huge super-states forecast in James Burnham's *Managerial Revolution*. One cannot draw their exact boundaries as yet, but one can see more or less what areas they will comprise. And if the world does settle down into this pattern, it is likely that these vast states will be permanently at war with one another, though it will not necessarily be a very intensive or bloody kind of war. Their problems, both economic and psychological, will be a lot simpler if the doodlebugs are more or less constantly whizzing to and fro.

If these two or three super-states do establish themselves, not only will each of them be too big to be conquered, but they will be under no necessity to trade with one another, and in a position to prevent all contact between their nationals. Already, for a dozen years or so, large areas of the earth have been cut off from one another, although technically at peace.

Some months ago, in this column, I pointed out that modern scientific inventions have tended to prevent rather than increase international communication. This brought me several angry letters from readers, but none of them were able to show that what I had said was false. They merely retorted that if we had socialism, the aeroplane, the radio, etc. would not be perverted to wrong uses. Very true, but then we haven't socialism. As it is, the aeroplane is primarily a thing for dropping bombs and the radio primarily a thing for whipping up nationalism. Even before the war there was enormously less contact between the peoples of the earth than there had been thirty years earlier, and education was perverted, history rewritten and freedom of thought suppressed to an extent undreamed of in earlier ages. And there is no sign whatever of these tendencies being reversed.

176. Orwell's baby stepson Richard.

Maybe I am pessimistic. But, at any rate, those are the thoughts that cross my mind (and a lot of other people's too, I believe) every time the explosion of a V bomb booms through the mist.

* * *

A little story I came upon in a book. Someone receives an invitation to go out lion-hunting. 'But,' he exclaims, 'I haven't lost any lions!'

As I Please 58

9 February 1945

Every time I wash up a batch of crockery I marvel at the unimaginativeness of human beings who can travel under the sea and fly through the clouds, and yet have not known how to eliminate this sordid time-wasting drudgery from their daily lives. If you go into the Bronze Age room in the British Museum (when it is open again) you will notice that some of our domestic appliances have barely altered in three thousand years. A saucepan, say, or a comb, is very much the same thing as it was when the Greeks were besieging Troy. In the same period we have advanced from the leaky galley to the 50,000-ton liner, and from the ox-cart to the aeroplane.

It is true that in the modern labour-saving house in which a tiny percentage of human beings live, a job like washing-up takes rather less time than it used to. With soap flakes, abundant hot water, plate racks, a well-lighted kitchen, and – what very few houses in England have – an easy method of rubbish disposal, you can make it more tolerable than it used to be when copper dishes had to be scoured with sand in porous stone sinks by the light of a candle. But certain jobs (for instance, cleaning out a frying-pan which has had fish in it) are inherently disgusting, and this whole business of messing about with dish-mops and basins of hot water is incredibly primitive. At this moment the block of flats I live in is partly uninhabitable: not because of enemy action, but because accumulations of snow have caused water to pour through the roof and bring down the plaster from the ceilings. It is taken for granted that this calamity will happen every time there is an exceptionally heavy fall of snow. For three days there was no water in the taps because the pipes were frozen: that, too, is a normal, almost yearly experience. And the newspapers have just announced that the number of burst pipes is so enormous that the job of repairing them will not be completed till the end of 1945 –

when, I suppose, there will be another big frost and they will all burst again. If our methods of making war had kept pace with our methods of keeping house, we should be just about on the verge of discovering gunpowder.

* * *

To come back to washing-up. Like sweeping, scrubbing and dusting, it is of its nature an uncreative and life-wasting job. You cannot make an art out of it as you can out of cooking or gardening. What, then, is to be done about it? Well, this whole problem of housework has three possible solutions. One is to simplify our way of living very greatly; another is to assume, as our ancestors did, that life on earth is inherently miserable, and that it is entirely natural for the average woman to be a broken-down drudge at the age of thirty; and the other is to devote as much intelligence to rationalising the interiors of our houses as we have devoted to transport and communications.

I fancy we shall choose the third alternative. If one thinks simply in terms of saving trouble and plans one's home as ruthlessly as one would plan a machine, it is possible to imagine houses and flats which would be comfortable and would entail very little work. Central heating, rubbish chutes, proper consumption of smoke, cornerless rooms, electrically warmed beds and elimination of carpets would make a lot of difference. But as for washing-up, I see no solution except to do it communally, like a laundry. Every morning the municipal van will stop at your door and carry off a box of dirty crocks, handing you a box of clean ones (marked with your initial of course) in return. This would be hardly more difficult to organise than the daily diaper service which was operating before the war. And though it would mean that some people would have to be full-time washers-up, as some people are now full-time laundry-workers, the all-over saving in labour and fuel would be enormous. The alternatives are to continue fumbling about with greasy dish-mops, or to eat out of paper containers.

* * *

A sidelight on the habits of book reviewers.

Some time ago I was commissioned to write an essay for an annual scrapbook which shall be nameless. At the very last minute (and when I had had the money, I am glad to say) the publishers decided that my essay must be suppressed. By this time the book was actually in the process of being bound. The essay was cut out of every copy, but for technical reasons it was impossible to remove my name from the list of contributors on the title page.

Since then I have received a number of press cuttings referring to this book. In each case I am mentioned as being 'among the contributors', and not one reviewer has yet spotted that the contribution attributed to me is not actually there.

* * *

Now that 'explore every avenue' and 'leave no stone unturned' have been more or less laughed out of existence, I think it is time to start a campaign against some more of the worn-out and useless metaphors with which our language is littered.

Three that we could well do without out are 'cross swords with', 'ring the changes on', and 'take up the cudgels for'. How lifeless these and similar expressions have become you can see from the fact that in many cases people do not even remember their original meaning. What is meant by 'ringing the changes', for instance? Probably it once had something to do with church bells, but one could not be sure without consulting a dictionary, 'take up the cudgels for' possibly derives from the almost obsolete game of singlestick. When an expression has moved as far from its original meaning as this, its value as a metaphor – that is, its power of providing a concrete illustration – has vanished. There is no sense whatever in writing 'X took up the cudgels for Y'. One should either say 'X defended Y' or think of a new metaphor which genuinely makes one's meaning more vivid.

In some cases these overworked expressions have actually been severed from their original meaning by means of a misspelling. An example is 'plain sailing' (plane sailing). And the expression 'toe the line' is now coming to be spelled quite frequently 'tow the line'. People who are capable of this kind of thing evidently don't attach any definite meaning to the words they use.

* * *

I wonder whether people read Bret Harte[177] nowadays. I do not know why, but for an hour past some stanzas from 'The Society upon the Stanislaus' have been running in my head. It describes a meeting of an archaeological society which ended in disorder:

> Then Abner Dean of Angel's raised a point of order, when
> A chunk of old red sandstone took him in the abdomen;
> And he smiled a kind of sickly smile, and curled upon the floor,
> And the subsequent proceedings interested him no more.

It has perhaps been unfortunate for Bret Harte's modern reputation that of his two funniest poems, one turns on colour prejudice and the other on class snobbery. But there are a number that are worth rereading, including one or two serious ones: especially 'Dickens in Camp', the now almost forgotten poem which Bret Harte wrote after Dickens's death and which was about the finest tribute Dickens ever had.

177. Bret Harte (1836–1902) was an American author and poet.

As I Please 59

16 February 1945

Last week I received a copy of a statement on the future of Burma, issued by the Burma Association, an organisation which includes most of the Burmese resident in this country. How representative this organisation is I am not certain, but probably it voices the wishes of a majority of politically-conscious Burmese. For reasons I shall try to make clear presently, the statement just issued is an important document. Summarised as shortly as possible, it makes the following demands: (i) An amnesty for Burmese who have collaborated with the Japs during the occupation. (ii) A statement by the British government of a definite date at which Burma shall attain Dominion status. The period, if possible, to be less than six years. The Burmese people to summon a Constituent Assembly in the meantime. (iii) No interim of 'direct rule'. (iv) The Burmese people to have a greater share in the economic development of their own country. (v) The British government to make an immediate unequivocal statement of its intentions towards Burma.

The striking thing about these demands is how moderate they are. No political party with any tinge of nationalism, or any hope of getting a mass following, could possibly ask for less. But why do these people pitch their claims so low? Well, I think one can guess at two reasons. To begin with, the experience of Japanese occupation has probably made Dominion status seem a more tempting goal than it seemed three years ago. But – much more important – if they demand so little it is probably because they expect to be offered even less. And I should guess that they expect right. Indeed, of the very modest suggestions listed above, only the first is likely to be carried out.

The government has never made any clear statement about the future of Burma, but there have been persistent rumours that when the Japs are driven out there is to be a return to 'direct rule', which is a polite name for military dictatorship. And what is happening, politically, in Burma at this moment? We simply don't know: nowhere have I seen in any newspaper one word about the way in which the reconquered territories are being administered. To grasp the significance of this one has to look at the map of Burma. A year ago Burma proper was in Japanese hands and the Allies were fighting in wild territories thinly populated by rather primitive tribes who have never been much interfered with and are traditionally pro-British. Now they are penetrating into the heart of Burma, and some fairly important towns, centres of administration, have fallen into their hands. Several million Burmese must be once again under the British flag. Yet we are told nothing whatever about the form of administration that is being set up. Is it surprising if every thinking Burmese fears the worst?

It is vitally important to interest the British public in this matter, if possible. Our eyes fixed on Europe, we forget that at the other end of the world there is a whole string of countries awaiting liberation and in nearly every case hoping for something better than a mere change of conquerors. Burma will probably be the first British territory to be reconquered, and it will be a test case: a more important test than Greece or Belgium, not only because more people are involved, but because it will be almost wholly a British responsibility. It will be a fearful disaster if through apathy and ignorance we let Churchill, Amery and co put across some reactionary settlement which will lose us the friendship of the Burmese people for good.

For a year or two after the Japanese have gone, Burma will be in a receptive mood and more pro-British than it has been for a dozen years past. Then is the moment to make a generous gesture. I don't know whether Dominion status is the best possible solution. But if the politically conscious section of the Burmese ask for Dominion status, it would be monstrous to let the Tories refuse it in a hopeless effort to bring back the past. And there must be a date attached to it, a not too distant date. Whether these people remain inside the British Commonwealth or outside it, what matters in the long run is that we should have their friendship – and we can have it if we do not play them false at the moment of crisis. When the moment comes for Burma's future to be settled, thinking Burmese will not turn their eyes towards Churchill. They will be looking at us, the Labour movement, to see whether our talk about democracy, self-determination, racial equality and what-not has any truth in it. I do not know whether it will be in our power to force a decent settlement upon the government; but I do know that we shall harm ourselves irreparably if we do not make at least as much row about it as we did in the case of Greece.

* * *

When asked, 'Which is the wisest of the animals?' a Japanese sage replied, 'The one that man has not yet discovered.'

I have just seen in a book the statement that the grey seals, the kind that are found round the coasts of Britain, number only ten thousand. Presumably there are so few of them because they have been killed off, like many another over-trustful animal. Seals are quite tame, and appear to be very inquisitive. They will follow a boat for miles, and sometimes they will even follow you when you are walking round the shore. There is no good reason for killing them. Their coats are no use for fur, and except for eating a certain amount of fish they do no harm.

They breed mostly on uninhabited islands. Let us hope that some of the islands remain uninhabited, so that these unfortunate brutes may escape being exterminated entirely. However, we are not quite such persistent slaughterers of rare animals as we used to be. Two species of birds, the bittern and the spoonbill, extinct for many years, have recently succeeded in re-establishing themselves in Britain. They have even been encouraged to breed in some places. Thirty years ago, any bittern that dared to show its beak in this country would have been shot and stuffed immediately.

* * *

The Gestapo is said to have teams of literary critics whose job is to determine, by means of stylistic comparison, the authorship of anonymous pamphlets. I have always thought that, if only it were in a better cause, this is exactly the job I would like to have.

To any of our readers whose tastes lie in the same direction, I present this problem: Who is now writing 'Beachcomber's' column in the *Daily Express*? It is certainly not Mr J. B. Morton, who was 'Beachcomber' until recently.[178] I have heard it is Mr Osbert Lancaster,[179] the cartoonist, but that was merely a piece of gossip, and I have not made any careful examination. But I would bet five shillings that the present 'Beachcomber', unlike Mr Morton, is not a Catholic.

---

178. For Beachcomber, see note 23.

179. Osbert Lancaster (1908–86) was a artist and writer, a cartoonist on the *Daily Express* from 1939 until his death.

You and the atom bomb

19 October 1945

Considering how likely we all are to be blown to pieces by it within the next five years, the atomic bomb has not roused so much discussion as might have been expected.[180] The newspapers have published numerous diagrams, not very helpful to the average man, of protons and neutrons doing their stuff, and there has been much reiteration of the useless statement that the bomb 'ought to be put under international control'. But curiously little has been said, at any rate in print, about the question that is of most urgent interest to all of us, namely: 'How difficult are these things to manufacture?'

Such information as we – that is, the big public – possess on this subject has come to us in a rather indirect way, apropos of President Truman's decision not to hand over certain secrets to the USSR. Some months ago, when the bomb was still only a rumour, there was a widespread belief that splitting the atom was merely a problem for the physicists, and that when they had solved it a new and devastating weapon would be within reach of almost everybody. (At any moment, so the rumour went, some lonely lunatic in a laboratory might blow civilisation to smithereens, as easily as touching off a firework.)

Had that been true, the whole trend of history would have been abruptly altered. The distinction between great states and small states would have been wiped out, and the power of the state over the individual would have been greatly weakened. However, it appears from President Truman's remarks, and various comments that have been made on them, that the bomb is fantastically expensive and that its manufacture demands an enormous industrial effort, such as only three or four countries in the world are capable of making. This point is of cardinal importance, because it may mean that the discovery of the atomic bomb, so far from reversing history, will simply intensify the trends which have been apparent for a dozen years past.

It is a commonplace that the history of civilisation is largely the history of weapons. In particular, the connection between the discovery of gunpowder and the overthrow of feudalism by the bourgeoisie has been pointed out over and over again. And though I have no doubt exceptions can be brought forward, I think the following rule would be

180. The United States Air Force dropped an atomic bomb on Hiroshima on 6 August 1945 and another on Nagasaki on 9 August 1945. They killed at least 110,000 people immediately and destroyed both cities. The Japanese government sued for peace. Another 230,000 people died in the next five years from injuries or radiation.

found generally true: that ages in which the dominant weapon is expensive or difficult to make will tend to be ages of despotism, whereas when the dominant weapon is cheap and simple, the common people have a chance. Thus, for example, tanks, battleships and bombing planes are inherently tyrannical weapons, while rifles, muskets, long-bows and hand-grenades are inherently democratic weapons. A complex weapon makes the strong stronger, while a simple weapon – so long as there is no answer to it – gives claws to the weak.

The great age of democracy and of national self-determination was the age of the musket and the rifle. After the invention of the flintlock, and before the invention of the percussion cap, the musket was a fairly efficient weapon, and at the same time so simple that it could be produced almost anywhere. Its combination of qualities made possible the success of the American and French revolutions, and made a popular insurrection a more serious business than it could be in our own day. After the musket came the breech-loading rifle. This was a comparatively complex thing, but it could still be produced in scores of countries, and it was cheap, easily smuggled and economical of ammunition. Even the most backward nation could always get hold of rifles from one source or another, so that Boers, Bulgars, Abyssinians, Moroccans – even Tibetans – could put up a fight for their independence, sometimes with success. But thereafter every development in military technique has favoured the state as against the individual, and the industrialised country as against the backward one. There are fewer and fewer foci of power. Already, in 1939, there were only five states capable of waging war on the grand scale, and now there are only three – ultimately, perhaps, only two. This trend has been obvious for years, and was pointed out by a few observers even before 1914. The one thing that might reverse it is the discovery of a weapon – or, to put it more broadly, of a method of fighting – not dependent on huge concentrations of industrial plant.

From various symptoms one can infer that the Russians do not yet possess the secret of making the atomic bomb; on the other hand, the consensus of opinion seems to be that they will possess it within a few years. So we have before us the prospect of two or three monstrous super-states, each possessed of a weapon by which millions of people can be wiped out in a few seconds, dividing the world between them. It has been rather hastily assumed that this means bigger and bloodier wars, and perhaps an actual end to the machine civilisation. But suppose – and really this is the likeliest development – that the surviving great nations make a tacit agreement never to use the atomic bomb against one another? Suppose they only use it, or the threat of it, against people who are unable to retaliate? In that case we are back where we were before, the only difference being that power is concentrated in still fewer hands and that the outlook for subject peoples and oppressed classes is still more hopeless.

When James Burnham wrote *The Managerial Revolution* it seemed probable to many Americans that the Germans would win the European end of the war, and it was therefore natural to assume that Germany and not Russia would dominate the Eurasian land mass, while Japan would remain master of east Asia. This was a miscalculation, but it does not affect the main argument. For Burnham's geographical picture of the new world has turned out to be correct. More and more obviously the surface of the earth is being parcelled off into three great empires, each self-contained and cut off from contact with the outer world, and each ruled, under one disguise or another, by a self-elected oligarchy. The haggling as to where the frontiers are to be drawn is still going on, and will continue for some years, and the third of the three super-states - east Asia, dominated by China - is still potential rather than actual. But the general drift is unmistakable, and every scientific discovery of recent years has accelerated it.

We were once told that the aeroplane had 'abolished frontiers'; actually it is only since the aeroplane became a serious weapon that frontiers have become definitely impassable. The radio was once expected to promote international understanding and co-operation; it has turned out to be a means of insulating one nation from another. The atomic bomb may complete the process by robbing the exploited classes and peoples of all power to revolt, and at the same time putting the possessors of the bomb on a basis of military equality. Unable to conquer one another, they are likely to continue ruling the world between them, and it is difficult to see how the balance can be upset except by slow and unpredictable demographic changes.

For forty or fifty years past, Mr H. G. Wells and others have been warning us that man is in danger of destroying himself with his own weapons, leaving the ants or some other gregarious species to take over. Anyone who has seen the ruined cities of Germany will find this notion at least thinkable. Nevertheless, looking at the world as a whole, the drift for many decades has been not towards anarchy but towards the reimposition of slavery. We may be heading not for general breakdown but for an epoch as horribly stable as the slave empires of antiquity. James Burnham's theory has been much discussed, but few people have yet considered its ideological implications - that is, the kind of world-view, the kind of beliefs, and the social structure that would probably prevail in a state which was at once *unconquerable* and in a permanent state of 'cold war' with its neighbours.

Had the atomic bomb turned out to be something as cheap and easily manufactured as a bicycle or an alarm clock, it might well have plunged us back into barbarism, but it might, on the other hand, have meant the end of national sovereignty and of the highly-centralised police state. If, as seems to be the case, it is a rare and costly object as difficult to produce as a battleship, it is likelier to put an end to large-scale wars at the cost of prolonging indefinitely a 'peace that is no peace'.

What is science?

26 October 1945

In last week's *Tribune*, there was an interesting letter from Mr J. Stewart Cook, in which he suggested that the best way of avoiding the danger of a 'scientific hierarchy' would be to see to it that every member of the general public was, as far as possible, scientifically educated. At the same time, scientists should be brought out of their isolation and encouraged to take a greater part in politics and administration.

As a general statement, I think most of us would agree with this, but I notice that, as usual, Mr Cook does not define science, and merely implies in passing that it means certain exact sciences whose experiments can be made under laboratory conditions. Thus, adult education tends 'to neglect scientific studies in favour of literary, economic and social subjects', economics and sociology not being regarded as branches of science. Apparently. This point is of great importance. For the word science is at present used in at least two meanings, and the whole question of scientific education is obscured by the current tendency to dodge from one meaning to the other.

Science is generally taken as meaning either (a) the exact sciences, such as chemistry, physics, etc, or (b) a method of thought which obtains verifiable results by reasoning logically from observed fact.

If you ask any scientist, or indeed almost any educated person, 'What is science?' you are likely to get an answer approximating to (b). In everyday life, however, both in speaking and in writing, when people say 'science' they mean (a). Science means something that happens in a laboratory: the very word calls up a picture of graphs, test-tubes, balances, Bunsen burners, microscopes. A biologist, an astronomer, perhaps a psychologist or a mathematician is described as a 'man of science': no one would think of applying this term to a statesman, a poet, a journalist or even a philosopher. And those who tell us that the young must be scientifically educated mean, almost invariably, that they should be taught more about radioactivity, or the stars, or the physiology of their own bodies, rather than that they should be taught to think more exactly.

This confusion of meaning, which is partly deliberate, has in it a great danger. Implied in the demand for more scientific education is the claim that if one has been scientifically trained one's approach to *all* subjects will be more intelligent than if one had had no such training. A scientist's political opinions, it is assumed, his opinions on sociological questions, on morals, on philosophy, perhaps even on the arts, will be more valuable than those of a layman. The world, in other words, would be a better place if the scientists were in control of it. But a 'scientist', as we have just seen, means in practice a specialist in one of the exact sciences. It follows that a chemist or a physicist, as such, is politically more intelligent than a poet or a lawyer, as such. And, in fact, there are already millions of people who do believe this.

But is it really true that a 'scientist', in this narrower sense, is any likelier than other people to approach non-scientific problems in an objective way? There is not much reason for thinking so. Take one simple test – the ability to withstand nationalism. It is often loosely said that 'Science is international', but in practice the scientific workers of all countries line up behind their own governments with fewer scruples than are felt by the writers and the artists. The German scientific community, as a whole, made no resistance to Hitler. Hitler may have ruined the long-term prospects of German science, but there were still plenty of gifted men to do the necessary research on such things as synthetic oil, jet planes, rocket projectiles and the atomic bomb. Without them the German war machine could never have been built up.

On the other hand, what happened to German literature when the Nazis came to power? I believe no exhaustive lists have been published, but I imagine that the number of German scientists – Jews apart – who voluntarily exiled themselves or were persecuted by the régime was much smaller than the number of writers and journalists. More sinister than this, a number of German scientists swallowed the monstrosity of 'racial science'. You can find some of the statements to which they set their names in Professor Brady's *The Spirit and Structure of German Fascism*.[181]

But, in slightly different forms, it is the same picture everywhere. In England, a large proportion of our leading scientists accept the structure of capitalist society, as can be seen from the comparative freedom with which they are given knighthoods, baronetcies and even peerages. Since Tennyson, no English writer worth reading – one might, perhaps, make an exception of Sir Max Beerbohm[182] – has been given a title. And those English scientists who do not simply accept the *status quo* are frequently communists, which means that, however intellectually scrupulous they may be in their own line of work, they are ready to be uncritical and even dishonest on certain subjects.[183] The fact is that a mere training in one or more of the exact sciences, even combined with very high gifts, is no guarantee of a humane or sceptical outlook. The physicists of half a dozen

181. Robert Brady, *The Spirit and Structure of German Fascism* (London: Victor Gollancz, 1937).

182. Max Beerbohm (1872–1956) was a satirist and caricaturist.

183. The most prominent British communist scientists of the 1940s were the physicist J. D. Bernal (1901–71), the geneticist J. B. S. Haldane (1892–1964) and the mathematician Hyman Levy (1889–1975).

great nations, all feverishly and secretly working away at the atomic bomb, are a demonstration of this.

But does all this mean that the general public should *not* be more scientifically educated? On the contrary! All it means is that scientific education for the masses will do little good, and probably a lot of harm, if it simply boils down to more physics, more chemistry, more biology, etc, to the detriment of literature and history. Its probable effect on the average human being would be to narrow the range of his thoughts and make him more than ever contemptuous of such knowledge as he did not possess: and his political reactions would probably be somewhat less intelligent than those of an illiterate peasant who retained a few historical memories and a fairly sound aesthetic sense.

Clearly, scientific education ought to mean the implanting of a rational, sceptical, experimental habit of mind. It ought to mean acquiring a *method* – a method that can be used on any problem that one meets – and not simply piling up a lot of facts. Put it in those words, and the apologist of scientific education will usually agree. Press him further, ask him to particularise, and somehow it always turns out that scientific education means more attention to the sciences, in other words – more *facts*. The idea that science means a way of looking at the world, and not simply a body of knowledge, is in practice strongly resisted. I think sheer professional jealousy is part of the reason for this. For if science is simply a method or an attitude, so that anyone whose thought-processes are sufficiently rational can in some sense be described as a scientist – what then becomes of the enormous prestige now enjoyed by the chemist, the physicist, etc and his claim to be somehow wiser than the rest of us?

A hundred years ago, Charles Kingsley[184] described science as 'making nasty smells in a laboratory'. A year or two ago a young industrial chemist informed me, smugly, that he 'could not see what was the use of poetry'. So the pendulum swings to and fro, but it does not seem to me that one attitude is any better than the other. At the moment, science is on the upgrade, and so we hear, quite rightly, the claim that the masses should be scientifically educated: we do not hear, as we ought, the counter-claim that the scientists themselves would benefit by a little education. Just before writing this, I saw in an American magazine the statement that a number of British and American physicists refused from the start to do research on the atomic bomb, well knowing what use would be made of it. Here you have a group of sane men in the middle of a world of lunatics. And though no names were published, I think it would be a safe guess that all of them were people with some kind of general cultural background, some acquaintance with history or literature or the arts – in short, people whose interests were not, in the current sense of the word, purely scientific.

184. Charles Kingsley (1819–75) was a novelist and Christian socialist, best known for his 1863 fable for children, *The Water Babies*.

Good bad books

2 November 1945

Not long ago a publisher commissioned me to write an introduction for a reprint of a novel by Leonard Merrick. This publishing house, it appears, is going to reissue a long series of minor and partly-forgotten novels of the twentieth century. It is a valuable service in these bookless days, and I rather envy the person whose job it will be to scout round the threepenny boxes, hunting down copies of his boyhood favourites.

A type of book which we hardly seem to produce in these days, but which flowered with great richness in the late nineteenth and early twentieth centuries, is what Chesterton called the 'good bad book': that is, the kind of book that has no literary pretensions but which remains readable when more serious productions have perished. Obviously outstanding books in this line are *Raffles* and the *Sherlock Holmes* stories, which have kept their place when innumerable 'problem novels', 'human documents' and 'terrible indictments' of this or that have fallen into deserved oblivion. (Who has worn better, Conan Doyle or Meredith?) Almost in the same class as these I put R. Austin Freeman's earlier stories – *The Singing Bone*, *The Eye of Osiris* and others – Ernest Bramah's *Max Carrados*, and, dropping the standard a bit, Guy Boothby's Tibetan thriller, *Dr Nikola*, a sort of schoolboy version of Huc's *Travels in Tartary*, which would probably make a real visit to Central Asia seem a dismal anticlimax.

But apart from thrillers, there were the minor humorous writers of the period. For example, Pett Ridge – but I admit his full-length books no longer seem readable – E. Nesbit (*The Treasure Seekers*), George Birmingham, who was good so long as he kept off politics, the pornographic Binstead ('Pitcher' of the *Pink 'Un*), and, if American books can be included, Booth Tarkington's Penrod stories. A cut above most of these was Barry Pain. Some of Pain's humorous writings are, I suppose, still in print, but to anyone who comes across it I recommend what must now be a very rare book – *The Octave of Claudius*, a brilliant exercise in the macabre. Somewhat later in time there was Peter Blundell, who wrote in the W. W. Jacobs vein about Far Eastern seaport towns, and who seems to be rather unaccountably forgotten, in spite of having been praised in print by H. G. Wells.

However, all the books I have been speaking of are frankly 'escape' literature. They form pleasant patches in one's memory, quiet corners where the mind can browse at odd moments, but they hardly pretend to have anything to do with real life. There is another kind of good bad book which is more seriously intended, and which tells us, I think, something about the nature of the novel and the reasons for its present decadence. During the last fifty years there has been a whole series of writers – some of them are still writing – whom it is quite impossible to call 'good' by any strictly literary standard, but who are natural novelists and who seem to attain sincerity partly because they are not inhibited by good taste. In this class I put Leonard Merrick himself, W. L. George, J. D. Beresford, Ernest Raymond, May Sinclair, and – at a lower level than the others but still essentially similar – A. S. M. Hutchinson.

Most of these have been prolific writers, and their output has naturally varied in quality. I am thinking in each case of one or two outstanding books: for example, Merrick's *Cynthia*, J. D. Beresford's *A Candidate for Truth*, W. L. George's *Caliban*, May Sinclair's *The Combined Maze* and Ernest Raymond's *We, the Accused*. In each of these books the author has been able to identify himself with his imagined characters, to feel with them and invite sympathy on their behalf, with a kind of abandonment that cleverer people would find it difficult to achieve. They bring out the fact that intellectual refinement can be a disadvantage to a story-teller, as it would be to a music-hall comedian.

Take, for example, Ernest Raymond's *We, the Accused* – a peculiarly sordid and convincing murder story, probably based on the Crippen case. I think it gains a great deal from the fact that the author only partly grasps the pathetic vulgarity of the people he is writing about, and therefore does not despise them. Perhaps it even – like Theodore Dreiser's *An American Tragedy* – gains something from the clumsy long-winded manner in which it is written; detail is piled on detail, with almost no attempt at selection, and in the process an effect of terrible, grinding cruelty is slowly built up. So also with *A Candidate for Truth*. Here there is not the same clumsiness, but there is the same ability to take seriously the problems of commonplace people. So also with *Cynthia* and at any rate the earlier part of *Caliban*. The greater part of what W. L. George wrote was shoddy rubbish, but in this particular book, based on the career of Northcliffe, he achieved some memorable and truthful pictures of lower-middle-class London life. Parts of this book are probably autobiographical, and one of the advantages of good bad writers is their lack of shame in writing autobiography. Exhibitionism and self-pity are the bane of the novelist, and yet if he is too frightened of them his creative gift may suffer.

The existence of good bad literature – the fact that one can be amused or excited or even moved by a book that one's intellect simply refuses to take seriously – is a reminder that art is not the same thing as cerebration. I imagine that by any test that could be devised, Carlyle would be found to be a more intelligent man than Trollope. Yet Trollope has remained readable and Carlyle has not: with all his cleverness he had not even the wit to write in plain straightforward English. In novelists, almost as much as in poets, the connection between intelligence and creative power is hard to establish. A good novelist may be a prodigy of self-discipline like Flaubert, or he may be an intellectual sprawl like Dickens. Enough talent to set up dozens of ordinary writers has been poured into Wyndham Lewis's so-called novels, such as *Tarr* or *Snooty Baronet*. Yet it would be a very heavy labour to read one of these books right through. Some indefinable quality, a sort of literary vitamin, which exists even in a book like *If Winter Comes*, is absent from them.

Perhaps the supreme example of the 'good bad' book is *Uncle Tom's Cabin*. It is an unintentionally ludicrous book, full of preposterous melodramatic incidents; it is also deeply moving and essentially true; it is hard to say which quality outweighs the other. But *Uncle Tom's Cabin*, after all, is trying to be serious and to deal with the real world. How about the frankly escapist writers, the purveyors of thrills and 'light' humour? How about *Sherlock Holmes*, *Vice Versa*, *Dracula*, *Helen's Babies* or *King Solomon's Mines*? All of these are definitely absurd books, books which one is more inclined to laugh *at* than *with*, and which were hardly taken seriously even by their authors; yet they have survived, and will probably continue to do so. All one can say is that, while civilisation remains such that one needs distraction from time to time, 'light' literature has its appointed place; also that there is such a thing as sheer skill, or native grace, which may have more survival value than erudition or intellectual power. There are music-hall songs which are better poems than three-quarters of the stuff that gets into the anthologies:

Come where the booze is cheaper,
Come where the pots hold more,
Come where the boss is a bit of a sport,
Come to the pub next door!

Or again:

Two lovely black eyes –
Oh, what a surprise!
Only for calling another man wrong,
Two lovely black eyes!

I would far rather have written either of those than, say, *The Blessed Damozel* or *Love in the Valley*. And by the same token I would back *Uncle Tom's Cabin* to outlive the complete works of Virginia Woolf or George Moore, though I know of no strictly literary test which would show where the superiority lies.

Revenge is sour

9 November 1945

Whenever I read phrases like 'war guilt trials', 'punishment of war criminals' and so forth, there comes back into my mind the memory of something I saw in a prisoner-of-war camp in south Germany, earlier this year.

Another correspondent and myself were being shown round the camp by a little Viennese Jew who had been enlisted in the branch of the American army which deals with the interrogation of prisoners. He was an alert, fair-haired, rather good-looking youth of about twenty-five, and politically so much more knowledgeable than the average American officer that it was a pleasure to be with him. The camp was on an airfield, and, after we had been round the cages, our guide led us to a hangar where various prisoners who were in a different category from the others were being 'screened'.

Up at one end of the hangar about a dozen men were lying in a row on the concrete floor. These, it was explained, were SS officers who had been segregated from the other prisoners. Among them was a man in dingy civilian clothes who was lying with his arm across his face and apparently asleep. He had strange and horribly deformed feet. The two of them were quite symmetrical, but they were clubbed out into an extraordinary globular shape which made them more like a horse's hoof than anything human. As we approached the group, the little Jew seemed to be working himself up into a state of excitement.

'That's the real swine!' he said, and suddenly he lashed out with his heavy army boot and caught the prostrate man a fearful kick right on the bulge of one of his deformed feet.

'Get up, you swine!' he shouted as the man started out of sleep, and then repeated something of the kind in German. The prisoner scrambled to his feet and stood clumsily to attention. With the same air of working himself up into a fury – indeed he was almost dancing up and down as he spoke – the Jew told us the prisoner's history. He was a 'real' Nazi: his party number indicated that he had been a member since the very early days, and he had held a post corresponding to a General in the political branch of the SS. It could be taken as quite certain that he had had charge of concentration camps and had presided over tortures and hangings. In short, he represented everything that we had been fighting against during the past five years.

Meanwhile, I was studying his appearance. Quite apart from the scrubby, unfed, unshaven look that a newly captured man generally has, he was a disgusting specimen.

But he did not look brutal or in any way frightening: merely neurotic and, in a low way, intellectual. His pale, shifty eyes were deformed by powerful spectacles. He could have been an unfrocked clergyman, an actor ruined by drink, or a spiritualist medium. I have seen very similar people in London common lodging houses, and also in the Reading Room of the British Museum. Quite obviously he was mentally unbalanced - indeed, only doubtfully sane, though at this moment sufficiently in his right mind to be frightened of getting another kick. And yet everything that the Jew was telling me of his history could have been true, and probably was true! So the Nazi torturer of one's imagination, the monstrous figure against whom one had struggled for so many years, dwindled to this pitiful wretch, whose obvious need was not for punishment, but for some kind of psychological treatment.

Later, there were further humiliations. Another SS officer, a large brawny man, was ordered to strip to the waist and show the blood group number tattooed on his under-arm; another was forced to explain to us how he had lied about being a member of the SS and attempted to pass himself off as an ordinary soldier of the Wehrmacht. I wondered whether the Jew was getting any real kick out of this new-found power that he was exercising. I concluded that he wasn't really enjoying it, and that he was merely - like a man in a brothel, or a boy smoking his first cigar, or a tourist traipsing round a picture gallery - *telling* himself that he was enjoying it, and behaving as he had planned to behave in the days he was helpless.

It is absurd to blame any German or Austrian Jew for getting his own back on the Nazis. Heaven knows what scores this particular man may have had to wipe out; very likely his whole family had been murdered; and after all, even a wanton kick to a prisoner is a very tiny thing compared with the outrages committed by the Hitler régime. But what this scene, and much else that I saw in Germany, brought home to me was that the whole idea of revenge and punishment is a childish daydream. Properly speaking, there is no such thing as revenge. Revenge is an act which you want to commit when you are powerless and because you are powerless: as soon as the sense of impotence is removed, the desire evaporates also.

Who would not have jumped for joy, in 1940, at the thought of seeing SS officers kicked and humiliated? But when the thing becomes possible, it is merely pathetic and disgusting. It is said that when Mussolini's corpse was exhibited in public, an old woman drew a revolver and fired five shots into it, exclaiming, 'Those are for my five sons!' It is the kind of story that the newspapers make up, but it might be true. I wonder how much satisfaction she got out of those five shots, which, doubtless, she had dreamed years earlier of firing. The condition of her being able to get close enough to Mussolini to shoot at him was that he should be a corpse.

In so far as the big public in this country is responsible for the monstrous peace settlement now being forced on Germany, it is because of a failure to see in advance that punishing an enemy brings no satisfaction. We acquiesce in crimes like the expulsion of all Germans from East Prussia - crimes which in some cases we could not prevent but might at least have protested against - because the Germans had angered and frightened us, and therefore we were certain that when they were down we should feel no pity for them. We persist in these policies, or let others persist in them on our behalf, because of a vague feeling that, having set out to punish Germany, we ought to go ahead and do it. Actually there is little acute hatred of Germany left in this country, and even less, I should expect to find, in the army of occupation. Only the minority of sadists, who must have their 'atrocities' from one source or another, take a keen interest in the hunting-down of war criminals and quislings. If you asked the average man what crime Goering, Ribbentrop, and the rest are to be charged with at their trial, he cannot tell you. Somehow the punishment of these monsters ceases to seem attractive when it becomes possible: indeed, once under lock and key, they almost cease to be monsters.

Unfortunately, there is often a need of some concrete incident before one can discover the real state of one's feelings. Here is another memory from Germany. A few hours after Stuttgart was captured by the French army, a Belgian journalist and myself entered the town, which was still in some disorder. The Belgian had been broadcasting throughout the war for the European Service of the BBC, and, like nearly all Frenchmen or Belgians, he had a very much tougher attitude towards 'the Boche' than an Englishman or an American would have. All the main bridges into town had been blown up, and we had to enter by a small footbridge which the Germans had evidently made efforts to defend. A dead German soldier was lying supine at the foot of the steps. His face was a waxy yellow. On his breast someone had laid a bunch of the lilac which was blooming everywhere.

The Belgian averted his face as we went past. When we were well over the bridge he confided to me that this was the first time he had seen a dead man. I suppose he was thirty five years old, and for four years he had been doing war propaganda over the radio. For several days after this, his attitude was quite different from what it had been earlier. He looked with disgust at the bomb-wrecked town and the humiliation the Germans were undergoing, and even on one occasion intervened to prevent a particularly bad bit of looting. When he left, he gave the residue of the coffee we had brought with us to the Germans on whom we were billeted. A week earlier he would probably have been scandalised at the idea of giving coffee to a 'Boche'. But his feelings, he told me, had undergone a change at the sight of *ce pauvre mort* beside the bridge: it had suddenly brought home to him the meaning of war. And yet, if we had happened to enter the town by another route, he might have been spared the experience of seeing one corpse out of the - perhaps - twenty million that the war has produced.

Through a glass, rosily

23 November 1945

The recent article by *Tribune*'s Vienna correspondent[185] provoked a spate of angry letters which, besides calling him a fool and a liar and making other charges of what one might call a routine nature, also carried the very serious implication that he ought to have kept silent even if he knew that he was speaking the truth. He himself made a brief answer in *Tribune*, but the question involved is so important that it is worth discussing it at greater length.

Whenever A and B are in opposition to one another, anyone who attacks or criticises A is accused of aiding and abetting B. And it is often true, objectively and on a short-term analysis, that he is making things easier for B. Therefore, say the supporters of A, shut up and don't criticise: or at least criticise 'constructively', which in practice always means favourably. And from this it is only a short step to arguing that the suppression and distortion of known facts is the highest duty of a journalist.

Now, if one divides the world into A and B and assumes that A represents progress and B reaction, it is just arguable that no fact detrimental to A ought ever to be revealed. But before making this claim one ought to realise where it leads. What do we mean by reaction? I suppose it would be agreed that Nazi Germany represented reaction in its worst form or one of its worst. Well, the people in this country who gave most ammunition to the Nazi propagandists during the war are exactly the ones who tell us that it is 'objectively' pro-fascist to criticise the USSR. I am not referring to the left as a whole. By and large, the Nazi radio got more material from the British left-wing press than from that of the right. And it could hardly be otherwise, for it is chiefly in the left-wing press that serious criticism of British institutions is to be found. Every revelation about sins or social inequality, every attack on the leaders of the Tory Party, every denunciation of British imperialism, was a gift for Goebbels. And not necessarily a worthless gift, for German propaganda about 'British plutocracy' had considerable effect in neutral countries, especially in the earlier part of the war.

Here are two examples of the kind of source from which the Axis propagandists were

185. *Tribune*'s issue of 2 November 1945 had carried a critical piece on the Red Army in Austria by a 'special correspondent' that reported widespread rape. It provoked outrage from several *Tribune* readers.

liable to take their material. The Japanese, in one of their English-speaking magazines in China, serialised Briffault's *Decline and Fall of the British Empire.*[186] Briffault, if not actually a communist, was vehemently pro-Soviet, and the book incidentally contained some cracks at the Japanese themselves; but from the Japanese point of view this didn't matter, since the main tendency of the book was anti-British. About the same time the German radio broadcast shortened versions of books which they considered damaging to British prestige. Among others they broadcast E. M. Forster's *A Passage to India.* And so far as I know they didn't even have to resort to dishonest quotations. Just because the book was essentially truthful, it could be made to serve the purposes of fascist propaganda. According to Blake,

> A truth that's told with bad intent
> Beats all the lies you can invent,

and anyone who has seen his own statements coming back at him on the Axis radio will feel the force of this. Indeed, anyone who has ever written in defence of unpopular causes or been the witness of events which are likely to cause controversy, knows the fearful temptation to distort or suppress the facts, simply because any honest statement will contain revelations which can be made use of by unscrupulous opponents. But what one has to consider are the long-term effects. In the long run, can the cause of progress be served by lies, or can it not? The readers who attacked *Tribune*'s Vienna correspondent so violently accused him of untruthfulness, but they also seemed to imply that the facts he brought forward ought not to be published even if true. 100,000 rape cases in Vienna are not a good advertisement for the Soviet régime: therefore, even if they have happened, don't mention them. Anglo-Russian relations are more likely to prosper if inconvenient facts are kept dark.

The trouble is that if you lie to people, their reaction is all the more violent when the truth leaks out, as it is apt to do in the end. Here is an example of untruthful propaganda coming home to roost. Many English people of goodwill draw from the left-wing press an unduly favourable picture of the Indian Congress Party. They not only believe it to be in the right (as it is), but are also apt to imagine that it is a sort of left-wing organisation with democratic and internationalist aims. Such people, if they are suddenly confronted with an actual, flesh-and-blood Indian nationalist, are liable to recoil into the attitude of a Blimp. I have seen this happen a number of times. And it is the same with pro-Soviet propaganda. Those who have swallowed it whole are always in danger of a sudden

186. Robert Briffault (1876–1948) was a novelist, social anthropologist and surgeon. Born in France, he grew up in New Zealand and settled in Britain after serving on the western front in the First World War. *The Decline and Fall of the British Empire* (New York: Simon and Schuster, 1937) is a withering assault on imperialism and appeasement.

revulsion in which they may reject the whole idea of socialism. In this and other ways I should say that the net effect of communist and near-communist propaganda has been simply to retard the cause of socialism, though it may have temporarily aided Russian foreign policy.

There are always the most excellent, high-minded reasons for concealing the truth, and these reasons are brought forward in almost the same words by supporters of the most diverse causes. I have had writings of my own kept out of print because it was feared that the Russians would not like them, and I have had others kept out of print because they attacked British imperialism and might be quoted by anti-British Americans. We are told *now* that any frank criticism of the Stalin régime will 'increase Russian suspicions', but it is only seven years since we were being told (in some cases by the same newspapers) that frank criticism of the Nazi régime would increase Hitler's suspicions. As late as 1941 some of the Catholic papers declared that the presence of Labour ministers in the British government increased Franco's suspicions and made him incline more towards the Axis. Looking back, it is possible to see that if only the British and American peoples had grasped in 1933 or thereabouts what Hitler stood for, war might have been averted. Similarly, the first step towards decent Anglo-Russian relations is the dropping of illusions. In principle most people would agree to this: but the dropping of illusions means the publication of facts, and facts are apt to be unpleasant.

The whole argument that one mustn't speak plainly because it 'plays into the hands of' this or that sinister influence is dishonest, in the sense that people only use it when it suits them. As I have pointed out, those who are most concerned about playing into the hands of the Tories were least concerned about playing into the hands of the Nazis. The Catholics who said 'Don't offend Franco because it helps Hitler' had been more or less consciously helping Hitler for years beforehand. Beneath this argument there always lies the intention to do propaganda for some single sectional interest, and to browbeat critics into silence by telling them that they are 'objectively' reactionary. It is a tempting manoeuvre, and I have used it myself more than once, but it is dishonest. I think one is less likely to use it if one remembers that the advantages of a lie are always short-lived. So often it seems a positive duty to suppress or colour the facts. And yet genuine progress can only happen through increasing enlightenment, which means the continuous destruction of myths.

Meanwhile there is a curious backhanded tribute to the values of liberalism in the fact that the opponents of free speech write letters to *Tribune* at all. 'Don't criticise,' such people are in effect saying: 'don't reveal inconvenient facts. Don't play into the hands of the enemy!' Yet they themselves are attacking *Tribune*'s policy with all the violence at their command. Does it not occur to them that if the principles they advocate were put into practice, their letters would never get printed?

Freedom of the Park

7 December 1945

A few weeks ago, five people who were selling papers outside Hyde Park were arrested by the police for obstruction. When taken before the magistrates, they were all found guilty, four of them being bound over for six months and the other sentenced to forty shillings fine or a month's imprisonment. He preferred to serve his term.

The papers these people were selling were *Peace News*, *Forward* and *Freedom*, besides other kindred literature. *Peace News* is the organ of the Peace Pledge Union, *Freedom* (till recently called *War Commentary*) is that of the anarchists; as for *Forward*, its politics defy definition, but at any rate it is violently left. The magistrate, in passing sentence, stated that he was not influenced by the nature of the literature that was being sold; he was concerned merely with the fact of obstruction, and that this offence had technically been committed.

This raises several important points. To begin with, how does the law stand on the subject? As far as I can discover, selling newspapers in the street is technically an obstruction, at any rate if you fail to move when the police tell you to. So it would be legally possible for any policeman who felt like it to arrest any newsboy for selling the *Evening News*. Obviously this doesn't happen, so that the enforcement of the law depends on the discretion of the police.

And what makes the police decide to arrest one man rather than another? However it may be with the magistrate, I find it hard to believe that in this case the police were not influenced by political considerations. It is a bit too much of a coincidence that they should have picked on people selling just those papers.

If they had also arrested someone selling *Truth*, or the *Tablet*, or the *Spectator*, or even the *Church Times*, their impartiality would be easier to believe in.

The British police are not like the continental *gendarmerie* or Gestapo, but I do not think [*sic*] one maligns them in saying that, in the past, they have been unfriendly to left-wing activities. They have generally shown a tendency to side with those whom they regarded as the defenders of private property. Till quite recently 'red' and 'illegal' were almost synonymous, and it was always the seller of, say the *Daily Worker*, never the seller of say, the *Daily Telegraph*, who was moved on and generally harassed. Apparently it can be the same, at any rate at moments, under a Labour government.

A thing I would like to know – it is a thing we hear very little about – is what changes are made in the administrative personnel when there has been a change of government. Does a police officer who has a vague notion that 'socialism' means something against the law carry on just the same when the government itself is socialist? It is a sound principle that the official should have no party affiliations, should serve successive governments faithfully and should not be victimised for his political opinions. Still, no government can afford to leave its enemies in key positions, and when Labour is in undisputed power for the first time - and therefore when it is taking over an administration formed by Conservatives - it clearly must make sufficient changes to prevent sabotage. The official, even when friendly to the government in power, is all too conscious that he is a permanency and can frustrate the short-lived ministers whom he is supposed to serve.

When a Labour government takes over, I wonder what happens to Scotland Yard Special Branch? To Military Intelligence? To the Consular Service? To the various colonial administrations - and so on and so forth? We are not told, but such symptoms as there are do not suggest that any very extensive shuffling is going on. We are still represented abroad by the same ambassadors, and BBC censorship seems to have the same subtly reactionary colour that it always had. The BBC claims, of course, to be both independent and non-political. I was told once that its 'line', if any, was to represent the left wing of the government in power. But that was in the days of the Churchill government. If it represents the left wing of the present government, I have not noticed the fact.

However, the main point of this episode is that the sellers of newspapers and pamphlets should be interfered with at all. Which particular minority is singled out - whether pacifists, communists, anarchists, Jehovah's Witnesses or the Legion of Christian Reformers who recently declared Hitler to be Jesus Christ - is a secondary matter. It is of symptomatic importance that these people should have been arrested at that particular spot. You are not allowed to sell literature inside Hyde Park, but for many years past it has been usual for the paper-sellers to station themselves outside the gates and distribute literature connected with the open air meetings a hundred yards away. Every kind of publication has been sold there without interference.

As for the meetings inside the park, they are one of the minor wonders of the world. At different times I have listened there to Indian nationalists, temperance reformers, communists, Trotskyists, the SPGB, the Catholic Evidence Society, Freethinkers, vegetarians, Mormons, the Salvation Army, the Church Army, and a large variety of plain lunatics, all taking their turn at the rostrum in an orderly way and receiving a fairly good-humoured hearing from the crowd. Granted that Hyde Park is a special area, a sort of Alsatia where outlawed opinions are permitted to walk - still, there are very few countries in the world where you can see a similar spectacle. I have known continental Europeans, long before Hitler seized power, come away from Hyde Park astonished and even perturbed by the things they had heard Indian or Irish nationalists saying about the British empire. The degree of freedom of the press existing in this country is often overrated. Technically there is great freedom, but the fact that most of the press is owned by a few people operates in much the same way as state censorship. On the other hand, freedom of speech is real. On a platform, or in certain recognised open air spaces like Hyde Park, you can say almost anything, and, what is perhaps more significant, no one is frightened to utter his true opinions in pubs, on the tops of buses, and so forth.

The point is that the relative freedom which we enjoy depends on public opinion. The law is no protection. Governments make laws, but whether they are carried out, and how the police behave, depends on the general temper in the country. If large numbers of people are interested in freedom of speech, there will be freedom of speech, even if the law forbids it; if public opinion is sluggish, inconvenient minorities will be persecuted, even if laws exist to protect them. The decline in the desire for individual liberty has not been so sharp as I would have predicted six years ago, when the war was starting, but still there has been a decline. The notion that certain opinions cannot safely be allowed a hearing is growing. It is given currency by intellectuals who confuse the issue by not distinguishing between democratic opposition and open rebellion, and it is reflected in our growing indifference to tyranny and injustice abroad. And even those who declare themselves to be in favour of freedom of opinion generally drop their claim when it is their own adversaries who are being prosecuted.

I am not suggesting that the arrest of five people for selling harmless newspapers is a major calamity. When you see what is happening in the world today, it hardly seems worth squealing about such a tiny incident. All the same, it is not a good symptom that such things should happen when the war is well over, and I should feel happier if this and the long series of similar episodes that have preceded it, were capable of raising a genuine popular clamour, and not merely a mild flutter in sections of the minority press.

The sporting spirit

14 December 1945

Now that the brief visit of the Dynamo football team[187] has come to an end, it is possible to say publicly what many thinking people were saying privately before the Dynamos ever arrived. That is, that sport is an unfailing cause of ill-will, and that if such a visit as this had any effect at all on Anglo-Soviet relations, it could only be to make them slightly worse than before.

Even the newspapers have been unable to conceal the fact that at least two of the four matches played led to much bad feeling. At the Arsenal match, I am told by someone who was there, a British and a Russian player came to blows and the crowd booed the referee. The Glasgow match, someone else informs me, was simply a free-for-all from the start. And then there was the controversy, typical of our nationalistic age, about the composition of the Arsenal team. Was it really an all-England team, as claimed by the Russians, or merely a league team, as claimed by the British? And did the Dynamos end their tour abruptly in order to avoid playing an all-England team? As usual, everyone answers these questions according to his political predilections. Not quite everyone, however. I noted with interest, as an instance of the vicious passions that football provokes, that the sporting correspondent of the Russophile *News Chronicle* took the anti-Russian line and maintained that Arsenal was *not* an all-England team. No doubt the controversy will continue to echo for years in the footnotes of history books. Meanwhile the result of the Dynamos' tour, in so far as it has had any result, will have been to create fresh animosity on both sides.

And how could it be otherwise? I am always amazed when I hear people saying that sport creates goodwill between the nations, and that if only the common peoples of the

---

187. A team from Moscow Dynamo arrived in Britain in November 1945 to play four matches against top British teams – a tour supposed to symbolise the Anglo-Soviet wartime alliance. They drew 3-3 with Chelsea, beat Cardiff City 10-1 and Arsenal 4-3 and then drew with Rangers 2-2. The tour was surrounded by controversy. On purely sporting grounds, British football fans claimed that Dynamo were not a proper club side but a national team, and Dynamo made similar complaints about the Arsenal team they met, which included Stanley Matthews and Stan Mortensen, neither of them Arsenal players. Politically, the tour gave the right the opportunity to have a go at the Soviet Union at a time when it was otherwise infra dig. See *Passovotchka: Moscow Dynamo in Britain, 1945* by David Downing (London: Bloomsbury, 1999) for a detailed account.

world could meet one another at football or cricket, they would have no inclination to meet on the battlefield. Even if one didn't know from concrete examples (the 1936 Olympic Games, for instance) that international sporting contests lead to orgies of hatred, one could deduce it from general principles.

Nearly all the sports practised nowadays are competitive. You play to win, and the game has little meaning unless you do your utmost to win. On the village green, where you pick up sides and no feeling of local patriotism is involved, it is possible to play simply for the fun and exercise: but as soon as the question of prestige arises, as soon as you feel that you and some larger unit will be disgraced if you lose, the most savage combative instincts are aroused. Anyone who has played even in a school football match knows this. At the international level sport is frankly mimic warfare. But the significant thing is not the behaviour of the players but the attitude of the spectators: and, behind the spectators, of the nations who work themselves into furies over these absurd contests, and seriously believe – at any rate for short periods – that running, jumping and kicking a ball are tests of national virtue.

Even a leisurely game like cricket, demanding grace rather than strength, can cause much ill-will, as we saw in the controversy over body-line bowling and over the rough tactics of the Australian team that visited England in 1921. Football, a game in which everyone gets hurt and every nation has its own style of play which seems unfair to foreigners, is far worse. Worst of all is boxing. One of the most horrible sights in the world is a fight between white and coloured boxers before a mixed audience. But a boxing audience is always disgusting, and the behaviour of the women, in particular, is such that the army, I believe, does not allow them to attend its contests. At any rate, two or three years ago, when Home Guards and regular troops were holding a boxing tournament, I was placed on guard at the door of the hall, with orders to keep the women out.

In England, the obsession with sport is bad enough, but even fiercer passions are aroused in young countries where games-playing and nationalism are both recent developments. In countries like India or Burma, it is necessary at football matches to have strong cordons of police to keep the crowd from invading the field. In Burma, I have seen the supporters of one side break through the police and disable the goalkeeper of the opposing side at a critical moment. The first big football match that was played in Spain about fifteen years ago led to an uncontrollable riot. As soon as strong feelings of rivalry are aroused, the notion of playing the game according to the rules always vanishes. People want to see one side on top and the other side humiliated, and they forget that victory gained through cheating or through the intervention of the crowd is meaningless. Even when the spectators don't intervene physically they try to influence the game by cheering their own side and 'rattling' opposing players with boos and insults. Serious sport has nothing to do with fair play. It is bound up with hatred, jealousy, boastfulness, disregard of all rules and sadistic pleasure in witnessing violence: in other words it is war minus the shooting.

Instead of blah-blahing about the clean, healthy rivalry of the football field and the great part played by the Olympic Games in bringing the nations together, it is more useful to inquire how and why this modern cult of sport arose. Most of the games we now play are of ancient origin, but sport does not seem to have been taken very seriously between Roman times and the nineteenth century. Even in the English public schools the games cult did not start till the later part of the last century. Dr Arnold, generally regarded as the founder of the modern public school, looked on games as simply a waste of time. Then, chiefly in England and the United States, games were built up into a heavily-financed activity, capable of attracting vast crowds and rousing savage passions, and the infection spread from country to country. It is the most violently combative sports, football and boxing, that have spread the widest. There cannot be much doubt that the whole thing is bound up with the rise of nationalism – that is, with the lunatic modern habit of identifying oneself with large power units and seeing everything in terms of competitive prestige. Also, organised games are more likely to flourish in urban communities where the average human being lives a sedentary or at least a confined life, and does not get much opportunity for creative labour. In a rustic community a boy or young man works off a good deal of his surplus energy by walking, swimming, snowballing, climbing trees, riding horses, and by various sports involving cruelty to animals, such as fishing, cock-fighting and ferreting for rats. In a big town one must indulge in group activities if one wants an outlet for one's physical strength or for one's sadistic impulses. Games are taken seriously in London and New York, and they were taken seriously in Rome and Byzantium: in the Middle Ages they were played, and probably played with much physical brutality, but they were not mixed up with politics nor a cause of group hatreds.

If you wanted to add to the vast fund of ill-will existing in the world at this moment, you could hardly do it better than by a series of football matches between Jews and Arabs, Germans and Czechs, Indians and British, Russians and Poles, and Italians and Yugoslavs, each match to be watched by a mixed audience of 100,000 spectators. I do not, of course, suggest that sport is one of the main causes of international rivalry; big-scale sport is itself, I think, merely another effect of the causes that have produced nationalism. Still, you do make things worse by sending forth a team of eleven men, labelled as national champions, to do battle against some rival team, and allowing it to be felt on all sides that whichever nation is defeated will 'lose face'.

I hope, therefore, that we shan't follow up the visit of the Dynamos by sending a British team to the USSR. If we must do so, then let us send a second-rate team which is sure to be beaten and cannot be claimed to represent Britain as a whole. There are quite enough real causes of trouble already, and we need not add to them by encouraging young men to kick each other on the shins amid the roars of infuriated spectators.

Old George's Almanac

28 December 1945

Some weeks ago *Tribune* accepted an advertisement from Lyndoe, the world-famous astrologer. The advertisement was for Lyndoe's book of forecasts for 1946. It struck me at the time that it would be interesting at the end of the year to go through the book and test Lyndoe's predictions against the reality: and, if I should be spared until that date, I intend to do so. But it seems fairer all round to utter my own prophecies for the coming year at the same time. They will not be so comforting nor, probably, so detailed as Lyndoe's, but here they are for what they are worth:

International Relations. The conference of foreign ministers now proceeding in Moscow will be a flop, leading only to high-sounding statements and an all-round increase of ill-will. Thereafter the international situation will continue to deteriorate, though with a few deceptive intervals when things seem to improve. The governing facts will be that no one intends to surrender sovereignty and no one is yet ready for another war, and the general tendency will always be towards 'zones of influence' and away from co-operation. After much delay, work will be half-heartedly started on the building of the United Nations Organisation, but no one will believe that the UNO is actually going to amount to anything. As the year goes on there will be more and more tendency for the USA and the USSR to do a deal at the expense of Britain, the general terms of the bargain being American non-interference in Europe and the Middle East in return for Russian non-interference in China and Japan. Nevertheless the armaments race between Russia and America will continue without a check. There will be violent diplomatic battles over such strategic points as the Kiel Canal, Tangier, the Suez Canal and Formosa, but in each case the real control of the disputed area will remain with the power that happens to be nearest. The Dardanelles will pass under Russian control. Trieste will be declared an international port and later (probably not in 1946) annexed by Italy or Yugoslavia.

The Atomic Bomb. The Americans will continue to guard the secret, and the clamour for its revelation will continue. If at any moment it appears that some scientist or body of scientists is about to spill the beans, the cry will then be that the secret must be revealed only to the USSR and not to the world at large. Towards the end of the year there will be strong rumours that the Russians have the bomb already. There will then be other rumours to the effect that the real subject of dispute is not the bomb itself but a rocket capable of carrying it several thousand miles. Attempts to apply atomic energy to industry will get nowhere, but the piling-up of bombs will continue. Professor Joad and others will sign manifestos demanding that the bomb be put under international control, and many pamphlets will be published pointing out that atomic energy, properly used, could be 'a boon to mankind'. Unsuccessful efforts will be made to persuade the government to dig shelters 500 feet deep. In all countries the general public will gradually lose interest in the subject.

And here are my forecasts for individual countries, or such of them as I have space for:

The USA. For some months an all-round orgy of spending, followed by a sudden economic crisis and huge-scale unemployment, complicated by over-rapid demobilisation. Growth of a formidable fascist movement, probably under military leadership, and, parallel with and hostile to this, growth of a Negro fascist movement, affiliated to kindred movements in Asia. All-round increase in anti-British feeling, which will be the one point on which all American factions will be in agreement. Increase – simultaneously and in the same people – in isolationism and in imperialist sentiment.

The USSR. Continued mobilisation and armaments production on a huge scale, with resulting privation for the people at large. Starvation and homelessness throughout the devastated areas. Serious trouble with military deserters and returned prisoners, large numbers of whom will end by being deported to Siberia. Increase in pan-Slav feeling, and, simultaneously with this, a reversion to more revolutionary slogans for export purposes. Publication of new decrees guaranteeing freedom of speech and of the press. Continued exclusion of foreign observers, other than stooges.

Britain. No improvement in the conditions of daily life. Growing discontent over continuation of controls, slowness of demobilisation, and shortage of houses. Slight increase in anti-Semitism, growth of anti-American feeling, gradual waning of pro-Russian feeling. Renewed stew about the birthrate, leading to proposals – neither of which will be carried out – to subsidise maternity heavily and to encourage immigration from Europe. Chronic coal shortage, numerous unofficial strikes, and savage battles, unintelligible to the ordinary man, over the reconversion of industry. Towards the end of the year the opposition will begin to gain ground in by-elections, but there will be no come-back by the Conservatives. Instead there will appear a small but fairly active fascist movement, manned largely by ex-officers, and there will be symptoms of a serious split in the Labour Party.

Germany. Stagnation enlivened by banditry. At some time in the year the Allies will decide that Germany is a liability and begin a drive to restore the industrial plant which they have previously dismantled. The Czechs will also re-admit some of the Germans whom they have expelled. A powerful resistance movement will grow up, led at first by ex-Nazis but drawing into it former anti-Nazis of every colour. By the end of the year the majority of Germans will look back on the Nazi régime with regret. There will be renewed rumours that Hitler is alive.

France. Slow economic recovery, intellectual stagnation. Growth in the power of the Catholics as against the other factions. Increasing estrangement between socialists and communists. All-round growth of xenophobia. The one great political issue will be the question of the western bloc, but the forces will be so perfectly balanced that no decision will be reached.

India. One deadlock after another. Rioting, civil disobedience, derailment of trains, assassination of prominent Europeans, but no large-scale revolt. Sporadic fighting in Burma which will be attributed to dacoits and bands of uncaptured Japanese. Famine or near-famine conditions in south India, Malaya and parts of the Indonesian archipelago. Appearance all over Asia of fascist movements proclaiming the racial superiority of the coloured peoples. Within a few months Nehru will announce that the Labour Party is worse than the Conservative Party.

I could go on, but space is running out. Gazing into my crystal, I see trouble in China, Greece, Palestine, Iraq, Egypt, Abyssinia, Argentina and a few dozen other places. I see civil wars, bomb outrages, public executions, famines, epidemics and religious revivals. An exhaustive search for something cheerful reveals that there will be a slight improvement in the régimes of Spain and Portugal and that things will not go too badly in a few countries too small or remote to be worth conquering.

Messages for the new year are supposed to sound a note of uplift and encouragement, and it may be objected that my forecasts are unduly gloomy. But are they? I fancy it will turn out that I have been over-optimistic rather than the contrary. And to those who just can't face the future without a cheer-up message to aid them, I present this consideration: that even if everything I have predicted comes to pass - yes, and a lot of other horrors that I didn't get round to mentioning - 1946 will still be appreciably better than the last six years.

Freedom and happiness

4 January 1946

Several years after hearing of its existence, I have at last got my hands on a copy of Zamyatin's *We*, which is one of the literary curiosities of this book-burning age. Looking it up in Gleb Struve's *25 Years of Soviet Russian Literature*, I find its history to have been this:

Zamyatin, who died in Paris in 1937, was a Russian novelist and critic who published a number of books both before and after the revolution. *We* was written about 1923, and though it is not about Russia and has no direct connection with contemporary politics – it is a fantasy dealing with the twenty-sixth century AD – it was refused publication on the ground that it was ideologically undesirable. A copy of the manuscript found its way out of the country, and the book has appeared in English, French and Czech translations, but never in Russian. The English translation was published in the United States, and I have never been able to procure a copy: but copies of the French translation (the title is *Nous autres*) do exist, and I have at last succeeded in borrowing one. So far as I can judge it is not a book of the first order, but it is certainly an unusual one, and it is astonishing that no English publisher has been enterprising enough to re-issue it.[188]

The first thing anyone would notice about *We* is the fact – never pointed out, I believe – that Aldous Huxley's *Brave New World* must be partly derived from it. Both books deal with the rebellion of the primitive human spirit against a rationalised, mechanised, painless world, and both stories are supposed to take place about six hundred years hence. The atmosphere of the two books is similar, and it is roughly speaking the same kind of society that is being described, though Huxley's book shows less political awareness and is more influenced by recent biological and psychological theories.

In the twenty-sixth century, in Zamyatin's vision of it, the inhabitants of Utopia have so completely lost their individuality as to be known only by numbers. They live in glass houses (this was written before television was invented), which enables the political police, known as the 'Guardians', to supervise them more easily. They all wear identical uniforms, and a human being is commonly referred to either as 'a number' or 'a unif' (uniform). They live on synthetic food, and their usual recreation is to march in fours while the anthem of the Single State is played through loudspeakers. At stated intervals

188. Yevgeny Zamyatin's *We* was first published in an English translation by Gregory Zilboorg (New York: Dutton, 1924). A second edition in English did not appear until 1960.

they are allowed for one hour (known as 'the sex hour') to lower the curtains round their glass apartments. There is, of course, no marriage, though sex life does not appear to be completely promiscuous. For purposes of love-making everyone has a sort of ration book of pink tickets, and the partner with whom he spends one of his allotted sex hours signs the counterfoil. The Single State is ruled over by a personage known as the Benefactor, who is annually re-elected by the entire population, the vote being always unanimous. The guiding principle of the State is that happiness and freedom are incompatible. In the Garden of Eden man was happy, but in his folly he demanded freedom and was driven out into the wilderness. Now the Single State has restored his happiness by removing his freedom.

So far the resemblance with *Brave New World* is striking. But though Zamyatin's book is less well put together – it has a rather weak and episodic plot which is too complex to summarise – it has a political point which the other lacks. In Huxley's book the problem of 'human nature' is in a sense solved, because it assumes that by pre-natal treatment, drugs and hypnotic suggestion the human organism can be specialised in any way that is desired. A first-rate scientific worker is as easily produced as an epsilon semi-moron, and in either case the vestiges of primitive instincts, such as maternal feeling or the desire for liberty, are easily dealt with. At the same time no clear reason is given why society should be stratified in the elaborate way that is described. The aim is not economic exploitation, but the desire to bully and dominate does not seem to be a motive either. There is no power-hunger, no sadism, no hardness of any kind. Those at the top have no strong motive for staying at the top, and though everyone is happy in a vacuous way, life has become so pointless that it is difficult to believe that such a society could endure.

Zamyatin's book is on the whole more relevant to our own situation. In spite of education and the vigilance of the Guardians, many of the ancient human instincts are still there. The teller of the story, D-503, who, though a gifted engineer, is a poor conventional creature, a sort of Utopian Billy Brown of London Town, is constantly horrified by the atavistic impulses which seize upon him. He falls in love (this is a crime, of course) with a certain I-330 who is a member of an underground resistance movement and succeeds for a while in leading him into rebellion. When the rebellion breaks out it appears that the enemies of the Benefactor are in fact fairly numerous, and these people, apart from plotting the overthrow of the state, even indulge, at the moment when their curtains are down, in such vices as smoking cigarettes and drinking alcohol. D-503 is ultimately saved from the consequences of his own folly. The authorities announce that they have discovered the cause of the recent disorders: it is that some human beings suffer from a disease called imagination. The nerve-centre responsible for imagination has now been located, and the disease can be cured by X-ray treatment. D-503 undergoes the operation, after which it is easy for him to do what he has known all along that he ought to do – that is, betray his confederates to the police. With complete equanimity he watches I-330 tortured by means of compressed air under a glass bell:

> She looked at me, her hands clasping the arms of the chair, until her eyes were completely shut. They took her out, brought her to herself by means of an electric shock, and put her under the bell again. This operation was repeated three times, and not a word issued from her lips.
>
> The others who had been brought along with her showed themselves more honest. Many of them confessed after one application. Tomorrow they will all be sent to the Machine of the Benefactor.

The Machine of the Benefactor is the guillotine. There are many executions in Zamyatin's Utopia. They take place publicly, in the presence of the Benefactor, and are accompanied by triumphal odes recited by the official poets. The guillotine, of course, is not the old crude instrument but a much improved model which literally liquidates its victim, reducing him in an instant to a puff of smoke and a pool of clear water. The execution is, in fact, a human sacrifice, and the scene describing it is given deliberately the colour of the sinister slave civilisations of the ancient world. It is this intuitive grasp of the irrational side of totalitarianism – human sacrifice, cruelty as an end in itself, the worship of a leader who is credited with divine attributes – that makes Zamyatin's book superior to Huxley's.

It is easy to see why the book was refused publication. The following conversation (I abridge it slightly) between D-503 and I-330 would have been quite enough to set the blue pencils working:

> 'Do you realise that what you are suggesting is revolution?'
>
> 'Of course, it's revolution. Why not?'
>
> 'Because there can't be a revolution. Our revolution was the last and there can never be another. Everybody knows that.'
>
> 'My dear, you're a mathematician: tell me, which is the last number?'
>
> 'What do you mean, the last number?'
>
> 'Well, then, the biggest number!'
>
> 'But that's absurd. Numbers are infinite. There can't be a last one.'
>
> 'Then why do you talk about the last revolution?'

There are other similar passages. It may well be, however, that Zamyatin did not intend the Soviet régime to be the special target of his satire. Writing at about the time of Lenin's death, he cannot have had the Stalin dictatorship in mind, and conditions in Russia in 1923 were not such that anyone would revolt against them on the ground that life was becoming too safe and comfortable. What Zamyatin seems to be aiming at is not any particular country but the implied aims of industrial civilisation. I have not read any of his other books, but I learn from Gleb Struve that he had spent several years in

England and had written some blistering satires on English life. It is evident from *We* that he had a strong leaning towards primitivism. Imprisoned by the Czarist government in 1906, and then imprisoned by the Bolsheviks in 1922 in the same corridor of the same prison, he had cause to dislike the political régime he had lived under, but his book is not simply the expression of a grievance. It is in effect a study of the Machine, the genie that man has thoughtlessly let out of its bottle and cannot put back again. This is a book to look out for when an English version appears.

Pleasure spots

11 January 1946

Some months ago I cut out of a shiny magazine some paragraphs written by a female journalist and describing the pleasure resort of the future. She had recently been spending some time at Honolulu, where the rigours of war do not seem to have been very noticeable. However, 'a transport pilot . . . told me that with all the inventiveness packed into this war, it was a pity someone hadn't found out how a tired and life-hungry man could relax, rest, play poker, drink, and make love, all at once, and round the clock, and come out of it feeling good and fresh and ready for the job again'. This reminded her of an entrepreneur she had met recently who was planning a 'pleasure spot which he thinks will catch on tomorrow as dog racing and dance hall did yesterday'. The entrepreneur's dream is described in some detail:

> His blueprints pictured a space covering several acres, under a series of sliding roofs – for the British weather is unreliable – and with a central space over with an immense dance floor made of translucent plastic which can be illuminated from beneath. Around it are grouped other functional spaces, at different levels. Balcony bars and restaurants commanding high views of the city roofs, and ground-level replicas. A battery of skittle alleys. Two blue lagoons: one, periodically agitated by waves, for strong swimmers, and another, a smooth and summery pool, for playtime bathers. Sunlight lamps over the pools to simulate high summer on days when the roofs don't slide back to disclose a hot sun in a cloudless sky. Rows of bunks on which people wearing sun-glasses and slips can lie and start a tan or deepen an existing one under a sunray lamp.
>
> Music seeping through hundreds of grills connected with a central distributing stage, where dance or symphonic orchestras play or the radio programme can be caught, amplified, and disseminated. Outside, two 1,000-car parks. One, free. The other, an open-air cinema drive-in, cars queueing to move through turnstiles, and the film thrown on a giant screen facing a row of assembled cars. Uniformed male attendants check the cars, provide free air and water, sell petrol and oil. Girls in while satin slacks take orders for buffet dishes and drinks, and bring them on trays.

Whenever one hears such phrases as 'pleasure spot', 'pleasure resort', 'pleasure city', it is difficult not to remember the often-quoted opening of Coleridge's 'Kubla Khan'.

In Xanadu did Kubla Khan
A stately pleasure-dome decree:
Where Alph, the sacred river, ran
Through caverns measureless to man
Down to a sunless sea.
So twice five miles of fertile ground
With walls and towers were girdled round:
And there were gardens bright with sinuous rills,
Where blossomed many an incense-bearing tree;
And here were forests ancient as the hills,
Enfolding sunny spots of greenery.

But it will be seen that Coleridge has got it all wrong. He strikes a false note straight off with talk about 'sacred' rivers and 'measureless' caverns. In the hands of the above-mentioned entrepreneur, Kubla Khan's project would have become something quite different. The caverns, air-conditioned, discreetly lighted and with their original rocky interior buried under layers of tastefully-coloured plastics, would be turned into a series of tea-grottoes in the Moorish, Caucasian or Hawaiian styles. Alph, the sacred river, would be dammed up to make an artificially-warmed bathing pool, while the sunless sea would be illuminated from below with pink electric lights, and one would cruise over it in real Venetian gondolas each equipped with its own radio set. The forests and 'spots of greenery' referred to by Coleridge would be cleaned up to make way for glass-covered tennis courts, a bandstand, a roller-skating rink and perhaps a nine-hole golf course. In short, there would be everything that a 'life-hungry' man could desire.

I have no doubt, all over the world, hundreds of pleasure resorts similar to the one described above are now being planned, and perhaps are even being built. It is unlikely that they will be finished - world events will see to that - but they represent faithfully enough the modern civilised man's idea of pleasure. Something of the kind is already partially attained in the more magnificent dance halls, movie palaces, hotels, restaurants and luxury liners. On a pleasure cruise or in a Lyons Corner House one already get something more than a glimpse of this future paradise. Analysed, its main characteristics are these:

(a) One is never alone.
(b) One never does anything for oneself.
(c) One is never within sight of wild vegetation or natural objects of any kind.
(d) Light and temperature are always artificially regulated.
(e) One is never out of the sound of music.

The music - and if possible it should be the same music for everybody - is the most important ingredient. Its function is to prevent thought and conversation, and to shut out any natural sound, such as the song of birds or the whistling of the wind, that might otherwise intrude. The radio is already consciously used for this purpose by innumerable people. In very many English homes the radio is literally never turned off, though it is manipulated from time to time so to make sure that only light music will come out of it. I know people who will keep the radio playing all through a meal and at the same time continue talking just loudly enough for the voices and the music to cancel out. This is done with a definite purpose. The music prevents the conversation from becoming serious or even coherent, while the chatter of voices stops one from listening attentively to the music and thus prevents the onset of that dreaded thing, thought. For

> The lights must never go out.
> The music must always play,
> Lest we should see where we are;
> Lost in a haunted wood,
> Children afraid of the dark
> Who have never been happy or good.

It is difficult not to feel that the unconscious aim in the most typical modern pleasure resorts is a return to the womb. For there, too, one was never alone, one never saw daylight, the temperature was always regulated, one did not have to worry about work or food, and one's thoughts, if any, were drowned by a continuous rhythmic throbbing.

When one looks at Coleridge's very different conception of a 'pleasure dome', one sees that it revolves partly round gardens and partly round caverns, rivers, forests and mountains with 'deep romantic chasms' - in short, round what is called nature. But the whole notion of admiring nature, and feeling a sort of religious awe in the presence of glaciers, deserts or waterfalls, is bound up with the sense of man's littleness and weakness against the power of the universe. The moon is beautiful partly because we cannot reach it, the sea is impressive because one can never be sure of crossing it safely. Even the pleasure one takes in a flower - and this is true even of a botanist who knows all there is to be known about the flower - is dependent partly on the sense of mystery. But meanwhile man's power over nature is steadily increasing. With the aid of the atomic bomb we could literally move mountains: we could even, so it is said, alter the climate of the earth by melting the polar ice-caps and irrigating the Sahara. Isn't there, therefore, something sentimental and obscurantist in preferring bird-song to swing music and in wanting to leave a few patches of wildness here and there instead of covering the whole surface of the earth with a network of *Autobahnen* flooded by artificial sunlight?

The question only arises because in exploring the physical universe man has made no attempt to explore himself. Much of what goes by the name of pleasure is simply an effort to destroy consciousness. If one started by asking, what is man? what are his needs? how can he best express himself? one would discover that merely having the power to avoid work and live one's life from birth to death in electric light and to the tune of tinned music is not a reason for doing so. Man needs warmth, society, leisure, comfort and security: he also needs solitude, creative work and the sense of wonder. If he recognised this he could use the products of science and industrialism eclectically, applying always the same test: does this make me more human or less human? He would then learn that the highest happiness does *not* lie in relaxing, resting, playing poker, drinking and making love simultaneously. And the instinctive horror which all sensitive people feel at the progressive mechanisation of life would be seen not to be a mere sentimental archaism, but to be fully justified. For man only stays human by preserving large patches of simplicity in his life, while the tendency of many modern inventions - in particular the film, the radio and the aeroplane - is to weaken his consciousness, dull his curiosity, and, in general, drive him nearer to the animals.

The politics of starvation

18 January 1946

A few days ago I received a wad of literature from the Save Europe Now committee,[189] which has been attempting - without much encouragement from the government or help from the press - to increase the supply of food from this country to Europe. They quote a series of statements from authoritative sources, which I will come back to in a moment, and which go to show that whereas we are reasonably well off and the United States is enjoying an orgy of overeating, a good part of Europe is lapsing into brute starvation.

In the *Observer* of 13 January, however, I have just read a signed article by Air Chief Marshal Sir Philip Joubert, expressing the contrary opinion:

> To one returning from overseas in this seventh winter of war (writes Sir Philip), the appearance of the British people is tragic. They seem morose, lacking in spring; and laughter comes with difficulty. The children look pallid and suety - fat but not fit. They compare very ill with the rosy-cheeked youngsters of Denmark, who have all the meat and fat they need, with plenty of fruit in season.

His main thesis is that we need more meat, fats and eggs - i.e. more of the rationed foods - and less starch. The official figures showing that, in fact, we are healthier than we were before the war convey a false impression: first - this is a quite extraordinary argument - because health and nutrition were admittedly in a bad way before the war, so that the present improvement is nothing to write home about; secondly because the drop in the death-rate merely means a 'greater expectation of existence' and one must not 'confuse existence with life'. Unless we can attain 'liveliness, vitality, vigour', for which meat, fat, fruit and cane sugar are required, we cannot make the effort needed for the task of reconstruction. Sir Philip ends his article:

> As for those who would cut our present rations further so as to give more to the Germans, there must be many who would reply to their demands: 'I would sooner that my children, brought up in freedom and goodwill towards men, should enjoy full vigour than the Germans, who may be using their strength to make war on the world again in another generation.

189. The Save Europe Now committee was founded by Victor Gollancz (see Tribune biographies, pp. 393–4 of this volume) after he witnessed widespread starvation in occupied Germany.

It will be seen that he is assuming (a) that any further export of food means a cut in rations here, and (b) that it is only proposed to send food to Germany. And in fact that is the form in which the big public has heard of this project, although those responsible have emphasised from the start that they were only proposing a *voluntary* surrender of certain food-stuffs, by those sections of the population to whom it would do no harm, and were *not* proposing it for the sole benefit of Germany.

Now here are a few facts from the latest bulletin of the Save Europe Now committee. In Budapest, in November, the chemists were closing down for lack of supplies, the hospitals had neither windows, fuel nor anaesthetics, and it was calculated that the town contained 30,000 stray children, some of whom had formed themselves into criminal bands. In December, 'independent observers' considered that unless fresh food supplies were brought quickly, a million people would die of starvation in Hungary this winter. In Vienna (November) 'the food for hospital surgeons consists of unsweetened coffee, a very thin soup and bread. Less than 500 calories in all', while the Austrian Secretary of State, in December, described the thickly populated areas of eastern Austria as being menaced by 'boundless misery, epidemics, crime, physical and moral decline'. In Czechoslovakia, in November, the Foreign Minister appealed to Britain and the USA to send fats and meat to save 700,000 'very badly fed children, of whom fifty per cent already have tuberculosis'. In Germany, the Saar children are 'slowly starving'. In the British Zone, Field-Marshal Montgomery said that he was 'entirely dependent on imports of wheat if he was to maintain the present ration scales for the German people, ranging from 1,200 to 1,500 calories'. This was in November. About the same time General Eisenhower, speaking of the French Zone, said that 'the normal ration of 1,100 calories a day for the average consumer was consistently not met'. And so on. Meanwhile it appears that our own average consumption is about 2,800 or 2,900 calories a day, while the most recent figures of deaths from tuberculosis, and of deaths of mothers in childbirth and of children of all ages up to five, are the lowest ever recorded. As for the USA, consumption of butter has just risen largely and meat rationing has come to an end. The Secretary of Agriculture estimates that 'the lifting of rationing will make meat available for civilians at the rate of 165 lb. annually – the pre-war supply was in the neighbourhood of 125 lb.'.

Even if the above figures do not convey much impression, who has not seen the photographs of skeleton-like children in Greece and other places – children to whom no one would think of applying Sir Philip Joubert's term, 'suety'? Yet there has undoubtedly been considerable resistance to the idea that we should send more food to Europe. The Save Europe Now committee, though they are now pursuing more limited aims, started off with the suggestion that those who felt inclined should sacrifice their points, or some of their points, and that the government should forward the food so saved to the famine-stricken areas.[190] The scheme was discouraged officially, but it also had a cold reception from many private persons. People who would have been in a position to give it good publicity were frankly frightened of it, and the general public was allowed to imagine that what was proposed was to take food from British housewives in order to give it to German war criminals. Indeed, the whole manner in which this business has been discussed illustrates the curious dishonesty that infects every political issue nowadays.

There are two things that make what one might call the official left, Labour or communist, nervous of any scheme which might mean sending extra food to Germany. One is fear of the working-class reaction. The working classes, so it is said, would resent even a voluntary arrangement which meant, in effect, that people in the higher income groups, who buy unrationed foods and eat some of their meals in restaurants, should give up their surplus. The average woman in the fish queue, it is feared, would answer: 'If there's really any food to spare, let *us* have it. Or why not give it to the coal miners?' I don't know whether this would really be the reaction, if the issues were fully explained. I suspect that some of the people who argue thus have in mind the sordid consideration that if we are to sacrifice food in sufficient quantities, to make any difference, it would mean not merely giving up points but curtailing restaurant feeding. In practice, whatever it may be in intention, our rationing system is thoroughly undemocratic, and an all-round row on the subject of the export of food might draw attention to this fact. That is part of the reason, I think, why this question has not been fully discussed in print.

But another consideration, even less mentionable, also enters. Food is a political weapon, or is thought of as a political weapon. The hungriest areas are either in the Russian zone or in the parts of Europe that are divided between the USSR and the western Allies. Many people calculate that if we send more food to, say, Hungary, British or American influence in Hungary will increase: whereas if we let the Hungarians starve and the Russians feed them, they are more likely to look toward the USSR. All those who are strongly Russophile are therefore against sending extra food to Europe, while some people are probably in favour of sending food merely because they see it as a way of weakening Russian prestige. No one has been honest enough to avow such motives, but you have only to look through the lists of those who have – and of those who haven't – supported the Save Europe Now campaign to see how the land lies.

The folly of such calculations lies in supposing that you can ever get good results from starvation. Whatever the ultimate political settlement in Europe may be, it can only be worse if it has been preceded by years of hunger, misery, banditry and ignorance. Air

190. Basic foodstuffs were rationed by coupon but luxuries such as tinned fruit and tinned meat were rationed using a points system.

Marshal Joubert advises us to feed ourselves rather than feed German children who will be fighting against us a generation hence. This is the 'realistic' view. In 1918 the 'realistic' ones were also in favour of keeping up the blockade after the armistice. We did keep up the blockade, and the children we starved then were the young men who were bombing us in 1940. No one, perhaps, could and did foresee that the results of wantonly starving Germany, and of making a vindictive peace, would be evil. So also with raising our own rations, as we shall perhaps be doing before long, while famine descends on Europe. But if we do decide to do this, at least let the issues be plainly discussed, and let the photographs of starving children be well publicised in the press, so that the people of this country may realise what they are doing.

On housing

25 January 1946

The much-discussed Reilly Plan for rehousing[191] is in itself merely an effort to get rid of the waste, noise, drudgery and loneliness which are usual in any ordinary town or built-up area, without altogether sacrificing cultural continuity or the desire of the average human being to have 'a home of your own'.

This book,[192] written by an enthusiastic supporter of the Plan, develops its social and psychological implications. Sir Charles Reilly, who confesses that he did not originally foresee the far-reaching consequences deduced by his disciple – indeed he has slightly the air of a man who has mounted a hobby-horse which turns out to be a unicorn – contributes an Introduction.

In the Reilly Plan, the majority of the houses are not built along roads but round greens. A Reilly 'unit' consists of about 250 houses grouped round five or six greens: most of the greens are roughly oval in shape, and the number of houses surrounding them will vary from 30 to 60. Each unit has its own Community Centre, nursery school, shopping centre, restaurant and meals service, and is self-contained to the extent that no main traffic roads run through it. The houses run round the greens in long blocks; behind each house there is a small garden, but the front door gives straight on the green. They are warmed by 'area heating,' there is continuous hot water, and rubbish removal is done by suction. Some of the houses or flats have kitchens, some not. If you prefer to live in a kitchenless house, you can have all your meals delivered from the meals centre in thermos containers which are left on the doorstep like the milk, the dirty dishes being afterwards removed by the same agency. A town can be built up of as many Reilly 'units' as there is need and space for. Of course, any large town will have its central shopping and administrative area, but the main idea of the plan is to split the town up into self-contained communities, practically villages, of about 1,000 people each.

Supposing that it could actually be put into operation – and, according to Mr Wolfe,

191. The Reilly plan for housing was an unofficial report on post-war reconstruction based on a plan for Birkenhead by Sir Charles Reilly (1874–1948). Reilly had been Professor of Architecture at the University of Liverpool, and the plan envisaged houses being built around small village greens clustered around a community centre whose communal restaurant would obviate the necessity for kitchens in the houses.

192. Lawrence Wolfe: *The Reilly Plan* (London: Nicholson and Watson, 1945).

this method of rehousing is cheaper and quicker than the normal methods – the advantages of the plan are obvious. The proper provision of day nurseries near at hand, the 'area heating', the ability to get cheap meals at the Community Centre whenever you wanted them, the absence of noise and of anxiety about traffic (with towns so planned, there would be no danger of small children straying on to the motor roads), would take an immense load of unnecessary work off the housewife. Living round a green would almost certainly promote sociability, and it is an important detail that each of the Community Centres would only be serving about 1,000 people, all of whom might be expected to know one another by sight. The green spaces, the easily accessible playing fields, the absence of smoke, and the ever-running hot water would make for health and cleanliness, and the children would grow up in the constant society of others of the same age instead of being alternately nagged and coddled at home. Mr Wolfe is probably within his rights in claiming that in such communities there would be less drudgery, less disease, less ignorance, earlier marriages, a higher birthrate, less crime and fewer neuroses than we have at present. And yet!

Mr Wolfe uses the Reilly Plan as the occasion for an almost non-stop attack on what he calls 'isolationism': meaning not only the chaos and aimlessness of life in great cities, but the whole English tradition of having a home of your own and keeping yourself to yourself. He is probably right in saying that this has increased in recent years, and certainly right in saying that house-ownership, stimulated by the building societies (just before the war no less than 4 million people in Britain owned or were buying their houses), encourages it. Life in little family units, with few communal facilities, naturally increases the drudgery of household work, and the average woman is middle-aged at thirty, thanks to the labour of preparing six or seven meals a day in an inconvenient kitchen and looking after, say, two children. Mr Wolfe proceeds to build up a picture of Britain which would suggest that it is the most overworked, poverty-stricken, crime and disease-ridden country under the sun. What he does not say is that most of the social change of the present century has been in the direction which he advocates.

Life in Britain may be more 'isolationist' than it was, but it is also very much more comfortable and less laborious. As against thirty years ago, people are larger and heavier, live longer, work shorter hours, eat more, spend more on amusements, and have household facilities which their parents would have found unimaginable. By most of the standards which Mr Wolfe is applying, the mass of the people were far better off in 1939 than they had been in 1909, and though the war has diminished national 'real' income, it has also tended to produce greater equality. These facts are known to anyone whose memories go far back enough, but they can be checked by figures. A book to study side by side with Mr Wolfe's is *The Condition of the British People, 1911–45*, by Mark

Abrams,[193] recently published by Gollancz. This shows unmistakably the physical improvement that has taken place. It also shows, so far as one can draw an inference from its figures, that we have not grown any happier or any more conscious of a reason for living. The slump in the birthrate, which Mr Wolfe rightly deplores, has coincided with the rise in material standards. The recent Mass Observation book, *Britain and Her Birth-rate*, seems to show that the two phenomena are directly connected.

Evidently what is needed to change the existing trend is the growth of a sense of purpose, and it is not certain that this will happen merely because people are removed from their old-fashioned, isolated homes and resettled in labour-saving colonies where they will lose much of their privacy. Naturally Mr Wolfe claims that he has no wish to break up the family, but various of the innovations that he favours would tend to have that effect. He is remarkably enthusiastic about the kitchenless house and 'the abolition of the muddlesome, costly and wasteful apparatus of the kitchen'. The family that dispenses with its kitchen, he says, 'has a more attractive and comfortable home'. The food is delivered in a Thermos container 'shaped like a medium suitcase' which 'will keep the contents hot for several hours, even in cold weather, and even if left on the doorstep'. When you feel hungry just open the door, and there the stuff is. It is not stated whether you can choose what meals you will have, but presumably you cannot. You are, of course, using other people's crockery all the time, but it doesn't matter because it is sterilised in between-whiles.

It is perhaps hardly necessary to dwell on the objections to this kind of thing. What is more to the point is that nearly everyone, including the overworked housewives whom Mr Wolfe pities, would recoil from such a prospect. Comparatively few people, as a Gallup poll has just shown, even want their houses centrally heated. Furthermore, for the moment the main preoccupation is to get houses built and not sacrifice any that are still habitable.

Yet, sooner or later the replanning of whole areas will be possible, and then it will be necessary to decide once and for all whether the old style of house, and the old manner of arranging houses, is to survive. The question has not been properly thrashed out, and people have to fall back on instincts which may be partly perverted. They want to live near their work, but they want to live in houses and not in flats. They want day nurseries

193. Mark Abrams (1906–94) was a pioneer of opinion-polling and market research in Britain during the 1930s. From 1939 to 1945 he worked as an analyst and propagandist for the government. Abrams founded Research Services Limited in 1946 and during the 1950s and 1960s conducted most of the Labour Party's private polls. He was joint author (with Richard Rose) of *Must Labour Lose?* (Harmondsworth: Penguin, 1960), a post-mortem on Labour's 1959 general election defeat that played a big part in persuading Hugh Gaitskell to try to abandon Clause Four of the Labour Party constitution.

and welfare clinics, but they also want privacy. They want to save work, but they want to cook their own meals and not eat meals chosen by other people and delivered in Thermos containers. A deep instinct warns them not to destroy the family, which in the modern world is the sole refuge from the state, but all the while the forces of the machine age are slowly destroying the family. So they look on while our culture perishes, and yet irrationally cling to such fragments of it as the whitened doorstep and the open fireplace.

Even in the Reilly Plan a chunk of the old culture, in the form of a church, survives in each unit: and to judge from the sketches in this book, the churches are to be in the Gothic style. A question not asked by Mr Wolfe, and seldom asked by anybody, is why we are on earth at all, and, leading out of this, what kind of lives we want to live. Yet till we have an answer to this question we shall never solve our housing problem and are merely making it rather more likely that the atom bombs will solve it for us.

The cost of radio programmes

1 February 1946

In last week's *Observer*, Mr W. E. Williams, discussing the recent raising of radio licences from ten shillings to a pound, made the pertinent remark that 'the trouble with British broadcasting is that it is far too cheap'. It seems to me that his remark is worth expanding, because the relationship between the amount of money brought in by a radio programme, and the amount of work that can be put into it, is not generally grasped. Nor is it realised that the badness of many radio programmes is due to the fact that to write and produce them better would be impossibly expensive.

Radio-listening costs at most a few pence a day, and if you like you can keep your radio turned on for the whole twenty-four hours. As it is what might be called a low-pressure entertainment, not giving you nearly such acute pleasure as you get from watching a film or drinking a glass of beer, most people feel that they pay quite a high enough price for it. Actually, the tiny price that they pay, measured against the heavy cost of the mechanical side of broadcasting, makes for a dull, cut-off-the-joint type of programme, and discourages innovation and experiment. This is best illustrated by plays, features and short stories, because it is especially in this type of programme that the vast possibilities of radio have remained unrealised.

The writer of a play or feature which is to take 30 minutes is usually paid about 30 guineas. He may get rather more if he is a 'name', and he may get a small extra fee if his piece is re-broadcast: but, in general, 30 guineas is the most he can expect, and he may get much less, since many programmes of this type are written by salaried employees who turn out several of them a week. Even if he is not a salaried employee, he is not likely to have much choice about his subject or his manner of treating it. The need to produce fresh programmes every day means that schedules have to be produced months in advance, and nothing can be accepted unless it fits in with some predetermined series. If you get a good idea for a novel or magazine article you can sit down and write it without consulting anyone else, and if you make a good job of it you can probably sell it. It would be no use going on this principle with a radio programme. Either it fits in somewhere or other, or it is unsaleable, however good it may be in itself.

When this play, story or whatever it may be, is ready, it will in all probability go on the air only once. It is, therefore, impossible to spend much time and money in producing it. What actually happens is that it is broadcast by a company of stock actors who are taking part in several totally different programmes every week. They may be given copies of their parts a day or two before they go on the air, but quite often they arrive in the studio without even having heard the name of the programme in which they are to take part. In any case, there is no question of their learning their parts by heart: they simply read them from the typewritten script. The rehearsals, for a 30-minute programme, will probably take four, or at most, six hours. There is no time for more, and to do more on any one day would simply exhaust the actors and producer to no purpose. Finally the programme goes on the air, and there is an end of it. If it is ever re-broadcast, it will probably not be by a fresh performance, in which the actors might improve on their first effort, but by a mechanical recording of the first one.

Now compare this with what happens in the case of a stage play. Writing a play is speculative. Most plays fail to reach the stage, and many of those that do get acted are a flop. Still, anyone who writes a play hopes that it will run for months and bring him several hundred pounds: also, he can choose his theme, and within limits he can even vary the length to suit himself. Even on a one-act play, therefore, he will probably do weeks or months of work, and he will shed a drop of sweat on every semi-colon. Before the play opens there will be weeks of careful rehearsal, and the actors will not only be word-perfect, but will have studied their parts and done their best to pack the utmost significance into every speech. Produced in this manner, the play can be acted, whereas the average radio programme is merely read. Yet how would it be possible to take all this trouble with a programme which is to be broadcast only once, and which the public pays for at a much lower rate than it pays for drinking water?

Criticism of the BBC, both in the press and by the general public, is usually unfavourable, but what most people appear to demand is simply a better version of the programmes they are getting already. They want better music, funnier jokes, more intelligent discussions, more truthful news. What is much less often pointed out is that the radio as a medium of literary expression has been very little studied. The microphone is a new instrument, and it ought to call into being a new attitude towards verse, drama and stories. Actually very little thought has been given to this subject, and still less concrete experiment. When an experimental programme does get broadcast, it is usually because there happens to be inside the BBC some imaginative person who can pull the necessary wires and overcome bureaucratic opposition. There is nothing to tempt a freelance writer into trying innovations.

If a radio play, for instance, could be performed night after night for months, like a stage play, it would be possible to spend more money and do more work on it; and the radio play, as an art-form, might then begin to be taken seriously. However, there is an obvious reason why the same programme cannot be broadcast over and over again. This being so, serious work along certain lines is only possible if commercial considerations are ignored. This means, first of all, setting aside one wavelength for uncompromisingly 'highbrow' programmes. It is curious how strongly this idea is resisted, and by what people. Even Frederick Laws, of the *News Chronicle*, one of the best radio critics we have, has pronounced against it. Yet it is difficult to see how any genuinely new idea can be tested if every programme that goes on the air has to make an immediate appeal to millions, or at any rate, hundreds of thousands of people. There is enough fuss already over the meagre periods devoted to broadcasting poetry. In the long run, no doubt anything that is good becomes popular; but any innovation, in any of the arts, needs protection during its experimental stage. It is significant that during the war the most intelligent - though not the most technically efficient - broadcasting has been done on the overseas services, where no commercial consideration entered and, in many cases, a large audience was not aimed at. The other thing that is needed is more facilities for experiment - not experiment in the technical side of radio, of which there is no doubt plenty already, but experiment on the problem of adapting existing literary forms to the air. Various difficulties which may in reality be quite simple have never yet been overcome. To name just one (it is discussed in the introduction to Edward Sackville West's radio play, *The Rescue*): no one has yet discovered how to present a play or dramatised story in such a way that the audience can discover what is happening, without the use of a 'narrator' who ruins the dramatic effect. To solve such problems it would be necessary to make use of closed circuits and to employ teams of musicians, actors and producers - in other words, it would be necessary to spend a lot of money. But then oceans of money are spent already, and nearly all of it on rubbish.

The sort of competition that would be presented by 'sponsored' radio is not likely to have a beneficial effect on the BBC. It might tend to keep the BBC up to the mark in the matter of brightness and efficiency, but people who are broadcasting in order to advertise Bile Beans or Player's Cigarettes are not going to aim at the minority public. If the possibilities latent in radio are ever realised, it will be because the people who have ideas get a chance to test them and are not choked off by being told that this or that 'would not fit in' or 'would not have a wide enough appeal'. Also, it should be possible to produce a radio programme with the same care and seriousness as is devoted to a stage play, and the writer should receive a large enough fee to encourage him to spend sufficient time on the work. All of which demands money, and might even, lamentable though that would be, mean raising the price of a radio licence by a few shillings more.

Books v. cigarettes

8 February 1946

A couple of years ago a friend of mine, a newspaper editor, was firewatching with some factory workers. They fell to talking about his newspaper, which most of them read and approved of, but when he asked them what they thought of the literary section, the answer he got was: 'You don't suppose we read that stuff, do you? Why, half the time you're talking about books that cost twelve and sixpence! Chaps like us couldn't spend twelve and sixpence on a book.' These, he said, were men who thought nothing of spending several pounds on a day trip to Blackpool.

This idea that the buying, or even the reading, of books is an expensive hobby and beyond the reach of the average person is so widespread that it deserves some detailed examination. Exactly what reading costs, reckoned in terms of pence per hour, is difficult to estimate, but I have made a start by inventorying my own books and adding up their total price. After allowing for various other expenses, I can make a fairly good guess at my expenditure over the last fifteen years.

The books that I have counted and priced are the ones I have here, in my flat. I have about an equal number stored in another place, so that I shall double the final figure in order to arrive at the complete amount. I have not counted oddments such as proof copies, defaced volumes, cheap paper-covered editions, pamphlets, or magazines, unless bound up into book form. Nor have I counted the kind of junky books – old school text-books and so forth – that accumulate in the bottoms of cupboards. I have counted only those books which I have acquired voluntarily, or else would have acquired voluntarily, and which I intend to keep. In this category I find that I have 442 books, acquired in the following ways:

Bought (mostly second-hand)	251
Given to me or bought with book tokens	33
Review copies and complimentary copies	143
Borrowed and not returned	10
Temporarily on loan	5
Total	**442**

Now as to the method of pricing. Those books that I have bought I have listed at their full price, as closely as I can determine it. I have also listed at their full price the books that have been given to me, and those that I have temporarily borrowed, or borrowed and kept. This is because book-giving, book-borrowing and book-stealing more or less even out. I possess books that do not strictly speaking belong to me, but many other people also have books of mine: so that the books I have not paid for can be taken as balancing others which I have paid for but no longer possess. On the other hand I have listed the review and complimentary copies at half-price. That is about what I would have paid for them second-hand, and they are mostly books that I would only have bought second-hand, if at all. For the prices I have sometimes had to rely on guesswork, but my figures will not be far out. The costs were as follows:

	£	s	d
Bought	36	9	0
Gifts	10	10	0
Review copies, etc	25	11	9
Borrowed and not returned	4	16	9
On loan	3	10	0
Shelves	2	0	0
Total	**82**	**17**	**6**

Adding the other batch of books that I have elsewhere, it seems that I possess altogether nearly 900 books, at a cost of £165 15s. This is the accumulation of about fifteen years – actually more, since some of these books date from my childhood: but call it fifteen years. This works out at £11 1s a year, but there are other charges that must be added in order to estimate my full reading expenses. The biggest will be for newspapers and periodicals, and for this I think £8 a year would be a reasonable figure. Eight pounds a year covers the cost of two daily papers, one evening paper, two Sunday papers, one weekly review and one or two monthly magazines. This brings the figure up to £19 1s, but to arrive at the grand total one has to make a guess. Obviously one often spends money on books without afterwards having anything to show for it. There are library subscriptions, and there are also the books, chiefly Penguins and other cheap editions, which one buys and then loses or throws away. However, on the basis of my other figures, it looks as though £6 a year would be quite enough to add for expenditure of this kind. So my total reading expenses over the past fifteen years have been in the neighbourhood of £25 a year.

Twenty-five pounds a year sounds quite a lot until you begin to measure it against other kinds of expenditure. It is nearly 9s 9d a week, and at present 9s 9d is the equivalent of about 83 cigarettes (Players): even before the war it would have bought you less than

200 cigarettes. With prices as they now are, I am spending far more on tobacco than I do on books. I smoke six ounces a week, at half-a-crown an ounce, making nearly £40 a year. Even before the war when the same tobacco cost 8d an ounce, I was spending over £10 a year on it: and if I also averaged a pint of beer a day, at sixpence, these two items together will have cost me close on £20 a year. This was probably not much above the national average. In 1938 the people of this country spent nearly £10 per head per annum on alcohol and tobacco: however, 20 per cent of the population were children under fifteen and another 40 per cent were women, so that the average smoker and drinker must have been spending much more than £10. In 1944, the annual expenditure per head on these items was no less than £23. Allow for the women and children as before, and £40 is a reasonable individual figure. Forty pounds a year would just about pay for a packet of Woodbines every day and half a pint of mild six days a week – not a magnificent allowance. Of course, all prices are now inflated, including the price of books: still, it looks as though the cost of reading, even if you buy books instead of borrowing them and take in a fairly large number of periodicals, does not amount to more than the combined cost of smoking and drinking.

It is difficult to establish any relationship between the price of books and the value one gets out of them. 'Books' includes novels, poetry, text books, works of reference, sociological treatises and much else, and length and price do not correspond to one another, especially if one habitually buys books second-hand. You may spend ten shillings on a poem of 500 lines, and you may spend sixpence on a dictionary which you consult at odd moments over a period of twenty years. There are books that one reads over and over again, books that become part of the furniture of one's mind and alter one's whole attitude to life, books that one dips into but never reads through, books that one reads at a single sitting and forgets a week later: and the cost, in terms of money, may be the same in each case. But if one regards reading simply as a recreation, like going to the pictures, then it is possible to make a rough estimate of what it costs. If you read nothing but novels and 'light' literature, and bought every book that you read, you would be spending – allowing eight shillings as the price of a book, and four hours as the time spent in reading it – two shillings an hour. This is about what it costs to sit in one of the more expensive seats in the cinema. If you concentrated on more serious books, and still bought everything that you read, your expenses would be about the same. The books would cost more but they would take longer to read. In either case you would still possess the books after you had read them, and they would be saleable at about a third of their purchase price. If you bought only second-hand books, your reading expenses would, of course, be much less: perhaps sixpence an hour would be a fair estimate. And on the other hand if you don't buy books, but merely borrow them from the lending library, reading costs you round about a halfpenny an hour: if you borrow them from the public library, it costs you next door to nothing.

I have said enough to show that reading is one of the cheaper recreations: after listening to the radio probably *the* cheapest. Meanwhile, what is the actual amount that the British public spends on books? I cannot discover any figures, though no doubt they exist. But I do know that before the war this country was publishing annually about 15,000 books, which included reprints and school books. If as many as 10,000 copies of each book were sold - and even allowing for the school books, this is probably a high estimate - the average person was only buying, directly or indirectly, about three books a year. These three books taken together might cost £1, or probably less.

These figures are guesswork, and I should be interested if someone would correct them for me. But if my estimate is anywhere near right, it is not a proud record for a country which is nearly 100 per cent literate and where the ordinary man spends more on cigarettes than an Indian peasant has for his whole livelihood. And if our book consumption remains as low as it has been, at least let us admit that it is because reading is a less exciting pastime than going to the dogs, the pictures or the pub, and not because books, whether bought or borrowed, are too expensive.

Decline of the English murder

15 February 1946

It is Sunday afternoon, preferably before the war. The wife is already asleep in the armchair, and the children have been sent out for a nice long walk. You put your feet up on the sofa, settle your spectacles on your nose, and open the *News of the World*. Roast beef and Yorkshire, or roast pork and apple sauce, followed up by suet pudding and driven home, as it were, by a cup of mahogany-brown tea, have put you in just the right mood. Your pipe is drawing sweetly, the sofa cushions are soft underneath you, the fire is well alight, the air is warm and stagnant. In these blissful circumstances, what is it that you want to read about?

Naturally, about a murder. But what kind of murder? If one examines the murders which have given the greatest amount of pleasure to the British public, the murders whose story is known in its general outline to almost everyone and which have been made into novels and re-hashed over and over again by the Sunday papers, one finds a fairly strong family resemblance running through the greater number of them. Our great period in murder, our Elizabethan period, so to speak, seems to have been between roughly 1850 and 1925, and the murderers whose reputation has stood the test of time are the following: Dr Palmer of Rugeley, Jack the Ripper, Neill Cream, Mrs Maybrick, Dr Crippen, Seddon, Joseph Smith, Armstrong, and Bywaters and Thompson. In addition, in 1919 or thereabouts, there was another very celebrated case which fits into the general pattern but which I had better not mention by name, because the accused man was acquitted.

Of the above-mentioned nine cases, at least four have had successful novels based on them, one has been made into a popular melodrama, and the amount of literature surrounding them, in the form of newspaper write-ups, criminological treatises and reminiscences by lawyers and police officers, would make a considerable library. It is difficult to believe that any recent English crime will be remembered so long and so intimately, and not only because the violence of external events has made murder seem unimportant, but because the prevalent type of crime seems to be changing. The principal *cause célèbre* of the war years was the so-called Cleft Chin Murder, which has now been written up in a popular booklet; the verbatim account of the trial was published some time last year by Messrs Jarrolds with an introduction by Mr Bechhofer Roberts. Before returning to this pitiful and sordid case, which is only interesting from a sociological and perhaps a legal point of view, let me try to define what it is that the readers of Sunday papers mean when they say fretfully that 'you never seem to get a good murder nowadays'.

In considering the nine murders I named above, one can start by excluding the Jack the Ripper case, which is in a class by itself. Of the other eight, six were poisoning cases, and eight of the ten criminals belonged to the middle class. In one way or another, sex was a powerful motive in all but two cases, and in at least four cases respectability - the desire to gain a secure position in life, or not to forfeit one's social position by some scandal such as a divorce - was one of the main reasons for committing murder. In more than half the cases, the object was to get hold of a certain known sum of money such as a legacy or an insurance policy, but the amount involved was nearly always small. In most of the cases the crime only came to light slowly, as the result of careful investigations which started off with the suspicions of neighbours or relatives; and in nearly every case there was some dramatic coincidence, in which the finger of Providence could be clearly seen, or one of those episodes that no novelist would dare to make up, such as Crippen's flight across the Atlantic with his mistress dressed as a boy, or Joseph Smith playing 'Nearer, my God, to Thee' on the harmonium while one of his wives was drowning in the next room. The background of all these crimes, except Neill Cream's, was essentially domestic; of twelve victims, seven were either wife or husband of the murderer.

With all this in mind one can construct what would be, from a *News of the World* reader's point of view, the 'perfect' murder. The murderer should be a little man of the professional class - a dentist or a solicitor, say - living an intensely respectable life somewhere in the suburbs, and preferably in a semi-detached house, which will allow the neighbours to hear suspicious sounds through the wall. He should be either chairman of the local Conservative Party branch, or a leading Nonconformist and strong temperance advocate. He should go astray through cherishing a guilty passion for his secretary or the wife of a rival professional man, and should only bring himself to the point of murder after long and terrible wrestles with his conscience. Having decided on murder, he should plan it all with the utmost cunning, and only slip up over some tiny unforeseeable detail. The means chosen should, of course, be poison. In the last analysis he should commit murder because this seems to him less disgraceful, and less damaging to his career, than being detected in adultery. With this kind of background, a crime can have dramatic and even tragic qualities which make it memorable and excite pity for both victim and murderer. Most of the crimes mentioned above have a touch of this atmosphere, and in three cases, including the one I referred to but did not name, the story approximates to the one I have outlined.

Now compare the Cleft Chin Murder. There is no depth of feeling in it. It was almost chance that the two people concerned committed that particular murder, and it was only by good luck that they did not commit several others. The background was not domesticity, but the anonymous life of the dance-halls and the false values of the American film. The two culprits were an eighteen-year-old ex-waitress named Elizabeth Jones, and an American army deserter, posing as an officer, named Karl Hulten. They were only together for six days, and it seems doubtful whether, until they were arrested, they even learned one another's true names. They met casually in a teashop, and that night went out for a ride in a stolen army truck. Jones described herself as a strip-tease artist, which was not strictly true (she had given one unsuccessful performance in this line); and declared that she wanted to do something dangerous, 'like being a gun-moll'. Hulten described himself as a big-time Chicago gangster, which was also untrue. They met a girl bicycling along the road, and to show how tough he was Hulten ran over her with his truck, after which the pair robbed her of the few shillings that were on her. On another occasion they knocked out a girl to whom they had offered a lift, took her coat and handbag and threw her into a river. Finally, in the most wanton way, they murdered a taxi-driver who happened to have £8 in his pocket. Soon afterwards they parted. Hulten was caught because he had foolishly kept the dead man's car, and Jones made spontaneous confessions to the police. In court each prisoner incriminated the other. In between crimes, both of them seem to have behaved with the utmost callousness: they spent the dead taxi-driver's £8 at the dog races.

Judging from her letters, the girl's case has a certain amount of psychological interest, but this murder probably captured the headlines because it provided distraction amid the doodlebugs and the anxieties of the Battle of France. Jones and Hulten committed their murder to the tune of V-1, and were convicted to the tune of V-2.[194] There was also considerable excitement because – as has become usual in England – the man was sentenced to death and the girl to imprisonment. According to Mr Raymond, the reprieving of Jones caused widespread indignation and streams of telegrams to the Home Secretary: in her native town, 'She should hang' was chalked on the walls beside pictures of a figure dangling from a gallows. Considering that only ten women have been hanged in Britain this century, and that the practice has gone out largely because of popular feeling against it, it is difficult not to feel that this clamour to hang an eighteen-year-old girl was due partly to the brutalising effects of war. Indeed, the whole meaningless story, with its atmosphere of dance-halls, movie-palaces, cheap perfume, false names and stolen cars, belongs essentially to a war period.

Perhaps it is significant that the most talked-of English murder of recent years should have been committed by an American and an English girl who had become partly

194. For the V-1 and the V-2, see notes 130 and 152 respectively.

Americanised. But it is difficult to believe that this case will be so long remembered as the old domestic poisoning dramas, product of a stable society where the all-prevailing hypocrisy did at least ensure that crimes as serious as murder should have strong emotions behind them.

Do our colonies pay?

8 March 1946

I have before me a copy of *Socialist Commentary*,[195] the organ of the Socialist Vanguard Group, and another of *Bulletin*, the organ of the (American) Council on Jewish-Arab Co-operation.[196] From the first I take the following sentences:

> The balance sheet between Britain and India gives little support to the hypothesis that Britain is exploiting India . . . A merely 'moral' approach (to colonial problems) is insufficient, so long as many persons are hoodwinked into believing that [the] British economy is largely 'dependent' upon the possession of India and other colonies.

From the second I take the following:

> British governments pledged to maintain the empire have shown and can show no deviation in foreign policy regardless of political denomination . . . The British standard of living depends on the empire, and the empire must have permanent military installations in the far east.

Here, therefore, you have one writer in a left-wing paper flatly stating that British living standards are dependent on colonial exploitation, and another writer in another left-wing paper stating equally definitely that they are not so dependent. For the moment I am not concerned with the question of which of them is right, but with the fact that they can differ in this way. It is probably not important that one paper is British and the other American, since the writer in the British paper is an American, as it happens.

It should be noticed that the question of whether we are exploiting India, and the question of whether our prosperity depends on India, are separate. It may well be that we are exploiting India, but for the profit of a small minority, without benefit to the nation

195. *Socialist Commentary* was the journal of the Socialist Vanguard Group, which began as the British section of a German ethical socialist (but revolutionary) propaganda group, the Internationaler Sozialistischer Kampfbund. The SVG in the 1940s was an enthusiastic proponent of a federal Europe and staunchly anti-Stalinist. In the 1950s, it became the Socialist Union and played a major role in promoting revisionism in the Labour Party, collaborating with (among others) Mark Abrams (see note 193).

196. The *Bulletin of the Council on Jewish-Arab Cooperation* was published in New York from 1944 to 1949 by the linguist Zellig Harris (1909–92) and his wife Bruria. Harris, who taught Noam Chomsky, was a left-wing Zionist and libertarian socialist.

as a whole. And of these two questions, the second is the more immediately important. If it is really true that our comparative comfort is simply a product of imperialism, that such things as the Beveridge scheme, increased old age pensions, raising of the school-leaving age, slum clearance, improved health services and what-not are luxuries which we can only afford if we have millions of oriental slaves at our command - that, surely, is a serious consideration. For, as socialists, we want an improved standard of living for our own people, and, again as socialists, we want justice for the colonial peoples. Are the two things compatible? Whatever the rights and wrongs of the matter may be, one would at least think that this question could be authoritatively answered. The facts, which are chiefly statistical facts, must be ascertainable. Yet no agreed opinion exists. Those two flatly contradictory statements which I quoted above are typical of hundreds of others which I could collect.

I know people who can prove to me with pencil and paper that we should be just as well off, or perhaps better, if all our colonial possessions were lost to us; and I know others who can prove that if we had no colonies to exploit our standard of living would slump catastrophically. And curiously enough this division of opinion cuts right across political parties. Thus, all Tories are imperialists, but whereas some Tories assert that without our empire we should be ruined economically as well as militarily, others assert that the empire is a non-paying concern and that we only maintain it from motives of public spirit. Socialists of the extreme left, such as the ILP, usually take it for granted that Britain would be plunged into the blackest poverty if she stopped looting the coloured peoples, while others not far to the right of them declare that if only the coloured peoples were liberated, they would develop more rapidly and their productive power would increase, which would be to our own advantage. Among Asiatic nationalists the same division of opinion exists. The most violently anti-British ones declare that when India is lost the British will all starve to death, while others argue that a free and friendly India would be a much better customer for British goods than a hostile and backward dependency. And yet, as I said above, this is quite obviously not an insoluble question. The figures that would settle it once and for all must exist, if one knew where to look for them.

However, it is not necessarily the case that either of the two current opinions is the right one. The person who says, 'Yes, Britain depends on India' usually assumes that if India were free, British trade with India would cease forthwith. The person who says, 'No, Britain doesn't depend on India' usually assumes that if India were free, British-Indian trade would proceed as before, with no period of dislocation. My own view has always been (a) that over a long period we have definitely exploited, i.e. robbed, our colonial possessions, (b) that to some extent the whole British nation has benefited from this, in an economic sense, and (c) that we cannot make restitution to the colonial peoples without lowering our own standard of living for several years at the least. The really essential thing, almost never mentioned when this subject is raised, is the time factor. Quite likely it would be to our advantage to make an end of imperialism, but not immediately. There might be a long and uncomfortable transition period first. This is a bleak thought, and I believe that it is a half-conscious avoidance of it that makes almost all discussions of this question curiously unreal.

At the general election, for instance, the avoidance of imperial issues was quite astonishing. When foreign affairs were mentioned at all, the reference was almost invariably to the USSR or the United States. I don't think I ever heard any speaker on any platform mention India spontaneously. Once or twice, at Labour meetings, I tried the experiment of asking a question about India, to get an answer which sounded something like this: 'The Labour Party is, of course, in fullest sympathy with the aspiration of the Indian people towards independence, next question, please.' And there the matter dropped, with not a flicker of interest on the part of the audience. The handbook issued to Labour speakers contained 200 pages, out of which one not very informative page was devoted to India. Yet India has nearly ten times the population of Britain! The subjects which, in my experience, roused real passion were housing, full employment and social insurance. Who could have guessed, from the manner in which they were discussed, that these subjects were in any way bound up with our possession of colonies which give us raw materials and assured markets?

In the long run an evasion of the truth is always paid for. One thing that we are gradually paying for now is our failure to make clear to the British people that their prosperity depends partly on factors outside Britain. Extremists of both right and left have grossly exaggerated the advantages of imperialism, while the optimists who stand between them have talked as though military control over your markets and sources of raw material were of no importance. They have assumed that a liberated India would still be our customer, without considering what might happen if India passed under control of a foreign power, or broke up into anarchy, or developed a closed economy, or were ruled over by a nationalist government which made a policy of boycotting British goods. What we ought to have said throughout these last twenty years is something like this: 'It is our duty as socialists to liberate the subject peoples, and in the long run it will be to our advantage as well. But only in the long run. In the short run we have got to count with the hostility of these peoples, with the chaos into which they will probably fall, and with their frightful poverty, which will compel us to give them goods of various kinds in order to put them on their feet. If we are very lucky our standard of living may not suffer by the liberation of the colonies, but the probability is that it will suffer for years, or even for decades. You have got to choose between liberating India and having extra sugar. Which do you prefer?'

What would the average woman in the fish queue say if it were put to her like that? I am not certain. But the point is that it never has been put to her like that, and if she plumps for the extra sugar - as she may - when the moment of crisis comes, it will be because the issues have not been fully discussed beforehand. Instead, we have had such contradictory statements as I quoted above, both in the last analysis untrue, and both, in their different ways, tending to perpetuate imperialism.

In front of your nose

22 March 1946

Many recent statements in the press have declared that it is almost, if not quite, impossible for us to mine as much coal as we need for home and export purposes, because of the impossibility of inducing a sufficient number of miners to remain in the pits. One set of figures which I saw last week estimated the annual 'wastage' of mine workers at 60,000 and the annual intake of new workers at 10,000. Simultaneously with this – and sometimes in the same column of the same paper – there have been statements that it would be undesirable to make use of Poles or Germans because this might lead to unemployment in the coal industry. The two utterances do not always come from the same sources, but there must certainly be many people who are capable of holding these totally contradictory ideas in their heads at a single moment.

This is merely one example of a habit of mind which is extremely widespread, and perhaps always has been. Bernard Shaw, in the preface to *Androcles and the Lion*, cites as another example the first chapter of the Gospel of Matthew, which starts off by establishing the descent of Joseph, father of Jesus, from Abraham. In the first verse, Jesus is described as 'the son of David, the son of Abraham', and the genealogy is then followed up through fifteen verses: then, in the next verse but one, it is explained that as a matter of fact Jesus was *not* descended from Abraham, since he was not the son of Joseph. This, says Shaw, presents no difficulty to a religious believer, and he names as a parallel case the rioting in the East End of London by the partisans of the Tichborne Claimant, who declared that a British working man was being done out of his rights.

Medically, I believe, this manner of thinking is called schizophrenia: at any rate, it is the power of holding simultaneously two beliefs which cancel out. Closely allied to it is the power of ignoring facts which are obvious and unalterable, and which will have to be faced sooner or later. It is especially in our political thinking that these vices flourish. Let me take a few sample subjects out of the hat. They have no organic connexion with each other: they are merely cases, taken almost at random, of plain, unmistakable facts being shirked by people who in another part of their mind are aware of those facts.

Hong Kong. For years before the war everyone with knowledge of Far Eastern conditions knew that our position in Hong Kong was untenable and that we should lose it as soon as a major war started. This knowledge, however, was intolerable, and government after government continued to cling to Hong Kong instead of giving it back to the Chinese. Fresh troops were even pushed into it, with the certainty that they would be uselessly taken prisoner, a few weeks before the Japanese attack began. The war came, and Hong Kong promptly fell – as everyone had known all along that it would do.

Conscription. For years before the war, nearly all enlightened people were in favour of standing up to Germany: the majority of them were also against having enough armaments to make such a stand effective. I know very well the arguments that are put forward in defence of this attitude; some of them are justified, but in the main they are simply forensic excuses. As late as 1939, the Labour Party voted against conscription, a step which probably played its part in bringing about the Russo-German Pact and certainly had a disastrous effect on morale in France. Then came 1940 and we nearly perished for lack of a large, efficient army, which we could only have had if we had introduced conscription at least three years earlier.

The Birthrate. Twenty or twenty-five years ago, contraception and enlightenment were held to be almost synonymous. To this day, the majority of people argue – the argument is variously expressed, but always boils down to more or less the same thing – that large families are impossible for economic reasons. At the same time, it is widely known that the birthrate is highest among the low-standard nations, and, in our population, highest among the worst-paid groups. It is also argued that a smaller population would mean less unemployment and more comfort for everybody, while on the other hand it is well established that a dwindling and ageing population is faced with calamitous and perhaps insoluble economic problems. Necessarily the figures are uncertain, but it is quite possible that in only seventy years our population will amount to about eleven millions, over half of whom will be old age pensioners. Since, for complex reasons, most people don't want large families, the frightening facts can exist somewhere or other in their consciousness, simultaneously known and not known.

UNO. In order to have any efficacy whatever, a world organisation must be able to override big states as well as small ones. It must have power to inspect and limit armaments, which means that its officials must have access to every square inch of every country. It must also have at its disposal an armed force bigger than any other armed force and responsible only to the organisation itself. The two or three great states that really matter have never even pretended to agree to any of these conditions, and they have so arranged the constitution of UNO that their own actions cannot even be discussed. In other words, UNO's usefulness as an instrument of world peace is nil. This was just as obvious before it began functioning as it is now. Yet only a few months ago millions of well-informed people believed that it was going to be a success.

There is no use in multiplying examples. The point is that we are all capable of believing things which we *know* to be untrue, and then, when we are finally proved wrong, impudently twisting the facts so as to show that we were right. Intellectually, it is possible to carry on this process for an indefinite time: the only check on it is that sooner or later a false belief bumps up against solid reality, usually on a battlefield.

When one looks at the all-prevailing schizophrenia of democratic societies, the lies that have to be told for vote-catching purposes, the silence about major issues, the distortions of the press, it is tempting to believe that in totalitarian countries there is less humbug, more facing of the facts. There, at least, the ruling groups are not dependent on popular favour and can utter the truth crudely and brutally. Goering could say 'Guns before butter', while his democratic opposite numbers had to wrap the same sentiment up in hundreds of hypocritical words.

Actually, however, the avoidance of reality is much the same everywhere, and has much the same consequences. The Russian people were taught for years that they were better off than everybody else, and propaganda posters showed Russian families sitting down to abundant meals while the proletariat of other countries starved in the gutter. Meanwhile the workers in the western countries were so much better off than those of the USSR that non-contact between Soviet citizens and outsiders had to be a guiding principle of policy. Then, as a result of the war, millions of ordinary Russians penetrated far into Europe, and when they return home the original avoidance of reality will inevitably be paid for in frictions of various kinds. The Germans and the Japanese lost the war quite largely because their rulers were unable to see facts which were plain to any dispassionate eye.

To see what is in front of one's nose needs a constant struggle. One thing that helps toward it is to keep a diary, or, at any rate, to keep some kind of record of one's opinions about important events. Otherwise, when some particularly absurd belief is exploded by events, one may simply forget that one ever held it. Political predictions are usually wrong. But even when one makes a correct one, to discover *why* one was right can be very illuminating. In general, one is only right when either wish or fear coincides with reality. If one recognises this, one cannot, of course, get rid of one's subjective feelings, but one can to some extent insulate them from one's thinking and make predictions cold-bloodedly, by the book of arithmetic. In private life most people are fairly realistic. When one is making out one's weekly budget, two and two invariably make four. Politics, on the other hand, is a sort of sub-atomic or non-Euclidean world where it is quite easy for the part to be greater than the whole or for two objects to be in the same place simultaneously. Hence the contradictions and absurdities I have chronicled above, all finally traceable to a secret belief that one's political opinions, unlike the weekly budget, will not have to be tested against solid reality.

Some thoughts on the common toad

12 April 1946

Before the swallow, before the daffodil, and not much later than the snowdrop, the common toad salutes the coming of spring after his own fashion, which is to emerge from a hole in the ground, where he has lain buried since the previous autumn, and crawl as rapidly as possible towards the nearest suitable patch of water. Something – some kind of shudder in the earth, or perhaps merely a rise of a few degrees in the temperature – has told him that it is time to wake up: though a few toads appear to sleep the clock round and miss out a year from time to time – at any rate, I have more than once dug them up, alive and apparently well, in the middle of the summer.

At this period, after his long fast, the toad has a very spiritual look, like a strict Anglo-Catholic towards the end of Lent. His movements are languid but purposeful, his body is shrunken, and by contrast his eyes look abnormally large. This allows one to notice, what one might not at another time, that a toad has about the most beautiful eye of any living creature. It is like gold, or more exactly it is like the golden-coloured semi-precious stone which one sometimes sees in signet-rings, and which I think is called a chrysoberyl.

For a few days after getting into the water the toad concentrates on building up his strength by eating small insects. Presently he has swollen to his normal size again, and then he goes through a phase of intense sexiness. All he knows, at least if he is a male toad, is that he wants to get his arms round something, and if you offer him a stick, or even your finger, he will cling to it with surprising strength and take a long time to discover that it is not a female toad. Frequently one comes upon shapeless masses of ten or twenty toads rolling over and over in the water, one clinging to another without distinction of sex. By degrees, however, they sort themselves out into couples, with the male duly sitting on the female's back. You can now distinguish males from females, because the male is smaller, darker and sits on top, with his arms tightly clasped round the female's neck. After a day or two the spawn is laid in long strings which wind themselves in and out of the reeds and soon become invisible. A few more weeks, and the water is alive with masses of tiny tadpoles which rapidly grow larger, sprout hind-legs, then forelegs, then shed their tails: and finally, about the middle of the summer, the new generation of toads, smaller than one's thumb-nail but perfect in every particular, crawl out of the water to begin the game anew.

* * *

I mention the spawning of the toads because it is one of the phenomena of spring which most deeply appeal to me, and because the toad, unlike the skylark and the primrose, has never had much of a boost from poets. But I am aware that many people do not like reptiles or amphibians, and I am not suggesting that in order to enjoy the spring you have to take an interest in toads. There are also the crocus, the missel-thrush, the cuckoo, the blackthorn, etc. The point is that the pleasures of spring are available to everybody, and cost nothing. Even in the most sordid street the coming of spring will register itself by some sign or other, if it is only a brighter blue between the chimney pots or the vivid green of an elder sprouting on a blitzed site. Indeed it is remarkable how nature goes on existing unofficially, as it were, in the very heart of London. I have seen a kestrel flying over the Deptford gasworks, and I have heard a first-rate performance by a blackbird in the Euston Road. There must be some hundreds of thousands, if not millions, of birds living inside the four-mile radius, and it is rather a pleasing thought that none of them pays a halfpenny of rent.

As for spring, not even the narrow and gloomy streets round the Bank of England are quite able to exclude it. It comes seeping in everywhere, like one of those new poison gases which pass through all filters. The spring is commonly referred to as 'a miracle', and during the past five or six years this worn-out figure of speech has taken on a new lease of life. After the sorts of winters we have had to endure recently, the spring does seem miraculous, because it has become gradually harder and harder to believe that it is actually going to happen. Every February since 1940 I have found myself thinking that this time winter is going to be permanent. But Persephone, like the toads, always rises from the dead at about the same moment. Suddenly, towards the end of March, the miracle happens and the decaying slum in which I live is transfigured. Down in the square the sooty privets have turned bright green, the leaves are thickening on the chestnut trees, the daffodils are out, the wallflowers are budding, the policeman's tunic looks positively a pleasant shade of blue, the fishmonger greets his customers with a smile, and even the sparrows are quite a different colour, having felt the balminess of the air and nerved themselves to take a bath, their first since last September.

* * *

Is it wicked to take a pleasure in spring and other seasonal changes? To put it more precisely, is it politically reprehensible, while we are all groaning, or at any rate ought to be groaning, under the shackles of the capitalist system, to point out that life is frequently more worth living because of a blackbird's song, a yellow elm tree in October, or some other natural phenomenon which does not cost money and does not have what the editors of left-wing newspapers call a class angle? There is no doubt that many people think so. I know by experience that a favourable reference to 'nature' in one of my articles is liable to bring me abusive letters, and though the key-word in these letters is usually 'sentimental', two ideas seem to be mixed up in them. One is that any pleasure in the actual process of life encourages a sort of political quietism. People, so the thought runs, ought to be discontented, and it is our job to multiply our wants and not simply to increase our enjoyment of the things we have already. The other idea is that this is the age of machines and that to dislike the machine, or even to want to limit its domination, is backward-looking, reactionary and slightly ridiculous. This is often backed up by the statement that a love of nature is a foible of urbanised people who have no notion what nature is really like. Those who really have to deal with the soil, so it is argued, do not love the soil, and do not take the faintest interest in birds or flowers, except from a strictly utilitarian point of view. To love the country one must live in the town, merely taking an occasional week-end ramble at the warmer times of year.

This last idea is demonstrably false. Medieval literature, for instance, including the popular ballads, is full of an almost Georgian enthusiasm for nature, and the art of agricultural peoples such as the Chinese and Japanese centres always round trees, birds, flowers, rivers, mountains. The other idea seems to me to be wrong in a subtler way. Certainly we ought to be discontented, we ought not simply to find out ways of making the best of a bad job, and yet if we kill all pleasure in the actual process of life, what sort of future are we preparing for ourselves? If a man cannot enjoy the return of spring, why should he be happy in a labour-saving Utopia? What will he do with the leisure that the machine will give him? I have always suspected that if our economic and political problems are ever really solved, life will become simpler instead of more complex, and that the sort of pleasure one gets from finding the first primrose will loom larger than the sort of pleasure one gets from eating an ice to the tune of a Wurlitzer.[197] I think that by retaining one's childhood love of such things as trees, fishes, butterflies and – to return to my first instance – toads, one makes a peaceful and decent future a little more probable, and that by preaching the doctrine that nothing is to be admired except steel and concrete, one merely makes it a little surer that human beings will have no outlet for their surplus energy except in hatred and leader worship.

At any rate, spring is here, even in London N1, and they can't stop you enjoying it. This is a satisfying reflection. How many a time have I stood watching the toads mating, or a pair of hares having a boxing match in the young corn, and thought of all the

197. A cinema organ.

important persons who would stop me enjoying this if they could. But luckily they can't. So long as you are not actually ill, hungry, frightened or immured in a prison or a holiday camp, spring is still spring. The atom bombs are piling up in the factories, the police are prowling through the cities, the lies are streaming from the loudspeakers, but the earth is still going round the sun, and neither the dictators nor the bureaucrats, deeply as they disapprove of the process, are able to prevent it.

A good word for the Vicar of Bray

26 April 1946

Some years ago a friend took me to the little Berkshire church of which the celebrated Vicar of Bray was once the incumbent. (Actually it is a few miles from Bray, but perhaps at that time the two livings were one.) In the churchyard there stands a magnificent yew tree which, according to a notice at its foot, was planted by no less a person than the Vicar of Bray himself.[198] And it struck me at the time as curious that such a man should have left such a relic behind him.

The Vicar of Bray, though he was well equipped to be a leader-writer on *The Times*, could hardly be described as an admirable character. Yet, after this lapse of time, all that is left of him is a comic song and a beautiful tree, which has rested the eyes of generation after generation and must surely have outweighed any bad effects which he produced by his political quislingism.

Thibaw, the last King of Burma, was also far from being a good man. He was a drunkard, he had five hundred wives - he seems to have kept them chiefly for show, however - and when he came to the throne his first act was to decapitate seventy or eighty of his brothers. Yet he did posterity a good turn by planting the dusty streets of Mandalay with tamarind trees which cast a pleasant shade until the Japanese incendiary bombs burned them down in 1942.

The poet, James Shirley, seems to have generalised too freely when he said that 'Only the actions of the just | Smell sweet and blossom in their dust'. Sometimes the actions of the unjust make quite a good showing after the appropriate lapse of time. When I saw the Vicar of Bray's yew tree it reminded me of something, and afterwards I got hold of a book of selections from the writings of John Aubrey and reread a pastoral poem which must have been written some time in the first half of the seventeenth century, and which was inspired by a certain Mrs Overall.

Mrs Overall was the wife of a Dean and was extensively unfaithful to him. According to Aubrey she 'could scarcely denie any one', and she had 'the loveliest Eies that were ever seen, but wondrous wanton'. The poem (the 'shepherd swaine' seems to have been somebody called Sir John Selby) starts off:

198. 'The Vicar of Bray' is an English ballad that tells how the vicar of a Berkshire village kept his ecclesiastical living in the late seventeenth and early eighteenth centuries by changing his religious creed to match the preferences of successive monarchs.

Downe lay the Shepherd Swaine
So sober and demure
Wishing for his wench againe
So bonny and so pure
With his head on hillock lowe
And his arms akimboe
And all was for the losse of his
Hye nonny nonny noe . . .

Sweet she was, as kind a love
As ever fetter'd Swaine;
Never such a daynty one
Shall man enjoy again.
Sett a thousand on a rowe
I forbid that any showe
Ever the like of her
Hye nonny nonny noe.

As the poem proceeds through another six verses, the refrain 'Hye nonny nonny noe' takes on an unmistakably obscene meaning, but it ends with the exquisite stanza:

But gone she is the prettiest lasse
That ever trod on plaine.
What ever hath betide of her
Blame not the Shepherd Swaine.
For why? She was her owne Foe,
And gave herself the overthrowe
By being so franke of her
Hye nonny nonny noe.

Mrs Overall was no more an exemplary character than the Vicar of Bray, though a more attractive one. Yet in the end all that remains of her is a poem which still gives pleasure to many people, though for some reason it never gets into the anthologies. The suffering which she presumably caused, and the misery and futility in which her own life must have ended, have been transformed into a sort of lingering fragrance like the smell of tobacco-plants on a summer evening.

But to come back to trees. The planting of a tree, especially one of the long-living hardwood trees, is a gift which you can make to posterity at almost no cost and with almost no trouble, and if the tree takes root it will far outlive the visible effect of any of your other actions, good or evil. A year or two ago I wrote a few paragraphs in *Tribune* about some sixpenny rambler roses from Woolworth's which I had planted before the war. This brought me an indignant letter from a reader who said that roses are bourgeois, but I still think that my sixpence was better spent than if it had gone on cigarettes or even on one of the excellent Fabian Research Pamphlets.

Recently, I spent a day at the cottage where I used to live,[199] and noted with a pleased surprise – to be exact, it was a feeling of having done good unconsciously – the progress of the things I had planted nearly ten years ago. I think it is worth recording what some of them cost, just to show what you can do with a few shillings if you invest them in something that grows.

First of all there were the two ramblers from Woolworth's, and three polyantha roses, all at sixpence each. Then there were two bush roses which were part of a job lot from a nursery garden. This job lot consisted of six fruit trees, three rose bushes and two gooseberry bushes, all for ten shillings. One of the fruit trees and one of the rose bushes died, but the rest are all flourishing. The sum total is five fruit trees, seven roses and two gooseberry bushes, all for twelve and sixpence. These plants have not entailed much work, and have had nothing spent on them beyond the original amount. They never even received any manure, except what I occasionally collected in a bucket when one of the farm horses happened to have halted outside the gate.

Between them, in nine years, those seven rose bushes will have given what would add up to a hundred or a hundred and fifty months of bloom. The fruit trees, which were mere saplings when I put them in, are now just about getting in their stride. Last week one of them, a plum, was a mass of blossom, and the apples looked as if they were going to do fairly well. What had originally been the weakling of the family, a Cox's Orange Pippin – it would hardly have been included in the job lot if it had been a good plant – had grown into a sturdy tree with plenty of fruit spurs on it. I maintain that it was a public-spirited action to plant that Cox, for these trees do not fruit quickly and I did not expect to stay there long. I never had an apple off it myself, but it looks as if someone else will have quite a lot. By their fruits ye shall know them, and the Cox's Orange Pippin is a good fruit to be known by. Yet I did not plant it with the conscious intention of doing anybody a good turn. I just saw the job lot going cheap and stuck the things into the ground without much preparation.

A thing which I regret, and which I will try to remedy some time, is that I have never in my life planted a walnut. Nobody does plant them nowadays – when you see a walnut it is almost invariably an old tree. If you plant a walnut you are planting it for your grandchildren, and who cares a damn for his grandchildren? Nor does anybody plant a quince, a mulberry or a medlar. But these are garden trees which you can only be expected to plant if you have a patch of ground of your own. On the other hand, in any

199. Wallington in Hertfordshire. See note 42.

hedge or in any piece of waste ground you happen to be walking through, you can do something to remedy the appalling massacre of trees, especially oaks, ashes, elms and beeches, which has happened during the war years.

Even an apple tree is liable to live for about 100 years, so that the Cox I planted in 1936 may still be bearing fruit well into the twenty-first century. An oak or a beech may live for hundreds of years and be a pleasure to thousands or tens of thousands of people before it is finally sawn up into timber. I am not suggesting that one can discharge all one's obligations towards society by means of a private re-afforestation scheme. Still, it might not be a bad idea, every time you commit an antisocial act, to make a note of it in your diary, and then, at the appropriate season, push an acorn into the ground.

And, if even one in twenty of them came to maturity, you might do quite a lot of harm in your lifetime, and still, like the Vicar of Bray, end up as a public benefactor after all.

Confessions of a book reviewer

3 May 1946

In a cold but stuffy bed-sitting-room littered with cigarette ends and half-empty cups of tea, a man in a moth-eaten dressing-gown sits at a rickety table, trying to find room for his typewriter among the piles of dusty papers that surround it. He cannot throw the papers away because the wastepaper basket is already overflowing, and besides, somewhere among the unanswered letters and unpaid bills it is possible that there is a cheque for two guineas which he is nearly certain he forgot to pay into the bank. There are also letters with addresses which ought to be entered in his address book. He has lost his address book, and the thought of looking for it, or indeed of looking for anything, afflicts him with acute suicidal impulses.

He is a man of thirty-five, but looks fifty. He is bald, has varicose veins and wears spectacles, or would wear them if his only pair were not chronically lost. If things are normal with him he will be suffering from malnutrition, but if he has recently had a lucky streak he will be suffering from a hangover. At present it is half-past eleven in the morning, and according to his schedule he should have started work two hours ago; but even if he had made any serious effort to start he would have been frustrated by the almost continuous ringing of the telephone bell, the yells of the baby, the rattle of an electric drill out in the street, and the heavy boots of his creditors clumping up and down the stairs. The most recent interruption was the arrival of the second post, which brought him two circulars and an income tax demand printed in red.

Needless to say this person is a writer. He might be a poet, a novelist, or a writer of film scripts or radio features, for all literary people are very much alike, but let us say that he is a book reviewer. Half hidden among the pile of papers is a bulky parcel containing five volumes which his editor has sent with a note suggesting that they 'ought to go well together'. They arrived four days ago, but for forty-eight hours the reviewer was prevented by moral paralysis from opening the parcel. Yesterday in a resolute moment he ripped the string off it and found the five volumes to be *Palestine at the Crossroads*, *Scientific Dairy Farming*, *A Short History of European Democracy* (this one is 680 pages and weighs four pounds), *Tribal Customs in Portuguese East Africa*, and a novel, *It's Nicer Lying Down*, probably included by mistake. His review – 800 words, say – has got to be 'in' by midday tomorrow.

Three of these books deal with subjects of which he is so ignorant that he will have to read at least fifty pages if he is to avoid making some howler which will betray him not merely to the author (who of course knows all about the habits of book reviewers), but even to the general reader. By four in the afternoon he will have taken the books out of their wrapping paper but will still be suffering from a nervous inability to open them. The prospect of having to read them, and even the smell of the paper, affects him like the prospect of eating cold ground-rice pudding flavoured with castor oil. And yet curiously enough his copy will get to the office in time. Somehow it always does get there in time. At about nine pm his mind will grow relatively clear, and until the small hours he will sit in a room which grows colder and colder, while the cigarette smoke grows thicker and thicker, skipping expertly through one book after another and laying each down with the final comment, 'God, what tripe!' In the morning, blear-eyed, surly and unshaven, he will gaze for an hour or two at a blank sheet of paper until the menacing finger of the clock frightens him into action. Then suddenly he will snap into it. All the stale old phrases – 'a book that no one should miss', 'something memorable on every page', 'of special value are the chapters dealing with, etc, etc' – will jump into their places like iron filings obeying the magnet, and the review will end up at exactly the right length and with just about three minutes to go. Meanwhile another wad of ill-assorted, unappetising books will have arrived by post. So it goes on. And yet with what high hopes this down-trodden, nerve-racked creature started his career, only a few years ago.

Do I seem to exaggerate? I ask any regular reviewer – anyone who reviews, say, a minimum of 100 books a year – whether he can deny in honesty that his habits and character are such as I have described. Every writer, in any case, is rather that kind of person, but the prolonged, indiscriminate reviewing of books is a quite exceptionally thankless, irritating and exhausting job. It not only involves praising trash – though it does involve that, as I will show in a moment – but constantly *inventing* reactions towards books about which one has no spontaneous feelings whatever. The reviewer, jaded though he may be, is professionally interested in books, and out of the thousands that appear annually, there are probably fifty or a hundred that he would enjoy writing about. If he is a top-notcher in his profession he may get hold of ten or twenty of them: more probably he gets hold of two or three. The rest of his work, however conscientious he may be in praising or damning, is in essence humbug. He is pouring his immortal spirit down the drain, half a pint at a time.

The great majority of reviews give an inadequate or misleading account of the book that is dealt with. Since the war publishers have been less able than before to twist the tails of literary editors and evoke a paean of praise for every book that they produce, but on the other hand the standard of reviewing has gone down owing to lack of space and other inconveniences. Seeing the results, people sometimes suggest that the solution lies in getting book reviewing out of the hands of hacks. Books on specialised subjects ought to be dealt with by experts, and on the other hand a good deal of reviewing, especially of novels, might well be done by amateurs. Nearly every book is capable of arousing passionate feeling, if it is only a passionate dislike, in some or other reader, whose ideas about it would surely be worth more than those of a bored professional. But, unfortunately, as every editor knows, that kind of thing is very difficult to organise. In practice the editor always finds himself reverting to his team of hacks – his 'regulars', as he calls them.

None of this is remediable so long as it is taken for granted that every book deserves to be reviewed. It is almost impossible to mention books in bulk without grossly overpraising the great majority of them. Until one has some kind of professional relationship with books one does not discover how bad the majority of them are. In much more than nine cases out of ten the only objectively truthful criticism would be 'This book is worthless', while the truth about the reviewer's own reaction would probably be 'This book does not interest me in any way, and I would not write about it unless I were paid to'. But the public will not pay to read that kind of thing. Why should they? They want some kind of guide to the books they are asked to read, and they want some kind of evaluation. But as soon as values are mentioned, standards collapse. For if one says – and nearly every reviewer says this kind of thing at least once a week – that *King Lear* is a good play and *The Four Just Men* is a good thriller, what meaning is there in the word 'good'?

The best practice, it has always seemed to me, would be simply to ignore the great majority of books and to give very long reviews – 1,000 words is a bare minimum – to the few that seem to matter. Short notes of a line or two on forthcoming books can be useful, but the usual middle-length review of about 600 words is bound to be worthless even if the reviewer genuinely wants to write it. Normally he doesn't want to write it, and the week-in, week-out production of snippets soon reduces him to the crushed figure in a dressing-gown whom I described at the beginning of this article. However, everyone in this world has someone else whom he can look down on, and I must say, from experience of both trades, that the book reviewer is better off than the film critic, who cannot even do his work at home, but has to attend trade shows at eleven in the morning and, with one or two notable exceptions, is expected to sell his honour for a glass of inferior sherry.

As I Please 60

8 November 1946

Someone has just sent me a copy of an American fashion magazine which shall be nameless. It consists of 325 large quarto pages, of which no fewer than fifteen are given up to articles on world politics, literature, etc. The rest consists entirely of pictures with a little letterpress creeping round their edges: pictures of ball dresses, mink coats, step-ins, panties, brassieres, silk stockings, slippers, perfumes, lipsticks, nail varnish – and, of course, of the women, unrelievedly beautiful, who wear them or make use of them. I do not know just how many drawings or photographs of women occur throughout the whole volume, but as there are forty-five of them, all beautiful, in the first fifty pages, one can work it out roughly.

One striking thing when one looks at these pictures is the overbred, exhausted, even decadent style of beauty that now seems to be striven after. Nearly all of these women are immensely elongated. A thin-boned, ancient-Egyptian type of face seems to predominate: narrow hips are general, and slender non-prehensile hands like those of a lizard are everywhere. Evidently it is a real physical type, for it occurs as much in the photographs as in the drawings. Another striking thing is the prose style of the advertisements, an extraordinary mixture of sheer lushness with clipped and sometimes very expressive technical jargon. Words like suave-mannered, custom-finished, contour-conforming, mitt-back, innersole, backdip, midriff, swoosh, swash, curvaceous, slenderise and pet-smooth are flung about with evident full expectation that the reader will understand them at a glance. Here are a few sample sentences taken at random:

'A new Shimmer Sheen colour that sets your hands and his head in a whirl.' 'Bared and beautifully bosomy.' 'Feathery-light Milliken Fleece to keep her kitten-snug!' 'Others see you through a veil of sheer beauty, and they wonder why!' 'Gentle discipline for curves in lacy lastex pantie-girdle.' 'An exclamation point of a dress that depends on fluid fabric for much of its drama.' 'Suddenly your figure lifts . . . lovely in the litheness of a Foundette pantie-girdle.' 'Lovely to look at, lovelier to wear is this original Lady Duff gown with its shirred cap sleeves and accentuated midriff.' 'Supple and tissue-light, yet wonderfully curve-holding.' 'The miracle of figure flattery!' 'Moulds your bosom into proud feminine lines.' 'Isn't it wonderful to know that Corsees wash and wear and whittle you down . . . even though they weigh only four ounces!' 'The distilled witchery of one woman who was forever desirable . . . forever beloved . . . Forever Amber.' And so on and so on and so on.

A fairly diligent search through the magazine reveals two discreet allusions to grey hair, but if there is anywhere a direct mention of fatness or middle age I have not found it. Birth and death are not mentioned either: nor is work, except that a few recipes for breakfast dishes are given. The male sex enters directly or indirectly into perhaps one advertisement in twenty, and photographs of dogs or kittens appear here and there. In only two pictures, out of about three hundred, is a child represented.

On the front cover there is a coloured photograph of the usual elegant female standing on a chair while a grey-haired, spectacled, crushed-looking man in shirt-sleeves kneels at her feet, doing something to the edge of her skirt. If one looks closely one finds that actually he is about to take a measurement with a yard-measure. But to a casual glance he looks as though he were kissing the hem of the woman's garment - not a bad symbolical picture of American civilisation, or at least of one important side of it.

* * *

One interesting example of our unwillingness to face facts and our consequent readiness to make gestures which are known in advance to be useless, is the present campaign to Keep Death off the Roads.

The newspapers have just announced that road deaths for September dropped by nearly eighty as compared with the previous September. This is very well so far as it goes, but the improvement will probably not be kept up - at any rate, it will not be progressive - and meanwhile everyone knows that you can't solve the problem while our traffic system remains what it is. Accidents happen because on narrow, inadequate roads, full of blind corners and surrounded by dwelling houses, vehicles and pedestrians are moving in all directions at all speeds from three miles an hour to sixty or seventy. If you really want to keep death off the roads, you would have to replan the whole road system in such a way as to make collisions impossible. Think out what this means (it would involve, for example, pulling down and rebuilding the whole of London), and you can see that it is quite beyond the power of any nation at this moment. Short of that you can only take palliative measures, which ultimately boil down to making people more careful.

But the only palliative measure that would make a real difference is a drastic reduction in speed. Cut down the speed limit to twelve miles an hour in all built-up areas, and you would cut out the vast majority of accidents. But this, everyone will assure you, is 'impossible'. Why is it impossible? Well, it would be unbearably irksome. It would mean that every road journey took twice or three times as long as it takes at present. Besides, you could never get people to observe such a speed limit. What driver is going to crawl along at twelve miles an hour when he knows that his engine would do fifty? It is not even easy to keep a modern car down to twelve miles an hour and remain in high gear – and so on and so forth, all adding up to the statement that slow travel is of its nature intolerable.

In other words we value speed more highly than we value human life. Then why not say so, instead of every few years having one of these hypocritical campaigns (at present it is 'Keep Death off the Roads' – a few years back it was 'Learn the Kerb Step'), in the full knowledge that while our roads remain as they are, and present speeds are kept up, the slaughter must continue?

* * *

A sidelight on bread rationing. My neighbour in Scotland this summer[200] was a crofter engaged on the enormous labour of reclaiming a farm which has been derelict for several years. He has no helper except a sister, he has only one horse, and he possesses only the most primitive machinery, which does not even include a reaper. Throughout this summer he certainly did not work less than fourteen hours a day, six days a week. When bread rationing started he put in for the extra ration, only to find that, though he could, indeed, get more bread than a sedentary worker, he was not entitled to the full agricultural labourer's ration. The reason? That within the meaning of the act he is not an agricultural labourer! Since he is 'on his own' he ranks as a farmer, and it is assumed that he eats less bread than he would do if he were working for wages for somebody else.

* * *

When I was talking to some friends the other night, a question came up which we could none of us answer and which I should like someone to elucidate for me. The question is: on what principle are jurymen chosen? The theory is, I believe, that they are chosen at random from the whole population. At any rate, that is what trial 'by your peers' ought to mean in a democracy. But I have a strong impression – and my friends thought the same – that no one strictly describable as a working-man normally finds his way on to a jury. The people summoned as jurors always seem to be small business or professional men. Is there perhaps some property qualification which is not mentioned but is merely applied? I should like to know, because if the facts are what I think they are – that is, that

200. Orwell spent summer 1946 on the island of Jura, which he had first visited in autumn 1945. He rented a farmhouse, Barnhill, in the north of the island, to which he returned in April 1947. He left Barnhill in December 1947 seriously ill with tuberculosis and spent the rest of his life in sanatoriums and hospitals.

juries are drawn from the middle class while the accused in criminal cases often belong to the working class – they deserve more publicity than I have ever seen them get.

As I Please 61

15 November 1946

As the clouds, most of them much larger and dirtier than a man's hand, come blowing up over the political horizon, there is one fact that obtrudes itself over and over again. This is that the government's troubles, present and future, arise quite largely from its failure to publicise itself properly.

People are not told with sufficient clarity what is happening, and why, and what may be expected to happen in the near future. As a result, every calamity, great or small, takes the mass of the public by surprise, and the government incurs unpopularity by doing things which any government, of whatever colour, would have to do in the same circumstances.

Take one question which has been much in the news lately but has never been properly thrashed out, the immigration of foreign labour into this country. Recently we have seen a tremendous outcry at the TUC conference against allowing Poles to work in the two places where labour is most urgently needed – in the mines and on the land.

It will not do to write this off as something 'got up' by communist sympathisers, nor on the other hand to justify it by saying that the Polish refugees are all fascists who 'strut about' wearing monocles and carrying brief-cases.

The question is, would the attitude of the British trade unions be any friendlier if it were a question, not of alleged fascists but of the admitted victims of fascism? For example, hundreds of thousands of homeless Jews are now trying desperately to get to Palestine. No doubt many of them will ultimately succeed, but others will fail. How about inviting, say, 100,000 Jewish refugees to settle in this country? Or what about the displaced persons, numbering nearly a million, who are dotted in camps all over Germany, with no future and no place to go, the United States and the British Dominions having already refused to admit them in significant numbers? Why not solve their problems by offering them British citizenship?

It is easy to imagine what the average Briton's answer would be. Even before the war, with the Nazi persecutions in full swing, there was no popular support for the idea of allowing large numbers of Jewish refugees into this country: nor was there any strong move to admit the hundreds of thousands of Spaniards who had fled from Franco to be penned up behind barbed wire in France.

For that matter, there was very little protest against the internment of the wretched German refugees in 1940. The comments I most often overheard at the time were 'What did they want to come here for?' and 'They're only after our jobs'.

The fact is that there is strong popular feeling in this country against foreign immigration. It arises from simple xenophobia, partly from fear of undercutting in wages, but above all from the out-of-date notion that Britain is overpopulated and that more population means more unemployment.

Actually, so far from having more workers than jobs, we have a serious labour shortage which will be accentuated by the continuance of conscription, and which will grow worse, not better, because of the ageing of the population.

Meanwhile our birthrate is still frighteningly low, and several hundred thousand women of marriageable age have no chance of getting husbands. But how widely are these facts known or understood?

In the end it is doubtful whether we can solve our problems without encouraging immigration from Europe. In a tentative way the government has already tried to do this, only to be met by ignorant hostility, because the public has not been told the relevant facts beforehand. So also with countless other unpopular things that will have to be done from time to time.

But the most necessary step is not to prepare public opinion for particular emergencies, but to raise the general level of political understanding: above all, to drive home the fact, which has never been properly grasped, that British prosperity depends largely on factors outside Britain.

This business of publicising and explaining itself is not easy for a Labour government, faced by a press which at bottom is mostly hostile. Nevertheless, there are other ways of communicating with the public, and Mr Attlee and his colleagues might well pay more attention to the radio, a medium which very few politicians in this country have ever taken seriously.

* * *

There is one question which at first sight looks both petty and disgusting but which I should like to see answered. It is this: in the innumerable hangings of war criminals which have taken place all over Europe during the past few years, which method has been followed – the old method of strangulation, or the modern, comparatively humane method which is supposed to break the victim's neck at one snap?

A hundred years ago or more, people were hanged by simply hauling them up and letting them kick and struggle until they died, which might take a quarter of an hour or so. Later the drop was introduced, theoretically making death instantaneous, though it does not always work very well.

In recent years, however, there seems to have been a tendency to revert to strangulation. I did not see the news film of the hanging of the German war criminals at Kharkov, but the descriptions in the British press appeared to show that the older method was used. So also with various executions in the Balkan countries.

The newspaper accounts of the Nuremberg hangings were ambiguous. There was talk of a drop, but there was also talk of the condemned men taking ten or twenty minutes to die. Perhaps, by a typically Anglo-Saxon piece of compromise, it was decided to use a drop but to make it too short to be effective.

It is not a good symptom that hanging should still be the accepted form of capital punishment in this country. Hanging is a barbarous, inefficient way of killing anybody, and at least one fact about it – quite widely known, I believe – is so obscene as to be almost unprintable.

Still, until recently we did feel rather uneasy on the subject, and we did have our hangings in private. Indeed, before the war, public execution was a thing of the past in nearly every civilised country. Now it seems to be returning, at least for political crimes, and though we ourselves have not actually reintroduced it as yet, we participate at second hand by watching the news films.

It is queer to look back and think that only a dozen years ago the abolition of the death penalty was one of those things that every enlightened person advocated as a matter of course, like divorce reform or the independence of India. Now, on the other hand, it is a mark of enlightenment not merely to approve of executions but to raise an outcry because there are not more of them.

Therefore it seems to me of some importance to know whether strangulation is now coming to be the normal practice. For if people are being taught to gloat not only over death but over a peculiarly horrible form of torture, it marks another turn on the downward spiral that we have been following ever since 1933.

* * *

Quotation wanted.

A character in one of Chekhov's stories, I forget which, remarks: 'As Shakespeare says, "Happy is he who in his youth is young."' I have never been able to find this line, nor does it sound like Shakespeare. Possibly the translator retranslated it from the Russian instead of looking up the original. Can anyone tell me where it occurs?

Riding down from Bangor

29 November 1946

The reappearance of *Helen's Babies*, in its day one of the most popular books in the world - within the British empire alone it was pirated by twenty different publishing firms, the author receiving a total profit of £40 from a sale of some hundreds of thousands or millions of copies - will ring a bell in any literate person over thirty-five.[201] Not that the present edition is an altogether satisfactory one. It is a cheap little book with rather unsuitable illustrations, various American dialect words appear to have been cut out of it, and the sequel, *Other People's Children*, which was often bound up with it in earlier editions, is missing. Still, it is pleasant to see *Helen's Babies* in print again. It had become almost a rarity in recent years, and it is one of the best of the little library of American books on which people born at about the turn of the century were brought up.

The books one reads in childhood, and perhaps most of all the bad and good bad books, create in one's mind a sort of false map of the world, a series of fabulous countries into which one can retreat at odd moments throughout the rest of life, and which in some cases can even survive a visit to the real countries which they are supposed to represent. The pampas, the Amazon, the coral islands of the Pacific, Russia, land of birch-tree and samovar, Transylvania with its boyars and vampires, the China of Guy Boothby, the Paris of du Maurier - one could continue the list for a long time. But one other imaginary country that I acquired early in life was called America. If I pause on the word 'America', and, deliberately putting aside the existing reality, call up my childhood vision of it, I see two pictures - composite pictures, of course, from which I am omitting a good deal of the detail.

One is of a boy sitting in a whitewashed stone schoolroom. He wears braces and has patches on his shirt, and if it is summer he is barefooted. In the corner of the school room there is a bucket of drinking water with a dipper. The boy lives in a farm-house, also of stone and also whitewashed, which has a mortgage on it. He aspires to be President, and is expected to keep the woodpile full. Somewhere in the background of the picture, but completely dominating it, is a huge black Bible. The other picture is of a tall, angular man, with a shapeless hat pulled down over his eyes, leaning against a wooden paling and whittling at a stick. His lower jaw moves slowly but ceaselessly. At

201. *Helen's Babies* by John Habberton (1842–1921) was first published in 1876.

very long intervals he emits some piece of wisdom such as 'A woman is the orneriest critter there is, 'ceptin' a mule', or 'When you don't know a thing to do, don't do a thing'; but more often it is a jet of tobacco juice that issues from the gap in his front teeth. Between them those two pictures summed up my earliest impression of America. And of the two, the first - which, I suppose, represented New England, the other representing the south - had the stronger hold upon me.

The books from which these pictures were derived included, of course, books which it is still possible to take seriously, such as *Tom Sawyer* and *Uncle Tom's Cabin*, but the most richly American flavour was to be found in minor works which are now almost forgotten. I wonder, for instance, if anyone still reads *Rebecca of Sunnybrook Farm*, which remained a popular favourite long enough to be filmed with Mary Pickford in the leading part. Or how about the 'Katy' books by Susan Coolidge (*What Katy Did At School*, etc), which, although girls' books and therefore 'soppy', had the fascination of foreignness? Louisa M. Alcott's *Little Women* and *Good Wives* are, I suppose, still flickeringly in print, and certainly they still have their devotees. As a child I loved both of them, though I was less pleased by the third of the trilogy, *Little Men*. That model school where the worst punishment was to have to whack the schoolmaster, on 'this hurts me more than it hurts you' principles, was rather difficult to swallow.

Helen's Babies belonged in much the same world as *Little Women*, and must have been published round about the same date. Then there were Artemus Ward, Bret Harte, and various songs, hymns and ballads, besides poems dealing with the civil war, such as 'Barbara Fritchie' ('Shoot if you must this old grey head, But spare your country's flag, - she said') and 'Little Gifford of Tennessee'. There were other books so obscure that it hardly seems worth mentioning them, and magazine stories of which I remember nothing except that the old homestead always seemed to have a mortgage on it. There was also *Beautiful Joe*, the American reply to *Black Beauty*, of which you might just possibly pick up a copy in a sixpenny box. All the books I have mentioned were written well before 1900, but something of the special American flavour lingered on into this century in, for instance, the Buster Brown coloured supplements, and even in Booth Tarkington's 'Penrod' stories, which will have been written round about 1910. Perhaps there was even a tinge of it in Ernest Thompson Seton's animal books (*Wild Animals I Have Known*, etc), which have now fallen from favour but which drew tears from the pre-1914 child as surely as *Misunderstood* had done from the children of a generation earlier.

Somewhat later my picture of nineteenth-century America was given greater precision by a song which is still fairly well known and which can be found (I think) in the *Scottish Students' Song Book*. As usual in these bookless days I cannot get hold of a copy, and I must quote fragments from memory. It begins:

Riding down from Bangor
On an Eastern train,
Bronzed with weeks of hunting
In the woods of Maine
Quite extensive whiskers,
Beard, moustache as well
Sat a student fellow,
Tall and slim and swell.

Presently an aged couple and a 'village maiden', described as 'beautiful, petite', get into the carriage. Quantities of cinders are flying about, and before long the student fellow gets one in his eye: the village maiden extracts it for him, to the scandal of the aged couple. Soon after this the train shoots into a long tunnel, 'black as Egypt's night'. When it emerges into the daylight again the maiden is covered with blushes, and the cause of her confusion is revealed when

There suddenly appeared
A tiny little ear-ring
In that horrid student's beard!

I do not know the date of the song, but the primitiveness of the train (no lights in the carriage, and a cinder in one's eye a normal accident) suggests that it belongs well back in the nineteenth century.

What connects this song with books like *Helen's Babies* is first of all a sort of sweet innocence – the climax, the thing you are supposed to be slightly shocked at, is an episode with which any modern piece of naughty-naughty would *Start* – and, secondly, a faint vulgarity of language mixed up with a certain cultural pretentiousness. *Helen's Babies* is intended as a humorous, even a farcical book, but it is haunted all the way through by words like 'tasteful' and 'ladylike', and it is funny chiefly because its tiny disasters happen against a background of conscious gentility. 'Handsome, intelligent, composed, tastefully dressed, without a suspicion of the flirt or the languid woman of fashion about her, she awakened to the utmost my every admiring sentiment' – thus is the heroine described, figuring elsewhere as 'erect, fresh, neat, composed, bright-eyed, fairfaced, smiling and observant'. One gets beautiful glimpses of a now-vanished world in such remarks as: 'I believe you arranged the floral decorations at St Zephaniah's Fair last winter, Mr Burton? 'Twas the most tasteful display of the season.' But in spite of the occasional use of ''twas' and other archaisms – 'parlour' for sitting-room, 'chamber' for bedroom, 'real' as an adverb, and so forth – the book does not 'date' very markedly, and many of its admirers imagine it to have been written round about 1900. Actually it was written in 1875, a fact which one might infer from internal evidence, since the hero, aged twenty-eight, is a veteran of the civil war.

The book is very short and the story is a simple one. A young bachelor is prevailed on by his sister to look after her house and her two sons, aged five and three, while she and her husband go on a fortnight's holiday. The children drive him almost mad by an endless succession of such acts as falling into ponds, swallowing poison, throwing keys down wells, cutting themselves with razors, and the like, but also facilitate his engagement to 'a charming girl, whom, for about a year, I had been adoring from afar'. These events take place in an outer suburb of New York, in a society which now seems astonishingly sedate, formal, domesticated and, according to current conceptions, un-American. Every action is governed by etiquette. To pass a carriage full of ladies when your hat is crooked is an ordeal; to recognise an acquaintance in church is ill-bred; to become engaged after a ten days' courtship is a severe social lapse. We are accustomed to thinking of American society as more crude, adventurous and, in a cultural sense, democratic than our own, and from writers like Mark Twain, Whitman and Bret Harte, not to mention the cowboy and Red Indian stories of the weekly papers, one draws a picture of a wild anarchic world peopled by eccentrics and desperadoes who have no traditions and no attachment to one place. That aspect of nineteenth-century America did of course exist, but in the more populous eastern states a society similar to Jane Austen's seems to have survived longer than it did in England. And it is hard not to feel that it was a better kind of society than that which arose from the sudden industrialisation of the later part of the century. The people in *Helen's Babies* or *Little Women* may be mildly ridiculous, but they are uncorrupted. They have something that is perhaps best described as integrity, or good morale, founded partly on an unthinking piety. It is a matter of course that everyone attends church on Sunday morning and says grace before meals and prayers at bedtime: to amuse the children one tells them Bible stories, and if they ask for a song it is probably 'Glory, Glory Hallelujah'. Perhaps it is also a sign of spiritual health in the light literature of this period that death is mentioned freely. 'Baby Phil', the brother of Budge and Toddie, has died shortly before *Helen's Babies* opens, and there are various tear-jerking references to his 'tiny coffin'. A modern writer attempting a story of this kind would have kept coffins out of it.

English children are still Americanised by way of the films, but it would no longer be generally claimed that American books are the best ones for children. Who, without misgivings, would bring up a child on the coloured 'comics' in which sinister professors manufacture atomic bombs in underground laboratories while Superman whizzes through the clouds, the machine-gun bullets bouncing off his chest like peas, and platinum blondes are raped, or very nearly, by steel robots and fifty-foot dinosaurs? It is a far cry from Superman to the Bible and the woodpile. The earlier children's books, or books readable by children, had not only innocence but a sort of native gaiety, a buoyant, carefree feeling, which was the product, presumably, of the unheard-of freedom and security which nineteenth-century America enjoyed. That is the connecting link between books so seemingly far apart as *Little Women* and *Life on the Mississippi*. The society described in the one is subdued, bookish and home-loving, while the other tells of a crazy world of bandits, gold mines, duels, drunkenness and gambling hells: but in both one can detect an underlying confidence in the future, a sense of freedom and opportunity.

Nineteenth-century America was a rich, empty country which lay outside the main stream of world events, and in which the twin nightmares that beset nearly every modern man, the nightmare of unemployment and the nightmare of state interference, had hardly come into being. There were social distinctions, more marked than those of today, and there was poverty (in *Little Women*, it will be remembered, the family is at one time so hard up that one of the girls sells her hair to the barber), but there was not, as there is now, an all-prevailing sense of helplessness. There was room for everybody, and if you worked hard you could be certain of a living - could even be certain of growing rich: this was generally believed, and for the greater part of the population it was even broadly true. In other words, the civilisation of nineteenth-century America was capitalist civilisation at its best. Soon after the civil war the inevitable deterioration started. But for some decades, at least, life in America was much better fun than life in Europe - there was more happening, more colour, more variety, more opportunity - and the books and songs of that period had a sort of bloom, a childlike quality. Hence, I think, the popularity of *Helen's Babies* and other 'light' literature, which made it normal for the English child of thirty or forty years ago to grow up with a theoretical knowledge of racoons, woodchucks, chipmunks, gophers, hickory trees, water-melons and other unfamiliar fragments of the American scene.

As I Please 62

22 November 1946

The query I raised two weeks ago, about the methods used in selecting jurymen, is answered authoritatively by a contributor in this week's issue.[202] It also brought in a considerable stream of letters, nearly all of them enclosing a copy of a recently issued government form which has to be filled in by anyone claiming exemption from jury service. I had received a copy of this myself through the usual channels, and had immediately flung it into the wastepaper basket, but actually it contains most of the information that I wanted. Reading it through, I note with interest the qualifications needed by 'special jurors,' whatever 'special jurors' may be. They have to be read to be believed:

> The following jurors are qualified to be special jurors: Persons legally entitled to be called an 'Esquire' and persons of higher degree; bankers and merchants; occupiers of private dwelling-houses the net annual value of which is not less than £100 in towns containing, according to the last census, 20,000 inhabitants and upwards or £50 elsewhere; occupiers of premises other than a farm the net annual value of which is not less than £100; occupiers of farms the net annual value of which is not less than £300.

Study this paragraph in detail, and you will see that it has been worded, and very carefully worded, so as to exclude everyone who does not belong socially as well as financially to the upper crust. This form is being circulated after a Labour government with a crushing majority has been in office for fifteen months.

Several of the people who wrote to me stated that, so far as their own knowledge goes, manual workers are not in practice excluded from jury service, or are not always excluded. One correspondent, chairman of a Labour Party branch, adds that the trouble is not that manual workers are actually debarred from jury service, but that they dodge it whenever they can, for financial reasons. Jurors are not paid, so that serving on a jury

202. 'A Socialist Barrister' wrote: 'The astonishing, but quite incontrovertible answer to Orwell's query is that English law expressly provides for the exclusion from the jury in criminal trials (and indeed in civil cases also) of all who do not possess a definite interest in property of a prescribed minimum amount.' The property qualification was not abolished until the 1972 Criminal Justice Act.

means losing a day or two's wages. Incidentally, the fact that they are not paid gives them a strong motive for getting the job done as hurriedly as possible, and must have been responsible for many a wrong verdict.

How easy it would be to put this right by paying every juryman a reasonable fee – £1 a day, say – to compensate him for loss of time.

I notice that among the various categories of people exempted from jury service are 'Apothecaries certificated by the Court of Examiners of the Apothecaries Company' and pharmaceutical chemists generally. There seems to be an echo from *Pickwick Papers* here. At the hearing of Mrs Bardell's breach of promise case, it will be remembered, a chemist who is being sworn in for service on the jury remarks that 'there'll be murder before this trial's over', adding after he has taken the oath: 'I've left nobody but an errand boy in my shop. He's a very nice boy, my Lord, but he is not much acquainted with drugs; and I know that the prevailing impression on his mind is, that Epsom salts means oxalic acid; and syrup of senna, laudanum. That's all, my Lord.' Could it be, I wonder, that chemists earned their exemption as a result of some imaginative official happening to read this passage?

* * *

I wonder whether the ministry concerned has ever turned its thoughts towards peat as a source of domestic fuel. At this moment my coal cellar is empty, and judging by experiences last winter it will remain empty for a long time, but I am writing this beside a peat fire which warms the room comfortably enough. In London peat is fantastically expensive, but that is merely a racket which can be practiced because the price is not controlled and because people will pay anything sooner than freeze. I imagine that the natural price of peat would be somewhat less than that of coal, weight for weight.

There are enormous quantities of peat in Scotland, and it occurs in Wales and in a few parts of England. In Scotland it is dug in a very primitive way. The people scoop it out in small blocks with a kind of spade, and lay the blocks out on the grass to dry. When they are dry on one side they are placed upright in threes, then a little later they are built up into small piles, then into larger piles, and finally are carted home about two months after they are dug. All this has to be done in the spring and early summer, because at other times of year there is either too much rain, or the grass is too long, for the peat to get dry. I believe it used to be reckoned that if a family used no other fuel, it would mean a month's work, including drying and carting, to get a year's supply.

Of course, if peat were being dug in a big way, there would be no need to use these crude methods or to depend on fine weather for drying. People who are not accustomed to peat are sometimes put against it because they do not know the right way to light it, or do not realise that it must be stored in a dry place but with a few simple instructions it should be easy to popularise it as a domestic fuel. It gives out less heat than coal, but it is cleaner and easier to handle, and, unlike wood, it is suitable for small fireplaces. A few million tons of it a year would make a lot of difference if, as seems likely, we are never going to have quite enough coal again.

* * *

In current discussions of the Royal Commission that is to inquire into the press, the talk is always of the debasing influence exerted by owners and advertisers. It is not said often enough that a nation gets the newspapers it deserves. Admittedly, this is not the whole of the truth. When the bulk of the press is owned by a handful of people, one has not much choice, and the fact that during the war the newspapers temporarily became more intelligent without losing circulation, suggests that the public taste is not quite so bad as it seems. Still, our newspapers are not all alike; some of them are more intelligent than others, and some are more popular than others. And when you study the relationship between intelligence and popularity, what do you find?

Below I list in two columns our nine leading national daily papers. In the first column these are ranged in order of intelligence, so far as I am able to judge it: in the other they are ranged in order of popularity, as measured by circulation. By intelligence I do not mean agreement with my own opinions. I mean a readiness to present news objectively, to give prominence to the things that really matter, to discuss serious questions even when they are dull, and to advocate policies which are at least coherent and intelligible. As to the circulation, I may have misplaced one or two papers, as I have no recent figures, but my list will not be far out. Here are the two lists:

INTELLIGENCE	POPULARITY
1. *Manchester Guardian*	1. *Express*
2. *The Times*	2. *Herald*
3. *News Chronicle*	3. *Mirror*
4. *Telegraph*	4. *News Chronicle*
5. *Herald*	5. *Mail*
6. *Mail*	6. *Graphic*
7. *Mirror*	7. *Telegraph*
8. *Express*	8. *The Times*
9. *Graphic*	9. *Manchester Guardian*

It will be seen that the second list is very nearly – not quite, for life is never so neat as that – the first turned upside down. And even if I have not ranged these papers in quite the right order, the general relationship holds good.[203]. The paper that has the best reputation for truthfulness, the *Manchester Guardian*, is the one that is not read even by those who admire it. People complain that it is 'so dull'. On the other hand countless people read the *Daily* —— while saying frankly that they 'don't believe a word of it'.

In these circumstances it is difficult to foresee a radical change, even if the special kind of pressure exerted by owners and advertisers is removed. What matters is that in England we do possess juridical liberty of the press, which makes it possible to utter one's true opinions fearlessly in papers of comparatively small circulation. It is vitally important to hang on to that. But no Royal Commission can make the big-circulation press much better than it is, however much it manipulates the methods of control. We shall have a serious and truthful popular press when public opinion actively demands it. Till then, if the news is not distorted by businessmen it will be distorted by bureaucrats, who are only one degree better.[204]

As I Please 63

29 November 1946

Here is an analysis of the front page of my morning newspaper, on an ordinary, uneventful day in November 1946.

The big headline goes to the UN conference, at which the USSR is putting forward demands for an inquiry into the strength of Anglo-American forces in ex-enemy or allied countries. This is obviously intended to forestall a demand for inspection of forces inside the USSR, and it is plain to see that the resulting discussion will lead to nothing except recriminations and a prestige victory for this side or that, with no advance, and no attempt at any advance, towards genuine international agreement.

---

203. In fact, Orwell had got the order wrong for circulations: as he admitted in *Tribune* on 13 December 1946, 'the order of popularity of the penny papers runs *Express*, *Mirror*, *Herald*, *Mail*, *News Chronicle*'.

204. The Labour government set up a Royal Commission on the press in response to outrage among Labour Party members and the National Union of Journalists that the press in the run-up to the 1945 general election had been overwhelmingly Conservative - even though the public was overwhelmingly Labour. The Commons motion demanding it be set up was seconded by Michael Foot just before this piece was published. It was eventually appointed in April 1947 and reported in 1949.

The fighting in Greece is growing more serious. The constitutional opposition is swinging more and more towards support of the rebels, while the government is alleging that the so-called rebels are in fact guerrillas operating from across the frontier.

There is further delay in calling the Indian Constituent Assembly (this column has a footnote: 'Blood-bath in India: Page Two'), and Mr Gandhi has starved himself into a condition which is causing anxiety.

The American coal strike is continuing, and is likely to 'have disastrous effects on world grain supplies'. Owing to other recent strikes, the United States has cancelled delivery of two million tons of steel to Britain, which will further complicate the British housing problem. There is also an unofficial 'go slow' movement on the Great Western Railway.

Another bomb has gone off in Jerusalem, with a number of casualties. There is also news of various minor unavoidable calamities, such as a plane crash, the likelihood of floods all over England, and a collision of ships in the Mersey, with the apparent loss of 100 head of cattle, which I suppose would represent one week's meat ration for about 40,000 people.

There is no definitely good news at all on the front page. There are items, such as a rise in British exports during October, which look as if they might be good, but which might turn out to be bad if one had sufficient knowledge to interpret them. There is also a short statement to the effect that the occupying powers in Germany 'may' shortly reach a better agreement. But this is hardly more than the expression of a pious wish, unsupported by evidence.

I repeat that this pageful of disasters is merely the record of an average day, when nothing much is happening: and incidentally it occurs in a newspaper which, rather than most, tries to put a good face on things.

When one considers how things have gone since 1930 or thereabouts, it is not easy to believe in the survival of civilisation. I do not argue from this that the only thing to do is to abjure practical politics, retire to some remote place and concentrate either on individual salvation or on building up self-supporting communities against the day when the atom bombs have done their work. I think one must continue the political struggle, just as a doctor must try to save the life of a patient who is probably going to die. But I do suggest that we shall get nowhere unless we start by recognising that political behaviour is largely non-rational, that the world is suffering from some kind of mental disease which must be diagnosed before it can be cured. The significant point is that nearly all the calamities that happen to us are quite unnecessary. It is commonly assumed that what human beings want is to be comfortable. Well, we now have it in our power to be comfortable, as our ancestors had not. Nature may occasionally hit back with an earthquake or a cyclone, but by and large she is beaten. And yet exactly at the moment when there is, or could be, plenty of everything for everybody, nearly our whole energies have to be taken up in trying to grab territories, markets and raw materials from one another. Exactly at the moment when wealth might be so generally diffused that no government need fear serious opposition, political liberty is declared to be impossible and half the world is ruled by secret police forces. Exactly at the moment when superstition crumbles and a rational attitude towards the universe becomes feasible, the right to think one's own thoughts is denied as never before. The fact is that human beings only started fighting one another in earnest when there was no longer anything to fight about.

It is not easy to find a direct economic explanation of the behaviour of the people who now rule the world. The desire for pure power seems to be much more dominant than the desire for wealth. This has often been pointed out, but curiously enough the desire for power seems to be taken for granted as a natural instinct, equally prevalent in all ages, like the desire for food. Actually it is no more natural, in the sense of being biologically necessary, than drunkenness or gambling. And if it has reached new levels of lunacy in our own age, as I think it has, then the question becomes: what is the special quality in modern life that makes a major human motive out of the impulse to bully others? If we could answer that question - seldom asked, never followed up - there might occasionally be a bit of good news on the front page of your morning paper.

However, it is always possible, in spite of appearances, that the age we live in is not worse than the other ages that have preceded it, nor perhaps even greatly different. At least this possibility occurs to me when I think of an Indian proverb which a friend of mine once translated:

In April was the jackal born,
In June the rain-fed rivers swelled:
'Never in all my life,' said he,
'Have I so great a flood beheld.'

* * *

I suppose the shortage of clocks and watches is nobody's fault, but is it necessary to let their prices rocket as they have done in the last year or two?

Early this year I saw ex-army watches exhibited in a showcase at a little under £4 each. A week or two later I succeeded in buying one of them for £5. Recently their price seems to have risen to £8. A year or two ago, alarm clocks, which at that time could not be bought without a permit, were on sale at 16 shillings each. This was the controlled price, and presumably it did not represent an actual loss to the manufacturer. The other day I saw precisely similar clocks at 45 shillings – a jump of 180 per cent. Is it really conceivable that the cost price has increased correspondingly?

Incidentally, for 45 shillings you can, if you are on the phone, arrange for the telephone operator to call you every morning for nearly 18 months, which is a lot longer than the life of the average alarm clock.

* * *

Under the heading, 'The Return of the Jews to Palestine', Samuel Butler records in his *Note-Books*:

> A man called on me last week and proposed gravely that I should write a book upon an idea which had occurred to a friend of his, a Jew living in New Bond Street . . . If only I would help, the return of the Jews to Palestine would be rendered certain and easy. There was no trouble about the poor Jews, he knew how he could get them back at any time; the difficulty lay with the Rothschilds, the Oppenheims and such; with my assistance, however, the thing could be done.
>
> I am afraid I was rude enough to decline to go into the scheme on the ground that I did not care twopence whether the Rothschilds and Oppenheims went back to Palestine or not. This was felt to be an obstacle; but then he began to try and make me care, whereupon, of course, I had to get rid of him.

This was written in 1883. And who would have foreseen that only about sixty years later nearly all the Jews in Europe would be trying to get back to Palestine of their own accord, while nearly everybody else would be trying to stop them?

As I Please 64

6 December 1946

With great enjoyment I have just been rereading *Trilby*, George du Maurier's justly popular novel,[205] one of the finest specimens of that 'good bad' literature which the English-speaking peoples seem to have lost the secret of producing. *Trilby* is an imitation of Thackeray, a very good imitation and immensely readable – Bernard Shaw, if I remember rightly, considered it to be better than Thackeray in many ways – but to me

205. *Trilby* by George du Maurier was published in 1894 by Osgood, McIlvaine.

the most interesting thing about it is the different impressions one derives from reading it first before and then after the career of Hitler.

The thing that now hits one in the eye in reading *Trilby* is its anti-Semitism. I suppose, although few people actually read the book now, its central story is fairly widely known, the name of Svengali having become a by-word, like that of Sherlock Holmes. A Jewish musician - not a composer, but a brilliant pianist and music-teacher - gets into his power an orphaned Irish girl, a painters' model, who has a magnificent voice but happens to be tone deaf. Having hypnotised her one day to cure an attack of neuralgia, he discovers that when she is in the hypnotic trance she can be taught to sing in tune.

Thereafter, for about two years, the pair of them travel from one European capital to another, the girl singing every night to enormous and ecstatic audiences, and never even knowing, in her waking life, that she is a singer. The end comes when Svengali dies suddenly in the middle of a concert and Trilby breaks down and is booed off the stage. That is the main story, though of course there is much else, including an unhappy love affair and three clean-living English painters who make a foil for Svengali's villainy.

There is no question that the book is anti-Semitic. Apart from the fact that Svengali's vanity, treacherousness, selfishness, personal uncleanliness and so forth are constantly connected with the fact that he is a Jew, there are the illustrations. Du Maurier, better known for his drawings in Punch than for his writings, illustrated his own book, and he made Svengali into a sinister caricature of the traditional type. But what is most interesting is the divergence of the anti-Semitism of that date - 1895, the period of the Dreyfus case - and that of today.

To begin with, du Maurier evidently holds that there are two kinds of Jew, good ones and bad ones, and that there is a racial difference between them. There enters briefly into the story another Jew, Glorioli, who possesses all the virtues and qualities that Svengali lacks. Glorioli is 'one of the Sephardim' - of Spanish extraction, that is - whereas Svengali, who comes from German Poland, is 'an oriental Israelite Hebrew Jew'. Secondly du Maurier considers that to have a dash of Jewish blood is an advantage. We are told that the hero, Little Billee, may have had some Jewish blood, of which there was a suggestion in his features, and 'fortunately for the world, and especially for ourselves, most of us have in our veins at least a minimum of this precious fluid'. Clearly, this is not the Nazi form of anti-Semitism.

And yet the tone of all the references to Svengali is almost unconsciously contemptuous, and the fact that du Maurier chose a Jew to play such a part is significant. Svengali, who cannot sing himself and has to sing, as it were, through Trilby's lungs, represents that well-known type, the clever underling who acts as the brains of some more impressive person.

It is queer how freely du Maurier admits that Svengali is more gifted than the three

Englishmen, even than Little Billee, who is represented, unconvincingly, as a brilliant painter. Svengali has 'genius', but the others have 'character', and 'character' is what matters. It is the attitude of the rugger-playing prefect towards the spectacled 'swot', and it was probably the normal attitude towards Jews at that time. They were natural inferiors, but of course they were cleverer, more sensitive and more artistic than ourselves, because such qualities are of secondary importance. Nowadays the English are less sure of themselves, less confident that stupidity always wins in the end, and the prevailing form of anti-Semitism has changed, not altogether for the better.

* * *

In last week's *Tribune* Mr Julian Symons[206] remarked – rightly, I think – that Aldous Huxley's later novels are much inferior to his earlier ones. But he might have added that this kind of falling-off is usual in imaginative writers, and that it only goes unnoticed when a writer is, so to speak, carried forward by the momentum of his earlier books. We value H. G. Wells, for example, for *Tono-Bungay*, *Mr Polly*, *The Time Machine*, etc. If he had stopped writing in 1920 his reputation would stand quite as high as it does: if we knew him only by the books he wrote after that date, we should have rather a low opinion of him. A novelist does not, any more than a boxer or a ballet dancer, last for ever. He has an initial impulse which is good for three or four books, perhaps even for a dozen, but which must exhaust itself sooner or later. Obviously one cannot lay down any rigid rule, but in many cases the creative impulse seems to last for about fifteen years: in a prose writer these fifteen years would probably be between the ages of thirty and forty-five, or thereabouts. A few writers, it is true, have a much longer lease of life, and can go on developing when they are middle-aged or even old. But these are usually writers (examples: Yeats, Eliot, Hardy, Tolstoy) who make a sudden, almost violent change in their style, or their subject-matter, or both, and who may even tend to repudiate their earlier work.

Many writers, perhaps most, ought simply to stop writing when they reach middle age. Unfortunately our society will not let them stop. Most of them know no other way of earning a living, and writing, with all that goes with it – quarrels, rivalries, flattery, the sense of being a semi-public figure – is habit-forming. In a reasonable world a writer who had said his say would simply take up some other profession. In a competitive society he feels, just as a politician does, that retirement is death. So he continues long after his impulse is spent, and, as a rule, the less conscious he is of imitating himself, the more grossly he does it.

* * *

206 For Julian Symons see Introduction, note 4.

Early this year I met an American publisher who told me that his firm had just had a nine-months lawsuit from which it had emerged partially victorious, though out of pocket. It concerned the printing of a four-letter word which most of us use every day, generally in the present participle.

The United States is usually a few years ahead of Britain in these matters. You could print 'b——' in full in American books at a time when it had to appear in English ones as B dash. Recently it has become possible in England to print the word in full in a book, but in periodicals it still has to be B dash. Only five or six years ago it was printed in a well-known monthly magazine, but the last-minute panic was so great that a weary staff had to black the word out by hand.

As to the other word, the four-letter one, it is still unprintable in periodicals in this country, but in books it can be represented by its first letter and a dash. In the United States this point was reached at least a dozen years ago. Last year the publishing firm in question tried the experiment of printing the word in full. The book was suppressed, and after nine months of litigation the suppression was upheld. But in the process an important step forward was made. It was ruled that you may now print the first and last letters of the word with two asterisks in between, clearly indicating that it had four letters. This makes it reasonably sure that within a few years the word will be printable in full.

So does progress continue - and it is genuine progress, in my opinion, for if only our half-dozen 'bad' words could be got off the lavatory wall and on the printed page, they would soon lose their magical quality, and the habit of swearing, degrading to our thoughts and weakening to our language, might become less common.

As I Please 65

13 December 1946

A correspondent writes:

> I would be so pleased if you could draw attention to the problem which seems to be in danger of becoming completely neglected. Do MPs, or any other people in authority, realise the immense amount of time, energy and nervous force that many citizens have to lose through the appalling insufficiency of laundries?

I do not know whether MPs, as such, are aware of the present state of our laundry service, but anyone who has to fetch his washing for himself, at any rate in my district of London, will agree with every word that my correspondent says. Merely to get yourself 'taken on' by a laundry is a difficult feat, not to be achieved until you have lived several months in the district and practised a good deal of intrigue and flattery into the bargain. Then there are the slowness and irregularity of deliveries, the dreary waiting in queues on rainy winter mornings, the lost articles, the inefficient checking system, the smashed buttons, the handkerchiefs which come back hardly whiter than they went. And worst of all, perhaps, the difficulty of getting your own washing back when you are sent somebody else's by mistake, because it is always due to some shortcoming 'down at the works,' and the bored young woman behind the counter knows nothing about it.

All this is only too true. But my correspondent goes on:

> If MPs considered the people, would not one of their first tasks be to nationalise the laundries? The laundry should be as smooth-running as the postal service. Is it fantastic to suggest that everything which makes for the easier running of the home should be a prime concern of a people's government?

Unfortunately, nationalisation would not of itself make the laundries more efficient, any more than nationalising my typewriter would make it easier to write this article. Nationalisation is a long-term measure which in most cases does not affect an improvement but merely prepares the way for an improvement. Nationalising the coal mines, for instance, makes possible the heavy expenditure and the centralised control which are necessary before the mines can be brought up to date. But it will not for several years produce any more coal or make the lot of the miner any more bearable.

If the laundries were nationalised tomorrow they would have to carry straight on with the same personnel and equipment, and their efficiency would not greatly increase while the present shortages continue. The laundries are in a bad way because they lack soap, fuel, machinery, transport and, above all, labour. If they were given priority in any of these things, some other public utility would have to suffer. Everything leads back to the shortage of labour, which is made worse, in our present exhausted state, by the absence of any incentive to work long hours. We have entered on an uncomfortable reconstruction period which may last for years, and I wish the spokesmen of the government would say so more boldly. Otherwise great numbers of people may lose all enthusiasm for nationalisation, having looked forward to it as a sort of panacea, and then found that it makes no immediate difference.

But I do agree that when life becomes livable again, the laundry system needs thorough reorganisation. It is a disgrace, for instance, that there has never really been a way of getting babies' clothes washed outside the house. Before the war there existed – it may recently have started up again – a diaper service which delivered twelve clean 'nappies' daily. Only a few people could afford this luxury, and babies' clothes other than 'nappies' always had to be washed at home, because no laundry was cheap or rapid enough to deal with the vast quantity of pants, cot sheets and so forth that the average baby works its way through. What must have been the effect on our birthrate of that endless struggle with piles of dirty baby-linen in draughty stone-floored sculleries or in the tiny bathrooms of flats?

* * *

Recently I received a copy of Sir Stanley Unwin's interesting and useful book, *The Truth about Publishing*, which has appeared in a number of editions from 1926 onwards, and has recently been expanded and brought up to date. I particularly value it because it assembles certain figures which one might have difficulty in finding elsewhere. A year or so ago, writing in *Tribune* on the cost of reading matter, I made a guess at the average yearly expenditure on books in this country, and put it at £1 a head. It seems that I was pitching it too high. Here are some figures of national expenditure in 1945:

Alcoholic beverages	£685 millions
Tobacco	£548 millions
Books	£23 millions

In other words the average British citizen spends about 2d a week on books, whereas he spends nearly 10 shillings on drink and tobacco. I suppose this noble figure of 2d would include the amount spent on school textbooks and other books which are bought, so to speak, involuntarily. Is it any wonder that when recently a questionnaire was sent out by *Horizon*,[207] asking twenty-one poets and novelists how they thought a writer could best earn his living, not one of them said plainly that he might earn it by writing books?

* * *

When one reads the reports of UNO conferences, or international negotiations of any kind, it is difficult not to be reminded of L'Attaque and similar war games that children used to play, with cardboard pieces representing battleships, aeroplanes and so forth, each of which had a fixed value and could be countered in some recognised way. In fact, one might almost invent a new game called Uno, to be played in enlightened homes where the parents do not want their children to grow up with a militaristic outlook.

---

207. For *Horizon*, see note 39.

The pieces in this game are called the proposal, the *démarche*, the formula, the stumbling-block, the stalemate, the deadlock, the bottleneck and the vicious circle. The object of the game is to arrive at a formula, and though details vary, the general outline of play is always much the same. First the players assemble, and somebody leads off with the proposal. This is countered by the stumbling-block, without which the game could not develop. The stumbling-block then changes into a bottleneck, or more often into a deadlock or a vicious circle. A deadlock and a vicious circle occurring simultaneously produce a stalemate, which may last for weeks. Then suddenly someone plays the *démarche*. The *démarche* makes it possible to produce a formula, and once the formula has been found the players can go home, leaving everything as it was at the beginning.

At the moment of writing, the front page of my morning paper has broken out into a pink rash of optimism. It seems that everything is going to be all right after all. The Russians will agree to inspection of armaments, and the Americans will internationalise the atomic bomb. On another page of the same paper are reports of events in Greece which amount to a state of war between the two groups of powers who are being so chummy in New York.

But while the game of deadlocks and bottlenecks goes on, another more serious game is also being played. It is governed by two axioms. One is that there can be no peace without a general surrender of sovereignty: the other is that no country capable of defending its sovereignty ever surrenders it. If one keeps these axioms in mind one can generally see the relevant facts in international affairs through the smoke-screen with which the newspapers surround them. At the moment the main facts are:

(i) The Russians, whatever they may say, will not agree to genuine inspection of their territories by foreign observers.
(ii) The Americans, whatever they may say, will not let slip the technological lead in armaments.
(iii) No country is now in a condition to fight an all-out major war.

These, although they may be superseded later, are at present the real counters in the real game, and one gets nearer the truth by constantly remembering them than alternately rejoicing and despairing over the day-to-day humbug of conferences.

As I Please 66

20 December 1946

An advertisement in my Sunday paper sets forth in the form of a picture the four things that are needed for a successful Christmas. At the top of the picture is a roast turkey; below that, a Christmas pudding; below that, a dish of mince pies; and below that, a tin of ——'s Liver Salt.

It is a simple recipe for happiness. First the meal, then the antidote, then another meal. The ancient Romans were the great masters of this technique. However, having just looked up the word *vomitorium* in the Latin dictionary, I find that after all it does not mean a place where you went to be sick after dinner. So perhaps this was not a normal feature of every Roman home, as is commonly believed.

Implied in the above-mentioned advertisement is the notion that a good meal means a meal at which you overeat yourself. In principle I agree. I only add in passing that when we gorge ourselves this Christmas, if we do get the chance to gorge ourselves, it is worth giving a thought to the thousand million human beings, or thereabouts, who will be doing no such thing. For in the long run our Christmas dinners would be safer if we could make sure that everyone else had a Christmas dinner as well. But I will come back to that presently.

The only reasonable motive for not overeating at Christmas would be that somebody else needs the food more than you do. A deliberately austere Christmas would be an absurdity. The whole point of Christmas is that it is a debauch – as it was probably long before the birth of Christ was arbitrarily fixed at that date. Children know this very well. From their point of view Christmas is not a day of temperate enjoyment, but of fierce pleasures which they are quite willing to pay for with a certain amount of pain. The awakening at about 4 am to inspect your stockings; the quarrels over toys all through the morning, and the exciting whiffs of mincemeat and sage-and-onions escaping from the kitchen door; the battle with enormous platefuls of turkey, and the pulling of the wishbone; the darkening of the windows and the entry of the flaming plum pudding; the hurry to make sure that everyone has a piece on his plate while the brandy is still alight; the momentary panic when it is rumoured that Baby has swallowed the threepenny bit; the stupor all through the afternoon; the Christmas cake with almond icing an inch thick; the peevishness next morning and the castor oil on December 27th – it is an up-and-down business, by no means all pleasant, but well worth while for the sake of its more dramatic moments.

Teetotallers and vegetarians are always scandalised by this attitude. As they see it, the only rational objective is to avoid pain and to stay alive as long as possible. If you refrain from drinking alcohol, or eating meat, or whatever it is, you may expect to live an extra five years, while if you overeat or overdrink you will pay for it in acute physical pain on the following day. Surely it follows that all excesses, even a one-a-year outbreak such as Christmas, should be avoided as a matter of course?

Actually it doesn't follow at all. One may decide, with full knowledge of what one is doing, that an occasional good time is worth the damage it inflicts on one's liver. For health is not the only thing that matters: friendship, hospitality, and the heightened spirits and change of outlook that one gets by eating and drinking in good company are also valuable. I doubt whether, on balance, even outright drunkenness does harm, provided it is infrequent – twice a year, say. The whole experience, including the repentance afterwards, makes a sort of break in one's mental routine, comparable to a weekend in a foreign country, which is probably beneficial.

In all ages men have realised this. There is a wide consensus of opinion, stretching back to the days before the alphabet, that whereas habitual soaking is bad, conviviality is good, even if one does sometimes feel sorry for it next morning. How enormous is the literature of eating and drinking, especially drinking, and how little that is worth while has been said on the other side! Offhand I can't remember a single poem in praise of water, i.e. water regarded as a drink. It is hard to imagine what one could say about it. It quenches thirst: that is the end of the story. As for poems in praise of wine, on the other hand, even the surviving ones would fill a shelf of books. The poets started turning them out on the very day when the fermentation of the grape was first discovered. Whisky, brandy and other distilled liquors have been less eloquently praised, partly because they came later in time. But beer has had quite a good press, starting well back in the Middle Ages, long before anyone had learned to put hops in it. Curiously enough, I can't remember a poem in praise of stout, not even draught stout, which is better than the bottled variety, in my opinion. There is an extremely disgusting description in Ulysses of the stout-vats in Dublin. But there is a sort of back-handed tribute to stout in the fact that this description, though widely known, has not done much towards putting the Irish off their favourite drink.

The literature of eating is also large, though mostly in prose. But in all the writers who have enjoyed describing food, from Rabelais to Dickens and from Petronius to Mrs Beeton, I cannot remember a single passage which puts dietetic considerations first. Always food is felt to be an end in itself. No one has written memorable prose about vitamins, or the dangers of excess of proteins, or the importance of masticating everything thirty-two times. All in all, there seems to be a heavy weight of testimony on the side of overeating and overdrinking, provided always that they take place on recognised occasions and not too frequently.

But ought we to overeat and overdrink this Christmas? We ought not to, nor will most of us get the opportunity. I am writing in praise of Christmas, but in praise of Christmas 1947, or perhaps 1948. The world as a whole is not exactly in a condition for festivities this year. Between the Rhine and the Pacific there cannot be very many people who are in need of ——'s Liver Salt. In India there are, and always have been, about 10 million people who only get one square meal a day. In China, conditions are no doubt much the same. In Germany, Austria, Greece and elsewhere, scores of millions of people are existing on a diet which keeps breath in the body but leaves no strength for work. All over the war-wrecked areas from Brussels to Stalingrad, other uncounted millions are living in the cellars of bombed houses, in hide-outs in the forests, or in squalid huts behind barbed wire. It is not so pleasant to read almost simultaneously that a large proportion of our Christmas turkeys will come from Hungary, and that the Hungarian writers and journalists - presumably not the worst-paid section of the community - are in such desperate straits that they would be glad to receive presents of saccharine and cast-off clothing from English sympathisers. In such circumstances we could hardly have a 'proper' Christmas, even if the materials for it existed.

But we will have one sooner or later, in 1947, or 1948, or maybe even in 1949. And when we do, may there be no gloomy voices of vegetarians or teetotallers to lecture us about the things that we are doing to the linings of our stomachs. One celebrates a feast for its own sake, and not for any supposed benefit to the lining of one's stomach. Meanwhile Christmas is here, or nearly. Santa Claus is rounding up his reindeer, the postman staggers from door to door beneath his bulging sack of Christmas cards, the black markets are humming, and Britain has imported over 7,000 crates of mistletoe from France. So I wish everyone an old-fashioned Christmas in 1947, and meanwhile, half a turkey, three tangerines, and a bottle of whisky at not more than double the legal price.

As I Please 67

27 December 1946

Somewhere or other - I think it is in the preface to *Saint Joan* - Bernard Shaw remarks that we are more gullible and superstitious today than we were in the Middle Ages, and as an example of modern credulity he cites the widespread belief that the earth is round.

The average man, says Shaw, can advance not a single reason for thinking that the earth is round. He merely swallows this theory because there is something about it that appeals to the twentieth-century mentality.

Now, Shaw is exaggerating, but there is something in what he says, and the question is worth following up, for the sake of the light it throws on modern knowledge. Just why do we believe that the earth is round? I am not speaking of the few thousand astronomers, geographers and so forth who could give ocular proof, or have a theoretical knowledge of the proof, but of the ordinary newspaper-reading citizen, such as you or me.

As for the Flat Earth theory, I believe I could refute it. If you stand by the seashore on a clear day, you can see the masts and funnels of invisible ships passing along the horizons. This phenomenon can only be explained by assuming that the earth's surface is curved. But it does not follow that the earth is spherical. Imagine another theory called the Oval Earth theory, which claims that the earth is shaped like an egg. What can I say against it?

Against the Oval Earth man, the first card I can play is the analogy of the sun and moon. The Oval Earth man promptly answers that I don't know, by my own observation, that those bodies are spherical. I only know that they are round, and they may perfectly well be flat discs. I have no answer to that one. Besides, he goes on, what reason have I for thinking that the earth must be the same shape as the sun and moon?

I can't answer that one either. My second card is the earth's shadow: when cast on the moon during eclipses, it appears to be the shadow of a round object. But how do I know, demands the Oval Earth man, that eclipses of the moon are caused by the shadow of the earth? The answer is that I don't know, but have taken this piece of information blindly from newspaper articles and science booklets.

Defeated in the minor exchanges, I now play my queen of trumps: the opinion of the experts. The Astronomer Royal, who ought to know, tells me that the earth is round. The Oval Earth man covers the queen with his king. Have I tested the Astronomer Royal's statement, and would I even know a way of testing it? Here I bring out my ace. Yes, I do know one test. The astronomers can foretell eclipses, and this suggests that their opinions about the solar system are pretty sound. I am therefore justified in accepting their say-so about the shape of the earth.

If the Oval Earth man answers - what I believe is true - that the ancient Egyptians, who thought the sun goes round the earth, could also predict eclipses, then bang goes my ace. I have only one card left: navigation. People can sail ships round the world, and reach the places they aim at, by calculations which assume that the earth is spherical. I believe that finishes the Oval Earth man, though even then he may possibly have some kind of counter.

It will be seen that my reasons for thinking that the earth is round are rather precarious ones. Yet this is an exceptionally elementary piece of information. On most other questions I should have to fall back on the expert much earlier, and would be less able to test his pronouncements. And much the greater part of our knowledge is at this level. It does not rest on reasoning or on experiment, but on authority. And how can it be otherwise, when the range of knowledge is so vast that the expert himself is an ignoramus as soon as he strays away from his own speciality? Most people, if asked to prove that the earth is round, would not even bother to produce the rather weak arguments I have outlined above. They would start off by saying that 'everyone knows' the earth to be round, and if pressed further, would become angry. In a way Shaw is right. This is a credulous age, and the burden of knowledge which we now have to carry is partly responsible.

* * *

Opinions may differ about the verdict in Professor Laski's libel case.[208] But even if one feels that the verdict was technically justified, I think it should be remembered that Professor Laski took this action - in effect - on behalf of the Labour Party. It was an incident in the general election - a reply, felt at the time to be necessary, to the anti-Red propaganda of part of the Conservative press. It will therefore be extremely unfair if he is left to pay the very heavy costs unaided. May I remind everyone again that contributions should be sent to Morgan Phillips, Secretary, Labour Party, Transport House.

The Laski case will presumably lead to further discussions about the composition of juries, particularly special juries, but I wish it would have the incidental effect of drawing people's attention once again to the present state of the law of libel.

I believe the libel trade, like some other trades, went through a slack period during the war, but a few years before that the bringing of frivolous libel actions was a major racket and a nightmare to editors, publishers, authors and journalists alike. Some people used to declare that it would be better if the libel laws were abolished altogether, or at any rate greatly relaxed, so that newspapers had as much latitude as they used to have, for instance, in pre-war France. I cannot agree with this. Innocent people have a right to protection against slander. The racket arose not so much because the law is unduly strict as because it is possible to obtain damages for a libel from which one has not suffered any pecuniary loss.

208. For Harold Laski, see Introduction, note 30. Laski had sued the *Newark Advertiser* for reporting a speech he had made during the 1945 general election campaign in such a way that he appeared to have been advocating violent revolution. Laski lost. Orwell's use of his column to appeal for funds is generous, particularly as he considered Laski a Soviet fellow-traveller.

The sufferers are not so much the big newspapers, which have fleets of retained lawyers and can afford to pay damages, as publishers and small periodicals. I do not know the exact provisions of the law, but from interviews with terrified solicitors which I have sometimes had before a book went to press, I gather that it is almost impossible to invent a fictitious character which might not be held to be a portrait of a real person. As a result, a blackmailing libel action is an easy way of picking up money. Publishing houses and periodicals are often insured against libel up to a certain sum, which means that they will pay a smallish claim sooner than fight an action. In one case I have even heard of collusion being practised. A arranged to libel B, B threatened an action, and the pair of them split the proceeds.

It seems to me that the way to put this right is to make sure that a libel action cannot be profitable. Except where it can be shown that actual loss has been suffered, let no damages be paid. On the other hand, where a libel is proved, the guilty party should make a retractation in print, which at present does not usually happen. Big newspapers would be much more frightened of that than of paying out £100,000 damages, while, if no money payments were made, the motive for blackmailing actions would have disappeared.

* * *

A correspondent has sent me a copy of one of the disgusting American 'comics' which I referred to a few weeks ago.[209] The two main stories in it are about a beautiful creature called the Hangman, who has a green face, and, like so many characters in American strips, can fly. On the front page there is a picture of what is either an ape-like lunatic, or an actual ape dressed up as a man, strangling a woman so realistically that her tongue is sticking four inches out of her mouth. Another item is a python looping itself round a man's neck and then hanging him by suspending itself over a balustrade. Another is a man jumping out of a skyscraper window and hitting the pavement with a splash. There is much else of the same kind.

My correspondent asks me whether I think this is the kind of thing that should be put into the hands of children, and also whether we could not find something better on which to spend our dwindling dollars.

Certainly I would keep these out of children's hands if possible. But I would not be in favour of actually prohibiting their sale. The precedent is too dangerous. But meanwhile, are we actually using dollars to pay for this pernicious rubbish? The point is not completely unimportant, and I should like to see it cleared up.

---

209. See 'Riding down from Bangor' above, p. 323.

As I Please 68

3 January 1947

Nearly a quarter of a century ago I was travelling on a liner to Burma. Though not a big ship, it was a comfortable and even a luxurious one, and when one was not asleep or playing deck games one usually seemed to be eating. The meals were of that stupendous kind that steamship companies used to vie with one another in producing, and in between times there were snacks such as apples, ices, biscuits and cups of soup, lest anyone should find himself fainting from hunger. Moreover, the bars opened at ten in the morning, and, since we were at sea, alcohol was relatively cheap.

The ships of this line were mostly manned by Indians, but apart from the officers and the stewards they carried four European quartermasters whose job was to take the wheel. One of these quartermasters, though I suppose he was only aged forty or so, was one of those old sailors on whose back you almost expect to see barnacles growing. He was a short, powerful, rather ape-like man, with enormous forearms covered by a mat of golden hair. A blond moustache which might have belonged to Charlemagne completely hid his mouth. I was only twenty years old and very conscious of my parasitic status as a mere passenger, and I looked up to the quartermasters, especially the fair-haired one, as godlike beings on a par with the officers. It would not have occurred to me to speak to one of them without being spoken to first.

One day, for some reason, I came up from lunch early. The deck was empty except for the fair-haired quartermaster, who was scurrying like a rat along the side of the deck-houses, with something partially concealed between his monstrous hands. I had just time to see what it was before he shot past me and vanished into a doorway. It was a pie dish containing a half-eaten baked custard pudding.

At once glance I took in the situation – indeed, the man's air of guilt made it unmistakable. The pudding was a left-over from one of the passengers' tables. It had been illicitly given to him by a steward, and he was carrying it off to the seamen's quarters to devour it at leisure. Across more than twenty years I can still faintly feel the shock of astonishment that I felt at that moment. It took me some time to see the incident in all its bearings: but do I seem to exaggerate when I say that this sudden revelation of the gap between function and reward – the revelation that a highly-skilled craftsman, who might literally hold all our lives in his hands, was glad to steal scraps of food from our table – taught me more than I could have learned from half a dozen socialist pamphlets?

* * *

A news item to the effect that Yugoslavia is now engaged on a purge of writers and artists led me to look once again at the reports of the recent literary purge in the USSR, when Zoshchenko, Akhmatova and others were expelled from the Writers' Union.[210]

In England this kind of thing is not happening to us as yet, so that we can view it with a certain detachment, and, curiously enough, as I look again at the accounts of what happened, I feel somewhat more sorry for the persecutors than for their victims. Chief among the persecutors is Andrei Zhdanov,[211] considered by some to be Stalin's probable successor. Zhdanov, though he has conducted literary purges before, is a full-time politician with – to judge from his speeches – about as much knowledge of literature as I have of aerodynamics. He does not give the impression of being, according to his own lights, a wicked or dishonest man. He is truly shocked by the defection of certain Soviet writers, which appears to him as an incomprehensible piece of treachery, like a military mutiny in the middle of a battle. The purpose of literature is to glorify the Soviet Union; surely that must be obvious to everyone? But instead of carrying out their plain duty, these misguided writers keep straying away from the paths of propaganda, producing non-political works, and even in the case of Zoshchenko, allowing a satirical note to creep into their writings. It is all very painful and bewildering. It is as though you set a man to work in an excellent, up-to-date, air-conditioned factory, gave him high wages, short hours, good canteens and playing-grounds, a comfortable flat, a nursery-school for his children, all-round social insurance and music while you work – only to find the ungrateful fellow throwing spanners into the machinery on his very first day.

What makes the whole thing somewhat pathetic is the general admission – an honest admission, seeing that Soviet publicists are not in the habit of decrying their own country – that Russian literature as a whole is not what it ought to be. Since the USSR represents the highest existing form of civilisation, it is obvious that it ought to lead the

---

210. Mikhail Zoshchenko (1895–1958) was a Russian satirist. Anna Akhmatova (1889–1966) was a Russian poet. Her work was denounced as bourgeois by the communists in the early 1920s and she was not published again until 1940. She was again denounced in 1946 but was rehabilitated after Stalin's death.

211. Andrei Zhdanov (1896–1948), the political boss of Leningrad during the siege of 1941–4, was made responsible for cultural policy in the Soviet Union in the immediate post-war years and initiated a hardline clampdown on deviance from the Communist Party line in every area of intellectual activity, starting off with literature and then moving into philosophy and the natural sciences. Even to acknowledge western and Jewish influences on Russian culture was to invite denunciation and imprisonment for 'cosmopolitanism'. Zhdanov died in mysterious circumstances in 1948, but his cultural policy remained in place until the death of Stalin in 1953 (and was later revived).

world in literature as in everything else. 'Surely,' says Zhdanov, 'our new socialist system, embodying all that is best in the history of human civilisation and culture, is capable of creating the most advanced literature, which will leave far behind the best creations of olden times.' *Izvestia* (as quoted by the New York paper, *Politics*) goes further: 'Our culture stands on an immeasurably higher level than bourgeois culture . . . Is it not clear that our culture has the right not to act as pupil and imitator but, on the contrary, to teach others the general human morals?' And yet somehow the expected thing never happens. Directives are issued, resolutions are passed unanimously, recalcitrant writers are silenced: and yet for some reason a vigorous and original literature, unmistakably superior to that of capitalist countries, fails to emerge.

All this has happened before, and more than once. Freedom of expression has had its ups and downs in the USSR, but the general tendency has been towards tighter censorship. The thing that politicians are seemingly unable to understand is that you cannot produce a vigorous literature by terrorising everyone into conformity. A writer's inventive faculties will not work unless he is allowed to say approximately what he feels. You can destroy spontaneity and produce a literature which is orthodox but feeble, or you can let people say what they choose and take the risk that some of them will utter heresies. There is no way out of that dilemma so long as books have to be written by individuals.

That is why, in a way, I feel sorrier for the persecutors than for the victims. It is probably that Zoshchenko and the others at least have the satisfaction of understanding what is happening to them: the politicians who harry them are merely attempting the impossible. For Zhdanov and his kind to say, 'The Soviet Union can exist without literature' would be reasonable. But that is just what they can't say. They don't know what literature is, but they know that it is important, that it has prestige value, and that it is necessary for propaganda purposes, and they would like to encourage it, if only they knew how. So they continue with their purges and directives, like a fish bashing its nose against the wall of an aquarium again and again, too dim-witted to realise that glass and water are not the same thing.

* * *

From *The Thoughts of the Emperor Marcus Aurelius*:

> In the morning when thou risest unwillingly, let this thought be present – I am rising to the work of a human being. Why then am I dissatisfied if I am going to do the things for which I exist and for which I was brought into the world? Or have I been made for this, to lie in the bed-clothes and keep myself warm? – But this is more pleasant – Dost thou exist then to take thy pleasure, and not at all for action or exertion? Dost thou not see the little plants, the little birds, the ants, the spiders, the

> bees working together to put in order their several parts of the universe? And art thou unwilling to do the work of a human being, and dost thou not make haste to do that which is according to thy nature?

It is a good plan to print this well-known exhortation in large letters and hang it on the wall opposite your bed. And if that fails, as I am told it sometimes does, another good plan is to buy the loudest alarm clock you can get and place it in such a position that you have to get out of bed and go round several pieces of furniture in order to silence it.

As I Please 69

17 January 1947

The *Daily Herald* for 1 January 1947 has a headline MEN WHO SPOKE FOR HITLER HERE, and underneath this a photograph of two Indians who are declared to be Brijlal Mukerjee and Anjit Singh, and are described as having come 'from Berlin'. The news column below the photograph goes on to say that 'four Indians who might have been shot as traitors' are staying at a London hotel, and further describes the group of Indians who broadcast over the German radio during the war as 'collaborators'. It is worth looking a bit more closely at these various statements.

To begin with, there are at least two errors of fact, one of them a very serious one. Anjit Singh did not broadcast on the Nazi radio, but only from Italian stations, while the man described as 'Brijlal Mukerjee' is an Indian who has been in England throughout the war and is well-known to myself and many other people in London. But these inaccuracies are really the symptom of an attitude of mind which comes out more clearly in the phraseology of the report.

What right have we to describe the Indians who broadcast on the German radio as 'collaborators'? They were citizens of an occupied country, hitting back at the occupying power in the way that seemed to them best. I am not suggesting that the way they chose was the right one. Even from the narrow point of view which would assume that Indian independence is the only cause that matters, I think they were gravely wrong, because if the Axis had won the war – and their efforts must have aided the Axis to some extent – India would merely have had a new and worse master. But the line they took was one that could perfectly well be taken in good faith and cannot with fairness or even with accuracy be termed 'collaboration'. The word 'collaboration' is associated with people like

Quisling and Laval. It implies, first of all, treachery to one's own country, secondly, full co-operation with the conqueror, and thirdly, ideological agreement, or at least partial agreement. But how does this apply to the Indians who sided with the Axis? They were not being traitors to their own country - on the contrary, they were working for its independence, as they believed - and they recognised no obligation to Britain. Nor did they co-operate in the same manner as Quisling, etc. The Germans allowed them a separate broadcasting unit on which they said what they liked and followed, in many cases, a political line quite different from the Axis one. In my opinion they were mistaken and mischievous, but in moral attitude, and probably in the effects of what they did, they were quite different from ordinary renegades.

Meanwhile one has to consider the effect of this kind of thing in India. Rightly or wrongly, these men will be welcomed as heroes when they get home, and the fact that British newspapers insult them will not go unnoticed. Nor will the slovenly handling of the photographs. The caption 'Brijlal Mukerjee' appears under the face of a totally different person. No doubt the photograph was taken at the reception which the repatriated Indians were given by their fellow countrymen in London, and the photographer snapped the wrong man by mistake. But suppose the person in question had been William Joyce. In that case, don't you think the *Daily Herald* would have taken good care that it was photographing William Joyce and not somebody else? But since it's only an Indian, a mistake of this kind doesn't matter - so runs the unspoken thought. And this happens not in the *Daily Graphic*, but in Britain's sole Labour newspaper.

* * *

I hope everyone who can get access to a copy will take at least a glance at Victor Gollancz's recently published book, *In Darkest Germany* (Gollancz, 8/6). It is not a literary book, but a piece of brilliant journalism intended to shock the public of this country into some kind of consciousness of the hunger, disease, chaos and lunatic mismanagement prevailing in the British Zone. This business of making people conscious of what is happening outside their own small circle is one of the major problems of our time, and a new literary technique will have to be evolved to meet it. Considering that the people of this country are not having a very comfortable time, you can't, perhaps, blame them for being somewhat callous about suffering elsewhere, but the remarkable thing is the extent to which they manage to remain unaware of it. Tales of starvation, ruined cities, concentration camps, mass deportations, homeless refugees, persecuted Jews - all this is received with a sort of incurious surprise, as though such things had never been heard of before but at the same time were not particularly interesting. The now-familiar photographs of skeleton-like children make very little impression. As time goes on and the horrors pile up, the mind seems to secrete a sort of self-protecting ignorance which needs a harder and harder shock to pierce it, just as the body will become immunised to a drug and require bigger and bigger doses.

Half of Victor Gollancz's book consists of photographs, and he has taken the wise precaution of including himself in a good many of them. This at least proves that the photographs are genuine and cuts out the routine charge that they have been obtained from an agency and are 'all propaganda'. But I think the best device in the book, after innumerable descriptions of people living on 'biscuit soup', potatoes and cabbage, skim milk and ersatz coffee, was to include some menus of dinners in the messes provided for the Control Commission. Mr Gollancz says that he slipped a menu card into his pocket whenever he could do so unobserved, and he prints half a dozen of them. Here is the first on the list:

Consommé in cups

Fried Soles in Butter
Fresh Potatoes

Dutch Steak
Mashed Potatoes
Cauliflower

Raspberry Cream

Cheese

Coffee

* * *

These accounts of starvation in Europe seem to link up with a paragraph, headed 'This Week's Hint for Dog-Lovers', which I cut out of the *Evening Standard* just before Christmas:

> Your dog may also have that 'after Christmas hangover' feeling if you have been indulging him with too many titbits. Many owners like to give their pets 'a taste of everything', regardless of the fact that many of the items of Christmas fare are unsuitable for dogs.
>
> No permanent harm may be done, but if the dog seems dull, the tongue loses colour and the breath becomes offensive, a dose of castor oil is indicated.
>
> Twelve hours rest from food, followed by a light diet for a few days, usually effects a speedy cure – and from eight to twelve grains of carbonate of bismuth may be given

three times a day. The dog should be encouraged to drink barley water rather than plain water.

Signed by a Fellow of the Zoological Society.

* * *

Looking through what I have written above, I notice that I have used the phrase 'a totally different person'. For the first time it occurs to me what a stupid expression this is. As though there could be such a thing as a partially different person! I shall try to cut this phrase (and also 'a very different person' and 'a different person altogether') out of my vocabulary from now onwards.

But there are other words and phrases which obviously deserve to go on the scrap-heap, but which continue to be used because there seems to be no convenient substitute. An example is the word 'certain'. We say, for instance, 'After a certain age one's hair turns grey', or 'There will probably be a certain amount of snow in February'. In all such sentences 'certain' means uncertain. Why do we have to use this word in two opposite meanings? And yet, unless one pedantically says 'after an uncertain age', etc, there appears to be no other word which will exactly cover the required meaning.

As I Please 70

24 January 1947

Recently I was listening to a conversation between two small businessmen in a Scottish hotel. One of them, an alert-looking, well-dressed man of about forty-five, was something to do with the Federation of Master Builders. The other, a good deal older, with white hair and a broad accent, was some kind of wholesale tradesman. He said grace before his meals, a thing I had not seen anyone do for many a year. They belonged, I should say, in the £2,000-a-year and the £1,000-a-year income groups respectively.[212]

We were sitting round a rather inadequate peat fire, and the conversation started off with the coal shortage. There was no coal, it appeared, because the British miners refused to dig it out, but on the other hand it was important not to let Poles work in the pits because this would lead to unemployment. There was severe unemployment in Scotland

212. Compared with average earnings of £350 a year.

already. The older man then remarked with quiet satisfaction that he was very glad – 'varra glad indeed' – that Labour had won the general election. Any government that had to clean up after the war was in for a bad time, and as a result of five years of rationing, housing shortage, unofficial strikes and so forth, the general public would see through the promises of the socialists and vote Conservative next time.

They began talking about the housing problem, and almost immediately they were back to the congenial subject of the Poles. The younger man had just sold his flat in Edinburgh at a good profit and was trying to buy a house. He was willing to pay £2,700. The other was trying to sell his house for £1,500 and buy a smaller one. But it seemed that it was impossible to buy houses or flats nowadays. The Poles were buying them all up, and 'where they get the money from is a mystery'. The Poles were also invading the medical profession. They even had their own medical school in Edinburgh or Glasgow (I forget which) and were turning out doctors in great numbers while 'our lads' found it impossible to buy practices. Didn't everyone know that Britain had more doctors than it could use? Let the Poles go back to their own country. There were too many people in this country already. What was needed was emigration.

The younger man remarked that he belonged to several business and civic associations, and that on all of them he made a point of putting forward resolutions that the Poles should be sent back to their own country. The older one added that the Poles were 'very degraded in their morals'. They were responsible for much of the immorality that was prevalent nowadays. 'Their ways are not our ways,' he concluded piously. It was not mentioned that the Poles pushed their way to the head of queues, wore bright-coloured clothes and displayed cowardice during air raids, but if I had put forward a suggestion to this effect I am sure it would have been accepted.

One cannot of course, do very much about this kind of thing. It is the contemporary equivalent of anti-Semitism By 1947, people of the kind I am describing would have caught up with the fact that anti-Semitism is discreditable, and so the scapegoat is sought elsewhere. But the race hatred and mass delusions which are part of the pattern of our time might be somewhat less bad in their effects if they were not reinforced by ignorance. If in the years before the war, for instance, the facts about the persecution of Jews in Germany had been better known, the subjective popular feeling against Jews would probably not have been less, but the actual treatment of Jewish refugees might have been better. The refusal to allow refugees in significant numbers into this country would have been branded as disgraceful. The average man would still have felt a grudge against the refugees, but in practice more lives would have been saved.

So also with the Poles. The thing that most depressed me in the above-mentioned conversation was the recurrent phrase, 'let them go back to their own country'. If I had said to those two businessmen, 'Most of these people have no country to go back to', they would have gaped. Not one of the relevant facts would have been known to them. They would never have heard of the various things that have happened to Poland since 1939, any more than they would have known that the overpopulation of Britain is a fallacy or that local unemployment can coexist with a general shortage of labour. I think it is a mistake to give such people the excuse of ignorance. You can't actually change their feelings, but you can make them understand what they are saying when they demand that homeless refugees shall be driven from our shores, and the knowledge may make them a little less actively malignant.

* * *

The other week, in the *Spectator*, Mr Harold Nicolson was consoling himself as best he could for having reached the age of sixty. As he perceived, the only positive satisfaction in growing older is that after a certain point you can begin boasting of having seen things that no one will ever have the chance to see again. It set me wondering what boasts I could make myself, at forty-four, or nearly. Mr Nicolson had seen the Czar, surrounded by his bodyguard of enormous Cossacks, blessing the Neva. I never saw that, but I did see Marie Lloyd,[213] already almost a legendary figure, and I saw Little Tich – who, I think, did not die till about 1928, but who must have retired at about the same time as Marie Lloyd – and I have seen a whole string of crowned heads and other celebrities from Edward VII onwards. But on only two occasions did I feel, at the time, that I was seeing something significant, and on one of these occasions it was the circumstances and not the person concerned that made me feel this.

One of these celebrities was Pétain.[214] It was at Foch's funeral in 1929. Pétain's personal prestige in France was very great. He was honoured as the defender of Verdun, and the phrase 'They shall not pass' was popularly supposed to have been coined by him. He was given a place to himself in the procession, with a gap of several yards in front of and behind him. As he stalked past – a tall, lean, very erect figure, though he must have been seventy years old or thereabouts, with great sweeping white moustaches like the wings of a gull – a whisper of '*Voilà Pétain!*' went rippling through the vast crowd. His appearance impressed me so much that I dimly felt, in spite of his considerable age, that he ought still to have some kind of distinguished future ahead of him.

The other celebrity was Queen Mary.[215] One day I was walking past Windsor Castle when a sort of electric shock seemed to go through the street. People were taking their hats off, soldiers springing to attention. And then, clattering over the cobbles, there came

213. Marie Lloyd (1870–1922) and Little Tich (Harry Relph, 1867–1928) were music hall stars.

214. For Pétain, see note 20.

215. Queen Mary (1867–1953) was the wife of King George V.

a huge, plum-coloured open carriage drawn by four horses with postillions. I believe it was the first and last time in my life that I have seen a postillion. On the rear seat, with his back to the carriage, another groom sat stiffly upright, with his arms folded. The groom who sat at the back used to be called the tiger. I hardly noticed the Queen, my eyes fixed on that strange, archaic figure at the back, immobile as a wax-work, with his white breeches that looked as though he had been poured into them, and the cockade on his top-hat. Even at that date (1920 or thereabouts) it gave me a wonderful feeling of looking backwards through a window into the nineteenth century.

* * *

Some scraps of literary intelligence:

A few weeks ago I quoted an Indian proverb in this column, and erroneously said that it had been translated by a friend of mine. Actually the verse I quoted comes from Kipling. This illustrates something I have pointed out elsewhere – that Kipling is one of those writers whom one quotes unconsciously.

The *Partisan Review,* one of the best of the American highbrow magazines – rather like a synthesis of *Horizon* and *Polemic* – is to be published in London from February onwards.

Zamyatin's novel *We*, about which I wrote an article in *Tribune* a year or so ago,[216] is to be reissued in this country. A fresh translation is being made from the Russian. Look out for this book.

As I Pleased 71

31 January 1947

One's relations with a newspaper or a magazine are more variable and intermittent than they can be with a human being. From time to time a human being may dye his hair or become converted to Roman Catholicism, but he cannot change himself fundamentally, whereas a periodical will go through a whole series of different existences under the same name. *Tribune* in its short life has been two distinct papers, if not three, and my own contacts with it have varied sharply, starting off, if I remember rightly, with a rap on the knuckles.

I did not learn of the existence of *Tribune* till some time in 1939. It had started early

216. See 'Freedom and happiness' above, p. 272.

in 1937, but of the thirty months that intervened before the outbreak of war I spent five in hospital and thirteen abroad. What first drew my attention to it, I believe, was a none-too-friendly review of a novel of mine.[217] During the period 1939–42 I produced three or four books and reprints, and I think it is true that I never had what is called a 'good' review in *Tribune* until after I became a member of the staff. (The two events were unconnected, needless to say.) Somewhat later, in the cold winter of 1939, I started writing for *Tribune*, though at first, curiously enough, without seeing it regularly or getting a clear idea of what kind of paper it was.

Raymond Postgate,[218] who was then editor, had asked me to do the novel reviews from time to time. I was not paid (until recently it was unusual for contributors to left-wing papers to be paid), and I only saw the paper on the somewhat rare occasions when I went up to London and visited Postgate in a bare and dusty office near London Wall. *Tribune* (until a good deal later everyone called it 'the' *Tribune*) was at that time in difficulties. It was still a threepenny paper aimed primarily at the industrial workers and following more or less the Popular Front line which had been associated with the Left Book Club and the Socialist League. With the outbreak of war its circulation had taken a severe knock, because the communists and near-communists who had been among its warmest supporters now refused to help in distributing it. Some of them went on writing for it, however, and the futile controversy between 'supporters' and 'opposers' of the war continued to rumble in its columns while the German armies gathered for the spring offensives.

Early in 1940 there was a large meeting in a public hall, the purpose of which was to discuss both the future of *Tribune* and the policy of the left wing of the Labour Party. As is usual on such occasions nothing very definite was said, and what I chiefly remember is a political tip which I received from an inside source. The Norway campaign was ending in disaster, and I had walked to the hall past gloomy posters. Two MPs whom I will not name, had just arrived from the House.

'What chance is there,' I asked them, 'of this business getting rid of Chamberlain?'

'Not a hope,' they both said. 'He's solid.'

I don't remember dates, but I think it can only have been a week or two before Chamberlain was out of the premiership.

After that *Tribune* passed out of my consciousness for nearly two years. I was very busy trying to earn a living and write a book amid the bombs and the general disorganisation, and any spare time I had was taken up by the Home Guard, which was still an amateur force and demanded an immense amount of work from its members.

217. The review was by Winifred Horrabin (1892–1967), the novel *Coming Up for Air*.

218. For Raymond Postgate see Tribune biographies, pp. 397–8 of this volume.

When I became aware of *Tribune* again I was working in the Eastern Service of the BBC. It was now an almost completely different paper. It had a different make-up, cost sixpence, was orientated chiefly towards foreign policy, and was rapidly acquiring a new public which mostly belonged, I should say, to the out-at-elbow middle class. Its prestige among the BBC personnel was very striking. In the libraries where commentators went to prime themselves it was one of the most sought-after periodicals, not only because it was largely written by people who knew something at first hand about Europe, but because it was then the only paper of any standing which criticised the government. Perhaps 'criticised' is an over-mild word. Sir Stafford Cripps had gone into the government, and the fiery personality of Aneurin Bevan gave the paper its tone. On one occasion there were some surprisingly violent attacks on Churchill by someone who called himself 'Thomas Rainsboro''. This was obviously a pseudonym, and I spent a whole afternoon trying to determine the authorship by stylistic evidence, as the literary critics employed by the Gestapo were said to do with anonymous pamphlets. Finally I decided that 'Thomas Rainsboro'' was a certain W——. A day or two later I met Victor Gollancz, who said to me:

'Do you know who wrote those Thomas Rainsboro' articles in *Tribune*? I've just heard. It was W——.'

This made me feel very acute, but a day or two later I heard that we were both wrong.[219]

During this period I occasionally wrote articles for *Tribune*, but only at long intervals, because I had little time or energy. However, towards the end of 1943 I decided to give up my job in the BBC, and I was asked to take over the literary editorship of *Tribune*, in place of John Atkins, who was expecting call-up. I went on being literary editor, as well as writing the 'As I Please' column, until the beginning of 1945. It was interesting, but it is not a period that I look back on with pride. The fact is that I am no good at editing. I hate planning ahead, and I have a psychical or even physical inability to answer letters. My most essential memory of that time is of pulling out a drawer here and a drawer there, finding it in each case to be stuffed with letters and manuscripts which ought to have been dealt with weeks earlier, and hurriedly shutting it up again. Also, I have a fatal tendency to accept manuscripts which I know very well are too bad to be printed. It is questionable whether anyone who has had long experience as a

219. Thomas Rainsboro', who contributed several critical pieces on military strategy for *Tribune*, was the pen-name of Frank Owen (1905–79), editor of the *Evening Standard* (1937–41) and co-author (with Michael Foot and Peter Howard, using the collective pseudonym of 'Cato') of *Guilty Men* (London: Victor Gollancz, 1940), the bestselling polemical attack on the appeasers of the 1930s.

freelance journalist ought to become an editor. It is too like taking a convict out of his cell and making him governor of the prison. Still, it was 'all experience', as they say, and I have friendly memories of my cramped little office looking out on a backyard, and the three of us who shared it huddling in the corner as the doodlebugs came zooming over, and the peaceful click-click of the typewriters starting up again as soon as the bomb had crashed.

Early in 1945 I went to Paris as correspondent for the *Observer*. In Paris *Tribune* had a prestige which was somewhat astonishing and which dated from before the liberation. It was impossible to buy it, and the ten copies which the British Embassy received weekly did not, I believe, get outside the walls of the building. Yet all the French journalists I met seemed to have heard of it and to know that it was the one paper in England which had neither supported the government uncritically, nor opposed the war, nor swallowed the Russian myth. At that time there was - I should like to be sure that it still exists - a weekly paper named *Libertés*, which was roughly speaking the opposite number of *Tribune* and which during the occupation had been clandestinely produced on the same machines as printed the *Pariser Zeitung*.

Libertés, which was opposed to the Gaullists on one side and the communists on the other, had almost no money and was distributed by groups of volunteers on bicycles. On some weeks it was mangled out of recognition by the censorship; often nothing would be left of an article except some such title as 'The truth about Indo-China' and a completely blank column beneath it. A day or two after I reached Paris I was taken to a semi-public meeting of the supporters of *Libertés*, and was amazed to find that about half of them knew all about me and about *Tribune*. A large working man in black corduroy breeches came up to me, exclaimed 'Ah, vous êtes Georges Orrvell!' and crushed the bones of my hand almost to pulp. He had heard of me because *Libertés* made a practice of translating extracts from *Tribune*. I believe one of the editors used to go to the British Embassy every week and demand to see a copy. It seemed to me somehow touching that one could have acquired, without knowing it, a public among people like this: whereas among the huge tribe of American journalists at the Hotel Scribe, with their glittering uniforms and their stupendous salaries, I never encountered one who had heard of *Tribune*.

For six months during the summer of 1946 I gave up being a writer in *Tribune* and became merely a reader, and no doubt from time to time I shall do the same again; but I hope that my association with it may long continue, and I hope that in 1957 I shall be writing another anniversary article. I do not even hope that by that time *Tribune* will have slaughtered all its rivals. It takes all sorts to make a world, and if one could work these things out one might discover that even the —— serves a useful purpose. Nor is *Tribune* itself perfect, as I should know, having seen it from the inside. But I do think that it is the only existing weekly paper that makes a genuine effort to be both progressive and humane - that is, to combine a radical socialist policy with a respect for freedom of speech and a civilised attitude towards literature and the arts: and I think that its relative popularity, and even its survival in its present form for five years or more, is a hopeful symptom.

As I Please 72

7 February 1947

Recently I have been looking through Mr Peter Hunot's *Man about the House*, published a month or two back by the Pilot Press. Books telling you how to do household repairs are fairly numerous, but I think this is about the best I have seen. The author gathered his experience the hard way by taking over a nearly derelict house and making it habitable with his own hands. He thus concentrates on the sort of difficulties that do actually arise in real life, and does not, like the author of another book in my possession, tell you how to mend Venetian blinds while ignoring electrical fittings. I looked up all the domestic calamities that I have had to deal with during the past year, and found all of them mentioned, except mice, which perhaps hardly come under the heading of decorations and repairs. The book is also simply written and well illustrated, and takes account of the difficulty nowadays of getting hold of tools and materials.

But I still think that there is room for a very large, comprehensive book of this type, a sort of dictionary or encyclopaedia with every conceivable household job tabulated under alphabetical headings. You would then be able to look up 'Tap, how to stop a dripping', or 'Floorboards, causes of squeaking in', with the same certainty of getting the right answer as when you look up madeira cake or Welsh rarebit in Mrs Beeton's cookery book. The time was when the amateur handyman, with his tack hammer and his pocketful of rawlplugs, was looked on as a mere eccentric, a joke to his friends and a nuisance to his women-folk. Nowadays, however, you either do your repairs yourself or they don't get done, and most of us are still remarkably helpless. How many people even know how to replace a broken sash-cord, for instance?

As Mr Hunot points out, much of the tinkering that now goes on would be unnecessary, or would be much easier, if our houses were sensibly built. Even so simple a precaution as putting fuse boxes in get-at-able places would save a lot of nuisance, and the miserable business of putting up shelves could be greatly simplified without any extra materials or radical change in methods. I hear rumours that the new houses now being built will have the pipes so placed that they will not freeze, but surely this cannot be true. There will be a snag somewhere, and the annual freeze-up will happen as usual. Burst water-pipes are a part of the English winter, no less than muffins or roasted chestnuts, and doubtless Shakespeare would have mentioned them in the song at the end of *Love's Labour's Lost*, if there had been water-pipes in those days.

It is too early to cheer, but I must say that up to date the phenomena of the freeze-up have been less unpleasant than those of 1940. On that occasion the village where I lived was not only so completely snowed up that for a week or more it was impossible to get out of it, or for any food vans to get in, but every tap and pump in the village froze so hard that for several days we had no water except melted snow. The disagreeable thing about this is that snow is always dirty, except just after it has fallen. I have noticed this even in the high peaks of the Atlas mountains, miles from human habitation. The everlasting snow which looks so virginal, is in fact distinctly grimy when you get close to it.

* * *

About the time when Sir Stafford Cripps came back from India,[220] I heard it remarked that the Cripps offer[221] had not been extended to Burma because the Burmese would have accepted it. I don't know whether any such calculation really entered into the minds of Churchill and the rest. It is perfectly possible: at any rate, I think that responsible Burmese politicians would have accepted such an offer, although at that moment Burma was in process of being overrun by the Japanese. I also believe that an offer of Dominion status would have been gladly accepted if we had made it in 1944 and had named a definite date. As it is, the suspicions of the Burmese have been well roused, and it will probably end by our simply getting out of Burma on the terms least advantageous to both countries.

If that happens, I should like to think that the position of the racial minorities could be safeguarded by something better than promises. They number ten to twenty per cent of the population, and they present several different kinds of problem. The biggest group, the Karens, are a racial enclave living largely within Burma proper. The Kachins and other frontier tribes are a good deal more backward and more different from the Burmese in customs and appearance. They have never been under Burmese rule - indeed, their territories were only very sketchily occupied even by the British. In the past they were well able to maintain their independence, but probably would not be able to do so

220. For Stafford Cripps see Tribune biographies, pp. 390–1 of this volume.

221. For the Cripps offer, see note 122.

in the face of modern weapons. The other big group, the Shans, who are racially akin to the Siamese, enjoyed some faint traces of autonomy under British rule. The minority who are in the most difficult position of all are the Indians. There were over a million of them in Burma before the war. Two hundred thousand of them fled to India at the time of the Japanese invasion – an act which demonstrated better than any words could have done their real position in the country.

I remember twenty years ago a Karen remarking to me, 'I hope the British will stay in Burma for two hundred years.' 'Why?' 'Because we do not wish to be ruled by Burmese.' Even at the time it struck me that sooner or later it would become a problem. The fact is that the question of minorities is literally insoluble so long as nationalism remains a real force. The desire of some of the peoples of Burma for autonomy is genuine, but it cannot be satisfied in any secure way unless the sovereignty of Burma as a whole is interfered with. The same problem comes up in a hundred other places. Ought the Sudan to be independent of Egypt? Ought Ulster to be independent of Eire? Ought Eire to be independent of Britain? And so on. Whenever A is oppressing B, it is clear to people of goodwill that B ought to be independent, but then it always turns out that there is another group, C, which is anxious to be independent of B. The question is always how large must a minority be before it deserves autonomy. At best, each case can only be treated on its merits in a rough and ready way: in practice, no one is consistent in his thinking on this subject, and the minorities which win the most sympathy are those that have the best means of publicity. Who is there who champions equally the Jews, the Balts, the Indonesians, the expelled Germans, the Sudanese, the Indian Untouchables and the South African Kaffirs? Sympathy for one group almost invariably entails callousness towards another.

* * *

When H. G. Wells's *The Island of Doctor Moreau* was reprinted in the Penguin Library, I looked to see whether the slips and misprints which I remembered in earlier editions had been repeated in it. Sure enough, they were still there. One of them is a particularly stupid misprint, of a kind to make most writers squirm. In 1941 I pointed this out to H. G. Wells, and asked him why he did not remove it. It had persisted through edition after edition ever since 1896. Rather to my surprise, he said that he remembered the misprint, but could not be bothered to do anything about it. He no longer took the faintest interest in his early books: they had been written so long ago that he no longer felt them to be part of himself. I have never been quite sure whether to admire this attitude or not. It is magnificent to be so free from literary vanity. And yet, what writer of Wells's gifts, if he had had any power of self-criticism or regard for his own reputation, would have poured out in fifty years a total of ninety-five books, quite two thirds of which have already ceased to be readable?

As I Please 73

14 February 1947

Here are some excerpts from a letter from a Scottish nationalist. I have cut out anything likely to reveal the writer's identity. The frequent references to Poland are there because the letter is primarily concerned with the presence of exiled Poles in Scotland:

> The Polish forces have now discovered how untrue it is to say 'An Englishman's word is his bond'. We could have told you so hundreds of years ago. The invasion of Poland was only an excuse for these brigands in bowler hats to beat up their rivals the Germans and the Japs, with the help of Americans, Poles, Scots, Frenchmen, etc etc. Surely no Pole believes any longer in English promises. Now that the war is over you are to be cast aside and dumped in Scotland. If this leads to friction between the Poles and Scots so much the better. Let them slit each other's throats and two problems would be thereupon 'solved'. Dear, kind little England! It is time for all Poles to shed any ideas they may have about England as a champion of freedom. Look at her record in Scotland, for instance. And please don't refer to us as 'Britons'. There is no such race. We are Scots and that's good enough for us. The English changed their name to British, but even if a criminal changes his name he can be known by his fingerprints . . . Please disregard any anti-Polish statement in the —— —— ——. It is a boot-licking pro-English (pro-Moscow you would call it) rag. Scotland experienced her Yalta in 1707 when English gold achieved what English guns could not do. But we will never accept defeat. After more than two hundred years we are still fighting for our country and will never acknowledge defeat whatever the odds.

There is a good deal more in the letter, but this should be enough. It will be noted that the writer is not attacking England from what is called a 'left' standpoint, but on the ground that Scotland and England are enemies as nations. I don't know whether it would be fair to read race-theory into this letter, but certainly the writer hates us as bitterly as a devout Nazi would hate a Jew. It is not a hatred of the capitalist class, or anything like that, but of England. And though the fact is not sufficiently realised, there is an appreciable amount of this kind of thing knocking about. I have seen almost equally violent statements in print.

Up to date the Scottish nationalist movement seems to have gone almost unnoticed in England. To take the nearest example to hand, I don't remember having seen it mentioned *Tribune*, except occasionally in book reviews. It is true that it is a small movement, but it could grow, because there is a basis for it.[222] In this country I don't think it is enough realised – I myself had no idea of it until a few years ago – that Scotland has a case against England. On economic grounds it may not be a very strong case. In the past, certainly, we have plundered Scotland shamefully, but whether it is now true that England as a whole exploits Scotland as a whole, and that Scotland would be better off if fully autonomous, is another question. The point is that many Scottish people, often quite moderate in outlook, are beginning to think about autonomy and to feel that they are pushed into an inferior position. They have a good deal of reason. In some areas, at any rate, Scotland is almost an occupied country. You have an English or anglicised upper class, and a Scottish working class which speaks with a markedly different accent, or even, part of the time, in a different language. This is a more dangerous kind of class division than any now existing in England. Given favourable circumstances it might develop in an ugly way, and the fact that there was a progressive Labour government in London might not make much difference.

No doubt Scotland's major ills will have to be cured along with those of England. But meanwhile there are things that could be done to case the cultural situation. One small but not negligible point is the language. In the Gaelic-speaking areas, Gaelic is not taught in the schools. I am speaking from limited experience, but I should say that this is beginning to cause resentment. Also, the BBC only broadcasts two or three half-hour Gaelic programmes a week, and they give the impression of being rather amateurish programmes. Even so they are eagerly listened to. How easy it would be to buy a little good-will by putting on a Gaelic programme at least once daily.

At one time I would have said that it is absurd to keep alive an archaic language like Gaelic, spoken by only a few hundred thousand people. Now I am not so sure. To begin with, if people feel that they have a special culture which ought to be preserved, and that the language is part of it, difficulties should not be put in their way when they want their children to learn it properly. Secondly, it is probable that the effort of being bilingual is a valuable education in itself. The Scottish Gaelic-speaking peasants speak beautiful English, partly, I think, because English is an almost foreign language which they sometimes do not use for days together. Probably they benefit intellectually by having to be aware of dictionaries and grammatical rules, as their English opposite numbers would not be.

At any rate, I think we should pay more attention to the small but violent separatist

222. Scottish nationalism enjoyed significant support in the 1940s. The Scottish National Party won its first seat in the House of Commons in a 1945 by-election, and the pro-devolution Scottish Covenant Association, founded by the former SNP leader John McCormick to campaign for a Scottish assembly, gathered two million signatures in support of its proposals in 1949–50.

movements which exist within our own island. They may look very unimportant now, but, after all, the *Communist Manifesto* was once a very obscure document, and the Nazi Party only had six members when Hitler joined it.

* * *

To change the subject a bit, here is an excerpt from another letter. It is from a whisky distiller:

> We regret we are reluctantly compelled to return your cheque as owing to Mr Strachey's[223] failure to fulfil his promise to release barley for distilling in Scotland we dare not take on any new business . . . When you have difficulty in obtaining a drink it will be some consolation to you to know that Mr Strachey has sent 35,000 tons of barley to NEUTRAL Eire for brewing purposes.

People must be feeling very warmed-up when they put that kind of thing into a business letter which, by the look of it, is almost a circular letter. It doesn't matter very much, because whisky distillers and even their customers don't add up to many votes. But I wish I could feel sure that the people who make remarks like the one I overheard in the greengrocer's queue yesterday – 'Government! They couldn't govern a sausage-shop, this lot couldn't!' – were equally few in numbers.

* * *

Skelton is not an easy poet to get hold of, and I have never yet possessed a complete edition of his works. Recently, in a selection I had picked up, I looked for and failed to find a poem which I remember reading years ago. It was what is called a macaronic poem – part English, part Latin – and was an elegy on the death of somebody or other. The only passage I can recall runs:

> Sepultus est among the weeds,
> God forgive him his misdeeds,
> With hey ho, rumbelo,
> Rumpopulorum,
> Per omnia saecula,
> Saecula saeculorum.

It has stuck in my mind because it expresses an outlook totally impossible in our own age. Today there is literally no one who could write of death in that light-hearted manner. Since the decay of the belief in personal immortality, death has never seemed funny, and it will be a long time before it does so again. Hence the disappearance of the

223. For John Strachey, see Introduction, note 44.

facetious epitaph, once a common feature of country churchyards. I should be astonished to see a comic epitaph dated later than 1850. There is one in Kew, if I remember rightly, which might be about that date. About half the tombstone is covered with a long panegyric on his dead wife by a bereaved husband: at the bottom of the stone is a later inscription which reads, 'Now he's gone, too.'

One of the best epitaphs in English is Landor's epitaph on 'Dirce', a pseudonym for I do not know whom. It is not exactly comic, but it is essentially profane. If I were a woman it would be my favourite epitaph – that is to say, it would be the one I should like to have for myself. It runs:

Stand close around, ye Stygian set,
With Dirce in one boat conveyed,
Or Charon, seeing, may forget
That he is old and she a shade.

It would almost be worth being dead to have that written about you.

As I Please 74

21 February 1947 (*Manchester Evening News, for* Tribune)[224]

The following is an extract from George Orwell's page, 'As I Please', included each week in *Tribune*

The news that, for the second time in the last few months, a play banned from the stage is to be broadcast by the BBC (which will probably enable it to reach a much bigger public than it would if it were acted) brings out once again the absurdity of the rules governing literary censorship in Britain.

It is only stage plays and films that have to be submitted for censorship before they appear. So far as books go you can print what you like and take the risk of prosecution. Thus, banned plays like Granville Barker's *Waste* and Bernard Shaw's *Mrs Warren's Profession* could immediately appear in book form with no danger of prosecution, and no doubt sell all the better for the scandal that had happened beforehand. It is fair to

224. During the second half of February 1947, the government had suspended publication of the political weeklies and the trade press because of an extreme shortage of fuel. The *Manchester Evening News*, the *Daily Herald* and the *Observer* responded by offering space to *Tribune*.

say that, if they are any good, banned plays usually see the light sooner or later. Even *Waste*, which brought in politics as well as sex, was finally allowed to appear thirty years after it was written, when the topicality which gave it a good deal of its force had vanished.

The trouble with the Lord Chamberlain's censorship of plays is not that it happens, but that it is barbarous and stupid - being, apparently, done by bureaucrats with no literary training. If there is to be censorship, it is better that it should happen beforehand, so that the author may know where he stands. Books are only very rarely banned in Britain, but the bannings that do happen are usually quite arbitrary. *The Well of Loneliness*, for example, was suppressed, while other books on the same theme, appearing round about the same time, went unnoticed.

The book that gets dropped on is the one that happens to have been brought to the attention of some illiterate official. Perhaps half the novels now published might suffer this fate if they happened to get into the right hands. Indeed - though the dead are always respectable - I doubt whether Petronius, or Chaucer, or Rabelais, or Shakespeare would remain un-bowdlerised if our magistrates and police were greater readers.

As I Please 75

27/28 February 1947 (*Daily Herald and Manchester Evening News* for Tribune)[225]

Recently I was looking through a child's illustrated alphabet, published this year. It is what is called a 'travel alphabet'. Here are the rhymes accompanying three of the letters, J, N and U:

J for the Junk which the Chinaman finds
Is useful for carrying goods of all kinds.

N for the Native from Africa's land.
He looks very fierce with his spear in his hand.

U for the Union Jacks Pam and John carry
While out for a hike with their nice Uncle Harry.

225. This column appeared in two parts - the first in the *Daily Herald* of 27 February and the second in the *Manchester Evening News* of 28 February.

The 'native' in the picture is a Zulu dressed only in some bracelets and a fragment of leopard skin. As for the Junk, the detail of the picture is very small, but the 'Chinamen' portrayed in it appear to be wearing pigtails.

Perhaps there is not much to object to in the presence of the Union Jack. This is an age of competing nationalisms, and who shall blame us if we flourish our own emblems along with all the rest? But is it really necessary, in 1947, to teach children to use expressions like 'native' and 'Chinaman'?

The last-named word has been regarded as offensive by the Chinese for at least a dozen years. As for 'native', it was being officially discountenanced even in India as long as twenty years ago.

It is no use answering that it is childish for an Indian or an African to feel insulted when he is called a 'native'. We all have these feelings in one form or another. If a Chinese wants to be called a Chinese and not a Chinaman, if a Scotsman objects to being called a Scotchman, or if a Negro demands his capital N, it is only the most ordinary politeness to do what is asked of one.

The sad thing about this alphabet-book is that the writer obviously has no intention of insulting the 'lower' races. He is merely not quite aware that they are human beings like ourselves. A 'native' is a comic black man with very few clothes on; a 'Chinaman' wears a pigtail and travels in a junk– which is about as true as saying that an Englishman wears a top hat and travels in a hansom cab.

This unconsciously patronising attitude is learned in childhood and then, as here, passed on to a new generation of children. And sometimes it pops up in quite enlightened people, with disconcerting results; as for instance at the end of 1941, when China officially became our ally, and at the first important anniversary the BBC celebrated the occasion by flying the Chinese flag over Broadcasting House, and flying it upside-down.

* * *

One thing one notices in these days when typewriters have become so scarce is the astonishing badness of nearly everyone's handwriting.

A handwriting which is both pleasant to look at and easy to read is now a very rare thing. To bring about an improvement we should probably have to evolve a generally accepted 'style' of writing such as we possessed in the past and have now lost.

For several centuries in the Middle Ages the professional scribes wrote an exquisite script, or rather a series of scripts, which no one now living could equal. Then handwriting declined, reviving in the nineteenth century after the invention of the steel pen. The style then favoured was 'copperplate'. It was neat and legible, but it was full of unnecessary lines and did not fit in with the modern tendency to get rid of ornament wherever possible. Then it became the fashion to teach children script, usually with disastrous results. To write script with real neatness one practically has to learn to draw, and it is impossible to write it as rapidly as a cursive hand. Many young or youngish people now make use of an uneasy compromise between script and copperplate, and indeed there are many adult and fully literate people whose handwriting has never properly 'formed'.

It would be interesting to know whether there is any connection between neat handwriting and literary ability. I must say that the modern examples I am able to think of do not seem to prove much. Miss Rebecca West has an exquisite handwriting, and so has Mr Middleton Murry. Sir Osbert Sitwell, Mr Stephen Spender, and Mr Evelyn Waugh all have handwritings which, to put it as politely as possible, are not good. Professor Laski writes a hand which is attractive to look at but difficult to read. Arnold Bennett wrote a beautiful tiny hand over which he took immense pains. H. G. Wells had an attractive but untidy writing. Carlyle's writing was so bad that one compositor is said to have left Edinburgh in order to get away from the job of setting it up. Mr Bernard Shaw writes a small, clear but not very elegant hand. And as for the most famous and respected of living English novelists, his writing is such that when I was at the BBC and had the honour of putting him on the air once a month there was only one secretary in the whole department who could decipher his manuscripts.[226]

As I Please 76

7 March 1947

One of *the* great faults of the present government is its failure to tell the people what is happening and why. That is so generally agreed that in itself it is hardly worth saying over again. However, with the wartime machinery of propaganda largely scrapped, and the press under control of private owners, some of whom are none too friendly, it is not easy for the government to publicise itself. Posters – at any rate, posters like the present ones – will not achieve much, films are expensive, pamphlets and White Papers are not read by the big public. The most obvious means of publicity is the radio, and we are up against the difficulty that politicians in this country are seldom radio-conscious.

During the recent crisis, people were to be heard remarking that the minister of this

226. The novelist was E. M. Forster.

or that ought to 'come to the microphone' more frequently. But it is not much use coming to the microphone unless what you say is listened to. When I worked in the BBC, and frequently had to put eminent people on the air, I was struck by the fact that few professional politicians seemed to realise that broadcasting is an art that has to be learned, and that it is quite different from platform speaking. A first-rate performer in one medium may be hopeless in the other, unless re-trained. Ernest Bevin, for instance, is a good platform speaker but a poor broadcaster. Attlee is better, so far as his voice goes, but does not seem to have a gift for the telling phrase. Churchill's wartime broadcasts were good of their Corinthian kind, but Churchill, unlike most of the others, gives the impression of having studied microphone technique.

When a speaker is invisible, he not only cannot make use of his personal charm, if any, he also cannot make gestures to emphasise his points. He cannot act with his body, and therefore has to act much more elaborately with his larynx. A good exercise for anyone trying to improve his microphone delivery is to have one of his speeches recorded, and then listen to it. This is an astonishing and even shocking experience. Not only does one's voice, heard externally, sound completely different from what it sounds like inside one's skull, but it always sounds much less emphatic. To sound natural on the air one has to have the impression, internally, that one is overacting. If one speaks as one would in everyday life, or on a platform, one always sounds bored. That, indeed, is the impression that the majority of untrained broadcasters do give, especially when they speak from scripts: and when the speaker sounds bored, the audience is apt to follow suit.

* * *

Some time ago a foreign visitor asked me if I could recommend a good, representative anthology of English verse. When I thought it over I found that I could not name a single one that seemed to me satisfactory. Of course there are innumerable period anthologies, but nothing, so far as I know, that attempts to cover the whole of English literature except Palgrave's *Golden Treasury* and, more comprehensive and more up-to-date, *The Oxford Book of English Verse*.

Now, I do not deny that *The Oxford Book* is useful, that there is a great deal of good stuff in it, and that every schoolchild ought to have a copy, in default of something better. Still, when you look at the last fifty pages, you think twice about recommending such a book to a foreigner who may imagine that it is really representative of English verse. Indeed, the whole of this part of the book is a lamentable illustration of what happens to professors of literature when they have to exercise independent judgment. Up to 1850, or thereabouts, one could not go very wrong in compiling an anthology, because, after all, it is on the whole the best poems that have survived. But as soon as Sir

Arthur Quiller-Couch reached his contemporaries, all semblance of taste deserted him.

The Oxford Book stops at 1900, and it is true that the last decades of the nineteenth century were a poor period for verse. Still, there were poets even in the nineties. There was Ernest Dawson – 'Cynara' is not my idea of a good poem, but I would sooner have it than Henley's 'England, My England' – there was Hardy, who published his first poems in 1898, and there was Housman, who published *A Shropshire Lad* in 1896. There was also Hopkins, who was not in print or barely in print, but whom Sir Arthur Quiller-Couch must have known about. None of these appears in *The Oxford Book*. Yeats, who had already published a great deal at that date, does appear shortly, but he is not represented by his best poems: neither is Kipling, who, I think, did write one or two poems (for instance, 'How Far Is St Helena') which deserve to be included in a serious anthology. And on the other hand, just look at the stuff that has been included! Sir Henry Newbolt's Old Cliftonian keeping a stiff upper lip on the North-West Frontier; other patriotic pieces by Henley and Kipling; and page after page of weak, sickly, imitative verse by Andrew Lang, Sir William Watson, A. C. Benson, Alice Meynell and others now forgotten. What is one to think of an anthologist who puts Newbolt and Edmund Gosse in the same volume with Shakespeare, Wordsworth and Blake?

Perhaps I am just being ignorant and there does already exist a comprehensive anthology running all the way from Chaucer to Dylan Thomas and including no tripe. But if not, I think it is time to compile one, or at least to bring *The Oxford Book* up to date by making a completely new selection of poets from Tennyson onwards.

* * *

Looking through what I have written above, I see that I have spoken rather snootily of Dawson's 'Cynara'. I know it is a bad poem, but it is bad in a good way, or good in a bad way, and I do not wish to pretend that I never admired it. Indeed, it was one of the favourites of my boyhood. I am quoting from memory:

> I have forgot much, Cynara! gone with the wind,
> Flung roses, roses, riotously with the throng,
> Dancing, to put thy pale lost lilies out of mind;
> But I was desolate and sick of an old passion,
> Yea, all the time, because the dance was long –
> I have been faithful to thee, Cynara! in my fashion.

Surely those lines possess, if not actual merit, at least the same kind of charm as belongs to a pink geranium or a soft-centre chocolate.

As I Please 77

14 March 1947

I have not yet read more than a newspaper paragraph about Nu Speling, in connexion with which somebody is introducing a bill in parliament, but if it is like most other schemes for rationalising our spelling, I am against it in advance, as I imagine most people will be.

Probably the strongest reason for resisting rationalised spelling is laziness. We have all learned to read and write already, and we don't want to have to do it over again. But there are other more respectable objections. To begin with, unless the scheme were rigidly enforced, the resulting chaos, with some newspapers and publishing houses accepting it, others refusing it, and others adopting it in patches, would be fearful. Then again, anyone who had learned only the new system would find it very difficult to read books printed in the old one, so that the huge labour of respelling the entire literature of the past would have to be undertaken. And again, you can only fully rationalise spelling if you give a fixed value to each letter. But this means standardising pronunciation, which could not be done in this country without an unholy row. What do you do, for instance, about words like 'butter' or 'glass', which are pronounced in different ways in London and Newcastle? Other words, such as 'were', are pronounced in two different ways according to individual inclination, or according to context.

However, I do not want to prejudge the inventors of Nu Speling. Perhaps they have already thought of a way round these difficulties. And certainly our existing spelling system is preposterous and must be a torment to foreign students. This is a pity, because English is well fitted to be the universal second language, if there ever is such a thing. It has a large start over any natural language and an enormous start over any manufactured one, and apart from the spelling it is very easy to learn. Would it not be possible to rationalise it by little and little, a few words every year? Already some of the more ridiculous spellings do tend to get killed off unofficially. For instance, how many people now spell 'hiccup' as 'hiccough'?

Another thing I am against in advance - for it is bound to be suggested sooner or later - is the complete scrapping of our present system of weights and measures.

Obviously you have got to have the metric system for certain purposes. For scientific work it has long been in use, and it is also needed for tools and machinery, especially if you want to export them. But there is a strong case for keeping on the old measurements for use in everyday life. One reason is that the metric system does not possess, or has not succeeded in establishing, a large number of units that can be visualised. There is, for instance, effectively no unit between the metre, which is more than a yard, and the centimetre, which is less than half an inch. In English you can describe someone as being five feet three inches high, or five feet nine inches, or six feet one inch, and your bearer will know fairly accurately what you mean. But I have never heard a Frenchman say, 'He is a hundred and forty-two centimetres high'; it would not convey any visual image. So also with the various other measurements. Rods and acres, pints, quarts and gallons, pounds, stones and hundredweights, are all of them units with which we are intimately familiar, and we should be slightly poorer without them. Actually, in countries where the metric system is in force a few of the old measurements tend to linger on for everyday purposes, although officially discouraged.

There is also the literary consideration, which cannot be left quite out of account. The names of the units in the old system are short homely words which lend themselves to vigorous speech. Putting a quart into a pint pot is a good image, which could hardly be expressed in the metric system. Also, the literature of the past deals only in the old measurements, and many passages would become an irritation if one had to do a sum in arithmetic when one read them, as one does with those tiresome verses in a Russian novel.

The emmet's inch and eagle's mile
Make lame philosophy to smile:

fancy having to turn that into millimetres!. . .

* * *

I have just been reading about a party of German teachers, journalists, trade-union delegates and others who have been on a visit to this country. It appears that while here they were given food parcels by trade unions and other organisations, only to have them taken away again by the Customs officials at Harwich. They were not even allowed to take out of the country the 15lb of food which is permitted to a returning prisoner of war. The newspaper reporting this adds without apparent irony that the Germans in question had been here 'on a six weeks' course in democracy'.

* * *

I wonder whether it would be possible, before the next bout of cold weather comes along, to do something about the racket in firewood? Last week I paid fifteen shillings for a hundred logs. They were very small logs, weighing I should say a pound to a pound and a half each, so that weight for weight they will have been twice or three times as expensive as coal. A day or two later I heard of logs being sold at a pound or thirty shillings a hundred. In any case, much of the wood that is hawked round the streets in cold weather is full of sap and almost unburnable.

Incidentally, does not the weather we have just been through reinforce my earlier plea for better use of our peat resources? At the time various people said to *me*: 'Ah, but you see, English people aren't used to peat. You'd never get them to use it.' During the last two weeks, most of the people known to me have used anything, not despising the furniture as a last resort. I kept going for a day myself on a blitzed bedstead, and wrote an article by its grateful warmth.

* * *

The other day I had occasion to write something about the teaching of history in private schools, and the following scene, which was only rather loosely connected with what I was writing, floated into my memory. It was less than fifteen years ago that I witnessed it.

'Jones!'

'Yessir!'

'Causes of the French revolution.'

'Please, sir, the French revolution was due to three causes, the teachings of Voltaire and Rousseau, the oppression of the nobles by the people and – '

At this moment a faint chill, like the first premonitory symptom of an illness, falls upon Jones. Is it possible that he has gone wrong somewhere? The master's face is inscrutable. Swiftly Jones casts his mind back to the unappetising little book, with the gritty brown cover, a page of which is memorised daily. He could have sworn he had the whole thing right. But at this moment Jones discovers for the first time the deceptiveness of visual memory. The whole page is clear in his mind, the shape of every paragraph accurately recorded, but the trouble is that there is no saying which way round the words go. He had made sure it was the oppression of the nobles by the people; but then it might have been the oppression of the people by the nobles. It is a toss-up. Desperately he takes his decision – better to stick to his first version. He gabbles on:

'The oppression of the nobles by the people and – '

'JONES!'

Is that kind of thing still going on, I wonder?

* * *

To forestall a flood of letters:

(a) As I have found out since writing my column last week, there are already several inclusive anthologies which deal with modern verse more satisfactorily than *The Oxford Book*; and

(b) 'Ernest Dawson' (for 'Dowson') was a misprint.

As I Please 78

21 March 1947

The atomic bomb is frightening, but to anyone who wants to counteract it by a different kind of fright I recommend Mr Mark Abrams's book, *The Population of Great Britain*, published in 1945.[227] This can be read in conjunction with the Mass Observation survey, *Britain and Her Birth-rate,* published about the same time, and other recent books on the same subject. They all tell more or less the same story, and it has very unpleasant implications for anyone who expects to be alive in 1970.

At present, as Mr Abrams's figures show, the age composition of our population is favourable, if one thinks in terms of labour units. We still have the benefit of the relatively high birthrate just before and just after the 1914–18 war, so that well over half our population is of working age. But the trouble is that we can't freeze the figures at this point. The working population grows older all the time, and sufficient children are not being born. In 1881, when our total population was only about two-thirds of what it is now, the number of babies (under four) was actually larger by about half a million, while the number of old people (over sixty-five) was less by something over three millions. In 1881 more than a third of the population was under fourteen: today the corresponding figure is less than a quarter. If there had been an old age pension in 1881, less than 5 per cent of the population would have been eligible for it: today more than 10 per cent are eligible for it. To see the full significance of this one has to look forward a bit.

By 1970, Mr Abrams calculates, the number of people over fifty-five may well be fourteen millions – this in a population which may be smaller than the present one. That is to say that about one person in three will be almost past work: or, to put it differently, that every two able-bodied people will be supporting one old person between them! When Mr Abrams produced his book, the birthrate had been rising during the later war years, and I believe it has again risen during 1946, but not to anywhere near replacement level: in any case the sudden jump in births may have happened merely because, owing to the war, people have been marrying earlier. The downward trend has been happening for more than half a century, and some of its effects cannot be escaped from, but the worst would be avoided if the birthrate reached and stayed at the point where the average family was four children, and not, as at present, a little over two. But this must happen

227. Mark Abrams, *The Population of Great Britain* (London: Allen and Unwin, 1945).

within the next decade; otherwise there will not be enough women of child-bearing age to restore the situation.

It is curious how little dismay the dropping birthrate caused until very recently. Even now, as the Mass Observation report brings out, most people merely think that it means a smaller population and do not realise that it also means an ageing population. Thirty years ago, even ten or fifteen years ago, to advocate smaller families was a mark of enlightenment. The key phrases were 'surplus population' and 'the multiplication of the unfit'. Even now there is strong social pressure against large families, not to mention the crude economic consideration. All writers on this subject seem to agree that the causes of the decline are complex and that it may not be possible to reverse the trend merely by family allowances, day nurseries, etc. But clearly there must be *some* financial inducement, because, in an industrialised society which is also socially competitive, a large family is an unbearable economic burden. At the best it means making sure that your children will start off with a poorer chance in life than you had yourself.

Over the past twenty-five years, what innumerable people must have kept their families down from directly economic motives! It is a queer kind of prudence if you consider the community and not the individual. In another twenty-five years the parents of today will be past work, and the children they have not had will not be there to support them. I wonder if the old age pension will stay at the equivalent of £1 a week when one person in three is in receipt of it?

* * *

I wonder if there exists – indeed I am sure something of the kind must exist – a short and simple textbook from which the ordinary citizen can get a working knowledge of the laws he lives under? Recently I had occasion to refer in this column to the rules governing the selection of juries. No doubt it was very ignorant on my part not to know that juries are picked out on a system that tends to exclude the working class; but evidently thousands of other people did not know it either, and the discovery came as a shock. Every now and again this kind of thing happens. By some chance or other – for instance, by reading the reports of a murder case – one finds out how the law stands on a certain subject, and it is frequently so stupid or so unfair that one would not have believed it if one had not seen it in black and white.

For instance, I have just been reading the government White Paper dealing with the confession made by David Ware in the Manchester murder case. Walter Rowland, since hanged, had been convicted of the murder, and Ware afterwards made a confession which Rowland's counsel attempted to use as evidence at the appeal. After reading the White Paper I have not the slightest doubt that the confession was spurious and that it was right to disregard it. But that is not the point. It came out in the appeal proceedings that the judges had no power to hear evidence of that kind. True or false, the confession could not be admitted as evidence. An innocent man might be convicted, the real criminal might make an unmistakably genuine confession, and the innocent man might still be hanged, unless the Home Secretary chose to intervene. Did you know that that is how the law stands? I certainly didn't, and the incident shows how rash it is to try to infer what the law would be on any given subject, using common sense as a starting-point.

Here is another instance, but in this case my ignorance is probably less excusable. In a recent *cause célèbre*, in which the accused was acquitted, it came out that the very heavy costs of the defence were paid by a Sunday paper. I confess that I had not realised until then that when you are found not guilty on a criminal charge, you still have to pay your own costs. I had vaguely imagined that when the Crown is discovered to be in the wrong, it pays up, like the unsuccessful claimant in a civil suit. However, it seems that if you are actually indigent, the Crown will provide you with counsel, but it takes care not to be seriously out of pocket by doing so. In this case, it is stated, the leading counsel briefed by the Sunday paper received about £500, whereas if briefed by the Crown he would have received less than £20. Apply that to an ordinary burglary or embezzlement case, where there is not much notoriety to be won, and see what it means to an indigent person's chance of getting the best possible defence.

* * *

What an outcry there has been over the suspension of the weekly papers! Even the *Smallholder* protested, and there was a very sharp editorial comment in *Practical Engineering*. The *Universe*, if I remember rightly, said that this was the prelude to the imposition of press censorship. And in general the idea seems to have seeped round that there was some kind of political motive for the suspension - the motive, presumably, being to prevent comment on the government's mistakes.

A well-known writer said to me that the banning of weekly papers was much the same kind of thing as the 'co-ordination' of the press in totalitarian countries. This seems to me the point at which suspicion turns into folly. Obviously there was no idea of silencing criticism, since the daily papers were left alone. The Beaverbrook press, for instance, is far more hostile to the government than any weekly paper of standing, besides having an enormously larger circulation. How much ignorant abuse Shinwell[228] might have escaped, if during the crisis he had made even one public appearance to explain what he was doing!

228. Emmanuel Shinwell (1884-1986) was Labour MP for Linlithgow 1922-4 and 1929-31, Seaham 1935-50 and Easington 1950-70. He was Minister of Power and Fuel 1945-7, Secretary of State for War 1947-50 and Minister of Defence 1950-1. He served as chairman of the Parliamentary Labour Party in the 1960s and was made a life peer in 1970.

As I Please 79

28 March 1947

I have been reading with interest the February–March bulletin of Mass Observation, which appears just ten years after this organisation first came into being. It is curious to remember with what hostility it was greeted at the beginning. It was violently attacked in the *New Statesman*, for instance, where Mr Stonier[229] declared that the typical Mass Observer would have 'elephant ears, a loping walk and a permanent sore eye from looking through keyholes', or words to that effect. Another attacker was Mr Stephen Spender. But on the whole the opposition to this or any other kind of social survey comes from people of conservative opinions, who often seem to be genuinely indignant at the idea of finding out what the big public is thinking.

If asked why, they generally answer that what is discovered is of no interest, and that in any case any intelligent person always knows already what are the main trends of public opinion. Another argument is that social surveys are an interference with individual liberty and a first step towards totalitarianism. The *Daily Express* ran this line for several years and tried to laugh the small social survey unit instituted by the Ministry of Information out of existence by nicknaming it Cooper's Snoopers. Of course, behind much of this opposition there lies a well-justified fear of finding that mass sentiment on many subjects is not conservative.

But some people do seem sincerely to feel that it is a bad thing for the government to know too much about what people are thinking, just as others feel that it is a kind of presumption when the government tries to educate public opinion. Actually you can't have democracy unless both processes are at work. Democracy is only possible when the law-makers and administrators know what the masses want, and what they can be counted on to understand. If the present government paid more attention to this last point, they would word some of their publicity differently. Mass Observation issued a report last week on the White Paper on the economic situation. They found, as usual, that the abstract words and phrases which are flung to and fro in official announcements mean nothing to countless ordinary citizens. Many people are even flummoxed by the word 'assets', which is thought to have something to do with 'assist'!

The Mass Observation bulletin gives some account of the methods its investigators use, but does not touch on a very important point, and that is the manner in which social

229. G. W. Stonier (1903–85) was assistant literary editor of the *New Statesman*.

surveys are financed. Mass Observation itself appears to keep going in a hand-to-mouth way by publishing books and by undertaking specific jobs for the government or for commercial organisations. Some of its best surveys, such as that dealing with the birthrate, were carried out for the Advertising Service Guild. The trouble with this method is that a subject only gets investigated if some large, wealthy organisation happens to be interested in it. An obvious example is anti-Semitism, which I believe has never been looked into, or only in a very sketchy way. But anti-Semitism is only one variant of the great modern disease of nationalism. We know very little about the real causes of nationalism, and we might conceivably be on the way towards curing it if we knew more. But who is sufficiently interested to put up the thousands of pounds that an exhaustive survey would cost?

* * *

For some weeks there has been correspondence in the *Observer* about the persistence of 'spit and polish' in the armed forces. The last issue had a good letter from someone who signed himself 'Conscript', describing how he and his comrades were forced to waste their time in polishing brass, blacking the rubber hoses on stirrup pumps with boot polish, scraping broom handles with razor blades, and so on. But 'Conscript' then goes on to say: 'When an officer (a major) carried out routine reading of King's Regulations regarding venereal disease, he did not hesitate to add: "There is nothing to be ashamed of if you have the disease – it is quite natural. But make sure that you report for treatment at once."' I must say that it seems to me strange, amid the other idiocies mentioned, to object to one of the few sensible things in the army system, i.e. its straightforward attitude towards venereal disease. We shall never be able to stamp out syphilis and gonorrhoea until the stigma of sinfulness is removed from them. When full conscription was introduced in the 1914–18 war it was discovered, if I remember rightly, that nearly half the population suffered or had suffered from some form of venereal disease, and this frightened the authorities into taking a few precautions. During the inter-war years the struggle against venereal disease languished, so far as the civilian population went. There was provision for treatment of those already infected, but the proposal to set up 'early treatment centres', as in the army, was quelled by the puritans. Then came another war, with the increase in venereal disease that war necessarily causes, and another attempt to deal with the problem. The Ministry of Health posters are timid enough, but even these would have provoked an outcry from the pious ones if military necessity had not called them into being.

You can't deal with these diseases so long as they are thought of as visitations of God, in a totally different category from all other diseases. The inevitable result of that is concealment and quack remedies. And it is humbug to say that 'clean living is the only real remedy'. You are bound to have promiscuity and prostitution in a society like ours, where people mature sexually at about fifteen and are discouraged from marrying till they are in their twenties, where conscription and the need for mobility of labour break up family life, and where young people living in big towns have no regular way of forming acquaintanceships. It is impossible to solve the problem by making people more moral, because they won't, within any foreseeable time, become as moral as all that. Besides, many of the victims of venereal disease are husbands or wives who have not themselves committed any so-called immoral act. The only sensible course is to recognise that syphilis and gonorrhoea are merely diseases, more preventable if not curable than most, and that to suffer from them is not disgraceful. No doubt the pious ones would squeal. But in doing so they might avow their real motives, and then we should be a little nearer to wiping out this evil.

* * *

For the last five minutes I have been gazing out of the window into the square, keeping a sharp look-out for signs of spring. There is a thinnish patch in the clouds with a faint hint of blue behind it, and on a sycamore tree there are some things that look as if they might be buds. Otherwise it is still winter. But don't worry! Two days ago, after a careful search in Hyde Park, I came on a hawthorn bush that was definitely in bud, and some birds, though not actually singing, were making noises like an orchestra tuning up. Spring is coming after all, and recent rumours that this was the beginning of another Ice Age were unfounded. In only three weeks' time we shall be listening to the cuckoo, which usually gives tongue about the fourteenth of April. Another three weeks after that, and we shall be basking under blue skies, eating ices off barrows and neglecting to lay up fuel for next winter.

How appropriate the ancient poems in praise of spring have seemed these last few years! They have a meaning that they did not have in the days when there was no fuel shortage and you could get almost anything at any time of year. Of all passages celebrating spring, I think I like best those two stanzas from the beginning of one of the Robin Hood ballads. I modernise the spelling:

> When shaws be sheen and swards full fair,
> And leaves both large and long,
> It is merry walking in the fair forest
> To hear the small birds' song.
>
> The woodwele sang and would not cease,
> Sitting upon the spray,
> So loud he wakened Robin Hood
> In the greenwood where he lay.

But what exactly was the woodwele? The Oxford Dictionary seems to suggest that it was the woodpecker, which is not a notable songster, and I should be interested to know whether it can be identified with some more probable bird.

As I Please 80

4 April 1947

The Royal Commission on the Press[230] is now getting to work, after mysterious delays. Presumably it will be a long time before it reaches any definite conclusions, and still longer before its findings are acted upon. Nevertheless, it seems to me that now is the time to start discussing the problem of preserving a free press in a socialised economy. Because, unless we become aware of the difficulties before they are actually upon us, the ultimate condition of the press in this country will be worse than it need be.

During the fuel crisis I remarked to several people on the badness of government publicity, to be met each time with the answer that the present government has hardly any organs of expression under its control. That, of course, is true. I then said, 'Why not take over the *Daily* —— and run it as a government organ?' This suggestion was always greeted with horror. Apparently to nationalise the press would be 'fascism', while 'freedom of the press' consists in allowing a few millionaires to coerce hundreds of journalists into falsifying their opinions. But I pass over the question of how free the British press is at present. The point is, what will finally happen if the present trend towards nationalisation continues?

Sooner or later, it seems to me, the press is certain to be nationalised, so far as its major organs go. It could hardly continue to exist as a huge patch of private enterprise, like a sort of game reserve, in the middle of a collectivised economy. But does that mean that *all* channels of expression will ultimately be under the control of bureaucrats? Some such thing could quite easily happen if the people most concerned are indifferent to their fate. One can quite well imagine newspapers, periodicals, magazines, books, films, radio, music and the drama all being lumped together and 'co-ordinated' under the guidance of some enormous Ministry of Fine Arts (or whatever its name might be). It is not a pleasant prospect, but I believe it can be averted if the danger is realised in advance.

What is meant by freedom of the press? The press is free, I should say, when it is easy

230. For the Royal Commission on the Press, see note 204.

and not illegal to get minority opinions into print and distribute them to the public. Britain is luckier in this respect than most countries, and it is fair to say that this is partly due to the variations that exist in the big commercial press. The leading daily papers, few though they are, contain more shades of difference than a government-controlled press would be likely to do. Still, the main guardians of minority opinion are the small independent weekly and monthly papers, and the book-publishing houses. It is only through those channels that you can make sure of getting a hearing for *any* opinion that does not express a libel or an incitement to violence. Therefore, if the big press is certain to be nationalised anyway, could not this principle be laid down in advance: that nationalisation shall only apply to so much of the press as comes under the heading of 'big business', while small concerns will be left alone?

Obviously the proprietor of a chain of a hundred newspapers is a capitalist. So is a small publisher or the owner-editor of a monthly magazine, strictly speaking. But you are not obliged to treat them both alike, just as in abolishing large-scale ownership of land you are not obliged to rob the smallholder or market gardener of his few acres. So long as a minority press can exist, and count on continued existence, even in a hole and corner way, the essential freedom will be safeguarded. But the first step is to realise that nationalisation is inevitable, and lay our plans accordingly. Otherwise the people specially concerned, the journalists, artists, actors, etc, may have no bargaining power when the time comes, and that unappetising Ministry of Fine Arts may engulf the whole lot of them.

* * *

Recently I was talking to the editor of a newspaper with a very large circulation, who told me that it was now quite easy for his paper to live on its sales alone. This would probably continue to be true, he said, until the paper situation improved, which would mean reverting to pre-war bulk, at enormously greater expense. Until then, advertisements would be of only secondary importance as a source of revenue.

If that is so – and I believe many papers could now exist without advertisements – is not this just the moment for an all-out drive against patent medicines? Before the war it was never possible to attack patent medicines in a big way, because the press, which would have had to make the exposure, lived partly off advertisements for them. As a start, some enterprising publisher might track down and reprint the two volumes of that rare and very entertaining book, *Secret Remedies.* This was issued, if I remember rightly, by the British Medical Association – at any rate, by some association of doctors – the first volume appearing about 1912 and the second during the nineteen-twenties.[231] It

231. In fact, the first volume appeared in 1909 and the second in 1912.

consisted simply of a list of existing proprietary medicines, with a statement of their claims, an analysis of their contents, and an estimate of their cost. There was very little comment, which in most cases was hardly necessary. I distinctly remember that one 'consumption cure' sold to the public at thirty-five shillings a bottle was estimated to cost a halfpenny.

Neither volume made much impact on the public. The press, for reasons indicated above, practically ignored both issues, and they are now so rare that I have not seen a copy for years. (Incidentally, if any reader has a copy I would gladly buy it - especially the second volume, which I think is the rarer.) If reissued, the book would need bringing up to date, for the claim to cure certain diseases is now forbidden by law, while many new kinds of rubbish have come on to the market. But many of the old ones are still there - that is the significant point. Is it not possible that the consumption of patent medicines might decrease if people were given a clearer idea of the nature and the real cost of the stuff they are pouring down their throats?

* * *

A few weeks back a correspondent in *Tribune* asked why we are not allowed to grow and cure tobacco for our own use, In practice, I think, you can do so. There is a law against it, but it is not strictly enforced - at any rate, I have certainly known people who grew their own tobacco, and even prepared it in cakes like the commercial article. I tried some once, and thought it the perfect tobacco for a non-smoker. The trouble with English tobacco is that it is so mild that you can hardly taste it. This is not, I believe, due to the lack of sun but to some deficiency in the soil. However, any tobacco is better than none, and a few thousand acres laid down to it in the south of England might help us through the cigarette shortage which is likely to happen this year, without using up any dollars or robbing the state of any revenue.

* * *

I have just been reading about the pidgin English (or 'beche-la-mar') used in the Solomon and New Hebrides Islands in the South Pacific. It is the lingua franca between many islands whose inhabitants speak different languages or dialects. As it has only a tiny vocabulary and is lacking in many necessary parts of speech, it has to make use of astonishing circumlocutions. An aeroplane, for instance, is called 'lanich (launch) belong fly allsame pigeon.' A violin is described thus: 'One small bokkis (box) belong whiteman all he scratch him belly belong him sing out good fella.'

Here is a passage in what seems, judging by the other extracts given, to be very high-class pidgin. It announces the Coronation of King George VI:

> King George, he dead. Number one son, Edward, he no want him clothes. Number two son he like. Bishop he make plenty talk along new King. He say: 'You look out good along all the people?' King he talk: 'Yes.' Then bishop and plenty government official and storekeeper and soldier and bank manager and policeman, all he stand up and sing and blow him trumpet. Finish.

There are similar pidgins, most of them not quite so bad, in other parts of the world. In some cases the people who first formed them were probably influenced by the feeling that a subject race ought to talk comically. But there are areas where a lingua franca of some kind is indispensable, and the perversions actually in use make one see what a lot there is to be said for Basic.

Afterword

George Orwell had mixed feelings about *Tribune*. As we have seen, he records: 'What first drew my attention to it, I believe, was a none-too-friendly review of a novel of mine.' He wrote that between 1939 and 1942 'I think it is true that I never had what is called a "good" review in *Tribune* until I became a member of the staff'. This, characteristically of the paper's enduring disdain for deference and its commitment to independent critical perspective, was in spite of the fact that he was a contributor from early 1940.

Orwell became a member of the staff at the end of 1943, leaving a 'wasted' two years at the BBC to become the paper's literary editor. With mixed feelings. It was not, in his own words, 'a period that I look back on with pride'.

By his own account he was 'no good at editing'. He could not turn down pieces that were lamentably unprintable, perhaps because of an empathy born of his own experience as a jobbing freelance. Orwell confessed to a 'physical inability to answer letters'. Unspeakably bad contributions were accepted, stuffed into desk drawers and never seen again until his successor came across them. It is typical of his and *Tribune*'s standing that, irrespective of being a 'bad' editor, Orwell, under the encouragement of Aneurin Bevan and (more sceptically, because of attitudes to the Soviet Union) Michael Foot, made *Tribune* a beacon of literary debate.

But it is not Orwell's brief period as a staff member of *Tribune* that defines his relationship with the paper or its relevance through him to the politics of the time and today. It was the 'As I Please' column that truly cemented his relationship with the paper and provided a platform for a courageous journalism which stamped a historical imprint on both his own and *Tribune*'s reputation for radical thought and reportage. *Tribune* did not then, and does not now, believe that Orwell was right in all of his views of the working class, his analysis of international affairs, particularly of what was to become the Cold War and the Middle East crisis, his version of all aspects of the Spanish civil war, on his attitude to 'Jews', or his alleged connections with authoritarian police and intelligence agencies.

Orwell's unsurpassed achievement in his regular *Tribune* column was to expose and delve into areas of life that would otherwise, to the disadvantage of wider knowledge and therefore the democratic process, go unexamined. From the earliest pieces on the discrimination and inequality among black American servicemen in Britain to taking the trouble to report police harassment of peace-campaigning paper sellers in Hyde Park, Orwell's reporting and commentary was brave, honest, enlightening and –

perhaps the greatest goal of any journalism – influential in changing political opinion.

In this there is a similarity but also a great difference between Orwell the author and Orwell the reporter. A contemporary author once asked, proffering the answer 'nothing', how much do we need to know about a writer personally? The answer in the case of an author of such global stature, influence and contradictions as George Orwell is, of course, everything.

Enigma is a common characteristic assigned to Orwell by his biographers. Obviously, one of them, Richard Rees, is right in his *George Orwell: Fugitive from the Camp of Victory*, that 'no full explanation of a man is ever possible'. Every biography provides a different insight. But nothing provides a deeper insight into the contemporary thoughts of a person on the great, or not so great but fundamentally important, events of a writer's time than what they thought and wrote at the time. This collection of Orwell's writing for *Tribune*, one of the 'happiest professional' times of his life, provides one of the most important pieces in the jigsaw. Here, in continuity and with a retrospect which he could not guard, is Orwell with his shield down.

And, in the engagement of dialogue with readers, his pen raised both in anger and respect, his legacy remains a hallmark of *Tribune*.

In characteristically iconoclastic style which perhaps was intended to outmatch *Tribune*'s own irreverence, Orwell gave his own verdict on us, with which I trust we remain true:

> *Tribune* is not perfect, as I should know, but I do think it is the only existing paper that makes a genuine effort to be both progressive and humane – that is, to combine a radical socialist policy with a respect for freedom of speech and a civilised attitude towards literature and the arts.

Chris McLaughlin

Tribune biographies

Evelyn Anderson (1909–77)

Tribune assistant editor 1943–6, joint editor 1946–52

Anderson was born Lore Seligmann to a German Jewish family and joined the German Communist Party (KPD) while a student in Frankfurt in 1927. She abandoned the KPD two years later for the German Social Democratic Party and on Hitler's rise to power in 1933 left Germany for Britain, where she became a prominent member of the small group of socialist exiles from Nazism in Britain that included Julius Braunthal and Franz Borkenau.

Her long article 'The Underground Struggle in Germany', published under the pseudonym Evelyn Lend, occupied nearly the whole of an issue of *Fact*, edited by Raymond Postgate, in 1938. She revisited the subject in *Hammer or Anvil?: The Story of the German Working Class Movement* (London: Victor Gollancz, 1945), which Orwell's wife Eileen helped edit and which Orwell reviewed in the *Manchester Evening News*.

She became Evelyn Anderson on marrying a BBC journalist, Paul Anderson (no relation to the editor of this volume), and joined *Tribune* in 1943 as assistant editor, taking particular responsibility for foreign affairs. She became a close friend of Orwell when he joined the paper later the same year, and her strong antipathy to communism played a major role in determining the paper's political stance in the late 1940s – though she was considered obsessive about eastern Europe by some members of staff. She later collaborated with the historian Walter Laquer on *A Dictionary of Politics* (London: Weidenfeld and Nicolson, 1971).

Aneurin Bevan (1897–1960)

Tribune editor 1941–5, director 1937–45

Born in Tredegar, south Wales, into a nonconformist Independent Labour Party family, Bevan followed his father down the pit at the age of thirteen and by the age of twenty was a prominent activist and orator in the miners' trade union the South Wales Miners' Federation. He won a scholarship to the Central Labour College in London in 1919, returning to south Wales (and unemployment) two years later. He became a union official in 1926, was elected to Monmouthshire County Council in 1928 and in 1929 won the Commons seat of Ebbw Vale for Labour.

He established a reputation as a firebrand left-winger in Parliament – for a brief period as an ally of Sir Oswald Mosley – and, after 1931, when Labour's representation in the Commons was reduced to fifty-two, became a key player on the Labour left both in Parliament and as an ally of Sir Stafford Cripps in the Socialist League, the main left pressure group among individual Labour Party members. He married Jennie Lee in 1934. Bevan was a member of *Tribune*'s editorial board from the start in 1937, and like Cripps was expelled from the Labour Party in early 1939 for backing a Popular Front against fascism and appeasement – although unlike Cripps he was soon allowed back.

During the Second World War, Bevan emerged from Cripps's shadow. He took control of *Tribune* on Cripps's departure for Moscow in 1940, sacking the pro-communist editor H. J. Hartshorn and installing Raymond Postgate in his place to ensure the paper took a pro-war line. Then, at the very end of 1941, after he and Postgate fell out, he took on the editorship himself, although the everyday work of putting out the paper was done by Jon Kimche and Evelyn Anderson. Meanwhile, from the back benches in the Commons, Bevan established himself as the de facto leader of the opposition to Winston Churchill's coalition government, consistently criticising it for failures of war policy and, after the Soviet Union entered the war in 1941, pressing for the opening of a second front.

Bevan became Minister of Health after the 1945 Labour landslide, overseeing the creation of the National Health Service. He resigned from the government in 1951, in protest at the introduction of prescription charges, along with John Freeman and Harold Wilson, and, after Labour lost the 1951 general election, was the figurehead of a left-wing Labour rebellion, largely organised around *Tribune*, demanding a less pro-American foreign policy and a domestic programme of widespread nationalisation. He had the Labour whip withdrawn in 1955 after leading a Commons revolt on the hydrogen bomb. But later the same year, after Hugh Gaitskell beat him to the Labour leadership on the retirement of Clement Attlee, Bevan joined the shadow cabinet, becoming shadow Foreign Secretary in 1956. And in 1957 he dismayed his core supporters, including *Tribune*, by disavowing unilateral nuclear disarmament on the grounds that it would 'send a British Foreign Secretary naked into the conference-chamber'. Bevan became Labour's deputy leader in 1959 and died the next year at the age of sixty-two.

On Bevan, see Michael Foot, *Aneurin Bevan* (two volumes, London: MacGibbon and Kee, 1962 and London: Davis-Poynter, 1973) and John Campbell, *Nye Bevan and the Mirage of British Socialism* (London: Weidenfeld and Nicolson, 1987).

Sir Stafford Cripps (1889–1952)

Chairman of *Tribune* board 1937–40

A leading barrister from a well-to-do family with strong Labour connections – his father, Lord Parmoor, was a minister in the 1924 and 1929–31 Labour governments, and his mother's sister was Beatrice Webb – Cripps joined the Labour Party in 1929, became Solicitor-General in the dying days of the 1929–31 Labour government, won the seat of Bristol East in a by-election and in the 1931 general election was one of only three former ministers to be re-elected as Labour MPs. During the 1930s, he became undisputed leader of the Labour left – in which role he set up *Tribune* in 1937 and bankrolled it from his fabulous legal earnings until 1940 – and came increasingly under the influence of Harry Pollitt, general secretary of the Communist Party. He was expelled from the Labour Party in 1939 for advocating a Popular Front with the Liberals and the Communists against the Chamberlain government.

In 1940, Winston Churchill made him ambassador to the Soviet Union (at which point Cripps broke his links with *Tribune* for good) and Cripps returned from Moscow in early 1942 to popular acclaim – wholly undeserved – as the man who had persuaded Stalin to enter the war on the Allied side.

With the war going badly for Britain – within days of his return the Japanese took Singapore – he appeared to many, not only on the left, as a potential replacement for Churchill. But Churchill saw him off: he gave Cripps a post in the War Cabinet and sent him to India, then in danger of Japanese invasion, with the task of talking the Indian political class round to support for the Allied war effort in return for something short of independence after the war.

The Cripps mission to India was a failure: all it generated was a resolution from the Indian National Congress demanding immediate independence and a massive civil disobedience campaign led by Mahatma Gandhi. Cripps was made minister for aircraft production when he returned to London.

Cripps rejoined the Labour Party in 1945 and was appointed President of the Board of Trade after the Labour general election victory of that year, returning to India in 1946 in an unsuccessful attempt to negotiate a settlement to obviate partition. He became Chancellor of the Exchequer in 1947, retiring on grounds of ill health in 1950. He was succeeded as Labour MP for Bristol South East (as his constituency had become) by the young Anthony Wedgwood Benn (as he then styled himself). There are several biographies of Cripps, the best of which are Simon Burgess, *Stafford Cripps: A Political Life* (London: Victor Gollancz, 1999) and Peter Clarke, *The Cripps Version: The Life of Stafford Cripps* (London: Allen Lane, 2002).

Michael Foot (b. 1913)

Tribune journalist 1937–8, joint editor 1948–52 and editor 1955–60

Born into a prominent Liberal family – his father Isaac was Liberal MP for Bodmin 1922–4 and 1929–35 – Foot joined the Labour Party soon after leaving Oxford University and fought Monmouth unsuccessfully for Labour in the 1935 general election. He worked as a researcher for Sir Stafford Cripps on the book *The Struggle for Peace* (London: Victor Gollancz, 1936) and spent six months as a trainee journalist for the *New Statesman and Nation* but was not taken on permanently. He joined the staff of *Tribune* for its launch in January 1937.

He had been there a little over eighteen months when Cripps fired William Mellor as editor – and Foot walked out in protest. Thanks to Aneurin Bevan, who introduced him to Lord Beaverbrook, owner of the *Daily Express* and the *Evening Standard*, Foot was not out of work for long. Beaverbrook was so impressed with him on their first meeting that he hired him as a feature writer on the *Standard*. Foot worked for the *Standard* until 1944, from 1942 as editor, resigning to join the *Daily Herald* and to fight (and win) Plymouth Devonport in the 1945 general election.

While at the *Standard*, he and two other Beaverbrook journalists, Frank Owen, editor of the *Standard*, and Peter Howard of the *Daily Express*, co-wrote (under the pen name 'Cato') a book-length assault for the Left Book Club on the appeasers of the 1930s, *Guilty Men* (London: Victor Gollancz, 1940) that became an instant bestseller. Two further Left Book Club books by Foot, both written under the pen name 'Cassius', were almost as successful: *The Trial of Mussolini* (London: Victor Gollancz, 1943), an account of an imagined war crimes trail of the Italian dictator, and *Brendan and Beverley* (London: Victor Gollancz, 1944), a satire warning that the Tories would fight a dirty general election campaign. Foot's involvement with *Tribune* was revived after Bevan dumped H. J. Hartshorn as editor in 1940, but it was only after Foot became an MP in 1945 (and Bevan joined the Cabinet) that he became a key player in the paper's life. Foot joined the board and took over Bevan's role of political director of the paper, persuaded Jon Kimche to return as editor in 1946 and, after Kimche left in 1948, became joint editor with Evelyn Anderson.

He gave up the editorship to Bob Edwards in 1952 but returned after losing his Devonport seat in the 1955 general election, resigning again as editor when, after Bevan's death, he was elected MP for Bevan's seat of Ebbw Vale in 1960.

Foot remained heavily involved in *Tribune* through the 1960s and early 1970s, then joined Harold Wilson's government in 1974 as employment secretary. In 1976, James Callaghan made him leader of the House of Commons. Foot was Labour leader between 1980 and 1983 and retired as an MP in 1992. His books include biographical works on Jonathan Swift, Aneurin Bevan, Lord Byron and H. G. Wells and several volumes of essays. See Mervyn Jones, *Michael Foot* (London: Victor Gollancz, 1994).

T. R. (Tosco) Fyvel (1907–85)

Tribune literary editor 1945–50

Born into a Jewish family in Cologne – his father a Viennese-born journalist, businessman and Zionist publicist, his mother Russian by birth – Fyvel lived a peripatetic existence as a child, at first in Germany. The family relocated to Zurich on the outbreak of war in 1914 and then moved to London in 1920. Fyvel was subsequently educated at a minor English public school and Cambridge University. A left-wing Zionist, he spent two years in Palestine in the late 1930s, writing a book on the Jewish–Arab–British conflict there, *No Ease in Zion*, which was published in 1938 by Fredric Warburg, who also published Orwell's *Homage to Catalonia.* (Its US publisher was Alfred A. Knopf, whose UK representative was Raymond Postgate.)

Fyvel met Orwell through Warburg early in 1940, and the three men collaborated on a series of radical books on war aims that came out in 1941 under the imprint Searchlight, one of which was Orwell's polemic *The Lion and the Unicorn.* Like Orwell, Fyvel was convinced in 1940–1 of the potential for a revolution in Britain, and his book *The Malady and the Vision* (London: Secker and Warburg, 1940) contains a critique of British politics very much in line with Orwell's. Later in the war, Fyvel served as a psychological warfare officer in the British army in north Africa and Italy. It was Fyvel who recommended Orwell as *Tribune* literary editor to Jon Kimche. When Orwell decided to give up the literary editorship of *Tribune*, Fyvel took over.

After leaving *Tribune*, Fyvel enjoyed a long career as a broadcaster and writer. In 1952, he was a co-founder (with Warburg, Malcolm Muggeridge, Stephen Spender and Michael Oakeshott) of *Encounter*, the Cold War current affairs monthly that (it later transpired) was subsidised by the CIA, and he contributed regularly to its early issues before joining the BBC in 1954. He was literary editor of the *Jewish Chronicle* 1973–83.

Fyvel wrote one of the best accounts of Orwell's later years, *George Orwell: A Personal Memoir* (London: Weidenfeld and Nicolson, 1982). On his political influence on Orwell, see John Newsinger, *Orwell's Politics* (Basingstoke: Macmillan, 1999). Several autobiographical essays were published posthumously as *And There My Trouble Began* (London: Weidenfeld and Nicolson, 1986).

Victor Gollancz (1893–1967)

Tribune director 1938–42

The son of a wholesale jeweller, Gollancz studied at Oxford University and joined the army as an officer after the outbreak of the First World War, in which role he was put in charge of officer training courses at Repton School. After the war he was hired by the publisher Ernest Benn to work for his company Benn Brothers. Gollancz made a massive success of a line of art books, then did the same with a fiction list but broke with Benn and set up his own company in 1927. Victor Gollancz Limited was an instant commercial triumph – largely because of the phenomenal sales of Dorothy Sayers's Lord Peter Wimsey thrillers, though its current affairs titles also did surprisingly well.

But as the international crisis of the 1930s deepened, Gollancz, by now a convinced pacifist and socialist and increasingly sympathetic to the Communist Party, decided that it was not enough just to publish left-wing titles in the normal way. In 1936, he announced the creation of a book club to publish cheap editions of radical books, the Left Book Club (LBC) – and within a year 40,000 people had signed up.

The LBC gave Gollancz significant political clout on the left, and when *Tribune* turned out to be rather less of a runaway success than its founders had hoped, they turned to him for help, offering him a place on the board and regular pages in the paper for the LBC in return for *Tribune* being promoted to LBC members. He agreed on condition that William Mellor be removed as editor. Stafford Cripps – who like Gollancz thought the left should ally itself with the Liberal Party and moderate Tories in a Popular Front against appeasement, a position that Mellor opposed – promptly fired Mellor and hired the communist fellow-traveller H. J. Hartshorn to replace him. The formal *Tribune*–LBC link was severed the next year, but Gollancz remained a major player in the paper's politics until 1942. Most importantly, he was the co-author (with Aneurin Bevan, George Strauss and Raymond Postgate) of the July 1940 *Tribune* manifesto that marked the paper's definitive break with the Communist Party over the war.

Orwell's relationship with Gollancz was fraught at the best of times. Gollancz published all but one of Orwell's books before 1940 – *Down and Out in Paris and London* (1933), *Burmese Days* (1934), *A Clergyman's Daughter* (1935), *Keep the Aspidistra Flying* (1936), *The Road to Wigan Pier* (1937), *Coming Up for Air* (1939) and the collection of essays *Inside the Whale* (1940) – and in 1941 he included two Orwell essays in *Betrayal of the Left*, the book that most comprehensively spells out the disgust of the British democratic left at the Hitler–Stalin pact and the CPGB's defeatism as displayed in the People's Convention of January 1941. But Gollancz also infamously added an introduction to *The Road to Wigan Pier* disowning Orwell's criticisms of the left, and he turned down both *Homage to Catalonia* and *Animal Farm* on political grounds. Orwell never trusted his judgement. 'It's frightful that people who are so ignorant should have so much influence,' he wrote to Geoffrey Gorer in 1940, incredulous at Gollancz asking him whether the Soviet secret police had really operated in Spain during the Spanish civil war. See Ruth Dudley Edwards, *Victor Gollancz: A Biography* (London: Victor Gollancz, 1987).

Jon Kimche (1909–94)

Tribune assistant editor 1942–5, joint editor 1946–8

A Swiss Jew, Kimche arrived in England at the age of twelve, joining the Independent Labour Party as a young man. He met Orwell in 1934 when they worked together in a Hampstead bookshop, Booklover's Corner, and they met again when Kimche, as chairman of the ILP Guild of Youth, visited Barcelona in 1937. He later managed the ILP's bookshop at 35 Bride Street, near Ludgate Circus. In the early war years he contributed articles on military strategy to the *Evening Standard*, and in 1942, on the recommendation of Michael Foot, who had met him through the ILP bookshop, was hired by Aneurin Bevan as assistant editor of *Tribune*.

In fact, he was editor in all but name: Bevan was described in the paper as its editor but in fact had neither the time nor the technical expertise to do the job. Precisely why Kimche was not given the title is unclear, but it seems to have been because Bevan thought that having a foreign ILPer named as editor would not look good. (*Tribune* supported the Labour Party, from which the ILP had disaffiliated in 1932.) Kimche left *Tribune* to join Reuters in early 1945 but returned in 1946, though by now his primary interest was in the Middle East – specifically, in the creation of a Jewish state in Palestine.

He was fired from his *Tribune* job after disappearing from the office in December 1947 to negotiate the safe passage through the Bosporus and the Dardanelles straits of a ship with thousands of Jews aboard bound for Palestine.

From this point on, Kimche made a name for himself as a leftist polemicist for and critic of the state of Israel and as an analyst of Middle Eastern politics, writing several books and innumerable articles. He was editor of the *Jewish Observer and Middle East Review* 1952–67 and then Middle East correspondent of the *Evening Standard* until 1973. His brother David, who emigrated to Israel and with whom he co-authored two books, joined Mossad, the Israeli secret service, rising to become its deputy director in the 1970s, and was director-general of the Israeli foreign ministry 1980–7.

Jennie Lee (1904–88)

Tribune director 1945–64

The daughter of a Fife miner, Lee joined the Independent Labour Party as a young woman and won a scholarship to study at Edinburgh University. She became a teacher and won North Lanark for the ILP in 1929 at the age of 25, losing her seat in the 1931 general election and remaining with the ILP after it decided to disaffiliate from the Labour Party the following year. She married Aneurin Bevan in 1934. She fought and lost a by-election in Bristol Central in 1943 as an independent with Common Wealth support but returned to the Labour Party in late 1944 and was elected as Labour MP for Cannock in 1945. She held the seat until 1970, serving as arts minister in the 1964–70 Labour government – in which role she was responsible, *inter alia*, for setting up the Open University. Lee took over the 'As I Please' column from Orwell in 1945–6 and replaced Bevan on the *Tribune* board when he joined the government. See Patricia Hollis, *Jennie Lee: A Life* (Oxford: Oxford University Press, 1997).

William Mellor (1888–1942)

Editor of *Tribune* 1937–8

The son of a Unitarian minister, Mellor became a socialist while a student at Oxford University, where he met G. D. H. Cole, who was then establishing a reputation as the *enfant terrible* of the Fabian Society. Mellor and Cole both played major roles in the Guild Socialist movement, and from 1913 they wrote a column together for George Lansbury's *Daily Herald* that continued as a regular feature of the paper after it went weekly with the outbreak of the First World War. Mellor opposed the war and was briefly imprisoned as a conscientious objector.

He returned to the *Herald* as industrial editor when it went daily again in 1919, and a year later he was a founder member of the Communist Party of Great Britain, in which he briefly played a leading role, gaining a reputation for extravagantly enjoying spending its subsidies from Moscow. He resigned from the CPGB in 1924 when, on the insistence of the Communist International, it adopted a highly centralised Bolshevik organisational structure (and relative austerity). He succeeded Hamilton Fyfe as *Herald* editor in 1926, when the Trades Union Congress took over the paper. He was kicked upstairs in 1930 soon after Odhams Press took half-ownership with the TUC, becoming assistant managing director of Odhams. He was effectively second in command to Sir Stafford Cripps in the Socialist League from 1933 and was the first editor of *Tribune* in 1937.

An unapologetic hedonist with a volcanic temper, he was sacked in summer 1938 after falling out with Cripps over money and the latter's proposals for a Popular Front of socialist and non-socialist parties against fascism. For the last ten years of his life, though married with a family, he conducted an affair with the young Barbara Betts (later to become Barbara Castle), whom he employed as a journalist on *Tribune*. See Margaret Cole, 'William Mellor', in Joyce Bellamy and John Saville (eds), *Dictionary of Labour Biography*, vol. 4 (Basingstoke: Macmillan, 1977) and several (mainly unflattering) references in Kevin Morgan, *Bolshevism and the British Left, part 1: Labour Legends and Russian Gold* (London: Lawrence and Wishart, 2006).

Frederic Mullally (b. 1919)

Tribune assistant editor 1945–6

Born in London and educated at St Joseph's Academy and St Xavier College, Mullally started in journalism on the subs' desk of the Calcutta *Statesman*, becoming the editor of the *Sunday Standard* in Bombay at the age of nineteen. Returning to London, he worked as a freelance for the *Financial News* and the *News Review* and became a journalist on the Independent Labour Party's weekly, the *New Leader*, edited by Fenner Brockway, with whom he co-wrote a book on the arms trade, *Death Pays a Dividend* (London: Victor Gollancz, 1944).

He was hired by Aneurin Bevan to take the place of Jon Kimche when the latter left *Tribune* to join Reuters in 1945. While at *Tribune* he wrote two pamphlets, *Films: An Alternative to Rank* (London: Socialist Book Centre, 1946), a manifesto for reform of the film industry, and *Fascism inside England* (London: Claud Morris, 1946), a history of the British Union of Fascists. He left *Tribune* at the request of Hugh Cudlipp to write a column on the *Sunday Pictorial* (forerunner of the *Sunday Mirror*) in late 1946.

Mullally abandoned Fleet Street in 1955 to move to Malta and become a novelist, writing a string of sex-, action- and politics-packed thrillers starting with *Danse Macabre* (London: Secker and Warburg, 1959). His novel *Clancy* (London: Hart-Davis, 1971), which was turned into a BBC drama series in 1975, includes a thinly disguised portrait of *Tribune* in the 1940s: it becomes *Forum*, with Bevan appearing as Dai Owen, Orwell as Herbert Lowell and Evelyn Anderson as Margaret Robinson. During the 1970s, Mullally contributed the words to a satirical cartoon strip, 'Oh, Wicked Wanda', drawn by Ron Embleton, in the porn magazine *Penthouse*. He published a short memoir of his time on *Tribune*, 'Fleet Street in the Forties', in *British Journalism Review* (1999), vol. 10, no. 1.

Raymond Postgate (1896–1971)

Editor of *Tribune* 1940–1

The son of a classics professor, Postgate became a socialist as a youth in Liverpool before studying at Oxford University. A conscientious objector during the First World War, in 1918 Postgate married Daisy Lansbury, daughter of George Lansbury, who gave him a job as a sub-editor on the *Daily Herald*. (Postgate's sister Margaret married G. D. H. Cole the same year.)

Postgate was a founder member of the Communist Party of Great Britain in 1920, briefly editing its weekly, *The Communist*, but left in 1922 after falling out with the party leadership, returning to the *Herald*. He worked with Lansbury again on *Lansbury's Labour Weekly* (1925–7) then freelanced for ten years (earning the main part of his living as UK representative of the New York publisher Alfred A. Knopf) before becoming editor of the left-wing monthly *Fact* (1937–9) and then editor of *Tribune*. In 1932, along with the Coles and Hugh Dalton, he was a member of a New Fabian Research Bureau delegation to the Soviet Union and contributed a chapter on the media to the book *Twelve Studies in Soviet Russia* (London: Victor Gollancz, 1933).

He was an extraordinarily prolific writer. His books include crime thrillers – the best known is *Verdict of Twelve* (London: Collins, 1940) – as well as biographies of John Wilkes (1930), Robert Emmett (1931) and George Lansbury (1951) and several historical books, among them a social history of Britain co-authored with G. D. H. Cole, *The Common People* (London: Methuen, 1938). He is probably best known today as the creator of the *Good Food Guide*, the first of which appeared in 1951. See John and Mary Postgate, *A Stomach for Dissent: The Life of Raymond Postgate 1896–1971* (Keele: Keele University Press, 1994); Margaret Cole, 'Raymond Postgate', in Joyce Bellamy and John Saville (eds), *Dictionary of Labour Biography*, vol. 4 (Basingstoke: Macmillan, 1977); and several references in Kevin Morgan, *Bolshevism and the British Left, part 1: Labour Legends and Russian Gold* (London, Lawrence and Wishart, 2006).

George Strauss (1901–93)

Tribune director 1937–45, chairman of board 1940–5

Born into a Jewish business family in London, Strauss was educated at Rugby School and joined the family firm of metal merchants, A. Strauss and Co, in 1920. His father Arthur, a Conservative MP who switched to Labour and lost his seat, funded his early political career, starting with a disastrous attempt to win Stoke Newington for Labour at the age of twenty-one in 1922 (the younger Strauss was so frightened by the rough and tumble of election campaigning that he withdrew from the contest before polling day). He represented North Lambeth (1925–31) and South East Southwark (1932–46) on the London County Council and was Labour MP for Lambeth North (1929–31 and 1934–50) and Lambeth Vauxhall (1950–79).

He was a parliamentary private secretary to Herbert Morrison as Minister of Transport from 1929 to 1931 and later played the same role during the Second World War to Sir Stafford Cripps when he returned to government. In 1945 he became a junior minister in the Ministry of Transport, handing his directorship of *Tribune* to his wife Patricia. He was Minister of Supply from 1947 to 1951, in which role he was responsible for the nationalisation of the iron and steel industries, and as a backbencher many years later he was responsible for the 1968 Bill that abolished theatre censorship. He became a supporter of Hugh Gaitskell in the 1950s, opposing unilateral nuclear disarmament and supporting abandonment of Clause Four of the Labour constitution. He later backed British membership of the EEC. He was Father of the House of Commons from 1974 to 1979.

An immensely rich man throughout his life, with a London residence in Kensington and a country house in Sussex, he put up a third of the working capital to launch *Tribune* in 1937 and covered its losses through the war years. His uncompleted autobiography is held at the Churchill Archives Centre in Cambridge, which is drawn on extensively in Kevin Morgan, *Bolshevism and the British Left, part 1: Labour Legends and Russian Gold* (London, Lawrence and Wishart, 2006).

Bibliography

Apart from Davison's *Complete Works*, I have also made extensive use of several other books that deserve more credit than footnotes where there are particular points that require reference:

Biographies and memoirs of Orwell

Gordon Bowker, *George Orwell* (London: Little, Brown, 2003)

Audrey Coppard and Bernard Crick (eds), *Orwell Remembered* (London: Ariel, 1984)

Bernard Crick, *George Orwell: A Life* (Harmondsworth: Penguin, 1982)

T. R. Fyvel, *George Orwell: A Personal Memoir* (London: Hutchinson, 1982)

John Newsinger, *Orwell's Politics* (Basingstoke: Macmillan, 1999)

Michael Shelden, *George Orwell: The Authorised Biography* (London: Heinemann, 1991)

D. J. Taylor, *Orwell: The Life* (London: Chatto and Windus, 2003)

Stephen Wadhams, *Remembering Orwell* (Harmondsworth: Penguin, 1984)

George Woodcock, *The Crystal Spirit: A Study of George Orwell* (London: Jonathan Cape, 1967)

Books on *Tribune* and the Labour left

Paul Addison, *The Road to 1945: British Politics and the Second World War* (London: Jonathan Cape, 1975)

Angus Calder, *The People's War: Britain 1939–45* (London: Jonathan Cape, 1969)

John Campbell, *Nye Bevan and the Mirage of British Socialism* (London: Weidenfeld and Nicolson, 1987)

Ruth Dudley Edwards, *Victor Gollancz: A Biography* (London: Victor Gollancz, 1987)

Michael Foot, *Aneurin Bevan 1897–1945* (London: MacGibbon and Kee, 1962)

Douglas Hill, *Tribune 40: The First Forty Years of a Socialist Newspaper* (London: Quartet, 1977)

Mark Jenkins, *Bevanism: Labour's High Tide* (Nottingham: Spokesman, 1979)

Bill Jones, *The Russia Complex: The British Labour Party and the Soviet Union* (Manchester: Manchester University Press, 1977)

Mervyn Jones, *Michael Foot* (London: Victor Gollancz, 1994)

Ben Pimlott, *Labour and the Left in the 1930s* (Cambridge: Cambridge University Press, 1977)

Jonathan Schneer, *Labour's Conscience: The Labour Left 1945–51* (London: Unwin Hyman, 1988)

Index